To
The Library
Campbell College
From
J. M. Price

SOUTHWESTERN MEN
and
THEIR MESSAGES

SOUTHWESTERN MEN

and

THEIR MESSAGES

Edited by

J. M. PRICE

Director, School of Religious Education

Southwestern Baptist Theological Seminary

Kansas City, Kansas

Central Seminary Press

1948

Printed by
Central Seminary Press
Kansas City, Kansas
U.S.A.

To Those

Whom These

Have Taught

CONTENTS

Chapter Page

Foreword

Introduction

I. Charles T. Ball
Biographical Sketch by T. E. Durham 5
The Cross, Satan's Hour and the Power of Darkness

II. W. W. Barnes
Autobiographical Sketch 17
A Religion Adequate for Today

III. B. H. Carroll
Biographical Sketch by J. W. Crowder 29
My Infidelity and What Became of It

IV. W. T. Conner
Autobiographical Sketch 41
The Place of Prayer in the Christian Life

V. B. A. Copass
Autobiographical Sketch 53
Perfect Salvation

VI. J. W. Crowder
Autobiographical Sketch 63
Opportunity

VII. J. B. Gambrell
Biographical Sketch by E. C. Routh 75
Up Fool Hill, and Considering Circumstances

VIII. A. H. Newman
Biographical Sketch by Frederick Eby 87
The Christian Consciousness

IX. Jeff D. Ray
Biographical Sketch by L. R. Elliott 99
Christ's Redemption

CONTENTS CONTINUED

X. I. E. Reynolds
Autobiographical Sketch 109
Music Tendencies, and Music in Worship

XI. L. R. Scarborough
Biographical Sketch by P. F. Evans 119
Tears of Jesus

XII. C. B. Williams
Autobiographical Sketch 131
How Much More Then Is A Man Worth!

FOREWORD

Southwestern Baptist Theological Seminary commemorates its fortieth anniversary this year, thus rounding out four decades of service. During these years the institution has had some of the greatest leaders in the South and they have made invaluable contributions.

It seems fitting, therefore, to bring out at this time a volume giving brief but comprehensive biographies of the lives of early leaders together with an outstanding sermon, address, or article from each. It is felt that former students and friends everywhere will be interested in having these materials for permanent records.

In the nature of the case it was impossible to include in one volume all of those who have contributed to the life of the institution. Therefore, there have been chosen twelve leaders of the early days who were with it for a number of years and who are deceased, retired, or near the retirement age.

Half of the sketches are biographies and half autobiographies. Thanks are due to Revs. T. E. Durham, J. W. Crowder, E. C. Routh, Frederick Eby, L. R. Elliott and Perry Evans for writing the biographies respectively of Drs. Ball, Carroll, Gambrell, Newman, Ray and Scarborough. They have done this as a labor of love.

Thanks also are due to the various publishers who have given permission to quote from their books, and to the various friends who have given information, encouragement and assistance at every stage of the work. May the book be a credit to the persons included and a help to the readers.

J. M. Price

Seminary Hill, Fort Worth, Texas

INTRODUCTION

Biography is history embodied in pulsating life. The events which compose historical records are never fully understandable when detached from persons. They become intelligible and thrilling when we interpret them in relation to the human agents who have set them in motion. Neither can the basic principles underneath the facts of history be effectively demonstrated until enshrined in the lives of those who have made it. History would be immeasurable impoverished—indeed would not exist—without biography.

It is such a conviction which has inspired the publication of this volume consisting of biography and autobiography. In and through the lives of the twelve men presented, we may read the history of one of the most important periods in Southern Baptist annals.

Further, we not only view a period; we also find the secret of a strategic institution, Southwestern Baptist Theological seminary. Every one of these men has made distinctly enriching contributions to the origination, the growth, the present stage of achievement, and future progress of this institution. We cannot adequately appraise them apart from the Seminary, or the Seminary apart from them. The two are united in sacred bonds which cannot be broken.

This volume not only makes available the inspiring facts of biography and autobiography; it also supplies a key sermon or address revelatory of the best emphasis and thinking of these noble workmen, so zealous in their devotion to the will of the Lord. This makes the book factual, personal, and inspiring.

Dr. J. M. Price has rendered invaluable service in assembling and editing the materials herein contained. To him, and all who have brought it to realization, our heartiest congratulations and gratitude.

We shall never cease being thankful for he privilege of personal acquaintance with the men who are the subjects of the various chapters. They have been and are the source of immeasurable blessings to us personally, as they have been, and will continue to be, to uncounted individuals, living on through them for all time to come.

E. D. Head, President
Southwestern Baptist Theological Seminary
Fort Worth, Texas

CHAPTER I

CHARLES T. BALL

BIOGRAPHICAL SKETCH*

Charles Thomas Ball, clergyman, educator, author, lecturer and dynamic leader in the field of education, was born in Oxford, North Carolina, February 3, 1866. He received his basic education in the public schools of North Carolina, an A. B. from Wake Forest College in 1898, and the Th.M. from the Southern Baptist Theological Seminary in 1903. He married Mary Agnes Peterson of Winston-Salem, North Carolina, November 30, 1897, and to this union two children were born, Marie Elizabeth and Charles E. Ball, M.D.

He became the dean of the Bible Department of Simmons College, now Hardin-Simmons University, in 1904 and served through 1911. He moved to Fort Worth, Texas, and became professor of Comparative Religion and Missions in the Southwestern Baptist Theological Seminary, heading that department from 1911 through 1919. He inaugurated the Extension Work of the Seminary and directed it in connection with the Missions Department. He organized the Baptist Student Missionary Movement in 1912, and directed its activities through 1919, promoting the movement throughout the South. He became the Executive Secretary of the American Baptist Student Union in 1920 and did a noble work with and for students throughout the nation for about five years.

Dr. Ball entered the pastorate of the Winsinoming Baptist Church of Philadelphia, Pennsylvania, in 1925, and rendered valuable service there. While pastor of this great church he turned his dynamic energies toward the establishment of a Baptist seminary in the city of brotherly love, Philadelphia. The

***By Rev. T. E. Durham, Pastor Arlington Heights Baptist Church, Fort Worth, Texas**

Baptists of that city followed his leadership in raising funds to build a great school, the Eastern Baptist Theological Seminary, and made him its first President in 1925. He raised large sums of money for its operation, and a million dollars endowment for its security. He selected a strong faculty and started a great school.

He had in his heart to establish a great university and turned his energies toward building such a school in Philadelphia. He had enough encouragement to give up the presidency of the Seminary and give his full time to establishing the Eastern University in 1926. He selected a faculty, secured buildings and began work, putting in a large extension department. However, he did not get the support from the city which he felt that his school was entitled to.

So when he received support and encouragement from Arlington, Virginia, to establish a university there, he moved the Eastern University from Philadelphia to Arlington in 1936 and it became the Arlington University. It was incorporated and chartered by the laws of Virginia. The school was growing and making splendid progress when Mrs. Ball became very ill, requiring much of his time and attention. His office sent out thousands of catalogues to ministers of all faiths in America and in England. With long experience he had made a strong university extension department, having students enrolled from this country and from England. His age and Mrs. Ball's illness clouded his greatest dream, namely, "a university near our Nation's Capitol, serving the English speaking world."

He was a thorough teacher, gifted in organizing preachers and students for effective achievements for the Master's cause. He was a tireless worker, preaching, teaching and lecturing. He was a writer of no mean ability. He has many laurels in his crown of achievement which will last for the ages to come. The Bible Department in Simmons College has become one of the honored Bible departments of our southwest. The department of Comparative Religion and Missions in the Southwestern Seminary encircles the earth with its influence, by its missionaries preaching and teaching the pure gospel of the Lord Jesus Christ to a needy world.

The Eastern Baptist Seminary has grown to be a strong

school, with a large endowment, receiving ample Northern Baptist support, with a recognized faculty of scholars, serving a large student body from this nation and other lands. The Baptist Student Missionary Movement was the forerunner of the Baptist Student Union which is one of our most influential agencies. It held effective national conventions both in Fort Worth, Texas, and Louisville, Kentucky, published a magazine and supported Dr. and Mrs. A. L. Aulick as field workers.

He was a good husband and a faithful father, providing well for his household. Mrs. Mary Agnes Ball was a devoted helpmeet to her gifted husband. She was a great Christian, a good mother, and an understanding, helpful neighbor, was an A.B. graduate of Salem College, Winston-Salem, North Carolina. She died May 10, 1943, after a long illness. Marie Elizabeth Ball, the only daughter, died at an early age. Dr. Charles Edward Ball, the only son, after attending Simmons and Baylor graduated at Jefferson Medical College, Philadelphia, and has grown to be a famous physician, an eye, ear, nose and throat specialist. Dr. Ball passed away on January 26, 1943. May he yet speak through his sermons for many years to come, and the Lord inspire the readers.

THE CROSS, SATAN'S HOUR AND THE POWER OF DARKNESS*

The text is Matt. 27:45,46. "Now from the sixth hour there was darkness over all the land until the ninth hour. And about the ninth hour Jesus cried with a loud voice saying, 'Eli, Eli, lama sabachthani, that is, 'My God, my God, why hast thou forsaken me?' "

Jesus went on the cross at nine o'clock in the morning, which was the sixth hour. There were three hours of day-light, in which there was gambling at the foot of the cross. Taunts, also, and insults were cast at Him by those who were passing, and a number of other happenings, including the seven words spoken by our Lord to those about Him. The darkness came at noon and lasted until the ninth hour, which was three o'clock in the afternoon.

It is my purpose at this time to undertake to give you a spiritual interpretation of the sufferings of our Lord and Master on the Cross. It is not my purpose to discuss His physical sufferings. Physical suffering and physical death were involved. They did drive nails through His hands and through His feet, and there was loss of blood and great bodily physical suffering; but in this discussion I am giving small attention to these because it is my conviction that our Lord thought very little about them.

In the garden our Lord prayed three times, "My Father, if it be possible let this cup pass from me. Nevertheless, not as I will, but as thou wilt." He knew that on the morrow He must meet in a death battle on the spiritual plane, during three hours of the densest darkness, the Old Serpent, Satan, the Devil, and solve for man and for God the problem of sin. This was a spiritual and not a physical conflict. But inquires one, "Was it not looking forward to and shrinking from suffering on the Cross and caused our Lord to pray in the Garden of Gethsemane, and sweat great drops of blood?" No, I cannot accept that view.

Our Lord suffered great agony in the garden the evening

*From *The Victorious Christ* by Charles T. Ball, American Publishing Co.

before the crucifixon and prayed three times to His father to deliver Him if in accordance with His will, because He knew that on the morrow He would face spiritual death, and actually die the second death, which means Hell and separation from God. He not only died the second death but went to Hell (Hades) for each of us. This He did in our stead.

Did you ever see God at His best? It has been said, and I think well, that all departments of nature sometime, somewhere, come to their highest and best expression. For example the highest and best expression of the vegetable kingdom is a full-blown rose; the highest and best expression of the mineral kingdom is a crystal of carbon; the highest and the best expression of animal nature is a well-bred horse; the highest and the best expression of Deity is a Man nailed to a Cross. Did you ever see God at His best? If you ever did, you saw a Man nailed to a Cross, by the eye of faith.

I wish to bring to you a few definite thoughts of this text that you can take home with you and remember and, I hope, profit by them.

First, it was a cry from the heart and lips of One who had had Himself put on the Cross to die under direct command from God the Father. John 16:17,18: "Therefore doth the Father love me, because I lay down my life that I might take it again. No one taketh it away from me, but I lay it down of myself. I have power to lay it down and I have power to take it again. The commandment received I from My Father."

Sometime, somewhere, back in the councils of eternity, before times eternal, God issued a command to His son to die for a lost world. True, there were men who thought they killed Him and the Devil did kill Him. But really and truly His death was the voluntary offering of Himself as a sacrifice for our sins. He did not die to make it possible for God to love lost sinners: for God loved them already so much that He commanded His only begotton Son to die for them. But He did die in order to make it right for God to save sinners. Scriptures put it in Romans 3:25,26: "Whom God set forth to be a propitiation, through faith in His blood, to show His righteousness at this present season; the showing, I say, of his righteousness at this present season; that He might Himself be just, and the justifier of Him that hath faith in Jesus Christ."

Second, it was a cry from the heart and lips of One who when He uttered it was being "made sin for us." II Cor. 5:21: "Him who knew no sin He made to be sin on our behalf, that we might become the righteousness of God in Him." This Scripture means and says that it was God the Father who put Jesus on the Cross. It was God the Father who "made Him to be sin." What does it mean? This is a great mystery. It means, in part at least, that the sinless Christ stepped into my shoes and took the responsibility for my sins. He became responsible to God in my stead.

Third, it was a cry from the heart and lips of One, who when He uttered it was tasting death for every man. (Hebrews 2:9). What do I mean by this? I mean that if you are His He was doing your dying, and left no dying for you to do. The death which Jesus died on the Cross for each of us was what the Bible sometimes calls the second death. It means Hell and eternal separation from God. This is why I say that when our Lord uttered this cry He was doing our dying and did not leave the smallest particle for us to do. If you are His, death, can never come near you, nor touch you.

Fourth, it was a cry from the heart and lips of One, who when He uttered it was overwhelmed in the mystery of doubt. Yes, He said, "Why" one time; but they were not His "doubts" nor His "whys." When He stepped into our shoes and took our place under the law He became responsible to God for our sins, and it was in this situation that He gave expression to our "doubts" and "whys." And because Jesus said "why" for us, because He mingled His voice with ours, God will hear when we say "why" and quiet our doubts and fears.

Fifth, it was a cry from the heart and from the lips of One, who when He uttered it was overwhelmed in the mystery of silence. It is noticeable and most amazing that after our Lord went on the Cross, no word came to Him from home. The Heavens were brass above His head.

It was easy enough for our Lord to hear from home before He went on the Cross. At His birth myriads of angels appeared on the scene. They had come from Heaven to celebrate this great event. They sang the songs He had heard in heaven around the throne. At His baptism the Holy Spirit appeared in the form of a dove to denote that the Spirit would be upon Him in all His fulness for His life work. The voice of the Father was also heard: "This is my beloved Son, in whom I am well pleased." On the mount of transfiguration the heavenly visitors, Moses and Elijah, appeared, and the voice of God was heard again saying: "This is my beloved Son, hear ye Him." And I believe that many times when our Lord was praying in the silent hours of the night and all alone, He heard the voice of His Father speaking to Him, and I doubt not that many times there were heavenly visitors.

Why this awful, dreadful silence in the hour when He most needed sympathy and when He was most misunderstood? It was because this One was as much man as if He had not been God, and at the same time as much God as if He had not been man, this One, the God-man, must of necessity perform this service for God and for man all alone.

Man could not help because of his guilt. He had sinned and lost his standing before God, and it was for him, it was to restore him, that the God-man was dying. God could not help because it was His holiness that had been outraged by man's sins. It must be done by One who represented both God and man and who was both God and man. Hence the silence! No word from Heaven, no help from man.

Sixth, it was a cry from the heart and lips of One, who when He uttered it was overwhelmed in the mystery of darkness. I believe this was the densest darkness this world will ever know. It was the darkest of the pit. It was the picture God gave of the sin that had put Jesus on the Cross.

No man saw the major sufferings of Jesus. The dense darkness concealed these evidences of suffering. The Scriptures tell us that it covered "all the land." Suffice it to say that it was Hell's hour and the power of darkness and the densest darkness the universe will ever know: the darkness of Hell!.

Seventh, it was a cry from the heart and lips of One who when He uttered it was fathoming the deepest abyss of sorrow. What is sorrow, anyhow? Did you ever try to analyze it? Someone has said that sorrow is the lack of something. The sorrowing soul lacks something that is necessary to its happiness.

As a pastor, I stood on one occasion with a young married couple before a little white casket which contained the body of thier first-born. They were sorrowing because they loved the child; it had gone from them.

Did our Lord lack something? When He was being "made sin" did God the Father turn from His dying Son? Was there a break in that high and holy fellowship that had never known a shock? Did it mean that God could not have fellowship with His own Son when He was being made sin? Did God turn from Him at this moment and did our Lord become conscious that He was "forsaken" even by His Father? "My God, my God, why hast thou forsaken me?"

When our Lord stood in our stead and took upon Himself the responsibility for our sins this act separated Him from God. When He uttered this cry He was experiencing the very worst there is in separation.

Eighth, it was a cry from the heart and lips of One, who when He uttered it was dying a death-destroying death. The Lord Jesus knew when He went on the Cross He would put death out of business. The apostle Paul bears record of this great fact in Second Timothy 1:10: "Our Saviour Jesus Christ, who abolished death and brought life and immortality to light through the gospel."

Not only did He abolish death, but destroyed the one through whom death came into the world. Hebrews 2:14: "Since the children are sharers in flesh and blood, He also, in like manner, partook of the same; that through death He might bring to naught him that had the power of death, that is, the Devil." Our Lord Jesus Christ partook of our nature, flesh, and blood, which involved death. This He did voluntarily for our sakes. He knew that He was stepping into the realm of death when He laid aside temporarily some of the privileges of Deity, emptied Himself, as told in Phil. 2:7,8. Our Lord's death was a voluntary act, a high and holy submission that Satan might slay Him. He knew all this was to be, and that it would fulfill the demands of the spiritual second death.

It was in this voluntary act of submission that He became our substitute, and this is what gives value to His death, which value He transfers to us and God accepts. He stood in our stead and experiences the second death for us. It was the knowledge that this would take place on the morrow that brought bloody sweat and great agony as He prayed the evening before in the garden. And it was the knowledge on His part that this act would save us from Hell and the Second Death that put joy in His sufferings. Our salvation was His joy in the midst of this suffering and death.

Now, since what I have said is true, and I believe in accordance with the teachings of the Scriptures, there are three great words with deep meaning that I must pronounce to you.

First, the death of our Lord was and is and will forever be, a vicarious death. He suffered and died the second death in our stead. He descended into the lower regions, that is into Hades, and came back for us. He rose from the grave also and ascended to the right hand of the Father for us.

Isaiah 53 is a great commentary on the vicariousness of the death of our Lord. We find in that great chapter the following expressions: "He was bruised for our iniquities;" "Jehovah hath laid on Him the iniquity of us all;" "When thou shalt make His soul an offering for sin;" "and He shall bear our iniquities." This great doctrine of substitution is found throughout the Scriptures. His death was vicarious. He died for our sins and in our stead.

Second, His death was atoning. He made atonement for our sins. Our Lord was the greatest bridge builder of the universe. He bridged with His own person the deep and yawning chasm that separated men from God. Jesus did not die to cause God to love lost sinners but rather God commanded Him to die. "God is love." the Scriptures tell us, but God is also justice, and He must have a just cause for saving before any man could be saved. God, as God the Father, could not go on the cross to die because He was the One whose holiness had been outraged by sin. No mere man could go on the cross and die and make atonement because it was man who had sinned. There must be one who represented both God and man; one who was as much God as if He had not been man. This One must make the atonement.

Let me call your attention again to this great Scripture found in Romans 3:25,26: "Whom God set forth to be a propitiation through faith, in His blood, to show His righteousness because of the passing over of the sins done beforetime, in the forbearance of God; for the showing, I say, of His righteousness at this present season; that He might Himself be just; and the justifier of Him that hath faith in Jesus."

A good Scotch woman lay dying. The Christian doctor knew that all the children could reach her bedside while she was still alive except the oldest daughter. She was too far away. After she had given her blessing to all the children present, the suggestion was made that she be asked whether or not she had a message to leave for Mary, who would probably reach home after her mother had gone. In her weakness the mother replied, "Yes, if I am gone when Mary arrives, tell her that the Bridge holds." Yes, it will hold for each of us also. Our Lord Jesus was the architect and the builder. The bridge will hold. He is the bridge. His death was an atoning death.

Third, His death was, and is, and always will be an expiatory death. It means that Jesus made expiation for our sins. Propitiation is a great New Testament word. Propitiate means "to satisfy, to appease, to purify."

Expiate, an Old Testament word, is a much stronger word. It means "to extinguish, put out of existence." So let us hold to our word expiate. The death of Christ was an expiatory death. On the Cross He expiated our sins; He extinguished them. He made them not to be; He put them out of existence.

In the Scriptures, in many places where God is spoken of as dealing with our sins, we find such expressions as:

Isaiah 44:22—"I have blotted out, as a thick-cloud, thy transgressions, and as a cloud, thy sins; return unto Me; for I have redeemed thee."

Isaiah 38:17—"Thou hast cast all my sins behind Thy back."

Psalms 103:12—"As far as the east is from the west, so far hath He removed our transgressions from us."

Micah 7:19—"Thou wilt cast all their sins into the depths of the sea."

Finally God says, Hebrews 8:12. "And their sins will I remember no more."

All the above can mean nothing less than that God chooses to put our sins out of His mind; not to remember our sins against us when, through Christ, we have become His own. That is, God chooses to forget our sins. A dying preacher said he could not make Christ remember that he had ever committed sin. Christ died to put away our sin. Praise His Holy Name.!

Chapter II

W. W. BARNES

AUTOBIOGRAPHICAL SKETCH

I was born February 28, 1883, in the village of Tiosnot (Elm City), formerly in Edgecombe, now in Wilson County, N.C. My father's and mother's people came from England to Isle of Wight County, Virginia, within a half-century after Jamestown was settled. For nearly a century they were active in the colony—members of the colonial legislature and the Governor's Council. They were members of the Church of England. Some, under the influence of the Great Awakening, became Baptists and left Virginia to settle in the new county of Edgecombe. Some were members of the Baptist church that left Isle of Wight in 1742 and settled where Scotland Neck now is.

My father was a physician and farmer, educated in Cincinnati and New York. He died when I was thirteen. Under the influence of a Missionary Baptist preacher, Elder Mark Bennett, my mother's grand-parents took the missionary side when the division occured in the 1830's. Most of her relatives took the anti-missionary side. Under the influence of Elder Bennett two of mother's aunts were sent to Chowan College in the 1850's. In due course mother went to Chowan, graduating in 1871. Since ladies did not speak in public, mother listened to her graduation address ("Hope") read by President W. M. Wingate of Wake Forest College. I have the address in her hand-writing.

My ancesters for eight or nine generations have been Baptists. Father's ancestor, Elder Jonathan Thomas, founded the church, known as Toisnot, now Wilson, in 1756. Mother had five great uncles who were preachers. Baptisticism is deeply ingrained in my blood. I became a Sunday school member the first Sunday in January, 1894. The church had seventy-seven members; the Sunday School averaged about sixty. The Rev. Q. C. Davis, father of Professor W. H. Davis of the Southern Seminary, had just resigned the pastorate and the son had just left the class. Mr. John Friend was the teacher. He was well named.

I revelled in the new atmosphere. The Sunday school lessons were studied daily with avidity. I joined the church during a revival and was baptized October 16, 1898 by the pastor, the Rev. M. L. Kesler. They made me a teacher in the spring of 1899 and superintendent in the fall. I served also as janitor (without wages), and led the singing. Later this church was my first pastorate. In fact, I functioned in every capacity except president of the Woman's Missionary Society. They never risked me in that place.

My formal education began in the country one-room school and was continued in the village school, supplemented by a private school, thus giving a school year of nine months. My real education was given me by my mother. She taught me mathematics (favorite in those years), English, Latin, and French. In my sixteenth and seventeenth years we read Church History together. Her volume is before me as I write on Wednesday, 18 June, 1947. (On Wednesday, 18 June, 1913, I came to Fort Worth to accept the Professorship of Church History. For these thirty-four years I have tried to interpret Church History in the light of her teachings.)

In August, 1900, I was licensed by the Elm City Church and entered Wake Forest College three weeks later. My college career was not particularly notable. Most of the time was given to study. Perhaps more should have been given to athletics and the literary society. I was fortunate in not having the multitudinous organizations that distract students today. The degrees of Bachelor of Arts and Master of Arts were received in 1904. Thirty years later, at the centennial celebration, the College conferred the Doctorate of Divinity.

The first year out of college I was tutor of the children of two American families near Santiago de Cuba, and the following year principal of a public school in my home county. There were three of us teaching—the daughter of a Primitive Baptist preacher, the daughter of a Freewill Baptist deacon and myself. We had frank and friendly discussions but no friction in school administration or religion. I was also pastor of my home church and of the church in Fremont, in the adjoining county to the south—two Sundays at each church.

In the fall of 1906 I entered the Southern Seminary at Louisville. I was fortunate in both college and seminary in having faculties of experience and wisdom. A few years after I left each school the faculties began to break up through death or retirement. I am grateful to a kind Providence for my opportunity in each school.

In February, 1909, I received the degree of Master in Theology from the Seminary and went to Havana, Cuba, to take charge of the Cuban-American College under the Home Mission Board. My duties were: to have direction of the school, teach the class of young ministers, and preach in English Sunday morning. My spare time was taken in assisting Dr. M. N. McCall in directing the mission work. Among the leaders of the Cuban work today are some of the ministers I taught then. Unavoidable circumstances led me to resign in May, 1912.

I returned to Louisville and completed graduate work with a major in Church History and minors in Hebrew and Sociology. On the day of graduation with the degree of Doctor of Theology came the inquiry concerning my advailibility for the Chair of Church History in Southwestern. Two days later the position was offered me. I held that Chair from 1913 to 1946, when I was transferred to the Research Professorship in Baptist History, a new chair in Baptist history. In preparation for this work I spent the calendar year, 1919, in Columbia, University majoring in American History, and much time since studying American secular and Christian history.

My experience of life, both as it has come and in retrospect, confirms me in the truth received from my mother that God's providence is sure.

A RELIGION ADEQUATE FOR TODAY*

John 14:6. "I am the way, the truth, and the life."

Man is a religious creature. The philosopher and man of letters, Ernest Renan, is quoted as saying "Man is incurably religious." This dictum of the unbelieving philosopher is proved to be correct by research into the life of all the peoples of the earth—the most highly civilized and the lowest in the stages of civilization. This being true, what sort of religion ought man to have? An adequate religion must satisfy man as he looks at the past; as he lives in present; as he faces the future. Such a religion must do four things for man.

I. As man looks at the past his religion must furnish to his intellect a reasonable explanation of the universe in which he lives.

Man's intellectual life is an important phase of his being. He must realize this even in his religious outlook. His theology is the result of his effort to rationalize the truths presented by his religion. In every religion, however naive and simple in its forms, there must be a sense of satisfaction concerning the world around us and the heavens above us. In the history of the religions of man there are many oddities, some of them downright foolish, in the explanations of the universe. In the religions of the ancient world—Babylonia, Assyria, Egypt, Greece, and Rome; among the Aborigines in North and South America; among the primitive peoples of Africa and Asia—in all of these there are found efforts to explain the universe. Among the intellectuals of Europe and America today there are efforts at such explanation. Some would explain the universe—its origin and its control—in terms of blind chance, materialistic fatalism. Others see a spiritual reality that furnishes an adequate answer to "the problem of the universe."

Christianity has its historical basis in the revelation in the Bible. There must be a starting point. The Bible begins with a statement magnificient in its simplicity: "In the beginning God." This starting point, when once it grips man's thought, is the answer to life's problems. The apostle puts his finger

*Radio address over KFJZ, Fort Worth, Texas, February 2, 1947

upon this fundamental principle when he said to King Agrippa: "'Why is it judged incredible with you if God doth raise the dead?" Given belief in God, any question of life, even the question of death, is answered.

The same apostle in another place sounds the depth of human thinking and reaches the height of intellectual achievement when he says: "For in him were all things created, in the heavens and upon the earth, things visible and things invisible, whether thrones or dominions or principalities or powers: all things have been created through him, and unto him; and he is before all things, and in him all things consist." (Colossians 1:16-17). If you, through that insight into reality called faith, have grasped that fundamental truth enunciated by Paul that there is One who stands at the center of this universe, who is the Author of its being and who controls its destiny, you can face a world torn to shreds. You can face your own small world going to pieces. The apostle was in a Roman prison facing the possibility of death by a Roman sword when he wrote those words just quoted. What did Rome matter? What mattered Roman soldiers and Roman prisons? Yea, what mattered death from a Roman sword when Paul knew Him who made all things and holds all things together?

II. Not only must a religion, to be adequate, furnish an explanation of the origin of the universe, but an adequate religion must furnish a sufficient moral guide for the present.

Man's need is primarily moral. His material resources may be limited, but if his moral values are clear and adequate, he is a man. An adequate religion must hold forth before man a high moral standard. Man never rises higher than his moral ideal, and those ideals must be buttressed by religion. In the history of nations their downgrade may be traced to a breakdown of their moral ideals which have weakened because their religious underpinning has given way. The Bible is *par excellance,* a Book of religion. Any history or geography or science included in the Bible is incidental to the moral development shown therein. Men have somtimes puzzled themselves over what they consider low moral standards and practices in the Old Testament, but I would remind you that the Christian religion comes to flower in the progressive revelation culminating in the New Testament. "God, having of old time spoken unto the fathers in the prophets by divers portions and in divers manners, hath at the end of these days spoken unto us in his Son, whom he appointed heir of all things, through whom also he made the worlds; who being the effulgence of his glory, and the very image of his substance, and upholding all things by the word of his power, when he had made purification of sins, sat down on the right hand of the Majesty on high." (Hebrews 1:1-3).

The Bible furnishes a moral guide to man floundering in his uncertainty. Man's chief difficulties with the Bible are not intellectual, but moral. When I see a man who is losing his grasp on spiritual, religious realities and places the cause therefor in his intellectual doubts concerning something he sees in the Bible, I know his moral foundations are giving way. I have seen the proof of this in many instances. He begins to slip morally. The Bible condemns his acts. He seeks to justify himself, to escape condemnation, by denying the truth of the Book which condemns his manner of life. He reads the Bible, or hears it read, and has a sense of obligation to a certain task. He is not willing to give himself to the task. He endeavors to by-pass the duty by denying the authority of Him who imposes the duty. He has his "doubts about the Bible."

Christianity, above all the religions in the history of man, puts before you and me a high moral standard and a perfect moral guide. For centuries men have paid their respect to Jesus of Nazareth. Christian, Jew and Pagan have recognized his moral perfection. For many years a great American daily paper has published an editorial tribute to Him at Christmas time. Last Christmas one of our Fort Worth daily papers published this editorial from the other daily. The French philosopher, Renan, whom I quoted at the beginning, paid his tribute by writing a volume dealing with Jesus. Many years ago a Jewish friend of mine, a man learned in eight languages, ancient and modern, assured me that he was so enamored with Jesus of Nazareth and His teachings that he read the Gospel stories each day in four or five languages in order that he might get every angle or phase of thought in Jesus' parables.

Some of Jesus' opponents testified that no man ever spake like this man.

The New Testament, in the Gospels and in the interpretations of Jesus given in the other books, holds before men of the first century and of all succeeding centuries the high moral ideal illustrated in the life and teachings of Jesus. No man ever went astray who seriously made Jesus his guide. I am not concerned about a man's theology, about his scientific opinions, about his economic theories, about any of his intellectual vagaries and outlooks, if he sincerely takes Jesus of Nazareth as his moral standard and guide. Christianity alone, among all the religions of the world, furnishes a guide to duty.

III. In the third place, an adequate religion must furnish for the present strength to perform one's duty to God and man.

Many a great thinker has left on record high thoughts concerning man and his relations and obligations to the Supreme Being and his relations and obligations to his fellow man. Marcus Aurelius, the Roman Emperor, has left us essays that point upward. Many religious teachers, founders of and leaders in some of the great religions of the world, have left us great teachings. Some of these teachings approximate teachings of Jesus, but none of these have been able in their own lives to illustrate their great ideals nor to inspire in their followers any great effort to achieve.

Study the record of Jesus as given us in the Gospels. Somehow he was able to touch the life of a tax-collector and make him fit to be a member of the apostolic band. He could call unknown fishermen from their boats and inspire them to go forth and win a hostile world, not afraid to stand before governors and kings. He could inspire a fallen woman, a social outcast, to new ideals and efforts at living. He could take the profane fisherman, Simon, and send him on a career of world-conquering fame. Did you ever notice the Gospel reference to the eye of Jesus? He must have had a penetrating eye. How many times reference is made to the fact that He looked at someone! He looked at the rich young man and saw his love of money. He put His finger on the sensitive spot in his soul. May we hope that the young man in after time was lifted up by that look! He looked at Nathanael and saw an Israelite in whom was no guile. And all of Nathanael's doubts fled. He looked at Peter who had just denied Him. The look crushed Peter and prepared him to see the risen Christ on Sunday following.

The apostle says, "I can do all things through Christ who strengtheneth me." That has been the experience of multitudes. Many a youth in whom man has seen little promise has become a William Carey, a David Livingstone. Millions whom the world has never recognized have received the inspiration and strength to meet life faithfully. Many of the men and women who have made our country great have found their source of strength and inspiration in Jesus of Nazareth.

Even beyond the bounds of organized Christianity much service to humanity has found its inspiration and its will to do in the life and teachings of Jesus. There were no orphanages, hospitals, or other houses for the care of man until He came. We have among us a great relief organization that serves the world in war and in peace that receives its very name from the cross of Jesus.

IV. An adequate religion must satisfy the intellectual craving for a tolerable explanation of the origin and continuance of the universe; must constitute a sufficient moral guide and give strength to perform the duties of the present life; so, also, in the fourth place, an adequate religion must give assurance for the future.

We are familiar today with the several security programs—the efforts of the political authorities in state and nation to give assurance for the future. The religious bodies of the United States have been hastened in their programs of security for their workers by the comparable efforts of the secular authorities. May I respectfully remind you that all of these efforts are based on secular and material foundations. The dollar bill that you have is not value in itself. It is a promise on the part of the United States government to pay the bearer on demand a silver dollar. That piece of paper, therefore, is of no more value than is the credit of the United States government. And we know from history, past and current, that nations rise and fall, they come and go. And those of us whose memories reach back fifteen years know how quickly material values fall and how helpless political governments are in the premises.

When I was a youth of twenty-one, the first year I was out of college (1904), I was tutor of the children of two American families in eastern Cuba. We lived ten miles north of Santiago, in the village of Dos Bocas, on the railroad between Havana and Santiago. The railroad, the river and the highway ran parallel to one another, following the winding valley between the two mountain ridges. Our home was situated up the mountain side, looking across the valley toward the west. The front yard was a beautiful flower garden. It was built up thirty feet above the river, supported by a massive stone wall. A stairway led down to a foot-bridge. Beyond the river, about twenty-five acres were planted in all manner of tropical fruits.

In the afternoon I used to watch the sun go down behind the ridge on the other side of the valley. The ridge was bordered by a fringe of bamboo that resembled a lace curtain up-right. By four o'clock the sun touched the bamboo fringe and slowly disappeared behind the curtain. Day after day, as I watched the approaching sunset, counting the minutes as the sun moved down the width of the bamboo, I resolved to go up the ridge some day to learn if I could see beyond the sunset.

One afternoon in October, as the sun touched the fringe atop the ridge, I sprang from my seat on the porch, hastened down the stone steps, across the bridge, through the orchard, across the highway and the railroad and up the path that wound like a thread up the mountain side. I looked back toward the residence. Night had settled in the valley—there is no twilight in the tropics—and was gradually reaching up the side of the mountain, approaching the residence.

As I reached the bamboo fringe and pushed through, a vision opened before me that has cheered me along the road for these four decades and more. Behind me was the valley of darkness, enveloping the place where I lived, whence I had just witnessed the set of the sun. Before me I saw the sun in all his brilliance shining up on a plain about ten miles wide. Magnificent royal palms dotted the landscape, hundreds of head of cattle were grazing on the luscious grass, millions of tropical flowers cast a riot of color, swarms of bees were extracting nectar. Beauty, abundance and peace reigned in every direction.

A lesson stamped itself upon my soul that afternoon and abides with me today. The day passes noontide and the shadows lengthen toward the east. We look at the path of life approaching the western horizon. The valley behind is filling with darkness; ahead are the light, the beauty, the abounding joy of eternal day. At eventide there shall be light.

Christianity looks to the future with assurance. Confucianism looks back to its founder; the glory of Buddhism is in the past; Mohammedanism had no higher word than that given by its leader a dozen centuries ago. Even Judaism has no message for the future. She looks back to Moses and endeavors to meet the present as well as possible. The Golden Age of Christianity is yet to be. Lord Tennyson looks forward to

"That far-off divine event
Toward which the whole creation moves."

William Cullen Bryant, watching a water-fowl wind its sure way through the unchartered skies, received a lesson for himself.

"He who from zone to zone
Guides through the boundless sky thy certain flight
In the long way that I must tread alone
Will lead my steps aright."

May I read you quotations from two philosophies of life that illustrate what I mean? There is a poem by Omar Khayyam, from ancient Persia, translated by Edward Fitzgerald. Two stanzas read as follows:

"We are no other than a moving row
Of Magic-Shadow shapes that come and go
Round with the Sun-illumined Lantern held
In Midnight by the Master of the Show.

And that inverted Bowl they call the Sky,
Whereunder crawling cooped we live and die,
Lift not your hands to *It* for help—for It
As impotently moves as you or I."

On the other hand listen to these words from James Russell Lowell:

"Truth forever on the scaffold,
Wrong forever on the throne;

Yet that scaffold sways the future,
And behind the dim unknown,
Standeth God within the shadow
Keeping watch above His own."

But one greater than all these poets that I have quoted, as he faced certain death, wrote: "I know whom I have believed and am persuaded that he is able to guard that which I have committed to him against that day." The apostle Paul wrote these words to his young fellow-laborer, Timothy, laid down his pen on the table and his head upon the Roman block and stepped out into eternity with assurance.

Chapter III

B. H. CARROLL

BIOGRAPHICAL SKETCH*

Benajah Harvey Carroll, of Irish descent, was born on a farm near Carrolton in Carroll County, Mississippi, December 27, 1843. He was the fifth son and seventh child in a family of twelve children. At seven he moved with the family to Arkansas, near Monticello and spent seven years more on a farm. He enjoyed fishing, hunting, and adventure. He delighted in story-telling and playing pranks.

In the fall of 1858 he moved with the family to Burleson County, Texas. Little is known of his early schooling, but it is known that he attended school at Monticello, Arkansas, and Caldwell, Texas. From his early life on he was an incessant reader. He said he began to read history at the age of four He was always a student. As a boy he taught school, and made the reputation then of being a born teacher.

In 1859, in his sixteenth year, he went to Baylor University at Old Independence. He was in Baylor less than two years and made a wonderful record as a student and debater. His speech on the campus of Baylor against the secession of Texas from the Union was a classic. His reading covered every branch of learning and his memory was most astounding. He averaged reading three hundred pages a day for more than fifty years, and often quoted from memory what he had not seen for forty years.

In 1861 he mustered into the Confederate Service at San Antonio, as a Texas Ranger, which service lasted one year and was filled with dangerous and thrilling adventures. In 1862 he joined the Seventeenth Regiment of the Texas Infantry at Aus-

*By Prof. J. W. Crowder, formerly Professor of English Bible, Southwestern Baptist Seminary.

tin. He served through the War and was severely wounded in the battle of Mansfield, Louisiana. He was highly commended by Colonel Allen for his courage, bravery, courtesy, and defense of the right. In the meantime he made some most remarkable war speeches and held some notable camp debates. In all his debates he took the more unlikely side, and always won.

In this four-year war period his infidelity had full sway, but he was converted in a Methodist Camp-Meeting in the summer of 1865. He was licensed to preach in 1866, and in November of the same year was ordained. On December 28 following, he was happily married to Miss Ellen Bell. To this marriage several children were born, three of whom are now living; Charles, a retired teacher and preacher, Katherine, a missionary, and Annie Louise. It proved to be a God-made match. She was a beautiful, loyal, devoted wife, mother, and Christian. After the death of his first wife, he married Miss Hallie Harrison, daughter of General Thomas Harrison, of Waco, Texas. To this union one son, Francis Harrison Carroll, was born. He is now a news columnist in California.

Immediately following his ordination, Dr. Carroll entered upon a most eventful and meaningful ministry. His first attempt was a combination of preaching and teaching, a failure financially but a success otherwise. He then tried preaching and farming, another failure financially. Then he said, "Come weal or woe, I shall give my life wholly to preaching the Gospel." This he did, and in 1870 he was called as assistant pastor of the First Baptist Church of Waco, and on January 1, 1871, he became full pastor. Thus he began a most remarkable pastorate, which continued twenty-eight years.

During his arduous pastoral work Dr. Carroll was outstanding as a denominational leader and champion of civic righteousness. His speeches and sermons did much to establish these causes. He was a commanding figure in the Texas and Southern Baptist Conventions, being six feet, four inches tall and very handsome. He standardized Baptist orthodoxy in the South and led many campaigns for righteousness and education, including the Prohibition Campaign in Texas in 1887, several for the payment of debts on Baylor University, the State Mission

Board, and Southwestern Seminary.

One of the greatest characteristics of Dr. Carroll was his co-operation with all organized Baptist work. Some of his most notable addresses were: one before the Southern Baptist Convention at Richmond, Virginia, on "The Wisdom of Mission Work in Texas"; another before the National Education Society at Birmingham, Alabama, in 1891, on "The Needless Multiplication of Colleges"; and his Centennial Address before the Southern Baptist Convention at Atlanta, Georgia, on "Home Missions in America for One Hundred Years."

He held two religious debates. One was with Dr. O. Fisher, a Methodist Bishop, on "Christian Baptism", "Infant Baptism", and "The Baptism in the Holy Spirit", The other was with Dr. Wilmeth, a disciple of Alexander Campbell, on "The Order of Repentance and Faith", "The Design of Baptism", and "The Setting Up of the Kingdom."

The most monumental work of B. H. Carroll is the Southwestern Baptist Theological Seminary. Along with this should be noted his literary productions, including *Interpretation of the English Bible* (seventeen volumes), eighteen volumes of sermons and fifteen volumes of other material (yet unpublished), which constitute an invaluable, enduring Carroll library.

Dr. Carroll died November 11, 1914 and was buried in Waco, Texas. A while before his death he prayed that he might recover so as to preach just one more sermon. He was indeed, "the colossus of Baptist history."

MY INFIDELITY AND WHAT BECAME OF IT*

There was nothing in my home life to beget infidelity. My father was a self-educated Baptist minister, preaching to village or country churches. My mother was a devoted Christian of deep and humble piety. There were no infidel books in our home library, nor in any other accessible to me. My teachers were Christians—generally preachers. There were no infidels of my acquaintance, and no public sentiment in favor of them. My infidelity was never from without, but always from within.

From unrembered time this skepticism progressed irregularly. Sometimes in one hour there would be more progress in extent and definiteness than in previous months. These short periods of huge advances were always sudden and startling. Place and circumstances had but little to do with them. The doubt was seldom germane to the topic under consideration. At times it came when I was in the Sunday School or hearing a sermon or bowed with the others in family prayer—more frequently when waking at night after healthful sleep, and still more frequently when rambling alone in the fields or woods or mountain heights.

Thus, before I knew what infidelity was, I was an infidel. My child-mind was fascinated by strange and sometimes horrible questionings concerning many religious subjects. Long before I had read the experiences of others, I had been borne far beyond sight of any shore, wading and swimming beyond my depth after solutions to such questions as the "philosopher's stone," the "elixir of life," and "the fountain of youth," but mainly the "chief good."

I understand now much better the character and direction of the questionings of that early period. I know now that I never doubted the being, personality and government of God. I was never an atheist or pantheist. I never doubted the existence and ministry of angels—pure spirits never embodied: I could never have been a Sadducee. I never doubted the essential distinction between spirit and matter: I could never have been a materialist.

*Address before Ministers' Institute in Nashville, February, 1892.
From *Sermons* by B. H. Carroll, American Baptist Publication Society. Used by permission.

And as to the origin of things, the philosophy of Democritus, developed by Epicurus, more by Lucretius, and gone to seed in the unverified hypothesis of modern evolutionists—such a godless, materialistic anti-climax of philosophy never had the slightest attraction or temptation for me. The intuitions of humanity preserved me from any ambition to be descended from either beast or protoplasm. I never doubted the immortality of the soul and conscious future existence. I never doubted the final just judgment by the Creator of the world.

But my infidelity related to the Bible and its manifest doctrines. I doubted that it was God's book; an inspired revelation of His will to man. I doubted miracles, the divinity of Jesus, and his vicarious expiation for the sins of man. I doubted any real power and vitality in the Christian religion. I never doubted that the Scriptures claimed inspiration, nor that they taught unequivocally the divinity and vicarious expiation of Jesus.

The trifling expedient of accepting the Bible as "inspired in spots" never occured to me. To accept, with Renan, its natural parts and arbitrarily deny its supernatural, or to accept the book as from God, and then strike at its heart by a false interpretation that denied the divinity and vicarious expiation of Jesus —these were follies of which I was never guilty. What anybody wanted, in a religious way, with the shell after the kernel was gone I never could understand.

While the beginnings of my infidelity cannot be recalled, I can give the date when it took tangible shape. I do know just when it emerged from choas and outlined itself in my consciousness with startling distinctness. An event called it out of the mists and shadows into conscious reality. It happened on this wise:

There was a protracted meeting in our vicinity. A great and mysterious influence swept over the community. Many people, old and young, joined the church and were baptized. Doubtless in the beginning of the meeting the conversions were what I would now call genuine. Afterwards many merely went with the tide. To me it was only a curious spectacle. I had manifested no special interest except once or twice mechanically and experimenally. I had no conviction for sin. I had not felt lost and did not feel saved. First one and then another catechized me.

"Don't you believe the Bible? "Yes." "Don't you believe in Jesus Christ?" "Y-e-s." "Well, dosen't the Bible say that whoever believes in Jesus Christ is saved?" "Yes."

Now, mark three things: First, this catechizing was by zealous church-members. Second, the answers were historical as from a textbook. Third, I was only thirteen years old. They reported to the preachers: "Here is a lad who believes the Bible, believes in Jesus Christ and believes that he is saved. Ought not such a one to join the church?" Now came the pressure of well-meant but unwise persuasion. The whole thing would have been exposed, if when I presented myself for membership, I had been asked to tell my own story without prompting or leading questions. I did not have any to tell and would have told none. But many had joined, the hour was late, the die was cast.

Until after my baptism everything seemed unreal, but walking home from the baptism the revelation came. The vague infidelity of all the past took positive shape, and would not down at my bidding. My answers had been educational. I did not believe that the Bible was God's revelation. I did not believe in miracles or the divinity or vicarious sufferings of Jesus. I had no confidence in conversion and regeneration. There was no perceptible change in my disposition or affections. What I once loved, I still loved; what I once hated, I still hated. It was no temporary depression as sometimes comes to genuine Christians.

Joining the church, with its assumption of obligations acted on me like a touch of Ithuriel's spear. I saw my real self. I knew that either I had no religion or it was not worth having. The sensation of actual and positive infideliy was so new to me that I hardly knew what to say about it. I felt a repugnance to parade it. I wanted time and trial for its verification. I knew that its avowal would pain and horrify my family and the church, yet honesty required me to say something.

So I asked that the church withdraw from me on the ground that I was not converted. This was not granted because the brethren thought that I mistook temporary mental depression for lack of conversion. They asked me to give it a trial; to read the Bible and pray. From that time on I read the Bible as never before—read it all many times; studied it in the light of my infidelity; marked its contradictions and fallacies, as they seemed to me, from Genesis to Revelation. Two years passed. In this interval we moved to Texas. In a meeting when I was fifteen years old, I was persuaded to retain membership for further examination.

Now came the period of reading Christian apologies and infidel books. What a multitude of them of both kinds! Hume, Paine, Volney, Bolingbroke, Rousseau, Voltaire, Taylor, Gibbon, and others, over against Watson, Nelson, Horn, Calvin, Walker and a host of others. In the meantime I was at college devouring the Greek, Roman and Oriental philosophies. At seventeen, being worn out in body and mind, I joined McCullough's Texas Rangers, the first regiment mustered into the Confederate service, and on the remote, uninhabited frontier pursued the investigation with unabated ardor.

Then came another event. It came from no sin on my part, but it blasted every hope and left me in Egyptian darkness. The battle of life was lost. In seeking the field of war, I sought death. By peremptory demand I had my church connection dissolved and turned utterly away from every semblance of Bible belief to infidelity. This time I brought it a broken heart and a disappointed life, asking for light and peace and rest. It was no no curious speculation; no tentative intellectual examination. It was a stricken soul, anxiously and earnestly seeking light.

As I was in the first Confederate regiment, so I was in the last corps that surrendered; but while armies grappled and throttled each other, a darker and deadlier warfare raged within me. My quest for the truth was sincere and unintermittent. Happy people whose lives are not blasted may affect infidelity, may appear to its oracles from a curious, speculative interest, and may minister to their intellectual pride by seeming to be odd.

It was not so with me. With all the earnestness of a soul between which and happiness the bridges were burned, I brought a broken and bleeding, but honest heart to every reputed oracle of infidelity. I did not ask life, fame or pleasure. I merely asked light to shine on the path of right. Once more I viewed the anti-Christian philosophies, no longer to admire them in what they destroyed, but to inquire what they built up, and offered to a hungry heart and blasted life. There now came to me a revelation as awful as when Mokanna, in Moore's *Lalla Rookh* lifted his veil for Zelica.

Why had I never seen it before: These philosophies were mere negations; they overturned but built up nothing. I say nothing; I mean nothing. To the unstricken, curious soul, they are as beautiful as the aurora borealis, shining on arctic icebergs. But to me they warmed and melted nothing. No flowers bloomed and no fruit ripened under their cheerless beams. They looked down on my bleeding heart as the cold, distant, pitiless stars have ever looked down on all human suffering. Whoever, in his hour of real need, rests on abstract philosophy, makes cold, hard granite his pillow. Whoever looks trustingly into its false faces, looks into the face of Medusa, and is turned to stone. They are all wells without water, and clouds without rain in a parching drouth.

In the soul's hour of need who can conjure by the name of Voltaire? Of what avail is Epicurus or Zeno, Huxley or Darwin? Here was my case: I had turned my back on Christianity, and had found nothing in infidelity; happiness was gone and death would not come.

The Civil War had left me a wounded cripple on crutches, utterly poverty-stricken and loaded with debt. The internal war of infidelity, after making me roll hopelessly the ever-falling stone of Sisyphus, vainly climb the revolving wheel of Ixion, and stoop like Tantalus to drink waters that ever receded, or reach out for fruit that could not be grasped, now left me bound like Prometheus on the cold rock, while vultures tore with beak and talons a life that could suffer, but could not die.

At this time, two books of the Bible took hold of me with unearthly power. I knew from my experience that they were neither fiction or allegory—Job and Ecclesiastes. Some soul had walked those paths. They were histories, not dreams and not mere poems. Like Job, I believed in God; and like him had cried: "Oh, that I knew where I might find him', that I might come even to his seat! . . . Behold, I go forward but he is not there: and backward, but I cannot perceive him: on the left hand, where he doth work, but I cannot behold him: he hideth himself on the right hand, that I cannot see him: but he knoweth the way that I take."

Like Job, I could not find answers in nature to the heart's sorest need and the most important questions; and, like Job, regarding God as my adversary, I had cried out for a revelation: "Oh, that one would hear me! behold, my desire is, that the Almighty would answer me, and that mine adversary had written a book. Surely I would take it upon my shoulder, and bind it as a crown to me." Like Job, I felt the need of a mediator, who as a man could enter into my case, and as divine could enter into God's case; and, like Job, I had complained: "He is not a man as I am, that I should answer him, and we should come together in judgment. Neither is there any daysman betwixt us, that might lay his hand upon us both."

Thus I approached my twenty-second year. I had sworn never to put my foot in another church. My father had died believing me lost. My mother—when does a mother give up a child?—came to me one day and begged, for her sake, that I would attend one more meeting. It was a Methodist camp meeting, held in the fall of 1865. I had not an atom of interest in it. I liked the singing, but the preaching did not touch me.

But one day I shall never forget. It was Sunday at eleven o'clock. The great, wooden shed was crowded. I stood on the out-skirts, leaning on my crutches, wearily and somewhat scornfully enduring. The preacher made a failure even for him. But when he came down, as I supposed to exhort as usual, he startled me not only by not exhorting, but by asking some questions that seemed meant for me.

He said: "You that stand aloof from Christianity and scorn us simple folks, what have you got? Answer honestly before God, have you found anything worth having?" My heart answered: "Nothing under the whole heaven; absolutely nothing." As if he had heard my unspoken answer, he continued: "Is there anything else out there with promise worth trying?" Again my heart answered: "Nothing, absolutely nothing. I have been to the jumping-off place on all these roads. They lead to a bottomless abyss." "Well, then," he continued, "admitting there's nothing there, if there be a God, mustn't there be a something somewhere? If so, how do you know it is not here? Are you willing to test it? I don't ask you to read any book, nor study any evidences, nor make any pilgrimages. Are you willing to try it now; to make a practical, experimental test, you to be the judge of the result?"

These calm and pertinent questions hit me with tremendous force, but I didn't understand the test. He continued: "I base my test on these two Scriptures: 'If any man willeth to do his will, he shall know of the doctrine whether it be of God'; "Then shall we know if we follow on to know the Lord.' " For the first time I understood the import of these Scriptures. I had never before heard of such a translation. In our version it says "If any man will do the will of God, he shall know of the doctrine whether it be of God." But the preacher quoted it: "Whosoever willeth to do the will of God," showing that the knowledge as to whether the doctrine was of God depended not upon external action or exact conformity with God's will, but upon the internal disposition. In the second Scripture was also new light: "Then shall we know if we follow on to know the Lord," which means that true knowledge follows persistence in the prosecution of it.

So, when he invited all who were willing to make an immediate experimental test to come forward and give him their hands, I went forward. I was not prepared for the stir which this created. My infidelity and my hostile attitude toward Christianity were so well known in the community that such action developed quite a sensation. Some even began to shout. Whereupon, to prevent misconception, I arose and stated that I was not converted; that my heart was as cold as ice; my action meant no more than that I was willing to make an experimental test of the truth and power of the Christian religion, and to persist in subjection to the test until a true solution could be found. This quieted matters.

The meeting closed without any change upon my part. The last sermon had been preached, the benediction pronounced and the congregation was dispersing. A few ladies only remained, seated near the pulpit and singing. Feeling that the experiment was ended and the solution not found, I remained to hear them sing. As their last song they sang:

O land of rest, for thee I sigh,
When will the moment come
When I shall lay my armor by
And dwell in peace at home.

The singing made a wonderful impression upon me. Its tones were as soft as the rustling of angels' wings. Suddenly there flashed upon my mind, like a light from heaven, this Scripure: "Come unto me all ye that labour and are heavy laden, and I will give you rest." I did not see Jesus with my eye, but I seemed to see him standing before me, looking reproachfully and tenderly and pleadingly, seeming to rebuke me for having gone to all other sources for rest but the right one, and now inviting me to come to Him. In a moment I went, once and forever, casting myself unreservedly for all time at his feet, and in a moment the rest came, indescribable and unspeakable, and it has remained from that day until now.

I gave no public expression of the change which had passed over me, but spent the night in the enjoyment of it and wondering if it would be with me when morning came. When the morning came, it was still with me, brighter than the sunlight and sweeter than the songs of birds, and now for the first time, I understood the Scripture which I had often heard my mother repeat: "Ye shall go out with joy, and be led forth with peace: the mountains and the hills shall break forth before you into singing, and all the trees of the field shall clap their hands" (Isa. 55:12).

When I reached home, I said nothing, but the experience could not be hidden. As I was walking across the floor on my crutches, an orphan boy whom my mother had raised called attention to the fact that I was both whistling and crying. I knew that my mother heard him, and to avoid observation, went at once to my room, lay down on my bed and covered my face with my hands. I heard her coming. She pulled my hands away and gazed long and steadfastly without a word. A light came over her face as the shining on the face of Stephen; and with trembling lips, she said: "My son, you have found the Lord." Her happiness was indescribable. I don't think she slept that night. She seemed to fear that she might dream and wake to find that the glorious fact was but a vision of the night.

I spent the night at her bedside reading *Pilgrim's Progress*. When I came with the pilgrims to the Beulah land, from which Doubting Castle could be seen no more forever, and which was within sight of the Heavenly City and within sound of the heavenly music, my soul was filled with a rapture and ecstacy of joy such as I had never before experienced. I knew then as well as I know now, that I would preach; that it would be my life work; that I would have no other.

Chapter IV

W. T. CONNER

AUTOBIOGRAPHICAL SKETCH

I was born January 19, 1877, in Cleveland County, Arkansas, between Pine Bluff and Warren. My father owned a small farm. He was married twice, and had one boy by his first wife and six boys and two girls by his second. Four boys and one girl survive.

We lived at the place indicated until I was about thirteen and then moved to the western part of the same country near Kingsland, where my father worked at a saw mill, hauling logs and lumber. When I was nearly sixteen we moved eight miles west of Abilene, Texas. I have lived in Texas ever since then, except three years in seminaries.

My earliest religious impressions go back to the church where my parents and grandmother belonged in Cleveland County, Arkansas. These impressions were deepened in Kingsland community, but I was not converted until I reached Texas and attended an old-time, hurrah, Methodist meeting in the summer of 1894.

The man who baptized me was W. M. Reynolds. In the summer of 1895 J. M. Reynolds, his brother, held a meeting in our church. He asked me if I thought I was called to preach. I answered in the affirmative. He arranged with the pastor and church to license me and helped to get started by making appointments in the adjoining communities. I shall always be grateful for his assistance. My impression to preach, however. runs back to the time when I was a small boy, and became a definite conviction soon after I was converted.

Up to the time that I began to try to preach, I had never gone to any but ungraded country schools on an average of three of four months a year and some years practically none. In '95 or '96 I went to Simmons College (now Hardin-Simmons University) for about two or three months. I attended one full session in '96 and '97 and most of '97-'98.

In the fall of 1898 I entered Baylor, borrowing money from C. P. Warren, the father-in-law of Dr. L. R. Scarborough. Then I dropped out and taught school two years to pay back a debt of fifty dollars. In the winter of '98-'99 I taught at Anderson's Chapel in Jones County and the next winter at Lawn in the southern part of Taylor County. During the winter that I taught in Jones County, I preached for the church at Tuscola, Texas, my first pretense at being a pastor. The next winter while living at Lawn, I preached for my home church in Caps, in the community where I had been converted.

During my first year in Baylor, I came in contact with John S. Tanner, the most dynamic teacher I ever knew. I had a year with him in English Bible and also studied college algebra and solid geometry with him.

The fall of 1901 I went back to Baylor and stayed until January, 1903, and dropped out to help a brother go there. He was called to preach but died in 1910 having contracted tuberculosis while at Simmons. I preached at Eagle Lake half-time and quarter-time each at Rock Island and East Bernard. In the fall of 1904 I went back to Baylor and graduated with the A.B. degree in 1906. Two women at Eagle Lake, Mrs. F. O. Norris and her sister, Mrs. Green, sent me over a hundred dollars to help on expenses in Baylor. In those days a hundred dollars was a hundred dollars.

Among those who graduated in the class of 1906 was Miss Blanche Horne, who later taught Latin in the high school at Hillsboro. On June 4, 1907 we were married. Dr. S. P. Brooks asked me to teach Latin in Baylor the following year since Dr. Daniel, the professor of Latin, was ill. I accepted on condition that he would let my wife teach half of it. He readily agreed because he knew she was the better Latin teacher. I stayed at Baylor and studied in what was then the Baylor Theological Seminary taking the Th.B. and A.M. degrees in 1908.

That fall I went to Rochester and graduated in 1909—no degree being given then on graduation. I stayed on a graduate scholarship another year, wrote a thesis at the suggestion of Professor Walter Rauschenbusch on the "Theology of Theodore Parker", and received the B.D. degree. In the late spring of 1910 I went to the University of Chicago and studied about two weeks under Dr. George B. Foster. About the first or the middle of June I came back to Texas and was Associational Missionary in the Alvarado (now Johnson County) Association.

In the fall of 1910 I succeeded Dr. Calvin Goodspeed as teacher of Theology at Southwestern and have taught ever since. I have had two periods of study away. One was six weeks in the summer of 1920 at the University of Chicago. The other was during most of 1914 at the Southern Seminary. I had a major in Theology with Dr. E. Y. Mullins, a minor in the philosophy of Religion with Dr. W. O. Carver, and a minor in the Phychology of Religion with Dr. B. H. De Ment.

In the summer of 1920 I received a D.D. degree from Baylor. I have engaged in numerous activities, including lectures at summer assemblies. Altogether I have written twelve books, including *Christian Doctrine, Revelation and God, The Faith of the New Testament* and *The Gospel of Redemption.*

In our family we have five daughters and one son, all grown and still living. Their names are: Mary, John Davis, Arnette, Blanche Ray, Neppie Lee and Sarah Frances. All are married except Neppie Lee, who teaches art in the University of Arkansas. We have five granddaughters and three grandsons.

THE PLACE OF PRAYER IN THE CHRISTIAN LIFE

The place of prayer in the Christian life is a vital one. Sometimes people raise the question as to whether or not it is legitimate for one to pray for salvation. To my mind there is no question about that. The question would rather be whether one is a Christian if he has not prayed at least in spirit.

Salvation comes from God. It comes as a free gift and if one has not at least assumed the attitude of asking for God's mercy, there would be a serious question as to whether he could be a Christian. God gives and we receive. If we want to receive, then we should ask. I do not mean by this that one should necessarily speak words aloud or that he should repeat a certain formula, but I do mean that the spirit of looking to God, asking for mercy, and depending on him must be in our hearts if we are to receive his mercy and salvation.

As to the place of prayer in the Christian life, I should say that it is essential. Prayer is of the very essence of the Christian life. It is not something to be added on or left off, as an appendage to the Christian life, but something that belongs to the very essence and nature of that life. Communion with God is essential in being a Christian. With this general statement, I would like for us to consider several phases of this matter of prayer.

There are certain principles underlying prayer. One might call them presuppostions or fundamental principles in relation to prayer. Let it be understood that I am discussing this matter from the standpoint of the Christian revelation of God.

One of these principles is that we should believe in the reality of God. To pray is to assume that there is a Power above and beyond man on which man is dependent and from which Men's blessings come. One could hardly pray if he did not believe that there was such a Power.. The Book of Hebrews tells us that one must believe that God is and that he is a rewarder of those that seek him. Here we are saying that underlying prayer is the implicit belief that such a Power exists and that man is related to that Power.

Moreover, prayer assumes that man is dependent. One of the deepest things in man's consciousness is the feeling of dependence. This feeling of dependence is so deeply embedded in man's consciousness that the German theologian Schleiermacher said that this sense of dependence was the essence of religion. He thus made religion universal. We might not care to make this the essence of religion with Schleiermacher, but we certainly could agree that this sense of dependence is deeply embedded in man's consciousness and is one of the reasons that prayer in some form is found among practically all peoples.

Another assumption underlying prayer is that God is personal. By this we are not to understand that God has the limitations of man. He is personal in the sense that he is intelligent and purposeful. He is not only intelligent, but he is the source of all intelligence in the universe. All the rational creatures of our universe have their being rooted in God. He is the source of all intelligence in life.

He is not purposeful in the sense that he has to question and debate and painfully work out his plans, but he is purposeful in the sense that he knows what he is about and moves toward the attainment of his fundamental intentions in relation to man and the world. He is personal in the sense that all finite personalities have the ground of their being in him and find their ultimate end in God. Some people have tried to maintain religion and even prayer in some form apart from belief in a personal God. But to say the least of it, prayer in the Christian sense without belief in the personality of God is impossible. What would thanksgiving or petition mean if there were no One to thank or no One from which we should ask.

Prayer also assumes that in some sense God is interested in man and in his welfare. The purpose of prayer is not to get God interested in man but to help in realizing the good will that God has toward man. One of the fundamental things in the Christians religion is God's love toward man. This love of God for man is expressed in the Greek New Testament by a word that means rational good will. Only once or twice do we find the verb used with reference to God's attitude toward man that denotes personal or intimate affection. Once or twice in the Gospel according to John such a word is used with reference to God's attitude toward the personal disciples of Jesus. In other places it is a word that means rational and purposeful good will. The New Testament gives us the impression that God from all eternity has had such good will toward man. In fact, in the First Epistle of John, we are told that God is love and the word used for love denotes this kind of good will.

So when we say that underlying prayer is the assumption that God has such good will toward man we are expressing what is implied in different ways in the New Testament with reference to this matter. Such an assumption does not necessarily belong to the general religious consciousness of mankind. It is an assumption involved in the Christian revelation of God.

The Christian assumption with reference to this matter is that God has a plan for our lives. Most any Christian whether he is Calvinistic or otherwise in his theology feels that somehow God has a plan for the life of each of his children and that prayer will help us to find and follow that plan. We are not to think of this plan as a dogmatic and arbitrary decree that interferes with our freedom or responsibilities with reference to our lives. Christians generally, however, do feel that by prayer and fellowship with God they can come into harmony with his will and find the direction in which he would have them go.

This is the direct contrary of what some people might think with reference to prayer. They might think of prayer as an effort on man's part to impose his plan and his will on God. People who misunderstand the nature and purpose of prayer have sometimes so spoken of it. They have denied the efficacy of prayer because they assumed that prayer was an effort to impose man's petty ideas and plans on God and bring God into line with these plans of man. The nature of prayer is just the opposite. It is not the purpose of prayer to bring God into line with man's ideas and purposes, but to bring man into harmony with God's plan and purpose for the one who prays.

Sometimes this question is raised with reference to prayer: If God is all-wise and good, if he knows what is best for us and wants to give us what is best, then why should we pray? Why not just leave God to give us what he knows to be best without trying to change or influence him in the matter?

Let me come back to emphasize that the teaching of Jesus is that God does know best. Jesus distinctly says that our

Father knows what we have need of before we ask him. Prayer, therefore, cannot be for the purpose of informing God. If we had to inform the Lord, we would in all likelihood misinform him. We would likely not give him true knowledge of the situation. If he were dependent on man's puny wisdom, he could not understand the true situation. He knows infinitely better what we need than we do. He looks ahead. He sees everything about us in true relation. He understands with a wisdom that is far above man.

Why, then, should we pray if God knows best what we need? Well, for one thing, Jesus wants us to come in our ignorance and blindness submitting ourselves to the infinite wisdom of God and trusting him to do what is best. We are to be enlightened by his wisdom, not that he is to be enlightened by ours.

Nor is the primary purpose of prayer to impose our wills on God. It is rather to bring us into line with his will and his purpose for us and our world. Jesus taught us to pray: "Thy kingdom come, thy will be done on earth as it is in heaven." The coming of his Kingdom means the reign of God in the hearts and lives of men. We are to pray for his will to be done in us and in the world in which we live.

Nor does this mean that we simply are to be passive in our attitude in regard to the matter. Our wills are to be active. We are to pray with energetic willing toward God and his work in the world. But while we are to be active and energetic, we are always to seek to bring our wills in line with his purposes and pray that our wills shall be done only as they are in line with his. We are to will in prayer but to will in harmony with the purposes of God and not contrary to his will I remember reading a statement from S. D. Gordon many years ago to this effect: that in prayer we do not work against God: we work *with* God. We are to pray as God's Spirit energizes in our hearts and brings us to will in harmony with him and his plan for us and the world. Jesus himself prayed: "Not my will, but thine be done" when such a prayer meant for agony and death. Such should be the Christian's attitude in prayer.

Let us come back to the question then: Since God knows and wills for us the best, why should we pray? We should pray on the ground that God in accomplishing his will in the world wants to take us into fellowship with him in bringing his purposes and plans. Prayer is the most personal act that a Christian ever performs in the religious life. It is the recognition of God as a Person of infinite knowledge and good will toward us and all mankind. It is our personal adjustment to him as such a Person. It is our effort to come into harmony with him as such a Person and try to help him work out his purposes and plans in our lives and the world.

We may not see all that God has in mind for us in willing that we should pray, but I think we can at least see this: Prayer is God's plan to take us up into fellowship with him in carrying out his purposes in the world. It might be put like this: In doing Christian work we do not simply find a general plan that God has laid down and seek to follow that plan by the use of our natural intelligence. God has, no doubt, such a general plan for each of us, but prayer makes God's plan for us intimate and personal. In prayer we seek to have such fellowship with God that we can work in intimate fellowship with him in carrying out his purposes in the world.

Take the matter of redemption which is central in the gospel of Christ. God's purpose for man is redemptive. He wants to take each of the sons of God into fellowship with himself in carrying out the purpose of redemption in relation to mankind. So when we ourselves experience redemption, he puts something of his own passion in our hearts for the salvation of others. In line with his purpose he prompts us by his Spirit to pray for others that they may be redeemed. He moves us to pray for those who are working as evangelists, missionaries, and in other forms of Christian service, for the redemption of men. In doing this, God takes us up into fellowship with himself and thereby transforms us more and more into his own image. The Spirit of Christ comes increasingly to possess us, move us, and control us in all our relations in life.

This means that to look on prayer simply as a means of getting "things" from God is to see prayer in a rather superficial light. I have read of prayer as a means of getting "things" from God. I do not mean to say that God does not sometimes give us things in answer to prayer, but I would say with emphasis that that is not the main purpose of prayer. The main purpose of prayer is to bring God himself into our lives and let God work out his purposes and plans in and through us. God himself is the answer to prayer. Prayer is not simply petition. It is much more than that. It includes adoration, thanksgiving, confession, intercession. In all of this, we are coming into fellowship with God and God himself is coming into our lives. As God comes into our lives, he transforms us more and more into the image of the living and redeeming Christ.

One reason, then, why God wants us to pray is for our own sakes. It brings us closer to himself. It makes us more like himself. He is thereby carrying out his purpose of good will concerning us.

Do not understand by this, however, what has sometimes been called the reflex influence of prayer. A man like Immanuel Kant, the great philosopher, says plainly in his lectures on ethics that the reflex influence of prayer is the only benefit. He means by this evidently that there is no direct communion or personal touch of the spirit of man with the Spirit of God. Prayer only helps man, so he evidently thinks, because it enables man to bring himself into a better state of mind and heart. Prayer would be only a man's effort to lift himself over the fence by his own bootstraps. I have not seen anybody able to get very high off the ground by such an effort. What I mean to say is that one reason God ordains for us to pray is because prayer brings us in fellowship with God and makes us like God. God himself is the answer to prayer.

I do not mean, however, that the blessing to the man who prays is the only benefit that comes from prayer. In ways that we do not understand God works his purposes in the lives of others in answer to our prayer. God energizes in the lives of others as we pray for them. One of the constant pleas of the apostle Paul was that his fellow Christians pray for him. He uses language that shows that he means that they agonize in prayer, that they thall labor in prayer. We can help other Christians around the world by praying for them. We can help men into the Kingdom of God by interceding for them.

I should like to emphasize also that there is what one might call a listening side to prayer. Some people consider one a good conversationalist if he will do all the listening and let them do all the talking. Some of us are like that in relation to God. We want God to listen and we want to do all the talking. In prayer we should listen for God's voice as he speaks to us. In fellowship with God in prayer there is light to be obtained on the problems and difficulties of life that can not be obtained any other way. If one wishes light from the face of God to illumine his way, he should listen attentively when he seeks to have fellowship with God.

Nor should we think of seeking God in prayer simply for our sakes. It is true that if we seek God and his will, abundant blessings will come to us. God is our chief need. In a true sense, God is our only need. But we have not yet been brought to the true view of the matter until we see that we should seek God for his own sake. We should adore and worship him because he is worthy of our adoration and worship. We should **make God the end** of prayer and worship, not man. If we seek God because of what he will do for us, we have not yet risen above the human plane. We should worship him for what he is within himself, not merely because of what he gives us. A good father or mother does not wish to be loved by a son or daughter for what the son or daughter thinks to get from loving the parent. True love is bestowed for the sake of the one loved, not for the sake of the lover.

One other word. How can one know about the reality and blessing of prayer? He can know in only one way, namely, by trying it. He cannot know by arguing. He cannot know merely by hearing about it. He cannot know even by reading the Bible. These things may give him suggestions, but he will really know for himself only as he tries it. Dr. S. P. Brooks told once about an incident that took place while he was a student in Baylor University. Brooks was a Christian. He had a friend who was not. This friend came to him one day and, calling him by his first name, said: "Palmer, do you suppose God would hear a man like me pray?" Those who knew Dr. Brooks will recognize his answer as characteristic of the man. He said: "The way to find out is to try." They went into the old tabernacle that used to stand back of where the First Baptist Church of Waco now stands. They got down on their knees and Brooks prayed, then the other man prayed, and God saved him. The way you find out about prayer is to try it out. There is no other way.

Chapter V

B. A. COPASS

AUTOBIOGRAPHICAL SKETCH

My ancestors came from Normandy to England in 1166. I have a book called *Brother Copass* written in England a century or so ago. The descendants of those who came with William have scattered over the countries wherever the English people have gone. My son, who was in World War II, found people by our name in New Zealand and Australia. My daughter found a number in the telephone directory in Vancouver, British Columbia. So gradually they drifted to the United States and to the South.

I was born in Clementsville, Tennessee, May 29, 1865. My parents were Charles Wesley and Lucinda (Bowman) Copass. Father's given name would suggest the vigorous Methodist heritage he had. I started life at the close of the Civil War when times were hard. Tennessee had seceded from the Union, was at the northern border of the Confederacy, and practically every square mile of land was fought over by the contending armies and the country largely laid waste. So I know from experience what it means to live under pinched conditions.

My early schooling was rather meager as educational facilities were very poor in our community in those difficult times. Our country schools were from three to five months in length. There were some years when they did not even open the schools due to financial difficulties. They were one-teacher schools with all classes reciting in the same room and we recited aloud while the others tried to carry on their studies. After some years in these irregular country schools I attended Willette Academy, a school founded and maintained for many years by the Baptists in those Tennessee hills.

We moved from Tennessee to Kentucky and much of my

early life was spent in that state. I attended Bethel College at Russelville, Kentucky, receiving the A.B. degree in 1890 and the A.M. in 1893. In 1898 the college conferred on me the D.D. degree. I attended the Southern Baptist Theological Seminary for three years (1891-1894) finishing the regular course of studies which later became the Th.M. course. In those days they did not give a degree, such not being considered as necessary to success as it is now. In the summer of 1919 I attended the University of Chicago.

I was ordained to the ministry July 20, 1889. My first pastorate was at Clinton, Kentucky (1894-96), where Clinton College was located. Some of the students there in those days became leaders later in different parts of the United States, such as Dr. E. B. Atwood, Professor of Bible, in Hardin-Simmons University. Other pastorates were at Los Angeles, California (1896-98); Marksbury, Kentucky (1898-1901; Waxahachie, Texas (1901-06); San Marcos, Texas (1906-12) and Denton, Texas (1912-13). The longest pastorate was at San Marcos where San Marcos Baptist Academy is located. Through the church there I had much to do in establishing and building the Academy. Two state schools are located at Denton, and I enjoyed contact with students at these places.

For four years (1914-18) I served as Associate Secretary of the State Board of Missions of the General Convention of Texas. During that time I had the privilege of being associated with Dr. J. B. Gambrell who was State Missions Secretary. It was the opportunity of a life time. He was a remarkable character and a counselor of rare ability. The experiences connected with this work throughout Texas, together with the pastorates held in various states, gave a fine background for teaching preachers in Southwestern Seminary as head of the Department of Old Testament Interpretation from 1918-1942. I had previously declined a similar position in another seminary.

On May 29, 1894 (my birthday anniversary) I was married to Miss Cloantha Williams, daughter of the vice-president of Bethel College. She died in 1902. Of the four children born to this union, three survive—Mrs. J. B. Kennedy, Jackson, Mississippi; Ben A., Iraan, Texas; and Mrs. A. J. Holgrean, Olympia, Washington. I was married to Miss Crickett Keys of Waxahachie, Texas, September 12, 1904. To this union three children were born, only one of whom, Lieut. Col. Mike Copass of Seattle, Washington, survives. My family has followed the Copass tradition of scattering to different parts of the country, only one being in Texas.

I am a Mason, a Democrat, a member of the Phi Gamma Delta Fraternity and the Texas Baptist Historical Society. My greatest pride and joy, however, have been in membership in a Baptist Church, for the hope of the world lies more in this institution than in all of the societies and fraternal organizations in existence. I have taken an active part in the prohibition movement and other activities for moral and social reform, as well as in the general work of the denomination.

Besides various articles written through the years for newspapers and magazines, I am the author of the following books: *The Message of Hosea* (1906), *A Manuel of Old Testament Theology* (1925), *Theology in Hebrew Words* (1934), *One God* (1935), *Amos* (1938), and *Isaiah, the Prince of Old Testament Prophets* (1943). I have done considerable lecturing at Bible institutes and assemblies.

I retired from teaching in 1942 and am now residing at my home near the Seminary, and doing the things which my physical strength permits. I have always tried to be faithful to every task imposed. Seminary Hill will continue to be the center of things for me until God calls me to go to Him.

PERFECT SALVATION*

"But of him are ye in Christ Jesus, who was made unto us wisdom from God, even righteousness and sanctification and redemption." I Cor. 1:30.

The merest glance at the text, shows two things, plainly evident: Salvation is all of God, and salvation is all through Jesus Christ. And the Christ preached by the Apostle, is the Christ of the Cross—"But we preach Christ crucified." "For I determined not to know anything among you save Jesus Christ, and Him crucified." The Christ of the resurrection was the Christ of the Cross. It was as if the Apostle was saying: "All the power that dwells in God to draw men out of sin, to holiness and to himself was actually in the cross."

And this general statement of the Apostle is all the more human and interesting, when we remember that the writer was dealing with a concrete and present situation. He had to deal there at Corinth with the two demands that always develop when human hearts come to deal with the question of religion. The demand for external manifestation of power, to prove the so-called religious message to be from God; and the demand for "wisdom," that will appeal to the speculative pride of the minds of men. "Jews ask for signs"— i.e., external manifestations of power; "Greeks seek after wisdom"—i.e., philosophic speculation concerning God, the universe and men.

In the presence of these organized demands the great apostle held up Jesus Christ—"Christ the power of God and the wisdom of God."

As the City of Corinth and the Church in Corinth were more largely Greek than Jew, emphasis is laid upon Christ as wisdom from God. Such is true in our text: "Who was made unto us wisdom from God." This indeed is the message of the text. The remaining portion of the text is but an explanation of "Christ Jesus—wisdom from God"—even righteousness and sanctification and redemption."

I. Righteousness

Christ Jesus, as wisdom from God, becomes to men and for

***Texas State Baptist Convention Sermon, preached at Fort Worth, Nov. 7, 1912.**

men righteousness. This one word raises by implication the whole question of man's sinfulness and his resultant separation from a holy God. It implies that, if man returns to God, he must have righteousness, and a righteousness, that he himself cannot acquire. Another must provide it for him. This, God himself did when He provided Christ Jesus, "Him who knew no sin, He (God) made to be sin on our behalf, that we might become the righteousness of God in Him."

This word of our text makes no reference to any change in the character of one who comes to God through Christ, but rather to His standing before God in Christ. God sees not man's sinfulness, but his own righteousness as manifested and applied in Jesus.

This manifestation and application of righteousness through Christ, makes possible and actual man's justification in the sight of God. As some one explains: "That judicial act of God, by which, on account of Christ to whom the sinner is united by faith, he declares that sinner to be no longer exposed to the penally of law, but to be restored to his favor. The reversal of God's attitude toward the sinner, because of the sinner's new relation to Christ. God did condemn, He now acquits."

A Greek once stood before a tribunal charged and proved guilty of treason against his country. The judge asked whether any one knew a reason why the prisoner should not be sentenced and ordered to execution. At this juncture a man stepped forth from the spectators and held up two stumps of arms. He said: "I gave my two hands in behalf of my country in honorable battle. The man is guilty, but he is my brother. I plead these two stumps of arms in behalf of my brother." That plea set his brother free. Even so, the Christ of the cross, the wisdom from God, the righteousness of God takes sinful man's place before God, and man goes free. Not because he actually is righteous, but because God in Christ is righteousness.

Anselm, Archbishop of Canterbury about 1100 A.D. wrote a tract called "Consolations for the Dying." In that tract he stated in a concise and striking way the truth of the thought before us. In the form of dialogue he put it: "Dost thou believe that the Lord Jesus died for thee? I believe it. Dost thou thank Him for His passion and death? I do thank Him. Dost thou believe that thou canst not be saved except by His death? I believe it. Come then while life remainest in thee; in His death alone place thy whole trust, in naught else place thy trust; to His death commit thyself wholly; with this alone cover thyself wholly. And if the Lord thy God will to judge thee, say: 'Lord, between thee and me, I present the death of our Lord Jesus Christ, not otherwise can I content with thee.' And if He shall say that thou art a sinner, say thou: 'Lord, I interpose the death of our Lord Jesus Christ between my sins and thee.' If He says that thou hast deserved condemnation, say: 'Lord, I set the death of our Lord Jesus Christ between my evil deserts and thee; and His merits I offer for those which I ought to have and have not.' If He shall say that He is wrath with thee, say: 'Lord, I oppose the death of our Lord Jesus Christ between thy wrath and me.' And when thou hast completed this, say again: 'Lord, I set the death of our Lord Jesus Christ between thee and me.'"

This glorious plea is made possible because "Christ Jesus is made unto us wisdom from God, even righteousness." Without this work of Christ in behalf of the sinner, justification before God would be utterly and forever impossible. Here is the dividing line between despair and hope; darkness and light; destruction and salvation.

II. Sanctification

Christ Jesus as wisdom from God becomes to the justified person, sanctification. Some people are much afraid of that word because certain other people have made extravagant, foolish, even sinful claims concerning it. But this good word is found throughout the Bible, from the first book to the last; and holds within its meaning a vital Bible doctrine. It teaches that salvation even for this life, is only begun at the moment of justification. When the soul accepts Christ by faith as a personal Saviour, the Divine life is implanted in that soul by the Holy Spirit. The Spirit who gave that life to the soul abides with it, nurtures it, trains it, develops it, until, in actual character, it is like unto Jesus Christ. In every warfare, struggle, heart longing and aspiration after God and holiness the spirit of God in Christ is present to strengthen, guide and give victory.

Thus we understand that "The work of Jesus (in behalf of the sinner) for this life is two-fold. It is a work accomplished for us, destined to effect reconciliation between God and man: it is a work accomplished in us, with the object of effecting our sanctification. By the one, a right relation is established between God and us; by the other, the fruit of the re-established order is secured. By the former the condemned sinner is received into a state of grace; by the latter the pardoned sinner is associated with the life of God." Justification is the photographer making the negative; sanctification is the photographer developing the negative into the finished picture. Justifictation is the woman placing leaven in the measure of meal; sanctification is the process whereby the whole becomes leavened.

In the latter portion of Rom. 7 the Apostle shows the hopelessness of the struggle for holiness, if the battle is fought alone. The most that can be accomplished is the cry: "Wretched man that I am! Who shall deliver me out of the body of this death?" But in chapter 8 a new personality enters the struggle. That personality is the Spirit of God; and in Him victory is assured. "There is therefore now no condemnation to them that are in Christ Jesus. For the law of the Spirit of Life in Christ Jesus has made me free from the law of sin and death." The saved man is under the law of the Spirit of life. He is therefore, free from the law of sin and death under which he once lived. The outworking and completion of that law of the Spirit must come. That completion is the fulness of the Christ life; or Christ-likeness in character.

We then, as Christians having this hope, are not to allow sin to reign in our mortal bodies. Sin is still there, and will be there so long as we are in this body of our humiliation, but it must be put under foot in the life and power of the Spirit. A struggle there will be, sharp and constant, but victory is sure.

A petulant woman once said to this speaker: "If I ever do become a Christian, I am going to be a good one." The speaker replied: "From the way you have been talking you will be a very poor one. You will spend life battling with your temper." Wide eyed she asked: "What then, is the use of religion?" To which we replied: "To insure us final victory over sin in the Holy Spirit. As you are, you are doomed to defeat here and hereafter. Your struggle is useless without Christ." And, friends, we are permitted to see those who have fought that battle long and arduously, and have almost won. There is almost a halo about their faces as their life's sun is setting.

This preacher was once sent for by an old man who was nearing the end of life's journey. He had a trust to commit to the younger man. As I entered his room he said: "I cannot talk much. First, kneel by my bedside and pray that God's will, in my case, may be done." After the prayer he said: "Now bend over me. Lift my arms about your neck and let me kiss your face. As I near the portal, God gives it to me to love my brethren better." As I looked into that old face, it seemed that I could see a little of the glory. His battle was almost won. His victory was almost complete. In a few days he saw face to face Him who was his sanctification.

III. Redemption

Christ Jesus as wisdom from God becomes to the justified, sanctified person redemption. In its full and complete significence redemption includes and covers all that has been said and more. It lies back of justification and sanctification, and makes both possible. But the Scriptures lay emphasis upon two points of application. An illustration of the first is found in Eph. 1:7 "In whom we have our redemption through His blood even the forgiveness of our trespasses according to the riches of His grace." The meaning here is too obvious to need discussion. But emphasis is also laid upon another point of application. An instance is found in Rom. 8:22-23, "For we know, that the whole creation groaneth and travaileth together in pain until now, and not only so, but ourselves also, who have the first fruits of the spirit, even we ourselves groan within ourselves, waiting for our adoption to-wit: The redemption of our body."

This latter is the sense in which the word is used in our text. The Apostle was looking to that final victory and deliverance from even the presence of sin; when the body too will be redeemed and made like unto the body of the glory of Jesus Christ.

Salvation is more than something past. "Salvation is something past, something present and something future. A past fact, justification; a present process, sanctification; a future consumation, redemption and glory." If the past fact has been accomplished within a soul, the present and the future are assured. "For our citizenship is in heaven; whence also we wait for a Savior, the Lord Jesus Christ; who shall fashion anew the body of our humiliation, that it may be conformed unto the body of His glory, according to the working whereby He is able even to subject all things unto Himself." These bodies of ours are now full of sin, pain and death. They will go to the grave and corruption, if our Lord delay His coming. But when He comes these bodies will be raised from the dead, and fashioned anew like unto the glorified body of Jesus Christ. We will be like Him, spirit and body and the salvation already begun and now in process will be complete.

This blessed hope is not only for the Christian personally, but it comforts in the tenderest and most sacred relations of life. Many persons in this audience know something of the sorrows and bereavements of the speaker since he has been in Texas, now eleven years. Four times has he seen the bodies of loved ones go to the grave. One of those deaths was so full of glory that he may be permitted to describe it. A little boy, his father's constant companion, was going. The little fellow was motherless. Just before he left he said: "Father, take me into your arms." After a few moments he said: "Put me into the bed again." He seemed to know that his father held his body on earth for the last time. Then he said: "I want father and auntie and Cloantha and Benjamin and Clarissa (the members of the family including the servant girl) to go with me." In a few moments his spirit went away and we carried the little body to the grave on the morrow. But, beloved, I shall see him again in the body. His body, no longer subject to pain and death, but glorified. Then we will part never again, but be together with Jesus who is our redemption.

We need to see the Christ as the center and sum of all things pertaining to the relation of God and men.

"What the hand is to the lute,
What the breath is to the flute,
What is fragrance to the smell;
What the spring is to the dell,
What the flower is to the bee,

That is Jesus Christ to me.

What the mother to the child,
What the Guide in pathless wild,
What is oil to troubled wave,
What is ransom to the slave,
What is water to the sea,
That is Jesus Christ to me.

And with this Saviour as our Saviour now and forever, and this message of Christ Jesus as wisdom from God even righteousness and sanctification and redemption, and in this power of the Holy Spirit, we are to go to a lost world and preach the Christ of the Cross as did the great Apostle at Ephesus and Corinth. We need no new message for the Twentieth Century, but the old story of abounding grace and redeeming love. We need to preach perfect and eternal salvation in the cross of Calvary.

"Exalt the cross! its awful shape
Athwart the blood red sky,
Shall turn the nations of the earth
To Him of Calvary.

Exalt the cross! its outstretched arms,
To all the world proclaim
The passion of a Savior's love,
The glory of his name.

Beyond all human ken,
Exalt the cross! its mystery,
Shall break the hearts, wash white the souls
Of multitudes of men.

Exalt the cross! its feebleness,
Transfigured Divine,
Shall shake the whole great teeming earth,
Christ conquers in this sign."

CHAPTER VI

J. W. CROWDER

AUTOBIOGRAPHICAL SKETCH

I was born of American parents on a farm near Hayesville, Tennessee, March 27, 1873. I lived and worked on this farm with the family of nine children until I was grown.

My family was poor and educational advantages were meager. My first school was the "Old Field School" three and one-half miles away. To this school I walked with my oldest brother when I was six years old. My first book was Webster's *Blue Back Speller*. After two years we were transferred to the Hayesville school, where we had college men for our teachers, one of whom especially inspired me with visions of the possibilities for a country boy.

Inspired thus, and stimulated by the examples of Abraham Lincoln and James A. Garfield, I split rails and did all kinds of farm work. Like Lincoln, I studied by the light of the fireplace, and like Garfield, the tow-boy, carried my books with me to my daily tasks. Having gone as far as possible in my studies with the constant calls from the farm, I bought my freedom from my father for three months, by which I was able to prepare for teaching in Tennessee. Then I entered High School at Lafayette, ten miles from home, and walked back for the week-ends in order to make my limited funds hold out.

I organized my first school at Hayesville, Tennessee, January 3, 1893. This was the beginning of a public service of fifty years—two in Tennessee, three in Kentucky, and forty-five in Texas.

In 1897 I came to Texas and taught in the public schools four years, during which time I entered the ministry. I was "liberated", or licensed, by the Weston Baptist Church, September 30, 1899; preached my first sermon October 6; was called to the pastorate of the Honey Creek Baptist Church, January 20, 1900; and was ordained March 3 of the same year. During more than forty years of ministry, I have held fourteen pastorates in Texas: six in Collin County, two in Hill, one in Freestone, one in Robertson, one in Ellis, two in Fort Worth, and one in Parker County.

I was married in Tennessee to Miss Allie May Morrow, June 1, 1897. To this union were born two children, Carroll and Noma, both of whom survive. On April 1, 1934, my first wife passed away. On May 11, 1935, I was married to Mrs. May Fair of Sherman, Texas, a registered nurse and welfare worker. We have lived on Seminary Hill twelve years.

In October, 1905, I moved from Celina to Waco for study in Baylor University, enrolling for an A.B. degree, including Latin and Greek. At the same time I became a student with Dr. B. H. Carroll and after four years of study received from his hand in 1908 the special degree of the English Bible (E.B.). In 1909 Dr. Carroll asked me to become his assistant in the English Bible Department of the Seminary, looking to becoming his successor as teacher. At first I declined intending to go to Yale after finishing in Baylor, but in response to his urgent request I reconsidered and decided to go with him. This Dr. W. W. Lackey has admirably expressed in verse thus:

"Eschewing fame and bright career,
He chose to walk with the greatest seer."

In 1910 I came with the Seminary to Fort Worth and finished my course in absentia in Baylor, receiving the Classical A.B. degree in 1911. In the meantime I was carrying forward my work on the Th.M. degree in the Seminary. This course was pursued until work in the following departments was finished: Church History, Homiletics, Systematic Theology, Missions, New Testament Greek, Hebrew and English Bible. In addition I did by correspondence one year each in Temple University, the University of Chicago, and Webster University for which the D.D. degree was received in 1934.

All my teaching in Tennessee, Kentucky and Texas was done under first grade certificates. During the four years with B. H. Carroll I made an average of 98 plus on the whole Bible and in Senior Greek, an average of 99½. My record in Baylor

University was summed up in the college annual, "Baylor Round-Up", for 1911 with the encomium, "He was a scholar, and a ripe and good one."

In 1901 Dr. Carroll appointed me custodian of his lectures on the English Bible, and, later, compiler and reviser of his manuscripts. Of the thirty-five volumes published, I have furnished the manuscripts for all except four, and now have the manuscripts for fifteen more, which I am editing for publication. Also have published the book: *Dr. B. H. Carroll the Colossus of Baptist History.*

At Dr. Carroll's death in 1914 I became Professor of English Bible in the Southwestern Baptist Theological Seminary and taught in this capacity for five years. Then I became director of the Seminary Extension Department, in which I labored twenty-four years. In the meantime I was made director of the Seminary's floral interests and labored in that field fifteen years, teaching Introductory Greek during this time.

On June 1, 1943, I retired from active service with the Seminary to finish the task assigned by Dr. Carroll. At this time the faculty of the Seminary in presenting publicly a gift expressed their approval of my service with emphasis on two words: "Faithful and Efficient."

OPPORTUNITY*

Text: "So then, as we have opportunity, let us work that which is good toward all men." Galatians 6:10.

Whatever Paul may have been discussing as a subject here, he enlarges in this text so as to include the great purpose of our lives—to do good toward all men. The rest of the sentence reads: "and especially toward them that are of the household of the faith." It is not this limited phase of the text, however, that we wish to consider this evening, but the broader phase which sets forth our duty "toward all men."

I offer as preliminary to this discourse two equations for your consideration, viz.:

1. Gifts and training equal ability.
2. Ability and opportunity equal responsibility.

By combining these two equations and then subtracting "ability" from both members, we have this equation:

Gifts and training and opportunity equal responsibility.

In this equation we see that opportunity has two antecedents—gifts and training. These terms stand in the order of their relations. Now let us give some attention to these antecedents.

What do we mean by gifts? Our gifts are the potentialities within us, whether latent or developed. These, whether developed, constitute the sum total of our power to do. They are of God. Paul said of Christ, "When he ascended on high he led captivity captive and gave gifts unto men." No one is responsible for a lack of them, but the responsibility rests upon him who has the gift.

Next, in order, is training. By this we mean education, that which develops the latent powers within us. That is the best training which recognizes God at every point, hence, Christian education is the best education. One may have great gifts and yet not have great ability, due to the lack of training. Effective training requires much study and diligent practice. Nor would we lose sight of the great fact that God not only

*Sermon preached before the Collin County Baptist Association at Melissa, Texas, September 8, 1903, and published in the *Baptist Standard* by request of the congregation.

gives gifts, but He gives opportunity for the development of them. At this point our responsibility begins.

Now let us consider

I. The source and nature of opportunity.

"As we have opportunity." The word here translated "opportunity" means "a fit or favorable time." Since this word enters very largely into our responsibility, we wish to note

1. Opportunities are God-given. We certainly are not living in a world of chance. All we have and are is of God, and therefore the glory belongs to Him. This is strikingly illustrated in the case of Joseph, who was sold into Egyptian slavery. It was a dark hour for him when his brothers exchanged him for twenty pieces of silver, and darker when belied and cast into prison. Then he interprets two dreams and is forgotten. After two full years the king dreams, and Joseph interprets his dreams by the power of God, for which he is promoted to second place in the kingdom. Did it come by chance? Nay; verily, "God was with him and prospered him."

We see the Son of God as He sat by the well at Sychar, wearied with His journey, while the disciples have gone into the city to buy food. A strange thing occurred—a woman came to draw water at noon, it being the custom to come in the early morning or late afternoon. Did it just happen? Nay; when we see the glorious results we understand that God was just giving His beloved Son opportunity.

When Paul saw the man of Macedonia and heard him calling for help, he understood that God was giving him opportunity to preach the Gospel unto the Macedonians. It has been said that we make our own opportunities, but in a very limited sense is this true—only in the sense of one opportunity being a stepping-stone to another.

2. Opportunities are successive. They do not all come at once, but only one at a time. Our great concern should be the present opportunity. Those of the past are gone forever; those of the future are yet to come. So, then, our concern should be for the thing in hand. They are successive, also, in the fact that one may be the door to another. The opportunity of today is so often the door to the one of tomorrow.

3. Opportunities for service were never more numerous than

they are today. If I were to name this age, I would call it the Age of Opportunity. Why the railroads? To send the Gospel to every nook and corner of the nation. Why the great steamers? To carry the missionaries to foreign lands. All the discoveries and inventions mean nothing less than opportunity.

Gray, in his "Elegy in a Country Churchyard," paid fine tribute to the capabilities of our less fortunate ancestors in the following stanza:

"Full many a gem of purest ray serene,
The dark unfathomed caves of ocean bear;
Full many a flower is born to blush unseen
And waste its sweetness on the desert air."

No poet will have the right to sing thus over our graves. If we close our eyes to the opportunities God has given us, let their song be the dirge of lost opportunities. The missionary opportunity is far greater now than ever before in the history of the world. God has opened the last door, and now missionaries may enter every nation under the canopy of heaven.

4. The value of an opportunity is measured by the value of the thing involved in the opportunity. One who neglects an opportunity to rescue a perishing child is regarded as a criminal, because of the value put upon human life. How much more should one be regarded a criminal who neglects an opportunity to rescue a perishing soul. Whoever has been instrumental in God's hand in leading a soul to Christ is far richer than one who has gained the whole world.

5. We must look for opportunities. We are not likely to enter an open door if we do not see it. After our Lord had revealed Himself to the Samaritan woman at the well of Sychar as the Messiah, and she had sped the good news into the city, the people came forth in multitudes to see the Prophet. Then He turned to His disciples and said, "Say not ye, there are yet four months, and then cometh the harvest? behold, I say unto you. Lift up your eyes, and look on the fields, they are white already unto harvest." This command seems to me to be very timely for our people today. "Lift up your eyes."

Why do we not lift up our eyes? The reason is that our eyes are fastened on the things of the world. There stands a man with a dollar in his hand. His eyes are fastened steadfastly on it. He does not lift them to see the opportunity to turn the dollar to the best account. While pressing men of this class to render unto the Lord that which is His, I have been asked, "Where is the Lord's post office?" To this I replied, "Wherever there is one who is in need, there God has a post office." Jesus said, "Inasmuch as ye did it unto one of these least, ye did it unto me." Why should Rockefeller, Carnegie, or we with our pittance, hesitate as to where we should invest our money so as to realize the greatest dividends? Austin Phelps says, "Vigilance is in watching opportunity; tact and daring, in seizing upon opportunity." Never was opportunity greater for people of means than it is today.

II. God's purpose in our lives and our responsibilities for our opportunities.

This thought is suggested by the second part of the text: "Let us work that which is good." It is, or should be, an important matter with us as to what we do with what God has given us. In giving us opportunities He has done it with a definite purpose and He will require their value at our hands. So, then,

1. Let us buy them up. We take this statement from Paul's language in Ephesians 5:16 and Colossians 4:5. In the body of the text they read: "Redeeming the time"; in the margin, "Buying up the opportunity." The word here translated "opportunity" is the same as the one in our text. The word translated "buying up" means "to save from being wasted," "to make the most of." It is evident that these passages refer only to present time and not to lost opportunities. We should enter the doors as they are opened to us.

2. This part of the text sets forth the positiveness of religion. Christianity has its positives as well as its negatives. Some people have what Sam Jones calls "gate-post" religion. They flatter themselves that they are religious because they do not steal, lie, swear, nor kill. Even the gate-post has the same of which to boast. The man who would convince the world that he is a Christian, let him show the spirit of our Lord, of whom it was said, "He went about doing good." It was this that convinced Nicodemus that he was a teacher "come from God."

So if we would convince the world that we are God's children, we must do it by the positiveness of our religion. It is common to hear the remark, "There is a good man," referring only to the man's negative goodness. It is not true. Men only are good who do good.

3. To this end we were created and recreated. I cannot conceive of a purpose of our existence in the world other than to glorify God. To this end He created man, and the Scriptures expressly declare that to this end we were recreated: "We are his workmanship, created in Christ Jesus for good works, which God afore prepared that we should walk in them." Again, Paul speaking of Christ, said, "Who gave himself for us, that he might redeem us from all iniquity, and purify unto himself a people for his own possession, zealous of good works." God saves people to serve him. This is the one divine purpose of our lives.

4. Let us look at a present condition. We have the name of being one of the best associations of the state. That is possible and probable, but we certainly cannot be satisfied with the compliments we receive. There are about seven thousand Baptists in this great county, and two or three thousand do all that is done in the name of this association. There are too many deserters in our Baptist army. It occurs to me that there is a great need for a course in court martialing and shooting. A man has no more right to desert a Baptist army in the heat of battle than he has to desert Uncle Sam in his conflict with the Spaniards or Filipinos. They are enrolled but not enlisted. O, for the power to enlist our people!

5. The unit of this organized force is the church. To the extent we ignore the development of the churches, to that extent we are weak. This text was written to the churches of Galatia. To this end Christ organized the church and died for it. The church that loses sight of the purpose of her existence has no right to exist.

Now let us consider

III. The extent and application of opportunities.

"Toward all men." This phase of the text recognizes

1. The relation that exists between all men. If there is a thing or being in the universe to which we bear no relation, then

toward that thing or being we owe no duty. I do not believe in the universal fatherhood of God, because Jesus said to a certain class of people to whom he preached, "Ye are of your father, the devil." But I do believe in the universal brotherhood of man as descended from a common parent. Wherever we meet one of Adam's posterity, we meet a brother. Our duty toward him is measured by the relation we sustain to him. This is plainly set forth by our Lord in his answer to the question, "Who is my neighbor?" in which he shows that this duty does not arise from race or nationality, but exists even between those who are at enmity.

2. It excludes selfishness. It is a lamentable fact that some of God's children have never arisen to the plane from which they can see beyond their own selfish interests and let their hearts throb in unison with their brethren for one common cause, even the cause of Christ. We should keep in mind that what we do in this selfish spirit is an abomination to God.

3. It sets forth the true idea of altruism. By this we mean the doctrine of "otherism." Often we hear it said that the Golden Rule is the true standard of life. Not so; it only purports to be a rule of reciprocation. By this rule we have as many standards as we have ideals of life; each one is to do to the other according to his own wish. Jesus came "not to be ministered unto, but to minister." We show His spirit in us by ministering to others. He said to His disciples, "A new commandment I give unto you, that ye love one another even as I have loved you." Here He makes His love the standard. We are wonderfully impressed with its meaning as we view the tragedy of the cross. There we see the righteous dying for the unrighteous. Even so, God is calling His people to the duty of giving their lives for a lost world. It is true that God calls just one here and there to die for His cause, but the greater call is to live for His cause. It is easier to die for Christ than it is to live for Him.

You ask, "Are we not to do good for ourselves?" I answer, that the higher purpose of life calls us to consider the needs of others, and the good we would do for ourselves should subserve the one great purpose to serve others. We are better enabled to do this as we consider the common fate of all. The poet has condensed it thus:

"The boast of heraldry, the pomp of power,
All that beauty, all that wealth e'er gave;
Await alike, the inevitable hour—
The paths of glory lead but to the grave."

This was recited by General Wolfe as he crossed the St. Lawrence the day before the Battle of Quebec. But I would rather have it said of me, "He went about doing good," than to have the laurels of Wolfe, Napoleon, or Alexander the Great. Their reward was of this world; ours is eternal.

4. It sets forth the missionary idea. I would not come before this intelligent body of Baptists with a message so limited in scope that I could not discuss the subject of missions without digression. I have the honor of being called a missionary by my churches. Some of my members inquire, "When are you going to let up on this missionary question?" I answer, "When Christ comes." If there is anything that characterizes us as a people, it is the fact that we are missionary. In this we are more like our Lord than in being Baptists. "As we have opportunity, let us work that which is good toward all men." In what can we do more good to a people than to give them the Gospel? Notice how broad the text in its application. "Toward all men." Christ died for the Hottentot, as He did for you and me. If we have the spirit of Christ, we will love them for whom He died. This is one of the greatest tests of our love.

5. The last thought is that our responsibility is co-extensive with our opportunities. The one who has neglected an opportunity to do good will never know his loss until he faces it in the eternal beyond. Lost opportunities will be thorns in our dying pillows. It is at the end that we shall look back over our lives to see the lost opportunities, which cause an expression of sadness to overshadow our brows; and if our friends inquire if we are afraid, we shall answer as did the dying young man who had done nothing for his Lord, "No; I am not afraid; Jesus saves me now, but oh, must I go and empty-handed?" "Alas! The number who will realize the truth of the poet with multiplied intensity:

"Of all sad words of tongue or pen,
The saddest are these: 'It might have been.' "

But with those who have been faithful to the trust committed to them, it will not be so. "They shall shine as the brightness of the firmament—and as the stars forever and ever."

Chapter VII

J. B. GAMBRELL

BIOGRAPHICAL SKETCH*

James Bruton Gambrell, descendant of French Huguenots, was born in Anderson County, South Carolina, August 21, 1841. When he was four years old his parents moved to northeast Mississippi.

Each day the father read the Bible, and he or an old Negro slave led in prayer. The family attended the Pleasant Ridge Church, the father missing only two Saturday meetings in twenty-five years. As a lad he was greatly influenced by reading a book, *Facts for Boys,* which he bought from a colporter for two dimes, the proceeds from the sale of two coon skins. He faced the decision between books and dogs, chose books, and borrowed and read all he could find.

He was converted at the age of fifteen and joined the Pleasant Ridge church. Determining to get an education he enrolled in a school taught by Professor R. M. Leavell at Cherry Creek when the war of the '60's began. He enlisted in the company organized by his teacher, Captain Leavell, and was sent to Virginia where he served first as a member of Pickett's division at Gettysburg, and later as a scout for Robert E. Lee. He was transferred to the Memphis section, where as captain, he organized and commanded a company of scouts. Returning to the Suffolk section in Virginia he married, on January 13, 1864, Miss Mary T. Corbell, a cousin of Mrs. George E. Pickett. They went to Mississippi to live in the latter part of 1866.

His first impression to preach came while in Mississippi. In December, 1866, he was licensed by the church where he

*By Dr. E. C. Routh, Editor "The Commission", Baptist Foreign Mission Board.

had been converted. In November, 1867, he was ordained by the Cherry Creek Church which he and Mrs. Gambrell had joined while teaching school at Wallerville. He counseled with General Mark P. Lowrey on the founding of Blue Mountain College. In 1870 he became pastor of the West Point church. Two years later he accepted the call of the Oxford Church and enrolled in the University of Mississippi. He attended his first Southern Baptist Convention at Charleston, South Carolina, in 1874.

In February, 1877, the *Baptist Record* was projected and he was asked to become editor. He served in that position fifteen years. During the greater part of that time he lived at Clinton where Mississippi College is located, served as pastor of the church and did field work for the college. As editor he fought against saloons. His oldest son, Roderick Dhu, publisher of a prohibition publication, was assassinated in that fight.

In 1891 at Birmingham, Dr. Gambrell and Dr. J. M. Frost were appointed a sub-committee on establishing the Sunday School Board, and after a full day of prayerful deliberation, submitted a report which led to the beginning. He was elected president of Mercer University in 1893. He resigned at the end of three years and agreed to accept the nomination of the Populist Party for governor of Georgia if it would declare for prohibition, but was ineligible because not a resident of the state six years.

In December, 1896, he began his greatest work as Secretary of Texas Baptists. They had reached a critical juncture due to division on the missionary program. Under his wise and tactful leadership they were unified. He said, "More people, a hundred to one, will join in a bear hunt than will turn out to kill a mouse." More than any other he set the pattern for a constructive co-operative plan of missionary work in Texas and the South. Under his leadership evangelistic efforts were expanded, the Baptist Education Commission constituted, the Texas Baptist Memorial Sanitarium built, and the Southwestern Baptist Theological Seminary established.

On February 10, 1910, he resigned as Secretary to accept the editorship of the *Baptist Standard* serving until December, 1914, when, following the consolidation of the state Mission and Education Boards he was elected Executive Secretary. For nearly four years he led Texas Baptists in their enlarged program.

During the World War period, characterized by tensions and discussions concerning Southwide boards, Dr. Gambrell was elected president of the Southern Baptist Convention at New Orleans and served four years. He handled a typically acute situation with gavel in hand, by saying, "Don't forget, brethren, that a hot box slows up the train." At the Atlanta Convention in 1919, when the Convention was invited to join the Inter-Church World Movement, Dr. Gambrell said: "Baptists never ride a horse without a bridle." He was famous for his aphorisms and stories, especially dog stories.

In June, 1918, he asked to be relieved of his heavy duties as Secretary and took up the professorship of Christian Ethics and Ecclesiology in Southwestern Seminary, to which he had given some time each week while editor-in-chief of the *Standard*. He continued thus until his death.

One of the most distinctive contributions of Dr. Gambrell was his European trip in 1920 with Drs. Mullins, Truett, Love. They attended a conference of European Baptists in London in July which resulted in the expansion of the Southern Baptist Missions to include Spain, Jugoslavia, Hungary, Rumania, Ukraine, and Palestine-Syria. He went on through Europe visiting practically all countries except Russia. Quite a trip for the veteran nearing his eightieth year!

A little while after he returned, his physical heart faltered for the first time. From his sick bed he sent his last message to the Southern Baptist Convention saying: "Do right and go forward." Then came the end of his earthly journey, June 10, 1921. We can still hear him saying to Southern Baptists: "Do right and go forward."

UP FOOL HILL*

Fool Hill lies just where the undulating lowlands of boyhood rise sharply up to the highlands of manhood. It is climbed only by big boys and the big boy is an institution in this world. He is, indeed, a series of personalities in one extraordinary combination. The only certain thing about him is his uncertainty. Like a spit-devil, he is loaded, and will go off with a spark, but just which way he will go is an unknown and an unknowable thing. But the chances are that he will go zigzag, and whichever way he does go you can trace him by the sparks.

When you notice the boy feeling of his upper lip, and a suspicion of something slightly darker than the skin appears, you may begin then to look sharp. The boy has come to the foot of fool hill, and will begin very soon to climb. The great problem is to get him up the hill in good repair. That done, you have blessed the world with a man.

Big boys are nearly certain to have the big-head. This is no bad sign. It is an inward sense of power, without the wisdom of discipline. Our boy entering the fool age is a caution. His voice is now fine and splitting, now coarse and grating. He begins a sentence coarse and ends fine, or fine and ends coarse. He is rank and sets digging to the world. All his judgments are pronounced and final. There is nothing he cannot decide instanter. He knows instantly and by intuition who is the greatest lawyer in the whole country, if he is a reading boy, or the best doctor. He can tell you who will be the next governor or anything else politicians are so anxious to know. He is authority on prize-fights, or cards, or anything else he knows nothing about. And when he pronounces on anything he has spoken. The governor is "Dick" somebody, and the supreme judge is "Tom". And, by the way, he often differs with these and other dignitaries. He sings in unearthly strains, with tendencies to the pathetic and the savage all in one breath.

With the big boy there is nothing medium. He uses adjectives freely and always in the superlative. He sees things in strong colors, for he is in the flood of passion. Fight! Yes, fight anything and on the shortest notice. He ought to fight to prove himself, so he feels. About this time his mind undergoes

*From *Parable and Precept* by J. B. Gambrell, Fleming H. Revell. Used by permission.

some radical changes. He wonders at the dullness and contrariness of his parents. It is a constant worry to him that he can't manage his father without a world of trouble, and he wonders what is the matter with "the old man" anyhow. Churches and Sunday schools are too dull for him, and the preacher is just nowhere. He can give him any number of pointers on theology and preaching.

Rushing on and into everything like mad, he stops short and bewails the coldness of this unfriendly world. Now he has more "dear friends" than he can shake a stick at; now he feels that he has not a friend in the world. He wants sympathy, while he tries the patience of everybody who has anything to do with him.

Such is the boy in the fool age. The great question is, what to do with him. He is climbing "fool hill" now, and the road is bad. Father, mother and friends are all anxious and sometimes vexed. Homes are deprived of all their peace by this great double-action marplot. But the question will not down. What shall we do with him? If he is turned loose now, he will be a wild engine on the track smashing things. If he is not handled wisely there will be a catastrophe. The ever-recurring question is: What shall be done with the big boy climbing fool hill? Often the impulse is to let the fool go. But that will not do. He is now like a green apple—sour, puckerish and unwholesome; but, like the apple, if we can save him, he will ripen into something good. We must save him. Saints and angels, help us to save this human ship in the storm, freighted with father's, mother's, sister's, brother's love, and with the infinite wealth of an immortal nature! We must save him for himself, his loved ones and his country.

The chances for saving him will depend mainly on what has been done for him before he struck fool hill. If, from infancy, he has been taught to revere sacred things, if he has been taught subjection to authority, if his mind has been stored with scripture texts, with noble poems, and recollections of the pure, the sweet, the good, you have in him the saving elements. We must never forget that in the final analysis every person saves or loses himself, no matter what influences help or hinder. A well-taught boy may climb this dubious hill without a bobble, but if the new life gains the temporary lead the chances are that the enduring good elements will reassert themselves and become paramount. Hence the transcendent importance of ballasting this ship betimes, before the storm sets in. Noble ambitions early planted and carefully nurtured are of great importance. During this period of trial, great wisdom and tact are needed. There must be a gradual lengthening of the ropes. If you tie this mustang up too tight he will break the rope, and maybe break his neck. It often happens that more can be done by indirection than otherwise. Some good woman, other than the boy's mother, may be a savior to him.

He feels his great importance, and you must recognize him. It is just here that the churches have failed and the saloons have succeeded. Show this embryonic governor that you recognize his parts and call on him for service. The harder the service the better he will like it. Get in with him, and do not be too critical, but pass his imperfections by. He will be nearly everything, but never mind; he only sees things large and sees them double and mixed, being now partly boy and partly man, and seeing with two sets of eyes.

You are fighting the devil for a soul, and you can't afford to be impatient, or give way to anger, when your fool boy takes an extra flounce. When he gets on a bad bent, give line, as the fisherman does when there is a hundred-pound tarpon on the other end of the line, but not too much. And remember all the while that time and heaven are on your side. With age comes discretion. Once up fool hill the road stretches away ever smoother and better to the pearly gates.

Our big boy is among us. His folly breaks into dudishness. He is an unturned cake, but likely there is good substance in him. He is worth cooking. If you see him on the street, take him by the hand and say a good word to him. His mother will be glad of it. Look him up and ask him to your house. Reach after his heart, for he has one. Two worlds are interested in that young fool, and underneath his folly there lies sleeping maybe a great preacher, teacher or other dignitary of the commonwealth.

CONSIDERING CIRCUMSTANCES AND CONDITIONS

"Overlooking fields" and "considering circumstances and conditions", have come to be vocational. We have people who do little else. Some of them have risen to the dignity of "experts." Others have become ministerial tramps, fleeing from place to place on account of "circumstances and conditions." So much do some dwell on "circumstances and conditions" that they have become enslaved to them.

Many of this class have trained their minds to see only the bad "circumstances and conditions". They "look over a field," see every bad thing, and make a map of the difficulties in their minds for future use. I know a preacher who has so bent his mind to this dolorous task that he can see nothing but difficulties in any place. He is not a pastor now. There were so many "circumstances and conditions" everywhere, that he quit, and the churches now have rest. No pulpit ought to sound like a frog pond. People won't hear a croaker long. The people have sense.

The tribe I am considering came down from antiquity. We read of them in Holy Writ The ten spies who took the heart out of Israel by reporting on the "circumstances and conditions" in the "Promised Land" were whipped by what they saw. The long-necked giants were a part of the circumstances. Only two of the spies could see above the "circumstances and conditions." They saw **God and the promises.** The ten were completely enslaved by the sight of their eyes and all their strength oozed out. They were in their own eyes as grasshoppers.

Another example of mental and spiritual subjugation to "circumstances and conditions" was the army of Israel when Goliath dared them. This great giant, and his big spear and loud mouth were circumstances that brought on a condition of fear, weakness and cowardly submission.

All Israel had the buck ague when David arrived. He gave very little time to "looking over the field", or considering "circumstnces and conditions." It was plain enough that these were bad. As Dr. Carroll would say, "the people were whipped inside." David, in the name of the Lord, took a rock and knocked Goliath in the head in quick order.

All the "circumstances and conditions" were the worst in the storm and shipwreck Paul was in. Paul got in connection with God and they all changed for good. What a blessing one brave soul is when "circumstances and conditions" are bad!

In religious matters the habit of forming conclusions from a mere human view of "circumstances and conditions" is utterly enslaving. The scheme of progress in religion as recorded in the Scriptures, implies a power above the human level, which changes "circumstances and conditions".

Materialist and near-sighted scientists are engaged in a huge effort to evolve the universe from the "circumstances and conditions" of matter. The true explanation of the material world is in the first sentence in the Bible: "In the beginning was God." God is the explanation of all religious success, as well as of creation,—not "circumstances and conditions."

There was a divided church, wasted and prostrated by internal wars. Several brethren went and "looked over the field." After considering the "circumstances and conditions" they said nothing could be done. The remnants were poor and without influence. The other people in town were strong and respectable. No one of standing would go about the little old neglected church. The "circumstances and conditions" made it impossible to do anything. They were very wise men of a very religiously ignorant sort.

Later came a young man who had a favorite text. "Have Faith in God." He never feared "circumstances or conditions." If he saw them nobody knew it. He preached and all prayed. God conquered and the "circumstances and conditions" didn't seem to amount to anything. The people flocked where God was. There is a great church there today.

"Circumstances and conditions" were very bad when Israel was at the Red Sea, but what difference did it make when God stretched out His mighty arm?

The burgomaster of Hamburg said to Oncken when Baptists in Germany were few and weak and persecuted: "As long as I can raise my finger I will put you down." With Germany against Oncken, the "circumstances and conditions" were very bad. Oncken replied to the burgomaster, "And as long as I can see God above your finger, I will preach." There are many

Baptists in Germany today. When God is in a situation "circumstances and conditions" conform to His will.

Two preachers went to a place in Texas to hold a meeting. They were told it was no use. Others had tried and failed. The people did not care for religion. There was one man there who would upset things, a sort of Goliath of Gath. The preachers paid no attention to "circumstances and conditions," but sailed in with the sword of the Spirit. Goliath was converted and scores of others. The "circumstances and conditions" were all changed gloriously.

Spurgeon wanted a great preaching place in London. But the people and most of the deacons said, "considering the circumstances and conditions' we can't build it. We are poor and have not the money." Spurgeon and six deacons prayed it out before God and triumphed in faith. A little later Spurgeon received $80,000 and never did know who sent it. The house was built, and "circumstances and conditions" improved steadily.

Near where I was raised was a community that was known as the worst "devil's den" in the country. It would have been the delight of the modern "sociological expert." There was the making of a book in it. A worse set of "circumstances and conditions" could not be found. A country preacher, after laying by his crop, took a Bible and hymn book and went to work. The devil's crowd cut saddles and bridles to pieces, shot guns around the meeting place at night, told the preacher to leave, but he cried to God and went on. In three weeks the devil's patch was cleaned up. Multitudes were converted and baptized, among them the leader of the devil's forces, and today the "circumstances and conditions" in that country are fine.

No man is going to earn his salt as a preacher if he can't see higher than "circumstances and conditions." The spirit of the times is trying to enslave the Christian world by involving its faith and everything in the doctrine of "circumstances and conditions." It is a cheat and a lie. God will make all things new by a power eternal in Himself. In these days of weakening faith the passing word in religion is that mighty word of Scripture, Power. Not influence, not education, but power, the power that brought Jesus from the dead, is to conquer. Without this power we are no-bodies in religion. With it "circumstances and conditions" are mere incidents of victory.

I say it with deep conviction, the supreme need of this age is the emancipation of the minds of men from "circumstances and conditions" and lifting of their minds to God, as the source of victory. Think of Paul's great words: "I can do all things through Christ who strengtheneth me." We must never get away from faith in the immanence of the divine in our work. Get down your Bible and read and ponder the eleventh chapter of Hebrews again and see how faith ranged above the "circumstances and conditions" in the days gone. These things were written for your instruction.

The subject draws me out. We must have the faith that dominates "circumstances and conditions" in order to have courage. My pencil point is now at the weakest place in the religious life of today. The "circumstances and conditions" are in modern life like the "perlice" in the story my good friend, Dr. Bernard, of Georgia, told of Irish bravery. An Irishman was saying that there were 100,000 as brave Irishmen as ever lived ready right then to fight for liberty. "Well, why don't they fight?" was asked. "They are afeard of the perlice," was the reply.

Preachers fear "circumstances and conditions." We must come back to simple faith and direct, personal effort. Waiting for "circumstatnces and conditions" to favor effort will never win. The farmer who keeps one eye on the clouds and the other on the wind will not make a crop. The farmer who industriously plows and plants and cultivates, believing in God and trusting Him for the increase will rarely have to buy corn. Walking by the sight of our eyes in religion will make pigmies of us all. We are to walk by faith, not by sight. It was because Moses saw Him who was invisible that he lived his wonder life.

If some preachers do not take a good steady look up, they are going to let "circumstances and conditions" keep them from taking collections. They will give down just when they ought to be strong in the Lord and in the power of His might. They will play the coward and begin a process of weakening within their own hearts, with God and the people. They will be "looking over another field" soon. Now is the time to rise above "circumstances and conditions" like men of God and do exploits.

Chapter VIII

A. H. NEWMAN

BIOGRAPHICAL SKETCH*

Reflection upon the life of Dr. Newman raises a baffling problem. Are some individuals placed in the course of history to perform specific tasks? It would seem that Paul was such an one. Martin Luther, Thomas Jefferson and Abraham Lincoln are other examples. Any time if crisis will call forth men of high ability who constitute the leaders of the age. It is interesting that the state of Georgia, just after the Civil War, produced a number of such personalities.

Dr. Newman, America's leading church historian, was born in the Edgefield District of South Carolina in 1852. His father was a farmer and harness maker who moved to Georgia after the Civil War. Young Albert learned to read at three. Later he was taught by several men, the most important being the Rev. E. A. Steed, a brilliant but somewhat eccentric man. Young Newman was so acquisitive that he was able to enter the junior year of Mercer University at seventeen and to graduate at the head of the class a few months before he was nineteen.

In 1872 he entered the Rochester Theological Seminary where he specialized in Hebrew and Old Testament Exegesis and graduated in May, 1875. The next year he studied Hebrew under Dr. Toy and New Testament Greek under Dr. Broadus at the Southern Baptist Seminary. He had extraordinary retentiveness, singular ability to acquire dead languages and undying devotion to truth.

In the fall of 1876 he returned to Rochester where he was made professor of Church History. In 1881 Dr. Newman transferred to Toronto Baptist College which later became McMaster

***By Dr. Frederich Eby, Professor of History and Philosophy of Education, University of Texas.**

University. First at the Rochester Seminary and then more fully at McMaster he found his task. With superb gifts for language he set about mastering the history of Christianity reading the original sources in Greek, Latin and German. It was the history of the origin and doctrines of the Baptists that presented his most unique opportunity.

Newman's ability as a scholar came to be recognized in a rather interesting way. In 1885 the fourth volume of Dr. Philip Schaff's monumental *History of the Christian Church* appeared Dr. Newman reviewed this book for the *Baptist Quarterly Review*. Dr. Schaff took him to task for some of his Scriptures, but nevertheless recognizing his exceptional scholarship, and invited him to edit St. Augustine's treatises on anti-Manicheanism. Some of these treatises had to be translated from the Latin by Dr. Newman himself. This work gave him a permanent place among the first scholars of the day.

At the suggestion of Dr. Newman the American Society of Church History promoted a series of histories of the Protestant denominations in the United States. He was invited to participate and in 1894 published his *History of the Baptist Churches in the United States*. No one had ever attempted to bring together in orderly fashion the facts of the opposition to infant baptism. This he did in *A History of Anti-pedo-baptism from the Rise of Pedo-baptism to* 1609, which was published in 1897.

The next effort was to write the history of the Christian Church. These two impartial volumes, written in splendid style, have been used as texts in many Baptist seminaries and also seminaries of other denominations. Just at the close of the century Dr. Newman with the colaboration of a group of leaders produced *A Century of Baptist Achievement*. This work laid the foundation for the establishment of the Baptist World Alliance which held its first session in London in 1905.

In 1901 Dr. Newman was asked by Dr. B. H. Carroll and President Oscar H. Cooper to assist them in building a great theological seminary at Baylor University. The Baptists of Texas were growing in numbers and wealth with unparalleled rapidity. The cities were increasing in population and culture. The large and cultured congregations demanded not only good but scholarly men as pastors. A seminary was imperative if Texas Baptists were to hold their people and advance. Dr. Newman saw the extraordinary opportunity and accepted the offer.

He gave up his teaching at Southwestern in 1913 and returned to Baylor where he gave a course in Church History. During 1917-18 he was visiting professor of Comparative Religion at Vanderbilt University. In 1921 President Rufus W. Weaver of Mercer University turned to Dr. Newman to assist him in developing a school of theology at that institution. He taught during the summer sessions at the University of Chicago, and finally closed his career by returning to McMaster University for the session of 1927-28.

Dr. Newman married Mary Augusta Ware, the daughter of a well-to-do plantation owner of Seale, Alabama, in 1873. Four children constituted the family: Dr. H. H. Newman, an authority in research, was Professor of Zoology at the University of Chicago until his retirement. The only daughter, Elizabeth, married Frederick Eby and has lived for many years in Austin, Texas. Dr. Henry Ware Newman after some years as a missionary in China is in medical practice in Austin. The youngest son, Albert Broadus, is with the College of the City of New York, and leader in the field of Chemical engineering.

Dr. Newman died at the home of his daughter, June 4, 1933. Mrs. Newman died the following January. His work still lives.

THE AUTHORITY OF CHRISTIAN CONSCIOUSNESS

By "authority" we understand "legal or rightful power", a "right to command." The correlative idea is that of obligation to obey. The king has authority over his subjects, the general over his soldiers, the parent over his child. Such authority, however, is purely derivative in its nature and hence is not absolute. The king's authority does not extend to the thoughts or the conscience of his subjects. At the utmost he can command only external obedience; he cannot command internal accord.

The question is not one of authority derived and limited, but of authority absolute; not of a right of Christian Consciousness to control one department of man's being, but of a right to control man's entire being—body, soul and spirit. The only authority that pertains to man's entire being, and that is absolute and final, is *the will of God*. The question for discussion, therefore, is whether or not Christian Consciousness is a trustworthy and infallible expression of God's will.

The *a priori* probability that God would reveal His will in a way that should be readily apprehended by His children is generally admitted. Has He left man to the gropings of reason? The utter failure of reason throughout the ages to gain any sufficient idea of what it concerns us, as immortal, spiritual beings to know, seems decisive against this method. Is conscience a sufficient revealer of God's will? The immortality of mankind, on the one hand, and the utter despair, resulting in asceticism on the other, point to a negative answer. Reason demands truth, but cannot find it. Conscience demands righteousness, but cannot realize. Revelation—above all God's perfect revelation of Himself in the Incarnate Christ—fulfills the demands of reason and of conscience.

I. It's Meaning

What, now, is Christian Consciousness? Consciousness, I take it, is essentially man's immediate knowledge of his own acts and states, the latter term including the impressions made upon him by God and His creatures. Christian Consciousness is the consciousness of a Christian. The Christian Consciousness differs from ordinary human consciousness in so far as a regenerate man differs from an unregenerate. I have attempted to define consciousness as a faculty; the term is likewise used to denote the deliverance of this faculty. The term Christian Consciousness is capable of a like employment. By a still further extension the term comes to designate the common Christian sentiment with reference to the matter of which Christian Consciousness takes cognizance. In this general sense the Christian Consciousness of the present generation would be the combined result of the Christian life and thought of the past eighteen centuries, and the Christian life and thought of the present.

Let us suppose a man combining in his own person all the good and bad qualities of humanity, converted to Christ in the apostolic time, subjected to the Judaizing processes of the early centuries, plunged at last into the depths of mediaeval bigotry and superstition, emancipated from bigotry and superstition through the study of the Bible and the influence of Greek and Arabic philosophy, subjected to the various influences of Lutheran and Calvinistic Protestantism, precipitated in turn into Socinian rationalism and indifferentism, and into hyper-Calvinistic fatalism, aroused thence into a state of frantic evangelistic enthusiasm. In a word, let us suppose him to have passed through every imaginable phase of Christian life and thought, to be still alive and resting at present in some of the multudinous religious parties. The experiences of the past would remain and would form a part of the contents of his Christian Consciousness.

The Divine element is permanent and unvarying. The impression made by the Divine element in consciousness will depend very largely upon the character of the individual, upon inherited and acquired capabilities and tendencies, and upon environment. Each Christian individual has a Christian Consciousness different from that of every other individual. Each age has a collective Christian Consciousness different from that of any other age. So far as there is agreement it depends upon the invariableness of the Divine element, likeness of natural and acquired dispositions, a common using of the experience of the past.

There are points in which Christians of all religious parties agree, and in which universal Christian Consciousness may be said to speak with one voice, but I am doubtful whether the contents of such a consensus would be very rich. There might be a considerable show of agreement in words, but the same form of words may express widely different conceptions in the minds of a number of individuals using it. We should expect that in those who are truly regenerate there would be agreement at least in the understanding of the fundamental truths of Divine revelation; but even here remarkable differences would appear.

For practical purposes, however, we are precluded from making use of the deliverances of the universal regenerate consciousness by the following considerations: 1. We cannot infallibly discriminate between the regenerate and the unregenerate. 2. Even in regenerate consciousness we cannot determine infallibly how much of consciousness is due to the regenerate principle, and how much is due to the natural man. 3. If these two difficulties were out of the way, it would be a practical impossibility to collect all these deliverances in such a way as to compare them. 4. Even if we had them collected and expressed in words, we could by no possibility determine the signification that any given form of words bore to the consciousness of each individual employing it. Practically, it is likely to mean, in the mouth of any individual user, the views that he and his set have come to entertain with reference to the great questions of theology, morals and religion.

The church historian can divide the eighteen Christian centuries into great epochs, and can characterize each epoch by a few general statements. If the middle ages are rightly characterized by intolerance, superstition and fanaticism; finding general expression in crusades, inquisition, and idolatry; the nineteenth century is no less characterized by tolerance, freedom from superstition and fanaticism, philanthrophy, scientific investigation, etc. Underlying the Christian life and thought of the middle ages, there must have been a general Christian Consciousness differing widely from that which underlies the Christian life and thought of the present. Philosophical views and scientific theories, while they are in part a product of the age in which they appear, exert in turn a vast influence upon the Christian Consciousness of the age.

II. It's Trustworthiness

How far and in what sense Christian Consciousness may be accepted as a trustworthy expression of the will of God. Here our best instructor will be the Word of God. To reach a satisfactory view of the relation between Christian Consciousness and the teaching of scripture as to the believer's special qualification for apprehending spiritual things, we should have a clear understanding of the scriptural representation of man in his unfallen, fallen, and regenerate states. I am inclined to accept the division of man's nature into body, soul, and spirit (*soma, psuche and pneuma*) as most in accord with scripture. and as best explaining the facts of man's unfallen, fallen, and regenerate states.

Psuche is the seat of personality, the immortal principle, and embraces intellect, emotion, and will. *Pneuma* is the Divine principle in man, manifesting itself chiefly in conscience, in aspirations after God, in communion with God, and in apprehension of spiritual things. In the unfallen man *soma* and *psuche* were under the control of *pneuma*. The subjection of *soma* and *psuche* to *pneuma* constituted man holy, and gave him blessed communion with God. The fall consisted in the fact that *psuche* emancipated itself from the control of *pneuma,* through which chiefly the will of God was made known. Though dethroned, *pneuma* persisted in the form of conscience and of a prompting toward godliness, more or less pronounced. *Psuche,* in so far as sensuality supplanted *pneuma* in its control, is represented as under the dominion of *sarx*. Yet the struggle between *pneuma* and *sarx* continues in the unregenerated man, intellect itself (*nous*), declaring the way of the *pneuma* to be the preferable way, but *sarx* prevailing over *pneuma,* and constituting the man *sarkical.*

When the unregenerated man is spoken of without special reference to his subjection to the *sarx,* he is said to be *psychical.* In regeneration man's *pneuma* is reinforced by the Divine *pneuma, sarx* is dethroned, and *psuche* and *soma* are brought under the dominion of the *pneuma*. Christ dwelling spiritually in the believer constitutes his true life. Yet the strivings of the *sarx* do not at once cease. Though it has received its death blow, it is tenacious of life. The believer does not once for all become what according to his profession he should be. The regenerate man is called *sarkical* or *psychical* on the other hand, and *spiritual* on the other, as the psychical or spiritual elements, including not mere sensuality, but a rebellious attitude of the intellect and will as well, are not, or are, in entire subjection to the spiritual. In the perfected state, *pneuma* becomes absolutely dominant, while in the finally impenitent *pneuma* remains as the Divine accuser, the "worm" that "dieth not."

What, then, shall we say of the authority of the consciousness of the regenerate man with reference to the things of God? The believer is said (I Cor. 2) to speak God's wisdom in a mystery, even the wisdom that hath been hidden. "We receive . . . the spirit, which is of God; that we might know the things that are freely given to us by God." "He that is spiritual judgeth all things, and he himself is judged of no man. For who hath known the mind of the Lord, that he should instruct Him? But we have the mind of Christ." Believers are spoken of as "reflecting in a mirror the glory of the Lord," and are said to be "transformed into the same image from glory to glory." Believers are said to "have an anointing from the Holy One," and to "know all things." The Apostle *knew* whom he had believed. "If any man willeth to do His (God's) will, he shall know of the doctrine."

I think we may safely say, that if in any given cause we could be perfectly sure that the *sarx* is in complete subjection and that the *pneuma* is absolutely dominant, that we are filled with the Spirit, that we have realized as complete a union with Christ as it is the privilege of the believer to enjoy. If we could say without reservation "to me living is Christ," in such case, I doubt not, our Christian Consciousness would express God's will in a highly authoritative form.

But, alas! those of us who are not hopelessly eccentric know too well how the *sarx* is still within us, and how incomplete is dominion of *pneuma*. And we cannot escape the conviction, based on experience and observation, that Christian Consciousness, while it has its important place in furnishing the believer with assurance of his acceptance with God, and of the reality of his personal appropriation of revealed truth, is exceedingly *variable* and *deceptive*. I believe that just in proportion to the height of the Christian's attainment in spiritual life will be his lack of confidence in the infallibility of the deliverance of his consciousness, and his sense of the need of a higher standard of appeal.

III. It's Perversions

1. Gnosticism. We should be scarcely justified in regarding the Gnostics of the first and second centuries as conscious deceivers. Many of them were no doubt wholly sincere in the belief that they had arisen above *pistis* to complete *gnosis*, and that they had found in Christianity a key to the mystery of the universe. Now no sane man of the present thinks that the slightest degree of authority is to be attached to the Christian Consciousness of a Basileides or a Valentinus. The fact is, they were woefully deceived, and lured multitudes of souls to destruction.

2. Montanism, in some respects the antithesis of Gnosticism, furnishes a still better illustration of the deceptiveness of Christian Consciousness, because we feel surer of the sincerity of its leading representatives, and because the movement involved a more direct appeal to the authority of Christian Consciousness. Montanism represents, on the one hand, a reaction against the growing secularization of the church and the speculative spirit of Gnosticism, and, on the other hand, a revival of heathen manticism, with its wild enthusiasm, ecstasy, visions, etc. Wrought up into a frenzy by zeal for reform, in view of the speedy approach of the end of the age, the Montanists supposed their fevered fancies to be the direct utterances of the promised Paraclete, who was to guide into all truth. Does any one now believe that Montanus and his prophetesses were inspired by the spirit of God in their unscriptural utterances?

3. Mysticism is another form of unwholesome dependence on Christian Consciousness widely different from either of those mentioned. Disgusted with the emptiness of forms and ceremonies and the corruption of church life, and imbued with semi-pantheistic, Neo-Platonic conceptions of God, man and the world, the mystic turned his thinking inward and sought fully to realize union and communion with God. By dint of profound and long-continued meditation men of strongly intuitional minds

were able to persuade themselves that they were so completely merged in Deity, that the deliverances of their consciousness were the very utterances of God. "God and I are one in knowing," wrote Master Eckart. "God's essence is His knowing, and God's knowing makes me know Him. Therefore is His knowing my knowing. The eye whereby I see God is the same eye whereby he seeth me. Mine eye and the eye of God are one eye, one vision, one knowledge, and one love . . . The inner voice is the voice of God." Few we take it, would venture to maintain that the pantheistic, often senseless, utterances of an Eckart, or a Suso, or even the more moderate and thoroughly devout utterances of a Tauler or a George Fox, are authoritative exponents of the Divine will.

4. The New Theology. It is in connection with the method of religious thought popularly known as the "New Theology" that the term Christian Consciousness is now most frequently used. Socinianism, Kantian and Hegelian philosophies, Colleridgeanism, German Biblical Criticism, New England Transcendentalism—these and other modes of thought, interacting and overlapping each other, have had much to do with the formation of the Christian Consciousness of the Andover School. The Andover Christian Consciousness so magnifies the love of God and the mercy of God as to lose sight, in a measure, of Gods punitive justice and of God's holiness, which is "a consuming fire." To quote the words of an Andover theologican: "The Christian thought of the mercy of God our Heavenly Father, has felt itself restrained by certain limitations which it is claimed the Bible puts upon the offer of the gospel to mankind, until now it can not help asking if there are any members of the human family who are shut out from the opportunities of grace, any who are left to be treated simply according to their actual deserts."

Now I have great respect for the Andover theologians, but does it not seem just a little presumptuous in them to set up their own religious sentiments in the face of the united sentiment of the most devout minds in all ages, nay, in the face of the Scripture itself, and to claim that these sentiments are the deliverances of Christian Consciousness? I had far rather trust the Christian Consciousness of a Smyth or a Munger. If Paul and John were Jews and had been subjected to the influences of their age, Smyth and Munger are nineteenth century Americans and have been subjected to influences even more likely to pervert their Christian Consciousness. Besides, the united Christian Consciousness of eighteen centuries has attested the special Divine inspiration of the Scriptures. When we hear of the Christian Consciousness of an individual of a faction setting itself up in opposition to Scripture, I think we are pretty safe in suspecting that *sarx* is lurking in the background.

CHAPTER IX

JEFF D. RAY

BIOGRAPHICAL SKETCH*

Jeff D. Ray is a colorful, many-sided man. Among the various worthwhile activities, his teaching young preachers how to preach is outstanding. He held the chair of Homiletics and Pastoral Duties at Southwestern Seminary from 1907 to his retirement in 1944. During that time he taught probably 5,000 students.

Preaching is his passion and it is emotional, building up a crescendo of emphasis spiraling to a climax. He has preached in nearly every county seat on the 16 railroads running out of Fort Worth and in many other towns and cities. He has preached many convention, commencement, and other occasional sermons. He has conducted many revivals. The latest one (1947), at 86 years of age, was in Orange, Texas, resulting in the salvation of souls, rededicated lives and the setting up of family altars.

Dr. Ray is a great lover of Christ, his gospel and his churches. He has cherished a deathless devotion to friends, such as "Judge" Fred Freeman and Dr. B. H. Carroll, being with the former like David with Jonathan, and with the latter like Timothy to Paul. "Lee" Scarborough, "Marse George" Truett and many others shared his devotion. Hosts of younger men look on "Uncle Jeff" as a spiritual father. His affection for his family was that of an old time Southern gentleman.

Among his characteristics, frankness and sincerity loom large. If he thought a colleague wrong he could be severe with him but the next day be as thoroughly apologetic if he had reason to revise his judgment. Another prominent trait is ideal-

*By Dr. L. R. Elliott, Librarian Southwestern Baptist Theological Seminary.

ism. He loves truth, beauty and honor. He used never to lock his office nor keep a record of the books he loaned from his library. He has paid thousands of bills without keeping a receipt. When a younger friend indignantly asked why he paid one a second time he replied, "Son, in order that the ministry be not blamed."

He wields a facile pen. He has written *The Highest Office*, 1923; *The Country Preacher*, *B. H. Carroll*, and *Trouble*, 1929; *Expository Preaching*, and *Meant for Men*, 1939; *The Scarlet Sin*, 1942. In addition he has contributed articles to both the religious and secular press. For ten years he has been a writer for the Fort Worth Star-Telegram. His column, "Your Problems and Mine" is well and widely known. He has written many feature articles on Baptist Conventions, local Texas history, and travel experiences. His writing is concise, streamlined. His sentences go in a straigth line, moving directly to the conclusion.

He is an effective public reader of the written Word. Thousands of Baptist convention messengers remember his forceful reading of the Scriptures. In chapel he read the Bible, Shakespeare (whose writing he regards as next to the Bible) Poe's "Raven", Longfellow's "Hiawatha" and other dramatic pieces. His purpose was to present truth through word pictures to the imagination as well as through logic to the reason.

Jefferson Davis Ray was born in Victoria, Texas, Nevember 24, 1860. His father fell in the War between the States. His mother, who was Ava Dollahite, heroically struggled against poverty to rear her children. He received a diploma from the National School of Oratory, Philadelphia, 1879, the A.B. from Baylor in 1882 and the D.D. in 1903. Other study was in the Southern Baptist Theological Seminary, 1895-97, and two summers in the University of Chicago.

His first wife, "the mother of my children," was Josephine Wood, whom he married in 1885. She died in 1918. Two children survive: Attorney Carroll Ray and Mrs. Josephine Freeman. His second wife was the dainty daughter of the old South, Lillian Spight. They were married in 1922 and she died in 1937. In 1938 he persuaded "Miss Georgia" Miller to resign as Dr. Scarborough's secretary and share his life and home.

He was ordained to the gospel ministry in 1882 and has served as pastor of Baptist Churches at Huntsville, Texas, 1882-85, 1889-95; Eminence, Kentucky, 1895-97; Caldwell, Texas, 1897-1901; Corsicana, Texas, 1901-03; Seventh and James Street Church, Waco, Texas, 1903-07. In 1886-89 he was director of Texas Baptist Sunday School and Colportage work. He was Baptist camp pastor at Camp Bowie, Fort Worth, during World War. I.

Dr. Ray is an humble man. He does not carry himself with the air of importance nor seems to realize that many Texas Baptists regard him as a prince of Israel. His famous dream underlines this trait. He dreamed that Dr. Truett and Dr. Scarborough had come to sojourn at his home. The time of their departure arriving his mother sent him to bridle and saddle their horses and hold them while the distinguished guests mounted and rode away. His well-remembered chapel speech, "Since I came," has deflated the ego of many a younger brother.

He has the insight to judge real rather than apparent values. When several names were mentioned for a vacant professorship and one seemed to gain the ascendency Dr. Ray remarked, "All the fine things you have said about this man are so. He knows more and can do less with it than any man you have named." When Baylor conferred the D.D. degree on him a brother chided him for his vanity. Dr. Ray replied: "Yes, Tom, I accepted the degree because the school I love and help wanted to show their appreciation. Nobody has paid attention to it and I have never referred to it. You refused a degree and have gone over the country bragging about it. Which of us is vain?"

Dr. Ray's hobby is working cross-word puzzles, and his recreation is walking. He probably participated in more Texas Baptist history than any man living. He is an honored and appreciated statesman. His influence for truth and righteousness reaches beyond the borders of time.

CHRIST'S REDEMPTION*

Text: "The redemption that is in Christ Jesus." Romans 3:24.

This text deals with a fundamental doctrine. Without the redemption that is in Christ Jesus religion offers no permanent basis for peace or joy, and no adequate motive for wholehearted service. Today I shall seek to show how the redemption in Christ touches us at four vital points: First, in giving us a new standing before God. Second, in giving us a new condition in the sight of God. Third, in giving us a new character from God. Fourth, in giving us a new fellowship with God.

I. A New Standing Before God.

Man's normal standing before God is expressed in the third chapter of John and the 18th verse: "He that believeth not is condemned already because he hath not believed in the name of the only begotten Son of God." Again in the 36th verse of the same chapter: "He that believeth not the son shall not see life, but the wrath of God abideth on him." And again, in the third chapter of Galatians, at the 10th verse: "They that are of the works of the law are under a curse, for it is written: Cursed is every one that continueth not in all the things that are written in the book of the law to do them."

We find for these scriptures that normally a man stands before God under the burden of condemnation, the weight of His curse, and the blight of His wrath, but the redemption that is in Christ Jesus gives him a new standing before God. We are delivered by this redemption from the weight of God's condemnation, for we find it set down at Romans 8:1 :"There is, therefore, now no condemnation to them that are in Christ Jesus." It removes the blight of God's wrath, for we find it said in First Thessalonians, the 5th chapter and 9th verse: "God hath not appointed us (that is, the believers) to wrath, but to obtain salvation by our Lord Jesus Christ." And it removes the weight of God's curse, for we find it written in Galatians 3:13: "Christ hath redeemed us from the curse of the law, being made a curse for us in our place."

You have read in *Les Miserables,* Victor Hugo's great

***Convention Sermon, Baptist General Convention of Texas, Nov. 8, 1902.**

work, the story of the French peasant who was cast from his cart and pinned beneath its wheels. A crowd of men gathered about and were vainly seeking to deliver the unfortunate teamster. Jean Valjean, once a convict in the galley ships, now the honored mayor of the city, comes upon the scene, and seeing that without immediate relief his fellow man is soon to be crushed to death, cast himself upon his breast and crawled in under the loaded cart, and with almost super-human strength lifted it from the unfortunate peasant and held it there until he struggled out free.

I was that peasant, crushed to death beneath the weight of sin. Jesus Christ was my Jean Valjean casting Himself in great humiliation upon the earth and bore for me the weight of sin and condemnation that crushed me down. He placed himself in my place of jeopardy, that I might stand in His place of liberty, that it might be fulfilled which was spoken by Isaiah the prophet: "Surely he hath carried our sorrows; he hath borne our griefs. . . The Lord hath laid on him the iniquity of us all."

II. A New Condition in the Sight of God.

My next point is that the redemption that is in Jesus Christ gives a new condition in the sight of God. Man's normal condition is one of uncleanness. Isaiah, the first chapter says: "The whole head is sick; the whole heart is faint; from the sole of the foot unto the head there is no soundness in it, but wounds and bruises and putrifying sores." Paul in the first chapter of Romans says: "Wherefore God gave them up to uncleanness through the lusts of their flesh."

Jesus Christ found me with the open token of sin upon my breast, like the unfortunate woman in the *Scarlet Letter* with the letter A—initial letter in adultery—on her breast. But in giving me a new standing before Him he did not doom me to go into heaven with this token of sin visible to the angels and the redeemed saints, but cleansed me from it. He did what patching up, working over, and mere reforming can never do. So what ocean waters cannot do for even what we call our slightest sin, the blood of Jesus Christ is able to do for that which we consider the deepest sin.

It was this to which Zechariah referred: "In that day there

shall be open to the house of David and to the inhabitants of Jerusalem a fountain for sin and uncleanness." Isaiah said: "Come, let us reason together. Though your sins be as scarlet, they shall be as white as snow. Though they be red like crimson, they shall be as white as wool." It was the tasting of this nectar that moved John to write: "And the blood of Jesus Christ his Son, cleanseth from all sin", and to picture the redeemed hosts as clothed in white garments.

It was this cleansing power of the blood of Jesus to which Paul referred in the 5th chapter and 21st verse of Second Corinthians, when he said: "He who knew no sin God hath made to be sin in our place, that we might be the righteousness of God in him." His power to cleanse led God to say in the Psalms: "As far as the east is from the west, so far have I removed your transgressions from you." How far is it from here to the east? Travel with the cable's speed a million years, you have not reached the east. How far is it from here to the west? Travel with a ligntning sweep a million years and you have not reached the west. What God means to say by that text is this: That the believer in Jesus Christ, as He looks upon that believer, has his sins removed from him by the limitless space of two infinities.

III. A New Character from God.

But I say not only that the redemption in Jesus gives us a new standing before God and a new condition in the sight of God, but also a new character from God. Man's normal character as it relates to God is that of open rebellion against Him, for we find it written in the 107th Psalm: "Because they rebelled against the words of God and condemned the counsel of the most high." And in the colossal eighth of Romans: "The carnal mind is enmity against God, is not subject to the law of God, neither indeed can be." Now, the carnal mind does not mean some awfully bad mind that only wicked people have, but the mind with which all of us were born. We hear some talk in these days about salvation by character. Now, there is in scripture taught a salvation by character, not that character that is the result of reforming the shattered fragments of man's fallen nature; but that character that is imparted through faith in Jesus Christ.

Salvation would be sadly incomplete if God had simply taken off my shoulders sin's burden, and washed from my heart sin's stain, and yet left in my heart the seeds of a nature fatally in love with sin. What were heaven to me if I shall be doomed to spend eternity there, out of rapport with God, loving the things that are evil? But we have a new character through Jesus Christ, and so Paul writes in Second Corinthians the 5th chapter: "Therefore if any man be in Christ Jesus he is a new creation. Behold, all things are passed away. All things are become new."

So the redemption that is in Christ Jesus, after lifting the cart of sin's burden that presses me down to death, and after washing the filth and mire of the streets from the garments that have been stained, gives a new nature, a new character from God. Zacchaeus was a tax tyrant, whose ear was deaf to the cry of the widow or the orphan's moan. One day he met Jesus in the thoroughfare and he believed in Him, and at once there was a change in his attitude to the suffering poor, for he said: "I give half my goods to feed the poor." At once there was a change in his thought about fair dealing between man and man, for he said: "If I have taken anything from any man by false accusation, behold, I restore it to him fourfold." He believed in Jesus and had received a new nature from Him, and he was but fulfilling the scripture that said: "It is no longer I that live, but Christ that liveth in me." It could be said of him: "He is a new creation." A similiar experience took place in the conversion of the Philippian jailor.

IV. A New Fellowship with God.

Now, brethren, the last point is that the redemption that is in Jesus Christ has wrought for us a new fellowship with God. Man's normal relation to God is not one of fellowship, for we find in the tenth chapter of Psalms: "The wicked through the pride of his countenance will not seek after God. God is not in all his thoughts." And we find it written in the second chapter of Ephesians: "At that time ye were without Christ, being aliens from the commonwealth of Israel, and strangers from the covenant of promise." So the Scriptures teach that man's normal condition is the condition of an alien and a stranger, and one who, when he looks upon his sins, instead of flying to God for forgiveness, flees from God as an avenging Nemesis.

We are not in fellowship with God by nature. We are aliens and strangers to God by nature. There is a fascinating fiction afloat which they call the universal fatherhood of God, and it teaches that all men are the children of God. Now, the Scriptures in every part of them stand squarely against any such fictitious assumption, however much it may appeal to the sentimental mind. "They that are the children of the flesh, these are not the children of God." Does that sound like the universal fatherhood of God for all men?" "But as many as received him, to them (and not to any others—to them) gave he power to become the sons of God." Paul says: "Ye are the children of God"—how? By a natural birth? By a sort of universal sentimental connection between us and the Creator? No. "Ye are the children of God through faith in the Lord Jesus Christ."

The man who, for whatever pretext or reason, rejects Jesus Christ, has no right to claim God as his father, and no right to call God his father. The Scriptures teach that the man that doeth unrighteousness is a child of the devil. The Scriptures teach that the men who sin are the children of wrath and not the children of God. Unless I mistake the signs of the times, the coming battleground of our Southern Baptists will find its scene just upon this doctrine. Gradually it is weaving its way into the teachings of many pulpits, and institutions of learning. Let our churches begin now to rid themselves of this heresy, if it exists, or to forearm themselves against it if they see it coming. Let all our preachers everywhere announce that God is the father only of the believer. Let every church steeple bear upon the banner that it floats to the breeze the motto: "No man is the son of God except as he has become such by believing in the Son of God."

Now, let us spend the few moments that shall be left in discussing the question of the blessings that flow to us from this redemption that is in Christ Jesus. For one thing this redemption blesses us when we mourn for sin. "As one whom his mother comforteth, so will I comfort you." There is one brought nigh unto us by the redemption that is in Christ Jesus more able to comfort than a mother, for when my father and my mother forsake me, then the Lord taketh me up.

But further than that, this redemption that is in Jesus Christ greatly comforts me when we come to the consideration of our own wickedness and unworthiness. Remembering all that God has done for us, recalling all his matchless mercies there comes a yearning impulse in our hearts to do something for him. Just as the little lad's paltry loaves and fishes fed the multitudes, so, out of the empty vessel that I shall bring, the feast of God's glory shall be supplied. We as well as Christ help to feed the hungry multitudes.

This redemption that is in Christ Jesus, and the fellowship that is built upon it, helps us when we come to face the unknown and uncertain future. You turn your face at the call of God's Spirit to a new and untried field, not knowing what awaits you there, except that experience and God's spirit teach you that hardship and toil and disappointment and suffering and homeless poverty await you there. But you go out, not as one who has no comfort, but you go out as one walking upon the clouds, upborne by the promise of God to those who go forth to preach his gospel: "Lo, I am with you always, even to the end of the world."

And so, brethren, when we look into the unknown future, the fellowship, the comradship, the presence of God—vouched to us by the presence of Christ—helps and comforts and buoys up our hearts. My tired little boy walking by me said: "I don't care if I do get tired, just so I am with you." I know not what the future holds for me; I know not what of homeless poverty; I know not what of sorrow and pain; I know not what of bereavement at the hand of death; I know not what of persecution from the wicked world; but this much I know, that in all I shall not be weary if Thou art with me.

But, further still, not only does this fellowship that is in Christ Jesus on account of his redemption, comfort us in the remnant of this life; but this fellowship comforts us in the hour of death. Israel's bard, realizing the fellowship of God in Jesus Christ, wrote: "Yea, though I walk through the valley of the shadow of death, I will fear no evil." No believer will ever die in the dark. It may be at midnight, and the natural eye may be glazed and sightless, but there shall be a supernal light, because it shall be the light of Him who bore our darkness that we might have His light. Darkness enveloped the cross when Jesus was crucified that light might flood the couch of the saint when he came to die. Thus, as he is my substitute in everything else, he will also be my substitute in bearing for me the otherwise darkness of the grave that I might have through him the everlasting light of his presence.

But, more still, the fellowship of God, based upon the redemption that is in Jesus Christ, helps us when we come to consider that unknown eternity. To every unbeliever, eternity is a leap in the dark. To every believer, eternity is but faith's taking hold of the hand of the Father and stepping out into undimmed light. Jesus said: "I go to prepare a place for you, and if I go and prepare a place for you, I will come again and receive you unto myself, that where I am there ye may be also." Heaven is where Jesus is just as happiness to a true wife is where her husband is. We tremble at the verge of eternity, but let us make the leap, and we shall find that underneath are the everlasting arms.

"All hail the power of Jesus' name
Let Angels prostrate fall,
Bring forth the royal diadem,
And crown Him Lord of all!
Let every kindred, every tribe,
On this terrestial ball,
To him all majesty ascribe
And crown Him Lord of all."

Chapter X

I. E. REYNOLDS

AUTOBIOGRAPHICAL SKETCH

I was born September 7, 1879, in Shades Valley, Alabama, five miles from Birmingham. Later we moved to a farm near Springville where I worked until I was twenty. I drove twenty-five miles in a wagon to Birmingham to secure work. My first job was carrying shingles at fifty cents per day. Later I built gin brushes for the Continental Gin Company at ten cents per hour.

While on the farm I attended community singing schools. In 1902 I attended a Normal Singing School taught by Prof. J. Henry Showalter, and a year later was secretary of another taught by him. I attended Mississippi College during the session of 1905-06. The next year I went to Moody Bible Institute to study music, but was unable to finish the course on account of my eyes. In 1911 I studied voice with George J. Parker of Boston and later with Dr. Andrew Hemphill of Fort Worth. I received the Mus.B. degree in 1918 from the Siegel-Myers University Correspondence School of Music. The degree of Mus.D. was conferred on me by the Southern School of Fine Arts in 1942.

My conversion was in a children's meeting in a Cumberland Presbyterian Church in my home community in Alabama, and six years later when my parents were converted I joined that church with them. In 1904 my wife and I joined the North Highlands Baptist Church in Birmingham and were baptized by Rev. Hatcher Watkins. I was a charter member of the Seminary Hill Baptist Church and served as chairman of its board of deacons.

Work as an evangelistic singer began with Rev. Otto Barber in 1904, and the next year I was employed in that capacity by the Mississippi Baptist State Mission Board. In 1906 I was associated with Rev. E. D. Solomon in revival work. Later I did evangelistic singing under Dr. E. B. Towner, Director of Music at Moody Bible Institute. In the winter of 1909 I was sent to the Panama Canal Zone in a similiar capacity by the Southern Baptist Home Mission Board. On returning in the spring I was put on the staff of the Home Mission Board as evangelistic singer with Dr. Weston Bruner, Superintendent of Evangelism.

I have directed choirs in several churches including the Twenty-seventh Street Baptist Church in Birmingham, the First Baptist Church, Wesson, Mississippi, and Seminary Hill and Broadway Baptist Churches in Fort Worth. Also I have directed the Seminary Choral Club in presenting at Christmas, commencement and other occasions *The Messiah* forty times, *The Elijah* and *Ruth* ten times each, and *The Creation, Holy City, King of Kings, Seven Last Words of Christ* and other outstanding selections from time to time.

My first marriage was in 1900 to Miss Velma Burns of Alabama who died along with our infant daughter in 1906. While attending the Southern Baptist Convention at Oklahoma City in May, 1912, I met Miss Lura Mae Hawk, a member of the choir of the First Baptist Church there, and we were married the following July. To this union was born a daughter, Lurames, now the wife of Lieut. Le Moyne Michels. They have two fine children.

In 1915 President L. R. Scarborough asked me to become head of the Department of Gospel Music of the Southwestern Baptist Theological Seminary. The work grew, other teachers were added, and curricula outlined leading to the Diploma and Bachelor's and Master's degrees in Sacred Music. In 1921 the department became a school and in 1926 George E. Cowden Hall was erected to house it. The faculty began with two and grew to be fifteen. The student body started with nine and has grown to two hundred. The school is a member of the Texas State Music Association and eligible for membership in the National Association of Schools of Music. It has enrolled more than 2,500 students during the years, and graduated over 250, who are now located in churches, schools, and on mission fields

From time to time I have held membership in a number of organizations of various kinds, including denominational groups, the Kiwanis Club, The Order of the Eastern Star, Knight Templars in the Masonic Order, Fort Worth Music Teachers' Association, (past president), Texas State Music Teachers' Association, Tri-State Church Music Association, National Music Education Conference, Authors' and Composers' Association of America and several others, local and general. I have served on the Southern Baptist Church Music Committee and spoken at Southern music conferences at Ridgecrest and the National Music Convention in Los Angeles. My name is in the *Encyclopedia of Musicians* and *Who's Who in America.*

Besides five mimeographed books used in class work at the Seminary I have published *Practical Church Music* (1925), *Ministry of Music* (1928), *Church Music* (1935), *Music and the Scriptures* (1942), and the *Choir in the Now Liturgical Church,* and served as an editor of *Jehovah's Praise, and Kingdom Songs.* Also I have written two sacred music dramas, four sacred music cantatas, and many anthems, hymns, and gospel songs, and articles on music for various denominational papers.

In the summer of 1945 I completed thirty years with Southwestern Baptist Theological Seminary, and retired as Director of the School of Sacred Music on account of health. I am now living at 801 Page St., Fort Worth, Texas, and giving my time as strength permits to writing, teaching in music training schools and lecturing in church music conferences.

CHURCH MUSIC TENDENCIES OF TODAY*

From the dawn of creation, when the morning stars sang together (Job 38:7), music has been a vital factor in religious worship. The kind of music used has depended very largely, if not entirely, upon the extent of the cultural development of the people by whom it was used. Without music, Christian worship and service would be bereft of one of their most helpful and powerful agencies in spreading the gospel of Christ. The music used in the Christian religion differs from that used in all other religions in that it is a means of praise, adoration, and exaltation of the King of Kings.

Andrew Law says, "Theology and music move hand in hand into time, and will continue eternally to illustrate, embellish, enforce, impress, and fix in the mind of the grand and great truths of Christianity." It seems to be part of the divine plan that music should be the handmaid of the churches. The Reverend David R. Breed, in his book on hymnology, *The History and Use of Hymns and Hymn Tunes,* says, "The fundamental difficulty is that we do not realize how much sacred song is to us, what it means, what it expresses, and what it is capable of accomplishing; and, therefore, it is pitiably neglected."

During the early centuries of Christianity, music was a powerful aid in carrying on the work of the churches. Under stress of bitter persecution some of the greatest hymns were given birth. It is said that the barbarians were won and transformed by the singing of Christian hymns. Edwards says, "It was the Hymns of Ambrose that conquered Constantine."

The Reformation directed by Luther was accomplished largely through the singing of Luther's hymns. Cardinal Cajetan said of him, "By his songs he has conquered us." and, in connection with the founding of Methodism by the Wesleys, it is said that when blood-thirsty crowds could not be quelled by John Wesley's black eyes or by Whitfield's compelling voice, they were known to turn and slink away when the truth was sung to them in Charles Wesley's hymns. Their leaders were known to weep and groan with remorse under the influence of Wesley's singing. They took the preacher by the hand and

*Article in *Music Journal,* November, 1945.

went away arm in arm, swearing by all that was good that not a hair of his head should be touched.

In the present age, no one would attempt to deny the power and influence of music in all Christian activity. An effective music program puts the worshipper in a receptive mood for the truths which the minister presents in his sermons. It also works on the emotions and affects the will in such a way that the individual is responsive to the teachings of Christ.

A very conservative estimate of the time consumed by the music program in each period of the church service—Sunday school, young people's meetings, evangelistic meetings, and all other activities—is about one-third of the whole time.

An impressive number of people are directly or indirecly connected with the music program as church music directors, choir directors, choir members, song leaders, accompanists, and leaders and performers on orchestral instruments. For instance, my own denomination, Southern Baptists, has over 25,000 churches and a membership of some 6,000,000 persons. Each of these churches has a choir director or song leader; each of them has an accompanist. Allowing an average of ten choir members for each of the 25,000 churches, there would be approximately 250,000 choir members, making a grand total of 300,000 people who are directly connected with the music program of the churches in the Southern Baptist Convention.

An imporant factor to be considered is the financial outlay for the music programs in the churches. Professor Augustine Smith, of Boston University, says that in the churches of America there is an annual outlay of $30,000,000 on religious music and that, because of the lack of standards, 90 percent of the amount is wasted. As applied to the Southern Baptist churches, the author believes that a conservative estimate of the cost of music programs, including hymnals, songbooks, choral music, cantatas, oratorios, instrumental music, instruments of various kinds, and the salaries of choir direrctors, song leaders, orchestra and band leaders, accompanists, soloists, quartets, and choirs would be $1,000,000 annually, or an average of $40 for each church. And if Professor Smith's statement that 90 per cent is lost because of inadequate and in-effective music programs is correct, then Southern Baptists are responsibile for wasting $900,000 a year.

Much has been said and written regarding the forms of music used in nonliturgical church programs, and much more could and should be said and written about them. The early Christians used the Psalms with tunes handed down from the Hebrew worship.

In the second century A. D. they began to compose their own songs, which expressed a distinctly Christian sentiment. In the fourth century the Roman Church, declared by the Roman emperor to be the Church of State, established all over its domain church music schools in which singers were trained to take charge of the music programs of the church. According to the records, for about one thousand years music was fostered entirely by the Roman church fathers.

In the sixteenth century Martin Luther broke away from the established forms and gave congregational singing to the people in their native tongue. Dr. Louis Benson, in his book *The English Hymn: Its Development and Use,* says that some other sects prior to the Reformation sang congregational songs in their own tongue. Luther wrote hymns based upon scriptural texts and set to tunes composed by himself, or to some of the German choral tunes. Other Protestant groups used the Psalms, unaltered, set to music. It was during the reign of Henry VIII that the Church of England came into existence, and it followed the forms of the Roman church to a great extent.

Isaac Watts appeared upon the scene the latter part of the seventeenth century with arrangements of the Psalms in metrical forms and hymns written on scriptural texts. Charles Wesley joined Watts in the early part of the eighteenth century, and together they brought in the era of English hymnody which earned them the title the Fathers of English Hymnody. The masses took to the hymn form, but the conservatives tried to stem the tide. Watts and Wesley were followed by hosts of other hymn writers. Hymn singing became universal in Protestant churches. Psalm singers were the last to adopt the hymns. The introduction of hymn singing and instruments in the churches brought about a great change in worship music. In the early part of the nineteenth century the gospel song was introduced in America.

At the present time the nonliturgical churches are widely divided in their likes, dislikes, and uses of church music. There are two distinct types, almost as far apart as the North and South Poles. The large urban churches with wealthy memberships desire a very formal type of service and a music program presented by the best trained choirs. The churches in smaller communities, with congregations made up of people who have had little opportunity to gain a knowledge and appreciation of music, prefer a simple type of music, often with little more than doggerel for words and with an ultra-rhythmical melody which appeals more to the physical than to the spiritual. In between these extremes is the great group of average churches, most of which eventually find themselves in one or the other of the extreme groups.

It is a sad fact that most of our churches become a prey to the commercial songbook publishers which usually means that they succumb to a poor grade of church music. In many of these there is opposition to the anthem on the grounds that it is not spiritual although the real truth is that most anthems are scriptural in nature, scriptures set to music. It is heartening indeed to note, however, that there is a definite trend in most of our churches, especially from the average church to the "First Churches," toward a better church music program, one that is more worshipful and less rhythmical, the norm being the standard hymn with opportunity for anthems and Gospel songs.

There is a growing demand in churches for music leadership trained in the Westminster Choir School, Christiansen Choir School, and similar superior choir schools. Another indication of the upward trend in church music throughout the country is that so many schools (the writer has noted twenty-three) are offering courses in church music and many of them offer church music degrees. The church leadership—preachers, education workers, and musicians—of the future must be able to promote and maintain programs commensurate with the ideals, standards, and appreciation of the young people of today. This applies to rural as well as urban communities.

SECURING BETTER MUSIC IN WORSHIP*

This is one of the most vital questions facing the churches of today, especially the non-liturgical churches. However, it is one of the most difficult to discuss because of its many angles and the differences of opinion on the subject. Too, it is a result that cannot be obtained overnight; to be lasting it must come by way of a gradual educational process. The speaker can bring only a few suggestions which are the result of study, observation and personal experience.

The first general suggestion relates to the matter of training and guiding our people into the knowledge of the purpose and mission of church music. That God gave it to be used as one medium through which to express our religious emotions—praise, adoration, joy, thanksgiving, devotion—must be impressed upon them. The mission of church music is the same as the mission of the church: to bring others into a fuller knowledge of Christ as Saviour, Master and Lord.

Also, the people should be taught to love and appreciate the better types of hymns. An appreciation of a thing is the greatest incentive to use it, and appreciation comes through education, influence and atmosphere or surroundings that are conducive to it. So we should teach good hymns to all age groups in our church life.

The churches, also, should have in them a church music educational program paralleling the secular music educational program just as they now have a religious educational program. By this means children and young people will be trained into an understanding of the best music. This will aid greatly in growing an appreciation for the better hymns. Results for helpfulness will follow.

Physical equipment should include an instrument—organ or piano in good repair and well tuned—, an adequate lighting system by which the singers can easily read music, and an abundant supply of worthy hymn books. The last-mentioned is important. Before we can have better hymn-singing we must have better hymnals from which to sing. Too many of our

*Address delivered at National Educators' Music Conference, Los Angeles, 1940.

non-liturgical churches, as in the case of our own denomination, are a prey to the cheap song book publishers.

The minister, his official board, and the church have much to do with inducing the use of better hymns in the church service. Unless there is a strong, sympathetic support of this movement little can be accomplished. In fact, the speaker believes the crux of the matter lies here. If the preacher has been the pastor of a church for sometime, the music conditions prevailing in the various departments of the church life are but reflections of his appreciation and desires.

Much depends upon the efficiency and ability of the music director and accompanist in securing the use of better hymns in the church service and related activities. In order to be a good salesman of any make of automobile, the salesman must first be sold on that particular car himself. Before the music leader will be able to get people to sing and enjoy and use better hymns he must be "sold" on them himself—have a love and appreciation for them.

The director, or song leader, must have had preparation for the work in his field—spiritually and mentally—with a physically fit body. Some of the essential qualifications are: magnetism, creative imagination, cheerfulness, a sense of humor, initiative and an earnest desire to leave off those personal habits which hinder his work.

Without a good accompanist it is practically impossible to carry on a successful music program. Church music playing is an art within itself and must be studied if perfected. The same religious and educational qualifications as those required for the director are desirable for the accompanist. Too, he or she must have a keen sense of measure and rhythm, be able to build a good accompaniment from the harmonies arranged for the voice parts, not drown out the voices, not sacrifice the spiritual for the artistic (but make the work more spiritual through artistic methods), be subordinate to the director, be able to memorize readily, make the best of the instrument at hand, and be on time and regular in attendance.

Following are some suggested methods which may be employed as an incentive to use better hymns in our church services:

1. Selection of hymns which produce an emotional reaction, instead of a physical reaction.

2. Selection of hymns appropriate for the occasion.

3. Teaching the congregation that in hymns the sentiment of the text is paramount, the music an aid in conveying the thought of the text, and the text and music properly suited to each other.

4. There should be variety in the rendering and use of hymns. This may be obtained by solos, duets, trios, quartets, women's voices, men's voices, children's voices, unison and antiphonal singing, humming back of solo voice, reading words while instrument plays, song sermons arranged homiletically around a given theme, or a song service built around a subject, and hymn-author studies with a brief biographical sketch before the hymn is sung.

5. Regardless of what method is employed the dignity of the occasion should be preserved. Uncouthness or vaudeville performance should never be reverted to in the singing of great religious hymns. Cheapness never aids the religious spirit on any occasion in any service. Stamping the foot, slapping the hands or the song book, yelling "sing it", whistling, or wearing a forced smile, attract the attention to the leader rather than what he is trying to do.

Let us "praise Jehovah in the beauty of holiness. . . Praise ye the Lord!"

Chapter XI

L. R. SCARBOROUGH

BIOGRAPHICAL SKETCH*

The Baptist world has a new reason for celebrating the Fourth of July, since on that day in 1870, in a humble home in Colfax, Louisana, Lee Rutland Scarborough was born. The parents were Mr. George W. and Mrs. Rutland Scarborough. He was a born leader of men. It made no difference with what group he associated, he became their leader.

His life may be divided into three periods. The first is that of preparation. An all-wise Father provided this preparation. God guided the Scarborough family to the big, open west near Anson, Texas, where they settled. Here, young Lee Rutland got the training that was indispensable to his future greatness. He lived in a dug-out. His early life was that of a typical cowboy. He was active in annual "round-ups", was a frequenter of the chuck wagon, followed cattle herds, and learned all the things incident to cowboy life, including "cutting out cows and calves", and "branding and marking".

In that period it was the "wild and woolly" west. Here the young lad learned to hunt wild game, turkey, deer, anthlope, and bear, and to ride. Someone has said, "He could ride anything that wore hair, whether cattle or horses". This outdoor life gave him a strong and healthy body. Few men could stand up under harder strain. God knew that a strong body would be needed when the young man became a national leader.

The young lad received such schooling as was common in that locality. He then went to Baylor University, receiving the B. A. degree in 1892. In 1896 he received the B. A. degree from Yale University, and went to Cameron, Texas, as pastor. Then he attended Southern Seminary one year. His mind had

*By Rev. Perry F. Evans, Field Representative Buckner Orphan's Home.

been set on becoming a great lawyer but God intervened. "You are a chosen vessel of mine to preach the unsearchable riches of Christ."

Perhaps his little semi-invalid mother did more to influence him religiously than any other person. But when he met and married Miss Neppie Warren, she, perhaps, had the greatest influence over him. "Behind the success of every man is a little woman, somewhere." Mrs. L. R. Scarborough is a most patient and Godly woman. She has never sought the limelight nor the spectacular. She has been content to live through her famous husband and six lovely children.

The second period is that of evangelism. In this realm Dr. Scarborough was perhaps greatest. He had few equals in the nation. His passion for the lost was supreme and challenging to the last degree. It was akin to Paul who said, "Brethren, my heart's desire and prayer to God for Israel is that they might be saved . . . I could wish myself accursed from Christ for my brethren in the flesh." Outside of Dr. George W. Truett, the writer of this article has never met another who had such an unutterable yearning for the lost. While in the pastorate he not only kept his church seeking them, but assisted scores of other Baptist pastors in revivals. He held some of the really great revivals of the nation.

His evangelistic efforts headed up in a constructive program. His revivals aided churches, hospitals, seminaries, and other agencies. He took into his warm heart all agencies. As president of Southwestern Seminary he continued to hold "The Chair of Fire," and from the classroom of evangelism went out men and women around the world fired with a passion to win the lost.

The third period of his life is that of kingdom building. Dr. Scarborough had no superior and few equals in all the South in this respect. While he was pastor of the great First Church, Abilene, he found time to raise money for two buildings for Simmons University. All of the buildings on the Southwestern campus are the results of his labors. Every brick in their walls is bathed with blood, sweat and tears.

Without doubt his greatest achievement in Kingdom building was his leadership in the Seventy-Five Million Campaign.

One day he told the writer: "Perry, my brethren tell me I must move my headquarters to Nashville, Tennessee." There he began the Herculean task of setting up an organization. In an almost unbelievably short time he swung into battle line the Baptists of the South, Marshalling his forces, including Baptist papers, the State Conventions, Training Unions, Sunday Schools and W.M.U.'s not only did he reach his goal but went far beyond securing gifts and pledges of ninety-two million dollars.

Some of his chief characteristics were his passion for the lost; already discussed; his optimism—Pollyana herself could have taken lessons from him: his keen sense of humor; even under the most trying circumstances; and his approachableness, being as much so as a little child.

Dr. Scarborough received the D.D. from Baylor and the LL.D. from Union University. He was president of the Texas Baptist Convention, and the Southern Baptist Convention, and vice-president of the Baptist World Alliance. He was author of *Recruits for World Conquests, With Christ after the Lost, Marvels of Divine Leadership, The Tears of Jesus, Prepare to Meet Thy God, Endued to Win, Christ's Militant Kingdom, Holy Places and Precious Promises, How Jesus Won Men, Ten Spiritual Ships, Products of Pentecost, My Conception of the Gospel Ministry. A Blaze of Evangelism across the Equator,* and *A Modern School of the Prophets.* He died at Amarillo, Texas, April 10, 1945, and was buried at Fort Worth.

THE TEARS OF JESUS*

John 11:35 — Jesus Weeping at the Gate of Death. "Jesus Wept."

Luke 19:41 — Jesus Weeping over a Doomed City. "When he was come near, he beheld the city, and wept over it."

Heb. 5:7 — Jesus Weeping over a Lost World. "He offered up prayers and supplication with strong crying and tears unto him that was able to save him from death, and was heard in that he feared."

We find in this first scripture Jesus weeping at the grave of Lazarus. In the second scripture we see Him weeping over a city which being doomed had rejected His message. And in the last scripture we find Him shedding tears and offering prayers in the days of His flesh over a ruined world for which He was to die.

We note in this second scripture that he was coming to Jerusalem for the last time. He had been out among the people for three and a half years, preaching, teaching, healing and performing many miracles. The blind could see when he touched their eyes; the lame could walk, the dumb could speak, and the dead came forth out of the grave at His word of authority and power. But He had come now to Jerusalem, for the last time. Just a few days afterwards he was to be crucified in the city he had come to save. Coming in that morning from the east side, with a great crowd meeting and following Him, praising God in accordance with the promises concerning Him, He saw that beautiful city with a wonderful history.

I am sure, since He knew all things, there was present in His mind the past history of triumphs and defeat, of prosperity and adversity. I am sure that He saw with His historic mind the things that had transpired in that city, where a great people had builded a great city, the center of the religious life of the world, where He had trained a race to be His chosen people. And as He looked upon that city the Scriptures say, "He wept." This Son of God, this Son of Man, seeing that city wept bitter, briny tears over what He saw. This is one of the three times

*From *The Tears of Jesus* by L. R. Scarborough, Baptist Sunday School Board. Used by permission.

in the Scriptures where it speaks of the tears of Jesus. On one occasion before this he stood at the grave of Lazarus, and wept, joined in the sorrow of the loved ones for the man who had been hospitable to Him, a man He loved. And there the Son of Man at the gate of death shed tears.

The other place where it speaks of His tears is where I read you from the 5th chapter of Hebrews. It says that "in the days of His flesh with strong supplication and tears he prayed unto Him Who was able to save Him from death." There in that case Jesus Christ not only wept over a lost city, but He wept over a lost world.

Now I want us to think for a little while of the weeping Saviour, the tears of Jesus Christ.

I. Why Are These Tears?

Who is this strange person who has filled all history and yet standing on the crest of the mountain we see weeping? His heart is torn and there comes from His eyes and from His heart tears that represent the attitude of His soul toward a lost city and toward a lost world. Who is He? Why He is the author of our Bible, the founder of our churches, a refuge to our souls, the hope of our resurrection, the builder of our heaven, and the source and provider of all our spiritual blessings. The Scriptures call Him our advocate, the anointed one, the balm in Gilead for our souls, the bread of life for our hopes, the corner stone and the foundation of our lives, the commander of God's army which is to conquer all sin, the counsellor and guide for our feet.

He is the founder on which we build and the fountain from which we drink. He is the hiding place for our tempest-tossed souls, the high priest of our communion with God. He is the Immanuel, the very presence of the Most High. He is King over Kings and Lord over Lords. He was the Lamb of God slain from before the foundation of the world as a sacrifice and atonement for our sins. He is the leader of God's mightiest hosts, the Lion of the Tribe of Judah. He it was that was the Man of Sorrows and who was aquainted with grief. He is the conquerer over sin and the enemies of God, the mediator between man and God, the messenger of God's covenant to a lost world, the Messiah of hope for a coming day of full redemption. He is the Prince of Life and the Prince of Peace, the redeemer, the rock of ages, the rose of Sharon, the scepter of Israel, the shepherd of God's sheep. He is God's only begotten and most beloved son.

Here on the mount overlooking Jerusalem He weeps with a heart full of compassion and love for a lost world, and establishes again the doctrine of the chief and central passion of the gospel wrought out in His ministry, death and intercession for a sin-cursed world. He is the mightiest among the mighty and loveliest among ten thousand, the maker and preserver of our lives and the Saviour of our souls. He it is that weeps over our sin, doom and destiny. It is in His hands that the reins of the universe are held. This man is the Son of God, is very God himself. He it is who controls all the things of our lives. And yet yonder in the city where He had taught and preached and was soon to be crucified, we see Him shedding the bitterest of tears. He is not some conqueror come to destroy, but a Saviour come to save. He will not call down the wrath of the clouds and gather the powers of the storms over them and die for them and save them. He it is that is weeping today over a lost world.

I raise another question.

II. Why These Tears?

Why is that this Son of Man, this Son of God, is weeping over the city of Jerusalem, and was constantly during the days of His flesh appealing unto God with strong supplications and tears? I say to you He is not weeping for Himself, though He sees the shadow of the cross just ahead of Him. He sees the dark, unspeakable sorrow of Gethsemane through which He is to go, the cruel crown of thorns which is to be pressed on His head, and already the piercing of the nails in His hands and the sword in His side. Yet He is not weeping over Himself. He is not weeping like a defeated conqueror. He was not weeping over a life of defeat, though in the eyes of the world He was living a life of defeat. He was not weeping because of His own failure or because of any discontent in His heart. Jesus was not weeping for Himself; but He was weeping because He saw some things from the Mount of Olivet. He was not weeping over that city which through the centuries had been builded by the sacrifices, and labors of His people. He was not weeping for its reputation, though He saw the ruin of that city about which He here prophesied. He was not weeping for the falling walls and the ruins of the Temple. Why was He weeping that day? What was it that He saw that caused the tears to come from His eyes? It is about that that I wish to speak to you.

I want if I can to bring you this day into a sympathetic attitude with Jesus Christ, as He stood on Mount Olive. What was it that brought the tears from His eyes and broke His heart? It lies in three directions. In the first place, he wept because He saw the spiritual condition of men. He saw men in their sins. He saw them in the darkness of their unbelief, in the night of their unfaith in Him, sinners, dead in trespasses and sins. He saw the wrath of God on them if the love of God was not in their hearts. He saw them rejecting the only light come to them. He saw them without hope and without God in the world. As He looked upon the soul of an unbeliever no wonder it brought a desire to be crucified for the life and salvation of that individual. The condition of men today ought to bring tears and burdens to the hearts of God's people.

I stood the other day by the side of a wife as she looked upon the pale, emaciated face of her loving husband. The doctors had just operated on him and said he had typhoid fever. At that time he was suffering from a hemorrhage which it looked like he could not stand. His face was white and his finger tips and toe tips seemed to be drained of blood. I stood by her side as we went into another room to pray. Oh, there was such a wringing of the wife's heart as she said, "He cannot stand the loss of blood! He cannot stand the battle of the germs of disease in his body!" She realized the condition of her husband.

I stood by the side of a mother as she looked into the face of her baby, dying as she thought. Her heart was wrung. The doctors had said, "He must die." She was torn by the realization of the condition of her child.

I will tell you, my friends, we need today to look into

the lives of the unsaved men all about us and see their peril and condition before Almighty God. Every man, woman and young person in this community without Jesus Christ in his heart by faith, is lost and dead in trespasses and in sins, is away from God and has no hope. The immoral decay of sin, is in every particle of his spirit. Shall we look on them unmoved while the Son of God seeing a lost and ruined city shed tears over its condition? I trust that God's people seeing the unsaved about them today and during this meeting will join the Saviour weeping over a lost world.

I shall never forget one Sunday afternoon, (after I had preached in the morning), when my first child, just five years of age, a little boy, as I was lying on my bed was sitting astride my body. Suddenly he changed the subject from what we had been talking about and looking into my face said with a trembling voice, "Daddy, I am lost. I want you to show me the way to Christ." I do not explain it. I only tell you the story. It was the first time I realized the spiritual condition of my child. It was the first time he had appealed to me from his own lost soul. From that time until he was saved I kept the prayers hot up, up to God. I carried him to the Saviour day by day. I believe it was because of the concern created in my heart that day that I kept the prayers hot. I want us in these days to remember the spiritual condition of every man that does not know Jesus Christ.

I think another thing that stirred the heart of Jesus was not only the condition of men, but the destiny of men. He saw the place to which these people were going when they were carried to the cemeteries. He the Son of God was thinking of where those people were going after death. And it is a matter that should stir our hearts. It is not what we possess here, not how much education or how little we have, but the question of destiny, of where we are going. This should be the important question. It matters not that we die. How little value there is to the bodies of men, how little value!

But my friends it is the eternal destiny of the soul that is the important question. I want us to know in the battle that we are going to fight here within the next few days that we are fighting a battle for the destinies of men. Every unsaved man in your community is going to hell. I do not know how you feel. I bless God I know there is a heaven for those who believe in Christ. I am going to preach the gospel on this point. I want us to see the destinies of men and be moved like our Saviour was moved.

There was another thing that stirred the heart of our Saviour and that was their refusal to hear Him and their rejection of Him. Oh, the saddest thing that can come to the heart of Jesus Christ is for Him to be rejected! I wonder what will be the attitude of the people of the community. He had wrought among them and yet they had rejected Him. I tell you, there is a demonstration on every hand that Jesus Christ is the Son of God and the Saviour of the world. I wonder what we will do with this demonstration the next few days.

This incident in the life of the Saviour but illustrates the care Jesus has for men.

III. The Savior's Care.

He has shown, not only in His earthly life and sacrificial death, but in His heavenly ministry for these twenty centuries how much He cares for men. Even the hairs of our heads are numbered and not a sparrow falls without His loving care. Every detail of our lives is of interest to the Saviour and all those things that make for our salvation and spiritual strength and service for Him are of the deepest concern to our Saviour's heart.

Does He not show in His attitude at Lazarus' grave that He loves and cares for the suffering loved ones at every grave? Does He not show by the many examples of healing, of raising the dead, of straightening the limbs of the crippled, opening the eyes of the blind and the ears of the deaf, that He cares for our bodies and our souls? Never a tear falls from the heart of a sorrowing widow nor from the penitent soul of the sick sinner that misses the loving eye of our Saviour. He has assured us by His multiplied providences of loving care. That is the beauty of that great picture on Mount Olivet. Jesus loves men and has a concern for their salvation. He has shown it in His creative power, in His preserving and providential power, in His earthly ministry and in His death on Calvary.

You and I should take up the work of Jesus Christ and

care for lost men. This is the message that I bring you this morning. This is the message—do you care for the lost men and women of this city? I wonder how many of you do. Will you stand with Jesus on Mount Olivet today and say, "We, too, will weep for our loved ones and join our Saviour in caring for their souls?"

Some time ago I was in a great convention. I spoke to that convention on compassion for the lost. It was some years ago when our boys were gathering in the army camps all over our country. In that crowd was a rather old, plainly dressed woman. She and her husband came down the aisle to shake hands with me. She took me by the hand and said, "Do you live at Fort Worth?" I said, "I do." Then she started to say, "My boy is in Camp Bowie near Fort Worth." She stopped and wept.

Seeing her weeping her husband came up and putting his arm around her, he said, "Mary, what's the matter?" She said, "I was thinking of our baby boy yonder in Camp Bowie. You know he isn't saved. We have written letters to him about it. We have prayed for him and others have prayed for him." She said "Here's a preacher that lives near where our soldier boy is and I was trying to put our boy, our baby boy, on the heart of this preacher." Then she turned to me in a way and with a question I shall never forget. I thought I loved lost men. For twenty-five years I have given strength without reservation to the winning of lost men to Christ. I thought I loved lost men. But this dear old mother looked up with all the love of a mother and said, "Preacher, do you love lost men?" Oh, that question rings in my heart today!

You have made great preparation for this meeting and I bless God for it. The great question now is, Do we love lost men? If we do, God help us to join Jesus Christ in soul-agony for them that we may win them to Him. I wonder how many of you can say: "Deep down in my heart I do have a tender, affectionate concern for the unsaved of this community and I can join with my Savior in a deep compassion for their salvation."

Listen to what God says, "They that sow in tears shall reap in joy. He that goeth forth and weepeth, bearing precious seed, shall doubtless come again with rejoicing, bringing his sheaves with him." God help us to be stirred in our souls for the lost of this community.

Chapter XII

C. B. WILLIAMS

AUTOBIOGRAPHICAL SKETCH

I was born in Cambden County, N. C., January 15, 1869. My father, Simeon Walston Williams, was distantly related to Roger Williams, father of religious liberty in America; William Williams, signer of the Declaration of Independence; Sir George Williams, founder of the Young Men's Christian Association; and William Williams, author of "Guide Me, O Thou Great Jehovah."

My mother, Mary Bray Williams, was descended from Prof. Thomas Bray of Cambridge University; Robert Bray, a naval officer whose ship (Columbia) carried the first American flag around the world; and William Bray, a charter member of Old Shiloh Church, the oldest Baptist Church in North Carolina, organized in 1727.

I taught in a country school when fifteen years of age at $20.00 per month and paid off the mortgage on the old family homestead. At eighteen I entered Wake Forest College with $48.00, borrowed $150.00 from the local educational board, and graduated with a debt of only $150.00. While in college I was active in debating and literary society work, and was valedictorian of the class of 1891. My four-year average scholastic record was 98½ which was not surpassed for forty years.

I was licensed to preach when seventeen years of age, and held several country church revivals that year. Three years later I was ordained by the Wake Forest Baptist Church, having been called as pastor of the church at Brasfield. For five years following graduation I was pastor of the Winton Baptist Church, principal of the school, and raised the money for a new school building.

In 1897 I entered Crozer Theological Seminary, specialized in the original languages of the Bible, and graduated in 1900 with the B.D. degree, my thesis being on "Evolution and God". Among the teachers there were Henry G. Weston, Bayard Taylor and Milton G. Evans. While there I was pastor of Baptist churches in Chester, Pa., and in nearby New Jersey cities.

Soon after graduating from Crozer I started for Texas, but stopped over in Locksburg, Arkansas, and served as principal of the high school for a year. After another year as pastor of the Olive Street Baptist Church in Texarkana, I was called to the pastorate of the First Baptist Church of Stephenville, Texas, and served for three years, when I accepted the pastorate at Rockdale. During this time I held revivals in Dublin, Lampasas, Brownwood and Trinity resulting in over 300 professions.

In 1905 Dr. B. H. Carroll, then Dean of the Theological School of Baylor University, wired me to meet him in Waco for an interview. I did, and before the day of consultation was over was elected to the chair of Greek New Testament and Interpretation and began work enthusiastically the following week. I was thus the first one brought in from the outside for Southwestern Seminary, Dr. B. H. Carroll and Dr. A. H. Newman being already connected with Baylor University. Others were soon added to the staff.

While teaching at Baylor I attended summer schools in the University of Chicago receiving the M.A. degree in 1907 and the Ph.D. in 1908. In 1916 I delivered the Baccalaureate address at Baylor and received the D.D. degree. In 1920 the trustees there voted to confer the LL.D., but being in a financial campaign as president of Howard College I was unable to be present to receive it.

While at Baylor the First Baptist Church of Waco offered me the pastorate at a salary of $4,000, but I declined and stayed with teaching at a $1,500 salary. After moving to Fort Worth I was called to the Broadway Baptist Church there and the First Baptist Church in Wichita Falls at salaries three times that of the Seminary salary. In nine years in Fort Worth I raised $75,000 for seminary expenses and endownment and witnessed in one service at the military camp 200 professions.

I was made the first librarian at Southwestern and catalogued the first 5,000 volumes of its excellent library, given by

Drs. A. J. Harris and A. H. Newman. From 1913 to 1919 I served as dean of the Seminary, and managing editor of the "Southwestern Journal of Theology" in addition to my teaching. Also I served during summers as dean of the Panhandle Bible Conference.

In 1919 I resigned my position at Southwestern to accept the presidency of Howard College. In two years there I paid off a debt of $60,000, raised an additional $300,000 for endowment, and got the college accredited by the Southern Association. I resigned the presidency of Howard in 1921 to return to teaching, research and writing.

I served as professor at Mercer University from 1921 to 1925 and at Union University from 1925 to 1938, when I retired from teaching. Then I served as pastor in Florida and North Carolina for seven years. I am now making my home at Pierson, Florida, and writing *An Estimate of the Greatness of Dr. B. H. Carroll.*

The books I have written are *A History of Baptists in North Carolina, The Function of Teaching in Christianity, New Testament History and Literature, Citizens of Two Worlds, An Introduction to New Testament Literature, The Evolution of New Testament Christology. A Translation of the New Testament in the Language of the People, New Testament Synonyms* and *The Galilean Wins.*

I have held membership in "The International Society of Biblical Literature and Exegesis", "The Victorian Institute", "The Philosophical Society of Great Britain", and others. I am also listed in *Who's Who in America, Who's Who in American Education, Who's Who in the American Clergy,* and *Who's Who Among North America Authors.*

HOW MUCH MORE THEN IS A MAN WORTH!

Matthew 12:12*

The Greek word "man" used here is a generic term. It embraces woman also, and so includes the whole human race. So the sentence would literally read, "How much more then is a human being worth!"

The Greeks, with all their culture and philosophy, had reached no adequate conception of the value of a man, unless he were a Greek. The Romans had no true conception of the real worth of a man, unless he were a Roman. Even the Jews, with a special revelation from God, had failed to reach an adequate conception of the value of a human being, unless he were a Jew.

Jesus, however, taught in universal terms that a human being, of whatever race, condition or character, is of supreme value. Jesus restored the paralyzed arm of a man on the Sabbath, which violated the Pharisaic law. So the Pharisee asked, "Is it lawful to heal on the Sabbath day?" Jesus reminded them that they would lift a sheep out of the pit on the Sabbath to keep if from dying and added "How much more then is a man worth!"

I. Some Human Estimates of the Worth of a Man

We start with the scientific man's estimate—the lowest estimate we know. Alfred Russell Wallace, who, simultaneously with Charles Darwin, gave to the world the theory of evolution, taught that a human being derived his soul directly from God by special creation, but that his body is the product of an evolutionary process. Charles Darwin, an extremist in evolution, still believed that the human being is a creature of God but through the evolutionary process. Thomas Huxley, though an agnostic, claims in his book, *Man's Position in Nature,* man as the climax of all life on earth. Even Ernest Haeckel, a radical German materialistic scientist, who kept a

*A sermon preached at various high school and college commencements and New Orleans Baptist Seminary.

life-size portrait of a monkey on the wall of his study to remind him of his supposed simian ancestors, still placed man in an exalted rank above the lower animals. Thousands of scientific men believe that God created man.

Next, we ask, what is the philosopher's estimate of man? Socrates, Plato, and Aristotle conceived of man as rational and immortal, and in some sense akin to Deity. Likewise, through the centuries following them most Greek, Roman, German, French, English, and American philosophers, think of man as a rational, immortal being. Borden P. Bowne, in his system of philosophy called Personalism, exalted a human being to the highest pinnacle and regarded man's personality as absolutely immortal and imperishable. Also William James in his Pragmatism taught that man alone of all God's creatures on earth is really worth while and that all the forces of nature and culture should conduce to his welfare.

What is the sociologist's estimate? Sociology is one of the latest children born into the family of sciences. But in the last half century sociologists have impressed on us that even a street waif with no bed but the pavement, no pillow but the rocks, is worth while. Even the deadbeat on the streets ought to be trained and given a place in the world.

What is the author's estimate? What does the literary man say? Robert Burns, in describing the struggles and sufferings of a human being, exclaimed: "A man's a man for a' that, for a' that." Man is made for something other than toil, sufferings and disappointment.

Carlyle said: "Man is the center of nature. That is, nature is not properly understood, with all her rivers and oceans, mountains and volcanoes, flowers and sunsets, without putting man at the very center.

Emerson put his estimate in these graphic words: "Man is an encyclopedia of facts." Man is the total expression of physical, intellectual, moral, and spiritual facts.

Pope in his "Essay on Man" says: "The proper study of mankind is man." Not nature, not philosophy, not even theology, but rather the origin, development, destiny and happiness of man.

Shakespeare exclaims in these matchless words:
"What a piece of work is a man! How noble in reason!
How infinite in faculties! In form and moving how
express and admirable! In action how like an angel!
In apprehension how like a god! The beauty of the world,
the paragon of animals."

II. The Divine Estimate of the Worth of a Man

I now come to emphasize the value God Himself puts upon His man. Go back to the Garden of Eden, and see what God did that last creation morning. He made man. He had to create the universe first, and get everything ready for this exalted being. By creating man last God would say to us, "Here is my best, my masterpiece." And I will not stickle if some keenwitted woman should remind me, "Did He not make woman last, and not man?" I will not retract my argument if you make woman God's masterpiece. But since the term "man" in the text includes woman as well as man, it still holds true that a human being is God's masterpiece in creation.

Out of what did God create man? The record says that He took of the clay of the garden and shaped it into the form of a man, i.e. his physical body. But that is not all of a man. The record says that God breathed into that body the Divine breath, and in this way Adam became "a living soul." So man is made of clay plus the breath of God, a thing not true of any other animal.

God also said to Adam, "Go and subdue all nature, and be the master of the world," which is a positive proof that God considers man the highest creature of all creation on earth.

But God's estimate may also be seen in His providence over the history of the world. It was Carlyle who said, "God did make this world, and He does forever govern it; the loud roaring loom of time, without its French revolutions, and without its Jewish revelations, weaves the vesture thou sees Him by." We might add to this marvelous statement that the history of the world, with its Greek and Roman, American and French, and German and South American revolutions, and with its Jewish and Christian revelations, has been directed by the hand of God for the improvement and happiness of man.

But the sublimest exhibition of God's evaluation of man is the Father's gift of His only begotten Son to die on Calvary, to redeem and save lost men. "For God so loved the world that He gave His only begotten Son, that whosoever believeth on Him might not perish but have eternal life." "When the fullness of time came, God sent forth His Son . . . that He might redeem them that were under the law, that we might receive the adoption of sons." Calvary is the most graphic expression of the Father's estimate of man.

What is the Son's estimate? It is His words that are spoken in our text. "How much then is a man of more value than a sheep?" Jesus recognized that man is the greatest animal that came from the creative hand. He is "a living soul." He is made "in the image of God." Then the actions of Jesus speak louder than His words. In life He lifted and comforted, He healed and taught and raised from the dead—all men were the objects of his deeds of mercy.

Horace Mann, the great educator, once delivered a dedicatory address for a million-dollar educational plant. A friend of his said to him, "Horace, like all the orators in your enthusiasm and flights of oratory you say things that are not so." Horace asked, "What did I say today that is not so?" "Oh, you said that if this million-dollar plant should save only one boy it would be money well spent. Bosh! You did not mean such a silly thing as that. The idea of a million-dollar plant saving only one boy and still being a good investment!" Horace pointed his finger in his face and said, "My friend, that depends on whose that boy might be. If it were your boy you would say so." Now Jesus Christ gave, for man's redemption, not millions of dollars, of silver and gold, not jewels and diamonds, but "Himself" to save man.

What is the Holy Spirit's estimate? The Spirit for these thousands of years has been moving up and down the world, from heart to heart, to convince men of sin, teach them the saving truths of the gospel, regenerate the soul, and transform the character and life so as to renew the image of God. How the living actions of the Triune God, the Father, the Son, the Holy Spirit, have demonstrated the lofty estimate of man's incalculable worth!

III. The Sphere of Man's Superior Worth

Wherein lies the superior worth of a man? Is it in his capacity to accumulate wealth? How often do you hear men say, "How much is Mr. Smith worth?" meaning to ask, "How large is his bank account, how many thousands of acres of land has he, how many bonds and stocks?" A man's intrinsic worth cannot be calculated by his capacity to accumulate wealth.

Nor does it lie in the structure of his physical body, though man's physical form is the most symmetrical and most beautiful of all the animals. He "is fearfully and wonderfully made," even from the physical point of view. And yet a lion is much stronger, an elephant is larger, a horse is much fleeter, an eagle can fly more gracefully and swiftly. In the physical realm man is not superior to the lower animals.

Where does his superiority lie? It begins to show itself in his intellect and capacity to think and reason. He can "think God's thoughts after Him." Consider the wonderful thinking of James Watt, who watched the kettle boil and the lid lift, discovered steam, and gave the mighty power to run our trains and ships and other machines; of Franklin, who caught the electric spark from the clouds and gave this mightier power to do man's work; of Morse, who sent the first message over the wires; of Edison, who has made electricity laugh and weep sing and preach; of Marconi, who made electricity encircle the globe without any wires; of Einstein who worked out a mathematical formula so comprehensive as to include the operations of all the laws of the universe; of Arthur Compton and a group of physicists who at last split the atom and produced atomic energy and the atomic bomb.

And what shall I say more! Man's intellectual and research powers seem almost infinite! I stand amazed as I think of what men may accomplish in the next five hundred years, if they continue as they have for the last one hundred. I suspect we shall be able to get into a rocket plane and fly to the moon today and return tomorrow in time to sleep at home. Men have accomplished more than a half dozen scientific miracles—many in the realm of transportation—as marvelous as that.

1. Man's Gift of Speech. He is the only animal on earth that can talk. What a privilege it is to be able to speak—to

put in language our thoughts and feelings! The little lamb can bleat and his mother understands this sheep language; the cow can low and her kind and her master knows her language; the horse can neigh and his fellows and his master recognizes what he means; the dove can coo and the dove family grasps the meaning of the cooing. The parrot approaches human speech, and can imitate, but she cannot express in words her own thoughts (if she has any). Man is the only animal on earth that can think his own thoughts and express them in words, in comprehensible articulate sounds.

A mother whispers words of love to her sobbing child and soothes its shattered nerves and broken heart; a friend speaks words of sympathy to a despairing comrade and lifts his soul to heights of hope. Demosthenes could with his dynamic words of eloquence so inspire the Athenians as to move them to desire to save their country from the ravages of Philip's invading phalanxes. Spurgeon with eloquent words of God's grace moved thousands to conversion to Christ and consecration to God. How much God's program of teaching and evangelizing missions depends upon man's gift of consecrated speech!

2. Man's Capacity for Knowing Right and Wrong. Man has a conscience and is the only being on earth that has such. A mule got mad this morning and kicked his master on the head and left him bleeding and suffering. He is not sorry for it. He has never felt that he did wrong in causing him pain and agony. He has no conscience. Man is the only moral being on earth.

3. Man's Capacity for Worshipping God. This capacity originates in his creation by God in His image. This capacity is universal. Charles Darwin in his voyage around the world reached the conclusion that there was only one or two tribes of savages in Patagonia that did not have some kind of religion. But modern anthropologists have discovered that there is not a single tribe in the jungles of Africa, or in Patagonia, that does not have some form of religion. In other words man is, distinctively, a religious animal. He can pray, he can worship, he can praise his Creator. So far as we know there is not a monkey in the heart of Africa that ever lifted his heart in prayer and praise to his Maker.

4. Man is Immortal. Man is so made as to live on forever. Physical death is not the end of his existence. Regardless of character his existence goes on forever. A human personality can never be destroyed. The pet dog who loves so tenderly, who would die to save his master from the ravages of wild beast, can never rise again to meet his master. That beautiful blooded horse that neighs for his master cannot rise from death to greet him on the other side. The little canary that sings those thrilling notes in the spring time to cheer the heart and make life happier has not a life beyond to sing for you. But you will live right on through death and throughout the ages of eternity.

5. Man is Capable of Eternal Life. This is many steps higher than immortality. All men are immortal. Only those who believe and live in Christ have "eternal life." Man is capable of being "born from above" and having and enjoying eternal life, which is fellowship with God, eternal union and harmony with Him throughout the ceaseless cycles of eternity. This is what the Apostle John means when he exclaims, "Behold, what manner of Love the father hath bestowed upon us, that we should be called children of God, and such we are. Beloved, now are we the children of God, and it is not yet made manifest what we shall be. We know that if He shall be made manifest, we shall be like Him, for we shall see Him as He is." This is eternal life—to be like God, and to see Him as He is through all the ages of eternity.

6. Man's Capacity for Service. In his capacity for eternal life we reached the climax of man's intrinsic worth, but his value of a "servant of all" puts the climax on his worth to the kingdom of God and to his fellowmen. A man, renewed and consecrated, like Paul or Peter or John; like Carey or Judson or Yates; like Spurgeon or Carroll or Truett, is God's most valuable possession, for it is through such as these that He is building His kingdom on earth and saving a world of sinners. The story is told that Gabriel asked Jesus when He ascended to heaven, "How are you going to carry on your work on the earth now?" Jesus replied, "I am depending on Peter, James and John, and the rest of them." "But, suppose they fail you," said Gabriel, then what?" Jesus replied, "I am depending on

them." We are His only dependence.

7. Three Inferences from Man's Superiority. First, he is worth saving phyically and socially. We can produce a stronger race of men by proper birth from proper parentage. If we try we can raise up a superior race of human beings in body and nerves and brains. Jesus looked upon that frail piece of mankind with a withered hand, and was moved with compassion. He must have his limb restored. So He spoke the word and made his withered arm and hand strong.

The church and school must co-operate with medical science and social workers in cleaning up our cities and country that our children may have a wholesome atmosphere in which to live. Our boys and girls must have a good birth and good places to live and play and train for manhood and womanhood.

Secondly, a man is worth saving intellectually and educationally. On John A. Broadus' tomb is this epitaph:

"On earth there is nothing great but man;
In man there is nothing great but mind."

There is nothing on earth that is really great but man, and nothing great in him apart from the soul (including the mind). Then Christian men and women should better support our public schools and colleges, our universities and seminaries, to train and develop the souls of our boys and girls.

Lastly, a man is worth saving spiritually and morally. This is our highest task. Let us build more churches, more Sunday schools. Let us pray that God may call more preachers, more evangelists, more missionaries to carry the gospel around the world, that all the nations and all the races may be brought into the kingdom and lifted to fellowship with God.

S0-BRX-607

For Gracie and the sister she loves.
They are the true heroes of our family.

notes left behind

135 days with Elena

Brooke & Keith Desserich

Thank you to our family and friends for their support
and influence in the publishing of this book.
A special thank you to Martha Montgomery,
Patricia Harman, Judy Woods Mullis and
Margaret Theile for their efforts in clarifying
Elena's message. And to Tiffany Kinzer who insisted
that this book be more than just for Gracie.

Published by Pen & Publish
Bloomington, Indiana
(812) 837-9226
info@PenandPublish.com
www.PenandPublish.com

ISBN 978-0-9817264-5-8

This book is printed on acid free paper.

Printed in the USA

Table of Contents

Forward 7

Chapter 1 – The Beginning 8

Chapter 2 – The "Honeymoon" 72

Chapter 3 – Life After Progression 116

Chapter 4 – Fearless 242

Book Club Discussion Questions 286

To Learn More. 287

Forward

We never intended to print the story you are about to read. When our daughter, Elena, was diagnosed with terminal brain cancer, she was only five. Her sister, Gracie, was only four. And while we knew Elena's death would be traumatic for both of us, we also knew that the loss of her sister and her memories would be even worse. Elena and Gracie had just become best friends. They took turns playing cook in the kitchen that Grandma had bought them for Christmas, they competed with each other to see who could jump the furthest off the dock into the water, and they played school (with Elena as the teacher and Gracie as the student). But just as Gracie would begin to know her sister, she would lose her forever…

That first night as Elena's heartbeat dropped and we soon learned her fate in the intensive care unit, we knew that a journal was the only answer. At least then, Gracie would come to know her sister in ways that she would never have remembered. So we wrote it for her, and only her, with an honesty that we began to question as more and more people found inspiration in the lessons of a 6-year-old girl. Still it was never for them, only for Gracie, and it always will be.

We call it "135 Days with Elena" because that is what we were told to expect in our first meeting with the doctors. And so from there we kept count – each day a gift and each one a memory. Each day also a reminder of the short time we have to live. Our only regret is that we didn't start sooner. With Elena and Gracie there is so much to love.

They say that facing death brings out the best and the worst in people. The amazing thing about Elena is that she never changed. She still smiled for pictures, loved babies and showed everyone the grace in humility. What you will read is very much the daughter we knew and the girl we adored. She will always be our hero. For Gracie, she will always be her best friend.

Chapter 1 – The Beginning

Nothing can convey the amount of love and joy that Elena brought to our family. She was our first and the cornerstone of our small family. Born just over five years ago on a snowy December morning, she became our hope and our dreams. And with the addition of her sister Gracie, our family was complete.

It all started the day after Thanksgiving. Without warning she lost her voice, developed a limp in her right leg and had spells of dizziness. At first we thought it was strep throat, then migraines, but three days later we were told it was a brain tumor. Finally, after two weeks of consultations, it was officially diagnosed as a diffuse brain stem glioma. Worse yet, it was most likely inoperable and they call her chances at survival "dismal." At that moment, life changed, but through it all, Elena exhibited a resiliency that we could not have imagined. She was a strong and serious girl with intelligence and wisdom to match. We were lucky to have her as part of our family.

Although we can't remember every moment of her little life, we can remember the nights. Nights started with a bath and a book. She'd always choose the biggest book and we'd always beg for the simple one. Somehow we'd always settle on "A Light in the Attic" or "One Fish, Two Fish, Red Fish, Blue Fish." We'd read and she would listen, but as the book dragged on and we would skip a page, she would catch us and turn the page back. What we wouldn't give to have those pages back. Then we'd end the night with a kiss, a tickle and a comment of how proud we were. Those were the nights we'd love to relive again. Now we pick the longest books we can find and enjoy every moment of every word.

So began her journey and her fight - one she would have the courage to win and where she would have all of our support. A little life; a lot of living.

Day 1 – November 29

It began early. We called it "binner." With her pick line installation scheduled for 7:00 a.m., the last time she could eat was 1:00 a.m. So at midnight I woke her up to a breakfast/dinner of yogurt – except the nurse forgot to order yogurt before the kitchen closed and we ended up with a meal of pudding and applesauce instead. From 1 a.m. to dawn we talked about "Alice in Wonderland," her new discovery of the television remote and what she always wanted to do. And although I couldn't always understand her words because of the tumor, I could usually understand her drawings. First came a circle with squiggly lines. This was where she wanted to go – the only problem was that I did not know what she was telling me. After several tries and more than enough frustration on her part, I figured out that she was talking about the "little restaurant" – the chili parlor a mile from our house. With this her face lit up as she told me she wanted spaghetti and cheese. This was a remarkably simple request and we added to the list. The next one was a bit harder: The Eiffel Tower. To this day, I still don't know where she came up with this one. Regardless, this was the list and what we needed to accomplish. From there the list continued to the "street of dresses," which I immediately recognized as a wedding dress district in our town, but I feigned ignorance. It had been the same street I deliberately drove down on the way home with the girls for the past five years, while telling them to pick out their dresses. Now she was asking me to take her in the same shops that I had always envisioned taking her to when she was engaged. Now I questioned if she would ever make it that far. Still, it went on the list.

As the night went on, we continued to talk. But with less than an hour of sleep, I honestly believed that we both felt more refreshed than any sleep could have offered. She wanted to talk and I wanted to listen. I hope that every night brings the same.

Later that day, her doctors made us aware of a program in Memphis that offered experimental brain stem treatments – the same treatments that were not available here at home. And by the end of the day, we received formal acceptance in the program and were booked for the first flight of the morning. Nothing was for sure, but Brooke and I felt that this might be her best chance.

That night the doctors sent us home for rest. Elena decorated the Christmas tree that the grandparents had hastily put up only minutes before. This had been one of Elena's requests and although time was limited, we took enough time before bed to find her Jesus and angel ornaments and hang them on the tree. In previous years, I'd always insisted on not putting up the tree before December 15th. This year it couldn't come soon enough.

Brooke read the girls a book before bed while Grandma and my aunt strung Christmas lights from the ceiling of their bedrooms. It was the longest book we could find.

Day 2 – November 30

The trip to Memphis was a long one. God love Elena and her desire to be pretty. To protect her from sickness, we took all of the necessary precautions from air scrubbing and cleaning the home to getting flu shots for the entire family. Lastly, we brought dust masks from the hospital to have Elena wear on the plane. She would have none of this. Of course, she did appreciate being wheeled around in a wheel chair like a queen on a throne, but to wear a dust mask was just too much. After all, how would her fellow passengers feel about her looks? After much prompting and prodding, we both ended up wearing masks. She said I looked silly.

Airline clearance was another issue. With Elena and her drugs, it took a good hour to get through security. It took another hour to get Mom past all the gift shops. Whatever Elena wanted she got as Mom caved and bought her a new Beanie Baby and ice cream. If we had passed any more gift shops through the terminal, I'm certain we would have gone broke.

Two hours later we were in Memphis. There we were introduced to the new hospital and our new regiment. Contrary to previous conversations, the pace was fast as Elena received the attention she needed to give us a fighting chance. Before the evening was out, we had had four consultations lasting over one hour each, two X-rays, an orientation, and a new home. She was exhausted and so was I. We ended the evening in the hotel room reading the "get well cards" from her classmates from kindergarten that I had smuggled into her bags. Finally, she crawled into bed clutching her cards beneath the covers. I'm still trying to figure out how to get them away from her before she falls asleep.

So far, so good. Two days into our time and we've met all the right people. We've even taken care of two of Elena's wishes – to put up the Christmas tree and go to the airport.

Day 3 – December 1

For the first time, we saw a picture of the tumor. It's not only large, but concealed within the walls of Elena's brain stem. The doctor says it is either a diffused glioma or a PNET tumor. The first has tiny boundaries with which to allow removal, even if it were possible, among the network of nerves in the brain stem. The second spreads throughout the spinal fluid, thus ensuring a long battle. Either way, the prognosis isn't good. Originally, we were told that we would have 3-6 months. It's little reassurance that now the doctors say possibly seven months to over a year. That's still not enough time to see my baby's driving lessons, first date, wedding or grandchildren. I guess anything is better than what we were originally told.

Elena's getting very tired now and has developed a fear of anyone with blue gloves. After all, these are the same hands that poked and prodded her for the past week. I think she fears the gloves over the shots at this point. She's also started to listen and ask questions. I've always known that Elena not only listened to our conversations, but now she's added to her vocabulary words such as "IV flushing," "MRI," and "CT scan." Along with it, she's realized that anyone who puts on blue gloves usually ends up hurting her. I'm thinking of buying a pack of clear gloves for the doctors in her wing just to calm her anxiety.

Tonight we decided to treat her to a dinner of her choice with her cousins. It was a good idea, but by the time we ended her doctors' appointments at 7:00 p.m., the dinner idea was a bit late. As a result, while she enjoyed the balloon art hat that we had made for her, she didn't make it far into the meal before she fell asleep on her aunt's shoulder. From there her fatigue only contributed to her condition and we ended up having to carry her out of the restaurant or risk her falling over her own feet. I know she needs the company, but right now I think she also needs the rest. She has had a rough week and it's just the beginning.

Day 4 – December 2

Today was a good day. It was Saturday and we didn't have to go to the hospital – all we had to do was make Elena smile. She was tired this morning, but also very hungry for waffles. After waking up at 6:00 a.m. from her open-eyed and teeth gnawing sleep, all she wanted was waffles with butter. At first we couldn't understand her with her limited voice, but thank goodness she could at least spell "WFL" to communicate her wishes. She had to have waffles with whip cream, chocolate chips and cherries for eyes – the same way that Allyson had her pancakes. And except for the cherries, she ate the entire thing. Must be the steroids working.

For the first time, Elena has now lost sensation in her thighs. Now she has a limp in her right leg, no gag reflex, limited ability in her right arm, loss of left eye peripheral vision, and reduced sensation in her legs. I know this because in an attempt to raise a smile, I tried to tickle her most ticklish part: her knees. It used to be that all I needed to do was motion towards her knees and I would instantaneously get a wide mouth smile. Now she simply looks at me with annoyance. I miss tickling my little girl. For a dad, it's always about more than horseplay – it's a way of expressing my love. I'll just have to find another way to make her smile.

Day 5 – December 3

A horse drawn carriage ride was her third choice after the "little restaurant" and the "Eiffel Tower." (I think part of it was due to the fact that when we read "Alice in Wonderland" that first night we skipped past "Cinderella" and an illustration of the pumpkin carriage.) Luckily, Memphis had plenty of them. So in the face of 20-degree wind chills, we made our way downtown to catch a horse drawn carriage ride. Instantly, the smile came back through the strain of anxiety that had recently robbed my little girl's face. It was back and I felt like a father again as we roamed the streets. And while bitterly cold, Elena's smile was enough to warm all of our hearts. I hope this will be a lasting memory.

From there, we went to the stuffed animal factory to create a bear of her choosing. Although one of her requests, this was far less satisfying for both of us in the Christmas rush. Packed into a store, we found nearly a 100 Christmas shoppers vying for first place in the commercialized race against time. And for the first time, I was jealous. I was jealous of their joy, jealous of their ignorance, jealous of their rushing. I wanted to be the one more concerned about getting to the next store rather than struggling to lock away every memory of a conceivably limited future. But instead, I realized that my family and I were the ones that truly appreciated the season and all that it meant. You see, her illness taught us to squeeze the very last sunlight out of every day and to see our children as more than just a Christmas list. And while I certainly still don't desire this lesson, I will never squander another day again. I think Elena also realized this and instead asked to leave and get an ice cream cone. We proceeded to leave, of course, after having convinced Gracie who already had her eyes on a ballerina outfit for her poodle animal.

What does all of this mean? I don't know and I don't think that every moment demands a lesson. All I know is that these memories need to last. Whether we go to the Eiffel Tower or to the grocery store, they both can be treasured moments if you make the most of them.

Day 6 – December 4

Today was Elena's birthday. Not really, but close enough. With the radiation treatments and biopsy happening this Wednesday, today was close enough for her grandparents and us. With a ten percent chance of complications from the biopsy, we all felt a party was in order. So after her morning appointments, we all headed off to lunch and then back to the room for presents. There she opened a guitar from her aunt and a digital camera from Grandma and Grandpa. Now we have pictures from her point of view. Too bad that every picture she takes is from the waist down.

Later that afternoon, we saw Grandma, Grandpa and Gracie leave for Cincinnati. With the biopsy in two days and a possible decision necessary on surgery, we felt that it was best to stay in Memphis with her and get Gracie back in her routine. It was a tough goodbye for all, but one that we knew had to occur. We already miss Gracie's charm and humor.

Day 8 – December 6

Last night we faced one big heart wrenching decision. In the end, we decided that the two-week delay in treating Elena's tumor was more than we were willing to risk. With her mouth now paralyzed and her being unable to swallow, we feared that waiting another two weeks for a biopsy would just be too much. Our hopes are that in treating this now with radiation, we will be able to recover many of her normal functions for the recovery period.

About midway through the day today, I noticed Elena was getting very quiet. I asked her what was wrong and she told me she was getting mad that everyone was talking about her and around her and no one was talking TO her. This is the new challenge. So I asked the doctors and nurses to talk directly to her, all while not going too far. We explain what will happen with radiation and how everything we are doing now will help her to get home and back to normal. We have a long six weeks ahead of us, but I think as the radiation begins, we will settle into our routine and she will start feeling better.

The prognosis has not changed, and we are still looking for a miracle, but we have found a tentative comfort in making a decision and moving forward to make Elena better. Though we still feel the anger and sadness, we force ourselves to stay positive. I am pretty sure that if there is any child who can beat this disease it's Elena.

Day 9 – December 7

I guess you could call it regret - possibly remorse. But without a conclusion it doesn't quite feel like either. Today while waiting for a procedure with Elena, I saw a mother and a son sitting across from us. He was about 11 years old and was obviously a brain cancer patient. Although in very good spirits, he had undergone just about every surgery and procedure that you could imagine. He had lost his hair from aggressive chemotherapy, was undergoing his last MRI and radiation treatments, and had a scar from the front of his brow to the back of his head with a shunt placed under the skin. Still, he had his personality and his sense of humor to go with the characteristic limp and facial paralysis that often comes with brain surgery.

Was this what my daughter would have looked like if we had chosen the biopsy, the surgery and the chemotherapy? And even if we had this option with the type of tumor she has, could the outcome have been worse? I guess we'll never know, but the one question I can't avoid is whether our decision to treat this as a glioma rather than performing the biopsy cheats her from a complete cure. Sure, the odds are overwhelming and a brain stem surgery almost never ends with a perfect conclusion. But then again, what are the odds of getting this type of tumor in the first place; in the worst possible place with one of the worst tumors out there? I guess, ultimately, it comes down to making the very best decision possible in enough time to prevent the inevitable complications that come with us exploring every option and doing every test. Still, these are questions that as a dad I will never escape.

Although she has had very few invasive procedures, Elena has had increasing difficulty with walking, talking and moving her right arm. Tomorrow we are fitting her for a wheel chair with a headrest because they tell me that her neck control will be the next to go. For the first time I've also noticed that she can no longer make the kissing sound when she presses her lips up against my cheek. I'm going to miss that the most. At least her spirit is strong and her punch is as well. Right now she wants Mom more than Dad; after all, Dad teases and tickles while Mom cuddles and cares. And right now she needs more cuddling than teasing. Still, I manage to get a smile every now and then; about as much as I get a punch from her still strong left arm when she wants me to quit bothering her. That's when I tell her that if she wants to punch and kick me, she has to do it with her right side – the side that has the partial paralysis. I figure there's more than one way to approach therapy.

With the tumor progressing, her speech is now very limited and you can see her actively counting the amount of times she chews her food so she doesn't choke. I think she's as much aware of her situation as we are. Her tongue and palate paralysis are also making it very difficult to understand her words. She's getting visibly frustrated now and with her right hand almost completely immobilized, she has difficulty in helping convey her thoughts with hand motions. Brooke and I are now trying to teach her sign language in the event that she loses speech altogether, as well as her sight. Hopefully she will never have to use it, but we are painfully aware that this might be her only connection to the outside world. She already knows the alphabet A-E and knows the signs for mother, father, thank you, tree, thirsty, hungry and proud. We use the sign for proud the most throughout the day. Brooke is teaching her the sign for bull-shit so at least she can curse when she gets frustrated. I don't think "shucks" has a sign. I keep telling her that as long as she keeps trying to tell us things, we'll keep working to understand, that way we'll never give up talking.

Elena told me that she wants to draw again. I figure this is a good way for her to communicate as well. Maybe she can use pictures the same way we use a journal to express ourselves. We're going out tomorrow to get paper and oil crayons; they'll give her the best colors and the best emotions.

Day 10 – December 8

Today she got wheels. After avoiding the issue for the past week, we finally went to see the hospital therapist to get a wheel chair. I guess we've known it was coming for the past week, but chose to characterize it as the after-effects of the anesthesia or exhaustion. Now we finally admit it is the tumor. There was no ignoring it when Elena woke up and her right hand was slightly bent with the fingers curled into her palm – the same way you often see with elderly patients with atrophy. She had the characteristic swelling of the right hand, the lint in the palm and the chapped fingers. We keep moisturizing her palm and trying to get her to move it, but it's no use. The therapist tells us that she will begin working with Elena next Tuesday, but that can't come soon enough; neither can the radiation.

In an effort to keep her hand active, we've started filling it with pudding cups and insisting that she feed herself. Actually, she insists on her independence as much as we do. Although not useful for many other things, her right hand is the perfect size to hold these cups and with her addiction to chocolate pudding, this comes in handy. Today alone she ate five pudding cups and three bowls of chocolate and vanilla swirl ice cream. Although we're trying to push vegetables, fruit and meat, with her swallowing issues we have a hard time getting her to eat them without choking. Besides that, it's really tough to avoid spoiling her right now. And we're not alone. With as many times as she has been in and out of the recovery room in the past week, the nursing staff has started to prepare swirl ice cream in advance of her procedures; just for her. For six years, Elena wanted nothing other than vanilla ice cream. Now all she wants is chocolate and vanilla swirl. Unfortunately, this is the one flavor they don't have. Still, that doesn't stop the nursing staff from mixing together a gallon of each flavor and freezing it in a special carton just for Elena. Now she not only has her own ice cream, but her own special shelf in the nurses' lunch freezer just for her.

Tonight Gracie arrived with Grandma and Grandpa and saw Elena at her worst. Hours after coming out of surgery and with steroids at an all-time high, she was in no mood for company, but a little Gracie time was exactly what she needed. Gracie has always been able to make Elena laugh, even in the worst of times. And today was one of those times. By the end of the evening they were laughing and fighting as usual. Gracie even had to try her hand at pushing Elena's wheel chair back and forth down the hallways until they both landed with a crash into the elevator wall. I think they both needed it, although Mom thought otherwise. Once again, Brooke was right and I was wrong.

Day 11 – December 9

For the past five years, we've never had a family portrait. It's not that we never had the time or the money, but that we always figured that next year would be the year to do it. For a family of schedules, budgets, and delayed gratification, it was never a priority – until now. This morning we finally had our picture taken – five years too late. We dressed up from the assortment of clothes we crammed into our bag just 10 days before and forced smiles that we didn't feel inside. Then something happened – we rediscovered each other. We discovered that Elena still had her infectious smile and model-like pose, Gracie was still the entertainer with her characteristic funny face and "antsy-pants" attention span. Mom was still the glue of the family with her beaming blue eyes and calming grace. I, on the other hand, was just the odd-male out. And for 20 minutes we lived as we had two weeks ago, from picture to picture, and remembered a family that had it all because we had each other.

The experience was one I wish we had had every year. Oh how I wish I could look back upon the past years and say, "Look at how young she was," or "She couldn't sit still then." Every picture tells a tale of the happier times – we just never took enough. And although the burdens of today will fade into what we will discover in the burdens of tomorrow, one thing will remain clear; the love expressed in those photos will help us overcome any challenge ahead. Take a picture.

Day 12 – December 10

It was just Elena and me today. Mom and Gracie left after breakfast and started the eight hour drive back home. She didn't want to leave, but with little money left and Gracie starting school on Monday, we knew we had no choice.

Looking back, we're still glad we made the decision we made. Had we decided on a biopsy or surgery, radiation and chemotherapy wouldn't have started until after Christmas, which would have been too late. We've already noticed a decreased gag and choking reflex this morning, which would have surely meant a feeding tube procedure if we weren't going for radiation tomorrow. All the nurses and doctors tell us that she'll probably get worse before she gets better, but this will lessen as the tumor shrinks over the next couple of weeks. Whether her paralysis and speech will improve is yet to be seen, but we're already reminding her that the wheel chair is only temporary. While she didn't want it in the first place, she now loves her new wheels. I think she likes getting pushed around all the time and getting all the attention she receives. But after one trip to the grocery store by myself, I can't wait to get rid of it. It's one thing to push a wheel chair, it's another to try pushing a shopping cart at the same time. After several attempts, we finally parked a cart at the end of the aisle and made trips back and forth. This worked until the third aisle when someone took off with our cart and the food in it. At that point, I figured just the basics were enough and went for the bread and yogurt and called it quits. Enough for one day.

Day 14 – December 12

Her new nickname is Fred. At least that's what I call her when she tries to ignore the doctors and nurses. And it always gets a reaction. At first a slap with her remaining powerful left hand and then a smile begins to creep into her lips.

At first, I introduced her as "Fred George" when the bus driver asked for her name and she responded by burying her face in her hand. I was not about to let her start out the day on a bad note.

From that point on, the name stuck. She was "Fred" to the receptionist, the nurses in radiation and just about anyone else who would listen. And by then, my little teenager started to crack. The slaps became more forceful and so did the smiles. I knew it would only be a matter of time. The remainder of the day went wonderfully well; her attitude was positive, she didn't fear the radiation treatments quite as much (I'm being gracious with this; it still took its share of tears as she was sedated), and she actually began to speak in her speech therapy class. This alone was no small feat for a girl who had not uttered one word for the past four days. The words weren't clear or even loud, but it was an effort nonetheless.

Then, as quickly as it started, our day at the hospital was over. But no matter how much she wanted to rest, she had to see the animals. So off to the zoo we went. For the next forty minutes, the trip went something like this: "Oh, see the hippo. Oh, see the giraffe. Oh, see the lion. Oh, see the pengu – never mind, they're not out." Thirty seconds per animal doesn't afford you much time for reflection – especially with storm clouds looming overhead. Then we saw the pandas, or shall I say P-A-N-D-A-S! Personally, I don't understand the lure of the panda. Why should they get their own house, their own velvet rope lines and their own monuments, while the poor elephants get nothing more than a stinky house? Shouldn't the peacock at least get a small shrine? Apparently, I am in the minority and the rest of the world is in awe of the black and white painted bears, including my daughter. For this we had to spend a good ten minutes admiring them, which meant we'd have to fast walk the zebras, the gorilla, and the antelope-looking thingies with the stripes (I think every zoo has thousands of these and no one knows what to call them) in order to catch up. Elena didn't care; these animals deserved a shrine in her mind as she pressed her nose up against the glass as close as she could without tipping over the wheel chair. And then came the smile. And then came the, "Dad – take a picture" remark. And then she was Elena. I like pandas a little more now.

From there, we headed out the gates towards our car, but not before running into three Amish men visiting a patient at the hospital. Three hours earlier, they had walked to the zoo and now were second-guessing their decision as storm clouds loomed. So, in our infinite wisdom, we thought we'd corrupt the Amish men and offer them a ride back to the house in our car. Elena thought this was hilarious. I'm not sure if she understood the intricacies of this gesture, but she kept right on laughing anyways. And as we took off, one of the men joked, "I guess you've never driven the Amish," and Elena burst out laughing and continued all the way home. For the entire trip, she laughed elbow-to-elbow with three Amish men in the backseat of the caravan. If there was ever a time for a picture, that would have been it. If only my camera battery would have allowed it. Oh well, that sort of thing happens every day. I'll get it next time.

Day 15 – December 13

Christmas is in full swing now at the hospital with donations coming in by the second and literally twenty or more toys for every patient. I think I have finally discovered the official Santa Claus imposter training camp as we've had visits from over five Santas in the past four days. This doesn't do much for our whole Santa legend in Elena's eye. I think she knows the truth, but she doesn't dare tell me. I think she thinks I still believe in him too and she doesn't want to spoil my Christmas.

Santa came again today. But by the fifth time, even Elena had reservations. With nothing left to do as we waited two hours for the next appointment, we decided to make the trip across campus. Apparently, we were not alone as we entered a line of hundreds also waiting for a chance to see Santa. Within minutes, Elena was at the head of the line, herded into the 0-6 age group. There she was given a toy and a book that she immediately opened to read. While a nice touch, this was unexpected – at least to us. From what we discovered, it was an annual event, as indicated by the crowd around us in the 0-6 line. Parents had not only known about it, but had actively prepped their children for the event by instructing them to pick out the "most valuable" or the "in-demand" toy of the season from the selection. At that point, it ceased to be about what made the children happy and more about what made the parents happy. There, all around me were children who had been dragged out of beds from chemotherapy for the event just so that they could claim a "prize" for the parents. And while some of these children chose to be there, there were also those who would have rather been in bed; anywhere but there. It almost seemed that the children were ashamed of their parents. I would be too. And not only had they planned for this event, but they also bragged to other families how they fooled a wish granting organization into believing that their 4 year old wanted to go to Las Vegas as a last wish. I don't know about you, but I find it very hard to believe that any 4-year-old chooses Las Vegas as their ideal vacation.

Was Elena thinking the same thing as I was? I don't know, but when it came time for her to choose, she chose the simplest $5 craft set on the table over a CD Radio, a Disney Arial musical instrument, an MP3 player and a Dora something-or-other in a giant box. With that, she asked to leave and motioned towards the door. I agreed. We left and sat on the grass reflecting on what we had just seen while we paged through the book.

Tragedy can both inspire and it can ruin lives. Some people use tragedy to exploit and the ramifications of these actions not only hurt their own reputations, but the impressions of their children as well. Other people respond to tragedy with escapism and spoil their children. I'm as guilty as the next person. In the face of Elena's situation, I want to take her away from it all and show her the world. I want to skip the next 6-months of school and never let her out of my sight. I want to buy her that puppy I told her I was allergic to, that special toy that I never had enough money for, and the prettiest clothes that didn't come from a used clothes store. I want to give her everything. But in doing so, I know that I would also take away everything. Normalcy is also a gift. She is homesick because she wants to go to school, because she wants her imperfect home, because she wants rules and discipline and because she wants her sister around. After all, in a way, our everyday lives are the lives we choose and hopefully the lives we've always wanted. This is the most that we can hope for; to be content with our lives and with ourselves. This is the gift I give my daughter and the gift I must keep giving her for the rest of her life, regardless of the length.

Elena wants to respect her family, wants to have her life back and doesn't want a toy or a trip in its place. In this way, her illness has taught us all a lesson in appreciation and giving thanks for what we already have. And although it may never be enough, it is what we need. We'll still take some vacations, we'll still treasure our time together, but from here on out, I will also honor her life as a 5-year-old from Cincinnati with a foundation firmly rooted in traditions and morals. She'll have her family, her home, her school, her friends and her life back after radiation and chemotherapy treatments end two weeks from now. And if she wants a puppy after that, who knows, I may have to give up my allergy. Normalcy doesn't mean I won't always spoil her.

Day 16 – December 14

Over the past fifteen days, I've learned a couple of rules about medicine. First, a good bedside manner in pediatrics should never be underestimated. We've encountered fantastically prestigious doctors who knew nothing about Dora or Barbie and felt the solution to every problem was another IV line stuck into my daughter. We've also encountered doctors who freely admitted they were out of guesses, but went out of their way to get to know Elena's birth date, that she preferred swirl ice cream over all others, and that she would always choose an Arial sticker over a Jasmine sticker any day. And more often than not, it was the doctor with the good bedside manner who had the best results. Not because of what they knew, but because of what they discovered as Elena would open up to them. After all, in order to be a good investigator you have to uncover all the facts.

The second thing I've learned about medicine is that in order for medicine to work well, the patient needs to take an active role. The patient should not only understand the disease, but know when to direct the process if necessary. After all, it is your body or your child at stake. It will never be as high of a priority to them as it is to you.

The third thing I've learned about medicine is that a good attitude and a positive outlook are critical to recovery. And while a disease may seem intimidating at first, there comes a time when you run out of tissues and you must work towards recovery. We're at this stage now.

The fourth thing I've learned about medicine is that strep throat causes brain tumors. Well, okay, maybe not, but it sure seems like it when you take your daughter to the hospital for a simple infection and you discover more than you ever wanted to know. I'm going for the MRI if Gracie ever gets a strep infection. Do you think it would be too much to just buy the machine and keep one in my basement just in case?

Seriously though, today was a day to say grace. Gracie Goose, specifically. And just as we discovered the importance of a positive outlook, Gracie came to save the day. You see, Elena and Gracie have never had anything in common other than their parents. Elena has brown hair; Gracie has blond hair. Elena has Dad's nose (God help her) and Gracie has Mom's nose. Elena is the safe child, while Gracie is the one who will keep me up at night for the rest of my life (probably on the front porch with a shotgun in hand – you can never trust the boys). Elena has poise and Gracie? Well she has a sparkling smile and not one ounce of grace. (I told Brooke that she'd never have it if we named her Grace, but I'm never one to say I told you so.) Elena likes fancy nails and dresses; Gracie loves remote control cars. Elena's serious and structured; Gracie is, well, Gracie. And she's just what Elena needs right now. After spending a week hearing about tumors, radiation and hair loss, while struggling to keep down every bite of yogurt, Elena needed a dose of Gracie's spontaneity and unorthodox love. Of course, Grandma's love didn't hurt either. And between the two of them they finally got Elena laughing and smiling within eight hours of their arrival. Before long, Elena was walking, talking, eating and smiling again. So what Dad and the doctors couldn't do in four days what Gracie and Grandma did in eight hours. And the recovery was miraculous. And while I'm sure the drug companies and the doctors will try and take credit for her improvement with the aid of radiation, dexamethasone, senna, odansetron and whatever else she takes, Elena also got a prescription for love. Of course Grandma and Mom used their own prescription. I'm sure the drug companies will immediately move to patent dress and shoe shopping when they discover the amount of improvement that Elena experienced after being led down the aisles of the local clothing stores in preparation for her big day at the Nutcracker on Saturday. It's amazing how much a red velvet dress and patent-leather red ballet shoes can do for cancer. Chances are it's probably also cheaper than most of the other drugs too.

Today was Gracie's big day and we all needed it. She has a way of stimulating excitement with her excessive energy and sparking smiles and with her simple, yet perceptive comments. One minute she told me, "Geez, Dad, you know we wouldn't need all these doctors for Elena if we could just get Jesus to come down and fix her," and then the next minute she was explaining to me the difference between the Hello Kitty sticker that she wanted to give me and the Barbie sticker that she stuck to my shirt. She'd never repeat the comment, never discuss it, and for the life of me I don't know where these moments of brilliance come from, but with Gracie you know it comes from the heart at that very minute. Her passion is in the here and now, and Lord knows we need every bit of it we can get. And just in case you're curious, the difference between a Hello Kitty sticker and the Barbie sticker is that I'm not a girl so I must have more in common with a cat. Flashes of brilliance indeed.

Day 18 – December 16

It must be the ruby red slippers. Elena wore them for the first time today and it made all the difference in the world. From morning till night, Elena walked nearly every hallway on her own power (of course with an overprotective Mom and Dad never leaving her side). Even when offered a ride on the wheel chair, she refused and kept right on going, struggling to lift the right leg against the strain of the paralysis and enduring atrophy. I think it was more a matter of will than a matter of strength today as her spirits were high, her determination strong and her fear of scuffing the shine of her brilliant new shoes. You see, Elena is one of those girls who prides herself on the shine of her shoes so I knew that with every step she tried a bit harder to avoid dragging the right foot. Either way, it worked and I'll buy her new shoes every day if it continues to deliver progress.

The voice was improved today as she forced herself to use it; mostly directed at Gracie in screams of "MINE." which were very clear indeed. The rest of the words and sentences were still mostly unclear, but the important part was that she tried. After all, therapy is more a struggle of determination than it is a matter of ability. Hopefully this will continue to improve over the next couple of days as Mom takes over.

And this is where I started eighteen days ago with a diagnosis and an unfamiliar new world. For the first time, I will leave Elena's side to head back to Cincinnati while Mom takes over for the next four days. Since we learned of the tumor eighteen days ago I've spent every night and every day by Elena's side. We've had conversations about lifetime wishes and arguments about Muppets; both with an intensity that I never before thought possible. She's a fan of Rizzo, while I'm partial to Gonzo. The rift could never be greater. At the same time, I learned more about my daughter in eighteen days than I'd learned about her in five years, eleven months and twenty-six days. She likes painting more than drawing, prefers nightgowns without sleeves and loves chocolate/vanilla swirl ice cream over everything else. If they don't have that, she'll take plain vanilla, but never chocolate ice cream alone. And in that time, I watched her progress from a limp and a weak voice to right side paralysis, limited left side vision and no voice at all. Now she has come full circle back to where we started with a right side limp and a weak voice. Physically, it is like the last eighteen days never happened, but in our minds we know better. At points, I even wondered if we would make it this far as we encountered internal bleeding scares, choking and a tumor which seemed to outrun the most aggressive steroid treatments that we could prescribe. While not something I wish to repeat, this time solidified our priorities and made us ready for the struggle ahead.

Today was also a day that taught us to embrace that struggle as we took Elena out on the town. First, she went with Mom, Gracie and Grandma for a manicure, pedicure and hairstyle. It was a chance to be pampered by the folks at the local beauty school and a moment to take pride in how she looked. And although the moment was fleeting due to the pain she experienced from the medicine she took that morning, it was enough to change her frame of mind and dissolve the glum look she had carried throughout the week. Once again she felt like a little girl as she showed off her fingernails and toenails to anyone who would stop to look. With a special trip to The Nutcracker tonight, the red nails and shoes to match were critical.

The Nutcracker has been a wish of Elena's for some time now, ever since she first saw the nutcrackers that we displayed on the fireplace mantle last year. And after Brooke explained the significance and the ballet connection, Elena was mystified. So when the first tree went up at the local hardware store after Halloween (hey, it's the store that I take her to the most), she knew it was time for The Nutcracker play. Now she would finally get to go to her first ballet in a real theater with a fancy dress, pretty nails and a hairstyle. And she was in heaven. Of course, she also wore the ruby red slippers to complete the outfit.

I'd love to say she was in awe of every minute or that she idolized every ballerina, but the truth was that she fell asleep after intermission in Mom's arms. Radiation takes its toll on a child in terms of exhaustion and this was its effect. But the impact was still there. It was an afternoon away from the anesthesia, the chemotherapy and the blood tests – and that's what mattered most. It was also a chance to cuddle in Mom's arms and I'm sure that was fine with Mom as well. Gracie, on the other hand, was a bundle of energy as she bounced between Grandma's lap and mine, mimicking the arm motions of every last solider, snowflake princess and sugar plum fairy on stage. Occasionally, she would grow tired of this as well, and would resort to rubbing Grandpa's beard and hair for good luck, kissing his cheek.

All in all, it was a good day. And the satisfaction I have in leaving tomorrow morning after seeing this improvement will be offset by the realization that according to the doctors, this progress might very well be temporary. It's always hard to see your once healthy daughter reduced to paralysis, an arsenal of drug treatments and a possible terminal illness all in a matter of days. I imagine it is much harder to see her improve to her previous perfection only to wonder how long it will last. Will it be three months, five months, seven months or possibly the rest of her life? She is definitely improving and from what I can see, she might regain all previously lost abilities. Our biggest fear is that after she improves she might quickly regress. For this reason, Brooke and I focus on her treatments, possible cures and on learning sign language as a method of communication if she were to lose her eyesight and ability to talk when the tumor returns again one day.

Of course, we will always pray for a miracle, but the reality is that we must also prepare for the inevitable. At the same time, we realize the lesson to be learned in terms of life's priorities and focusing on family above everything else. It has been eighteen days and we have our Elena back. It has been eighteen days and we now know her better than ever. And with these eighteen days in mind, we have also discovered a determination and will in our daughter that we never saw before. If this is any indication of her strength, I doubt we will ever need those sign language classes.

Day 19 – December 17

Elena and I took Dad and Gracie to the pancake house to meet with Grandma and Grandpa for the drive home. Elena decided to venture out of her comfort zone and risked ordering pancakes instead of waffles. We all watched as she took much bigger bites than she had been attempting for the last few weeks. It must have been comical watching three grown adults clapping as this almost six-year-old ate pancakes. After everyone had set left, Elena and I decided we needed to buy some gifts for the doctors and nurses who have been helping us. On the way to the Christmas section, we stopped by the jewelry section. Elena picked out a diamond heart necklace to give to Gracie for Christmas and an identical one for Mom and herself. She held on to that box so tightly you would have thought it was the Hope Diamond; probably to her it was just as priceless.

The rest of the day was full of laughing and joking, but best of all, Elena laughing without Keith or me standing on our heads and acting silly. Just honest laughing and smiling. The best part of all was putting her to bed. I asked if she wanted me to sleep in her bed and she just kept giggling and bobbing her head "yes" (no tickling required) and when the laughter stopped, she simply said, "I really like you Mom."

Day 20 – December 18

For the past few weeks, I have been wondering what Elena has been feeling as she stares off into space, not talking to anyone. Today was the first day I almost regretted that she could talk. I had to wake her at 5:45 a.m. this morning to take her drugs because she was moved to the first radiation treatment in the morning. As soon as she saw the Jell-O (which is her trigger to know that radiation will be happening in a few hours), she started staring off into space again. I sat on her bed and looked at her, asking what she was feeling. And out came the words I didn't want to hear. "I feel alone. I miss everyone. I miss my sister." You can't imagine how an adult manages a disease like this; try throwing it on the shoulders of a little five-year-old. She doesn't have the wisdom of age to try and deal with all the feelings and nasty things being done to her.

Whenever you think that there are not enough hours in your day, you haven't seen anything. We arrived at the hospital at 7:00 a.m. and didn't get home until 4:00 p.m. We had back-to-back appointments and the only reason we had time for lunch was because the speech therapist was out sick and her appointment was cancelled. The day seemed even more harried because Elena came out of sedation feeling really cranky and carried that throughout the day. She managed to sign the alphabet for her teacher before burying her head in her arms and refusing to acknowledge anything anyone tried to teach her. I couldn't even get a smile from her when about thirty people or more raved about her ruby slippers.

While I was waiting for her appointment to draw blood, I pulled out some Christmas cards I had bought for the doctors and started to fill one out. For the first time that day, Elena showed an interest in me and what I was doing. Looking at this newfound interest, I asked her if she wanted to sign her name to one. "Yes!" she said and promptly grabbed the entire box of Christmas cards from me. She could barely be stopped long enough to have the nurse take blood. When the nurse had finished, Elena licked the envelope and immediately handed the card over to the nurse who had just stuck her. Of course the nurse made a really big deal out of it and Elena smiled. She then promptly made herself at home at the nurses' desk and drew snowmen, trees and snowflakes all over the rest of my cards and handed them out to anyone who even looked at her. Not exactly what I had intended for the Christmas cards, but I think making her happy was a better purpose. From the look on his face, I don't think the janitor ever got a Christmas card before, but leave it to Elena to include everyone.

Remember when you were a kid at school and they asked you who your hero was? In elementary school, it was usually mom or dad. In grade school it was usually was a famous figure. Now that I am a mom, I can truly say no one is more my hero than that little girl in the ruby slippers handing out Christmas cards to strangers and dealing with her illness with such strength and grace.

Day 21 – December 19

She just keeps giving… Last night while working pretty late trying to get work from home done, Elena woke up. Sliding out of bed, she quietly walked over to my desk, grabbed the remaining unsigned Christmas cards and said, "I need my own chair." Apparently, the Christmas cards she had not given out weighed heavily on her mind and she felt the need to finish them immediately. So I set her up with a chair and a desk. For the next hour, she worked meticulously on those 10 last cards. I had to laugh as she had a ballpoint click pen and she kept clicking it on her lips like I always do. What a little adult she is. Thank goodness she hasn't gotten her father's grinch-iness for Christmas (though between me, you and the hundreds of people reading this, I think Daddy will be a pushover this year).

Day 23 – December 21

Six years – and yet the days seem to move faster than ever now. It is Elena's 6th birthday today and she started it out with a frown and bit of roid-rage. Not even the bus driver could coax a smile out of her on the lift ride into the bus. But her mood soon changed as we exited radiation recovery by noon and went to the cafeteria for lunch. There she had what she called a "small" breakfast of cheese eggs, yogurt, bowl of oatmeal and milk. Looked bigger to us. Then, no more than one hour later, she wondered what was for lunch.

From there, we went back to the hospital for a schedule and to hand out gifts to our angels of the brain tumor ward. Elena gave out her hand-written cards from her private stash and a bit of "bling" to the women in the form of a Christmas tree pin that she had picked out earlier that weekend. For the men she had a nutcracker in mind. She seems to have taken to the entire nutcracker theme as of late. She sleeps with a nutcracker at the head of her bed and insists that we put them on the mantel at home. This is her decoration and her mark on Christmas. I'm not sure of the symbolism, but it's her new Christmas tradition.

The staff of the brain cancer ward had their own party in mind as Elena's nurse headed up a birthday committee in Elena's honor. And there with the confetti that they had so eagerly manufactured from hole punching just about every piece of colored paper in the office earlier, they sang happy birthday to Elena and lightened our load with a flock of balloons large enough to start a voyage around the world. As we went from appointment to appointment, we spread the joy, dragging confetti from clinic to clinic as it rubbed off of our clothes and hair and fell from the wheel chair. I have no doubt that the janitor will easily be able to determine our schedule for the day. And with the balloons attached to every bar on the wheel chair, we completed the day and headed back to the room – but not before running into every wall, corner and person that we failed to see through the screen of balloons.

Today was also the day for our infamous zoo trip. And although we still don't know how the zoo staff heard about Elena, she enjoyed the trip never the less. With head in hands and her eyes half open (radiation has certainly made her more tired these days), we met up with the zookeeper for her adventure. From there we headed towards the giraffes. Gracie was first in line, ready and willing to ride the giraffes if offered. Elena was more hesitant, at first content to allow

Gracie to take over. But after feeding the first banana to the giraffe, Elena had to join in. From there she was hooked.

Next we went to see the polar bears and seals. Gracie would still have been more than willing to swim with the bears if allowed to, but instead we kept a safe distance behind the glass as the zookeeper sent the bears swimming for fish they prepared in advance. You can never quite understand the power of these animals until you look eye-to-eye at them four inches apart. The glass can't be thick enough.

Next we visited the pandas, complete with a trip behind the scenes to see their kitchen prep area, night cages and help feed them directly. Since we had never seen the panda and polar bear exhibits both open on the same day in our previous trips to the zoo (and having no real understanding of zoo matters), I figured that the pandas were nothing more than polar bears with black spray paint. After all, what a great way to increase ticket revenues? But once again I was proven wrong as we came face to face with the pandas and found them to be much smaller and much more docile than the polar bears. And although cautious with nothing more than a wire cage between them and the panda, they were impressed with the experience. Brooke, on the other hand, was awestruck as she kept telling Elena how exciting this was and how lucky she had been to see a panda this close. I guess we won't have to get Brooke a Christmas gift this year.

Tonight, Elena fell asleep smiling. Her voice has improved, she can now eat some real food, her right arm is starting to work again and she now walks around the room by herself. All is good and improving – thank God. Happy birthday, Elena!

Day 24 – December 22

Time is precious. I learned this being away from Elena for the past three days. And when I returned back to Memphis on Wednesday evening, I breathed a sigh of relief. Just as Brooke had discovered the previous week, when I went back to Cincinnati to work, I spent every minute thinking of Elena and wanting to be back in Memphis. And I mean every minute. You see, when I went back to Cincinnati I couldn't sleep. It wasn't because I wasn't tired or because I was just that busy, it was because I now see sleep as a waste of time. It's amazing how an experience such as this changes your philosophy on life. And while we never really slept in – 6:00 a.m. was "sleeping in" for us, even on the weekends; every minute that you spend away from your daughter with a critical illness is a minute that you lose. So what do you do? You clean the house, decorate her room, put up Christmas decorations and write a journal until 2:00 a.m. in the morning. And the most surprising thing is that we're not tired – this is just the new norm.

The same thing applies to the holiday spirit. Today, while waiting for the bus, Brooke and I wondered what we'd be doing now had Elena not developed cancer. We'd probably be running around town looking for that last-minute gift swearing to ourselves as we stood in line, waiting in traffic and working until 7:00 p.m. at night. We'd complain that we didn't have enough time, not enough money and not the perfect holiday decorations. Now, there's so much more to consider, but less to worry about. We look back at pictures from Halloween and think to ourselves how naïve and lucky we were, but never really knew it at the time. It's funny how you never know how much you can handle until it gets worse. And just when you get used to that, it happens again. But somehow, even with this experience you find a way to make it work because that is how you cope. Not because you deserve it or because you need the experience to set priorities, but because it's the human thing and it is life. And through this experience we will grow, find out what the holiday means and learn to expect more of each other. Together we will use this strain to make us stronger as a family and support each other when we break down. That is what a family does and how we cope.

Today we had doctor appointments until 11:00 a.m. and then got in the car and headed home as a family for the first time in about a month. And although it will take us over eight hours to get home, it is where we need to be. There we'll sleep as a family in our home, once again. I think this will be the first time in a long time that we'll truly rest. For my part, I'll spend the better part of the night lying in bed trying my best to stay awake and enjoy every last moment of having my family home for the holidays. If I sleep, it will just go too fast. Funny how time works.

Day 25 – December 23

Today was a day of hope. It was also the day of Elena's birthday party – two days late.Originally we planned on having Elena's birthday party at the local gymnastics romper room like just about every other suburban family, but in light of her condition and her wishes, we opted for the local chili parlor up the street to allow for her friends to visit. I think she enjoyed this best. So putting on her second best dress (sorry to all at the party, the best dress is for Christmas), she left with Mom for a morning at the spa where she had her nails shined and her hair curled. This was our attempt at a "redo" considering that her last beauty experience was interrupted by pain in her throat and stomach. This time it went off without a hitch and two hours later a freshly painted and curled girl was dropped off on the front porch by her Grandmother (Mom stayed behind for a little toe painting of her own). Gracie was in tow, complete with her own set of curls and the patented "Gracie Grin" as she stopped to pose before entering the front door.

Twenty minutes later, after an elaborate logistical dance involving bathroom breaks and discussions about how to best get nine people and three cars to the big event, we were on our way. And while I'm not sure that anyone has ever gone to the spa and dressed in their best clothes to go to a chili parlor, it is what made Elena happy and that's all that mattered.

On arrival, Elena shunned her wheel chair as she decided that today was the day to try her new leg brace. After all, what good were fancy clothes if you had to sit in them all day? But when she resisted holding our hands for balance, we finally understood her motives and resorted to corralling her on both sides with our hands in case she fell. She didn't. Somehow, the folks at the restaurant had gotten the impression that we had a party of 50 or less, but within a half an hour we filled up the party room and had started to conquer the rest of the restaurant as well. And by the end of the party, close to 80 people came to visit Elena in her first trip home. Family, friends, school teachers, co-workers (she comes to work with Mom and me in the morning and they consider her the "real" boss), more family and even people we never met before joined us in celebrating her birthday. Even her friends from her kindergarten class came. For the past week, these were the ones I heard about as she planned her visit home. Now I saw the joy on her face as she hugged each one, wishing she too could be outside on the school playground every morning freezing while waiting for the bell, as I imagine they must be doing this time of year. It was truly a day to remember even if it was nothing more than hot dogs and cheese.

Tonight Brooke cried. But unlike before, it wasn't because of anticipation or grief, but because she saw how many people truly cared. These are the tears we need more of every day to ensure that Elena wins her fight.

Day 26 – December 24

Merry Christmas-Eve. Tomorrow, Elena, Gracie and I will leave again to return to Memphis where Elena will continue her radiation treatments for the next month. Mom will stay at home for the next week to close out financial records for the company and develop new systems for it. It's only four days, but I don't envy her at all. Being in Memphis offers depression, isolation and fear. Cincinnati offers questions and uncertainty. One's certain, the other is unknown. It's the questions we fear most.

When you take care of Elena, you're focused on the present. What dosage of steroids is the right dose? What are the side-effects of chemotherapy? Can she handle the leg brace instead of the wheel chair? And each of these pursuits focuses your efforts on beating the disease one step at a time. At first you resent the monotony of the schedule as opposed to a quick and fast solution. Then, as you realize the scope of childhood cancer, it soon becomes a crutch as you can see daily improvement that forces you to believe Elena will win. Sometimes this improvement doesn't come and sometimes you see regression, but in the long run you see your daughter change and develop. One step at a time the depression will erode. The isolation and the fear, however, are always present.

In Cincinnati you are forced daily to come to terms with the future. This is probably the most painful part of it all. Here you drive past the school every morning and wonder if you'll get to help with Halloween snacks with Elena in first grade, if Gracie and she will appreciate sharing a bathroom when they're teenagers, and how you'll teach her to drive a stick-shift for the first time. Here reside the questions of the unknown that make it especially hard to continue daily activities. In time, this too will pass as she improves and we learn to live in Cincinnati day-to-day just as we do in Memphis. Perhaps this will happen as soon as February when she returns to Cincinnati and we can begin to live life again – but not in the same way.

I don't envy Brooke for the next week, but I know that I too will have the same duty the following week when I return to Cincinnati and she goes to Memphis. And for the next month, this will be our life. One day at a time.

Day 27 – December 25

Our gift was Elena this year. At 3:30 in the morning she woke us up to the sound of her voice when she came in to tell us that she wanted to watch cartoons. Her voice was clear and not nasal as it had been since Thanksgiving. And despite both of us being sound asleep, Brooke and I shot out of bed in amazement. A small piece of us wondered if it had all been just a bad dream and our daughter was fine after all. Then reality set in as she explained that her voice felt better and she had taken a drink of water and it helped her voice. And at 3:30 in the morning, we carried on a conversation. Her voice only lasted for a short time, but we ignored our blood-shot eyes and carried on the conversation – never mind that this was the first night that we could have slept more than four hours consecutively. How sweet the sound!

Christmas also brought many more gifts in the form of her continued walking, her eating nuts, fruits and pizza, and the first time she joined Gracie for tickle-time on the floor of the family room. But most of all, what I'll remember about this Christmas is making her smile.

At first it wasn't easy. When we dragged her out to church and then to my aunt's Christmas Eve celebration, she refused to participate and sat grudgingly with her head in her hands. No toy, person or visit from Santa could change her outlook. And although a visit from Sally (my aunt's 10-inch tall Chihuahua with a case of the shakes and beady eyes) induced a quick smile, it quickly faded as the never ending hunger pains set in for the fourth time in less than an hour. Food drive and the power of steroids!

No, above all, it was the things that she refused to do that gave her the most joy. You see, Elena never does anything of her own will. If you ask her to water ski, she refuses and says, "maybe tomorrow." If you ask her to read her reading primer she says, "I can't right now." If you ask her to try her bike without training wheels you get, "I'm too young." That's where Gracie comes in. You see, Gracie will do anything, anytime, regardless of whether she can do it right or whether she will get hurt. Act first, think later is Gracie's motto. Her other motto is, "I'm all right," when she picks herself up off the ground after falling. And while I cringe at the thought of her as a teenager, I love having her attitude right now.

When Elena says, "maybe tomorrow," I simply turn to Gracie and ask her. Not even a second passes before Elena reconsiders and turns competitive. Before long, she's waterskiing, riding that bicycle and sounding out every word. Now of course, Gracie can't ride that bike (balance is not her virtue), and Gracie can't read yet (although she's getting pretty close). But when I hold the back of the bike so it looks like she's doing it herself and when I act like Gracie is whispering the words in my ear, Elena immediately has to do one better. Sometimes I think Elena teaches Gracie caution, while Gracie teaches Elena courage. It's a great combination.

This time, it was driving. Yes, driving. You see, we had about thirty minutes to kill before church and I thought it would be a good idea to teach Elena how to drive. After all, I only have another ten years to teach her so I better get started. Mom, on the other hand, didn't agree. "What are you, stupid?" she asked. I too can be competitive, so off I went with my little stunt. After asking Elena and being turned down, I went to Gracie. All I needed to do was look at Gracie and she was immediately in my lap ready to go. And for the next ten minutes, Captain Zigzag was at the helm as we drove from one edge of the parking lot to the next and occasionally almost into a post or two. She loved it as she donned my sunglasses to get the complete effect.

Elena had to be next. She was labeled the Queen of the Grass as we took off through the abutting field and over a curb or two. She loved it. And for the next fifteen minutes she squealed, laughed and giggled. I think we'll have to do it again. Maybe tomorrow.

For most kids, gifts at Christmas would have been the most important thing of the holiday. For Elena, this Christmas was different. And while she opened the gifts, most were left by the edge of the tree as she moved on to the next. Instead, Elena got more joy out of my gift than any of the ones she received. Apparently, she and Mom went shopping together and decided that I needed a balloon animal kit. So for the next two hours, Christmas stopped while Elena and I sat next to each other laughing. I'm not ready for the restaurant circuit, but I do have a pretty good assortment of animals to choose from. I can make snakes, giraffes with short legs, dogs with long necks, horses with long necks and short legs, and even butterflies without wings that look like long-necked dogs. Not bad if I do say so myself. And it only takes two balloons to get one that doesn't pop. That's skill. Elena thinks I should make balloons for the doctors at the hospital tomorrow. I promise to as long as she promises to try the radiation without sedation. What she doesn't know is that I'll do it for nothing more than a smile. What a deal.

Day 28 – December 26

She certainly didn't want to be back. And although it was a short day, it was not easy. With three days of vacation from the hospital behind her, Elena made it very clear from 5:00 a.m. on that this was the last place she wanted to be. Just getting her out of bed at 5:00 a.m. proved impossible as she clung to her pillow squeezing out every last bit of sleep. And this was the same girl who came to our bedside every morning at 3:00 a.m. on weekends. The same medicine regiment that took no more than ten minutes over the weekend now took thirty minutes as she first refused the Jell-O that contained the pill, and then spit out the pill rather than swallowing it.

The radiation treatments came later that day. This too was difficult as I tried to continue the work that Brooke had started last week with getting her to stay still during the radiation treatments while awake. Up until now, Elena has needed sedation in order to remain still during her radiation treatments. And although the treatments last only ten minutes, the process can be scary for even an adult as a full size mesh mask is placed over your head and throat and then bolted to the table to immobilize the head to ensure direct targeting of the tumor.

Despite this, the advantages are significant. First, she would no longer require the use of a port and IV fluid, so she could avoid getting stuck every Monday morning and walking around for the entire week with an IV line sticking out of her chest. Second, she did not have to receive the dreaded "white medicine" they use to sedate her, thereby avoiding some nausea issues and an overall feeling of sluggishness throughout the day. Third, the entire process would last only ten minutes instead of two hours. Finally, (and most importantly) she would get to eat! Waffles, cheese eggs and even chocolate chip smiley face pancakes would all be possible without sedation. Both Brooke and I have tried to help Elena understand all of these advantages, even going so far as to create a chart on the back of the bedroom door showing good pictures when she learns to stay still and bad pictures when she needs the sleepy medicine. Hopefully, we will do better tomorrow. For tonight, she promises she will try harder.

After all of the excitement we thought it would be best to change the mood. For this, we turned to the local natural history museum. There, we took a tour of the evolution exhibit and the Christmas tree exhibit before making our way to the IMAX theater. Once inside, Elena began to complain of stomach pain before the lights dimmed. This was to be our first experience with the nausea that accompanies radiation. Without a bathroom in sight, I ended up using the only other thing I had – my hands. Eventually, this translated into my shirt, her shirt and her pants until we finally found the bathroom and attempted to clean up.

And there, in the men's bathroom as she stood in her underwear while I dressed her in the only change of clothes I had (an old diaper bag from Gracie's baby years that was in my car with two-year-old summer clothing), she asked the question. "Why does this have to happen to me?" she asked.

Not thinking much of the question, I answered to her that it happens to a lot of kids in the theater and it can also happen to most children who are getting radiation. Not satisfied with the answer, she touched my head and asked again, "No, Dad, why am I sick with the bump in my head when all of my friends are not?"

I had been asking the same question for a month. And somehow the answer never fits since it should never happen to any child in the first place. To simply pass it off as "odds" is to say that you'd be fine if it was someone else's child. To tag it as a "message from God" is to create a doubt of faith if you are the one who loses your child to the "message." In the end, I don't think you ever have an answer because there are no right answers. It happens and you learn to deal with it, fight it, or accept it – all very different responses by different people.

Now I'd love to tell you that I came up with a cute answer that tied it all together. And for the purposes of this journal, I'd like to at least find some meaning, but I have none. The truth is that I looked at my daughter, shrugged and said, "It will be all right," and hugged her. That's it. Someday, I hope to answer that question and in discovering it, improve her life, mine and a thousand others, but for now I'm forced to be humble and give her the reassurance she desperately needs. That's the mission of a father: to reassure and protect.

Day 29 – December 27

She can roll her tongue! I know it doesn't seem like a big deal to most people, but to me it is everything. You see, one of the first things that she lost when the tumor took over was the ability to roll her tongue. Then she lost her voice, her right hand, her right leg, her peripheral vision and her ability to swallow. So to get the tongue back is a very big deal. Sure, the leg is still a bit slow, but what this means to me is that we're getting everything back and Elena is getting better. Hopefully, it will all stay that way. I know every day from here on out will begin with me asking her to roll her tongue as she crawls out of bed. Who needs MRI and CT equipment when all you need is a roll of the tongue?

Day 30 – December 28

The day began at 3:00 in the morning. It seems that the ground turkey we ate last night wasn't so fresh after all. So for the better part of the morning, I spent quality time curled in a ball on the bathroom floor. Elena and Gracie, on the other hand, had no problems. Gracie never ate her dinner to begin with and only chose to indulge in ice cream. For the first time, I'm glad she only ate dessert. Elena, sick from radiation treatments, sat at the dinner table motionless and only ate a few graham crackers when prompted. Now it was her turn to be the parent.

So as I rushed off to the bathroom for the second, third, fourth and fifth times to clear out my stomach, Elena sat up in bed and instructed me to, "Try some Sprite," and, "Why don't you eat some graham crackers – it will settle your stomach." These were all the words I had used with her just the morning prior. Now those same words were being used to help me. Then, as if to cap it off, she remarked, "Now you know how I feel." How right she was and boy did she ever enjoy bossing me around. She even went so far as to come into the bathroom while I was curled up on the floor to tell me, "It would be all right," as she held my head.

So on we went through the day with me hunched over and pushing the wheel chair while Elena gave me tips on nausea. Just what I needed. Gracie followed with her aunt, all the while bounding through the halls as if she had just loaded up on a combination of caffeine and sugar sticks. You know – her normal walk. It was a painful day and as I write this, I'm still feeling the effects. Elena is telling me now that I should take some of her medicine – just what I need right now. Maybe she'll hide it in the Jell-O.

It's good to have Elena back. She was always the parent anyway. Tomorrow we go home for the holiday weekend.

Day 31 – December 29

All around us I see examples of determination, love, and commitment to living. They are the children age twelve and up; those who have been here before. They have experienced relapses; possibly for the second, third or even fourth time. And their wisdom and resolve are what drives us each and every day.

Today I sat on a bus with Elena as we traveled back to the house. In a nearby seat sat a father and a daughter. They too are heroes. He sat along the aisle, she sat next to the window – just as Elena and I sat behind them. She was about five years older than Elena and had been here before. Her father sat nearby supportingly, looking for conversation to break the thoughts of nausea that his daughter no doubtedly felt. During the five-minute-drive, barely a word was spoken between them, but I knew they did not need small talk to communicate. When we arrived, he rose, helped her to her feet and she stepped forward determined to leave the bus on her own power. I looked at Elena and saw her in five years. I wondered if we too would return, or would we experience a miracle and never return? Would she be a hero as well? And while I never want to see Elena go through a relapse, I realize that in her case the miracle might be just making it five years.

Elena is doing well today and I hope she will continue to improve over the coming months. Of course, we will have complications and side-effects, but regardless of the struggle, I pray we will succeed. I know she will be a hero. She already is.

Day 32 – December 30

I look out the window and have thoughts I should never have. I look back at my daughter lying in bed and compare what I see. Outside the hospital I see drug deals, prostitution and wasted opportunities. Inside our room I see a little girl fighting for her life. They have all the time in the world, while Elena's life might be reduced to days and hours. It isn't fair. I guess I shouldn't expect it to be.

It goes on 24-hours a day. On the streets outside the hospital, the comparisons are obvious. Elsewhere they are hidden. And now as a father wishing for just one more day, I do not see them as victims. I am frustrated and angry. But then again it doesn't make sense. Isn't her life more precious? As I said, these are questions I should never ask.

We all waste our time and our lives when we should aspire to do more. What we all wouldn't do for just one more day when it comes to an end. If only we knew. I know. The loss of a child represents every lesson we should learn and every moment we should cherish. But instead, we follow the foolish, ignore the clock, and cry victim when consequences fall. Yet these children get no such warning. Elena was never foolish, never ignored the clock, yet she is in the battle for her life. And so she becomes a lesson for us all. My price may be my daughter.

I will never understand and that's the irony of it all. The ultimate lesson here is one that I will never agree with or ever hope to find inspiration in. I don't fight to help other children because of Elena's lesson; I fight to help other children because I don't want the lessons to continue. I love my daughter and no lesson is worth her life. I will continue even if she loses her fight.

So many people tell me that they find honesty and meaning in her story. If it means that they will hug their children, create a legacy and help others, it would be a perfect tribute to Elena. If it is only a story, than the message is lost. Either way, to me the message is inconsequential – I do it because I don't want anyone else to go through what we have experienced. I guess in that way, there is a message, no matter how much I refuse it.

I will always remember these nights in the hospital as she slept softly and I sat by her side, peering into the darkness outside. It wasn't fair. No life is worth the life of a child. It doesn't make sense – but then again, it's not supposed to.

Day 33 – December 31

Today we learned an important lesson. In our efforts to avoid overlooking Gracie, we've tried to set up alone time between both Brooke and me. Too often this has resulted in Gracie still feeling left out and us feeling the exhaustion that comes with ping-pong parenting. What we didn't realize is that Gracie never craved individualized attention as much as she craved family time. Just as we want to, she also wants to be around Elena and be a family again. Individualized attention can never replace the family time that has made us strong until now.

In an attempt to spend some of this family time, Brooke and I decided to get back to basics and spend this Sunday in the same fashion we have hundreds of times before. So this afternoon we headed off to the children's museum and then to Grandpa-Grandpa's house for a simple family dinner. And just like every other Sunday, we crowded 16 – 20 people into a 10 foot by 12 foot room, and sat down for a dinner at a table that seats six. There we donned handcrafted New Year's Day Bengals hats in celebration and complained about the loss to the Steelers. In truth, I don't think we truly cared about the loss, but it was something to complain about on a miserable rainy Sunday.

There we were in our element; hot, cramped, loud and having a great time sharing stories, viewing photos and poking fun at our haircuts from the '80s. And to Elena and Gracie, this was their family as they too joined in popping noisemakers and stealing peanuts from the jars accumulating on the kitchen table made from an old countertop. Grandpa-Grandpa has a way of getting family together and making the simple cherished.

It was the right choice to spend the day as a family rather than pairing off with Brooke and Gracie and Elena and I. We were right to spend it doing what we had always done before. Elena and Gracie, even enjoyed being sisters again as they argued in the backseat all the way home.

Tomorrow, Brooke will leave with Elena for Memphis once again. Elena will not return until she finishes her treatments at the end of January. And although she will miss home, we are now halfway there.

Day 34 – January 1

This morning started in a flurry of activity. Everyone slept in today, then the girls came into our bedroom and we all slept in a little more. I remember just six months ago groaning when the girls woke us up early on the weekends and promptly ushered them upstairs to watch cartoons while we caught a few more minutes of sleep. Now we don't mind the wakeup call and snuggle up with them even longer.

Day 36 – January 3

I was approached twice today by fellow mothers remarking on how Elena has made such a wonderful recovery. I am torn. On one hand, I smile and think to myself that it truly is a miracle that these changes have occurred in two weeks. On the other hand, I hate to get too comfortable with the recovery. I keep finding myself forgetting that this may be temporary. I find myself slipping back into old habits of working when we get home rather than playing with her, reading a newspaper rather than squeezing every last ounce of conversation out of her, thinking about everything I left undone at home rather than what things I haven't done with Elena.

Those who know me best know I don't like surprises. I am the "read the last chapter of a book first" kind of girl. I need to know what is ahead of me so I can plan out each step to get there. I find myself in a weird sort of depression. I know what the future holds (or the most probable one) but I am paralyzed. I sit across from this little girl every day, cracking jokes and learning subtraction, and I have a horrible thought. These treatments have done wonderful things and fixed all the problems this tumor has caused, but did it make her too normal? I look at Elena and have a really hard time imagining that we could have a recurrence. Most look at that and say this is a good thing and positive thinking is the best course of action. I am scared that we will get too comfortable and this stupid tumor is going to broadside us. So do you live with the knowledge that it will grow again and try to cram a lifetime into a year? Or do you live with a positive outlook and maintain the status quo?

Aside from her ever growing cheeks and stealthy appetite, Elena is back to normal. It must be very weird for her to feel back to normal and still be stuck in a hospital. Actually, going home for the holidays helped her so much. She can now visualize herself getting better, going to school, playing with her sister and most importantly, being the "Razzle-Dazzle" girl of the week in her kindergarten class.

Day 41 – January 8

Today was a pretty easy going day. The wheel chair has now become a coat rack (as it should be), and we walked the hospital with pride. We did our radiation without a hitch as Mom read Elena "Junie B. Jones" books during the treatment. Even the technicians were laughing at the story. Elena held her head even higher as they told her she could eat breakfast tomorrow before treatments. No more fasting! I am quite sure she had the breakfast already planned five minutes after they told her that tidbit of news.

Elena worked very hard to keep me smiling today. She kept talking about how she needed the wagon to get her package at the front desk. Imagine my surprise when we got to the wagons and she wanted to pull it rather than sitting in it like every day for the last two months. Of course, she took out every corner on the way back to the room, but that was fine – she was walking.

Day 42 – January 9

Tonight Elena wants to write the journal. Here goes – I'll help spell:

Hi everybody!

- *I can't wait to come home.*
- *My favorite animal is a hummingbird but I don't have a feeder for one yet.*
- *I like to wear skirts and sparkly headbands.*
- *I like to read my animal book with all the animals inside.*
- *I like to watch cartoons when I get back from the hospital, my favorite show is "Go Diego Go" because it's all about a rescue and Diego really likes animals like me.*
- *My favorite thing to do with my Gracie is to play outside.*
- *My most favorite color is pink.*
- *My favorite part about school is eating lunch and being Razzle Dazzle.*

- *My most favorite season is summer because you get to go to the beach.*
- *Soccer is my favorite sport.*
- *The first thing I want to do when I get home is go to the beach.*
- *The one thing I wish I could do is swim with fish.*
- *The least favorite thing about the hospital is the needle in my port.*
- *I loved when everyone sang to me for my birthday.*

Day 44 – January 11

Elena and I got up extra early to go for an early morning radiation treatment today. Now early is a relative term when you think about the fact that Dad and Gracie got up at 2 a.m. to drive to Memphis. By the time we were done, Dad and Gracie were able to pick us up. Elena literally ran to see Daddy! We then went back to the house to get a snack while the girls played. Elena and Gracie and several other kids ran around the indoor play areas chasing each other. How much fun it was to watch Elena interact with other kids just like before. Once again, Gracie helped Elena come out of her shell and open up. Elena and Gracie then chased each other on tricycles and went up and down the playground. They even went on a hunt to find the resident kitty, but at the first sight of the two girls, that cat took off running. Smart move!

Later, we had two more appointments, so we left Gracie in charge of watching Grandma while the three of us went to physical therapy. Elena grabbed her new backpack from the school at the hospital, and rolled it right up to the shuttle stop as we tried to keep up. Elena climbed the shuttle stairs, sat down, showed Dad where to place her bag and started to chat with the driver about her day. Large and in charge! Keith couldn't stop laughing and Elena couldn't stop talking

We sailed through our appointments and hurried home to spend time with Gracie. Dad's 2:00 a.m. wake-up call finally caught up with him and he napped while we went to the craft room to share our newly purchased additions to the art supplies. I think Elena and Gracie depleted about half of those supplies in about an hour. Grandma is always the best at finding ways to divert our attention and finding new and creative things to do. While we were there, we met a little girl who was also in kindergarten and starting radiation next week. We shared our words of wisdom and Elena worked to ease the little girl's fears about radiation.

Day 45 – January 12

"You don't know me but..." It's the way most of the cards sent to Elena begin any more. And what started as an innocent journal for Gracie about her sister has now become so much more. Our daily journal started as a remembrance as we first came to grips with her illness, but it has now become the driving force in her recovery. Every day brings more cards, more letters and more e-mails than we can possibly read to her. Every day we pack cards for the hospital waiting room and pass the time reading to her the greetings from friends and family. It brings a smile to her and it brings encouragement to us. And now, for the first time, I can see the positive once again with the blessings of Elena's friends.

The cards come from all over: Ohio, Kentucky, Indiana, Iowa, Pennsylvania, Florida, Tennessee, Georgia, Alabama, New York, California, Washington, Maryland, Virginia, Michigan, Texas, Illinois, Arizona, Arkansas and plenty of other states I don't even remember at this time. Each one offers get well wishes, birthday greetings and holiday cheer. Some carry photographs, some carry children's drawings, and some carry small gifts, but all deliver smiles.

The cards now cover her door, obscure her bulletin boards and hang from the ceiling of her bedroom. Each of them carries a message – a message of hope. Hope for her health, hope for her happiness, hope for her future. For us, they carry us through every day. Thank you everyone.

Day 46 – January 13

Thank goodness we have at least another ten years to worry before they start driving. Maybe then they'll be able to recognize the difference between stop and go. Whoever thought it would be a good idea to arm children with a battery operated all-terrain vehicle never had to deal with Captain ZigZag (Gracie) and Queen of the Grass (Elena).

Today we spent the day in Alabama visiting my sister and her family. And although the visit did not start well with Elena having severe bouts of nausea and headaches requiring three separate calls to the emergency clinic, it ended perfectly with all four girls having a camp out on the floor of Allyson's room.

Elena, having discovered her new found freedom from steroids, seemed to be amazed at a feeling of "fullness" that accompanied breakfast. And after consuming three bowls of fruit salad and half a waffle, she told all within the sound of her voice that she was finally full. And following Mom's example, she has now decided to eat mostly fruits, vegetables and salads in an effort to lose the cheeks that she complains about daily. No problems there – Elena's never been one for junk food anyway.

From there, it was on to the all-terrain mini Jeep. After running over me, Michelle's foot, a ball and into the fence, she finally had enough experience to make it once around the yard. Of particular interest was her ability to chase me around the yard trying to run me over as I diligently tried to document the experience with a camera. It was her very own rebellion. All I know is that with a hill, a five foot wall and her horrible driving ability, she'll never see a mini Jeep in her backyard.

From there it was on to the Rocket Museum (I'm sure it has a formal name, but you get the idea). There Elena developed the theory that anything that was bigger than she was should be feared. Good luck overcoming this at a rocket museum. Suffice it to say, we didn't see much of the museum until Grandma made a deal to go on the zero-gravity ride provided that Elena agreed to be brave as well. So Grandma belted in and screamed her way up and down a 70 ft. rocket ride and Elena stopped squirming as she walked by the space shuttle. Once again, Elena won yet another bet.

Next were manicures and hairdos for the girls at a local beauty salon. Not only was this a welcome capstone to the day, but especially important to Elena as she became increasingly aware of her growing cheeks. Now, with new nails and curls, she was the bell of the ball. The cheeks no longer mattered.

Today was a good day. By 7 p.m., we finished the day with "The Little Mermaid" and dress-ups. Michelle and Allyson were unicorns, Gracie was a fairy and Elena was a bride. What a sight. What a day.

Day 47 – January 14

Do you ever know when you are experiencing a miracle? I guess I just expected more - maybe a flash of light, a clap of thunder or a visit from an angel. But maybe, just maybe, the angel is right here next to me.

It's true that Elena has come so far so fast. Of course, she also lost so much so quickly. But now she's back – smiles and all. And as I watch her run from swing to swing with her "Pippie Longstocking" tights, I truly begin to appreciate what we once had – all over again.

Today was a day to relax. Mom and Gracie left and after a picnic in the park, so did Grandma and Grandpa. It was back to Aunt

Jackie's house to relax and spend a couple of hours driving in the same loop around the backyard in the mini Jeep (boy does she love that thing). But after the fourth battery charge only lasted 20 minutes, she knew it was time to settle down with her cousins. I never thought we'd spend the second week of January on the back porch grilling out, but then again for Alabama, 70 degrees is a cold snap.

While the agenda was light, the memories were powerful. And somehow, some way, if I try hard enough, the day will never end. How do you know if a miracle is happening? You don't, but as a parent I'd just love to experience the peace of knowing that I'll get to see her graduation, wedding and her children. But for now, you focus on the many miracles that occur every day. 60 miracles in a minute, 3600 in an hour, 86,400 in a day – one miracle per second.

Day 48 – January 15

"Free at last… free at last!" I think Elena has listened to a bit too much television on Martin Luther King Day. Although certainly appropriate considering her improvement, I never figured I'd hear her singing this as she rode around Jackie's yard in circles on the mini Jeep.

Free at last, most certainly. With only ten days left before we leave the hospital and return home, Elena has become the elder stateswoman of the house. She knows the routine, knows her fellow patients and knows the staff. Upon arriving back at the house, she informed me that we were to eat dinner (the cheese pizza in the freezer was her choice), then check mail, and finally finish back at the room with a pint of ice cream and a Muppet movie. And although her head never crested the front counter as she asked for the mail and she couldn't get the security code to work when we made our way to the front door, it was clear that she was in charge. She chose the meal, she helped make it and she set the table. I figure either she feels that I'm in over my head, or she's on her way out. Maybe a bit of both. Finally, after dinner and on the way back to the room, she informed me that the ice cream was hers and that if I would like, I could go back to the kitchen and get the Oreos from the pantry. After all, she claimed Mom did this every night. Aha!! And all that talk about being good – now I understand how Mom made it through two weeks at the house.

Elena has improved greatly over the past weeks, but her walking and her balance are still missing. I was reminded of this as we approached the stairway to our second floor room. With a tug at my side, she again needed my help to climb the steps. I guess I could have taken the elevator, but without steps I would never get the opportunity to carry her and get free kisses. You see, every three steps require a kiss from Elena in order to continue. It's like Daddy fuel. And the way I figure it, with 24 steps total to the top, I get at least eight kisses every time. Of course, I usually fake a step just to get nine kisses. I think she knows, but gives it to me anyway. With as independent as Elena is getting, I can use all the opportunities I can get. Who needs Oreos when you get this?

Day 49 – January 16

I remember when Elena was intimidated by school. First, she was scared of daycare. Then she was scared of the first day of kindergarten. She wrapped her little arms around Mom's legs and shed the customary tears. Day two brought even more tears. I guess when you know what to expect, it can be even more fearful. Day three through day seven saw fewer tears, bashful hellos to teachers and friends and hand holding until everyone else entered the building. From day eight on it went much better. She still held our hands until the last possible moment and it still took at least five kisses and hugs before she would leave our side, but looking back I wish it would have taken at least six or more.

Yes, we were the "leftover parents"; the ones that still walked our children to the door when everyone else sought the protection of their warm cars when the cold temperatures came home to roost. Sure, there were a few more additions after weekends and absences, but we were the "regulars" of the group. To this day, I don't know if it was because she needed the support or whether we couldn't let go, but it doesn't matter now. I'll be there every morning from now until she goes to college, maybe even longer. Sure it's a little protective, but think of how much she'll appreciate it when she goes to high school and I'm walking five feet behind. She can look behind, introduce me to her friends and thank me for accompanying her. Okay… maybe not.

What was different about Elena was not how she entered school, but how she left. When most kids left screaming out the door, relieved to be finished, Elena would talk about how much she missed it the minute after she left. She'd tell me about art, about share-chair, about lunch and she'd tell me about her plans for tomorrow. To this day, I can't understand where the excitement disappeared between 3 p.m. and 8 a.m. the next day, but "my teacher did this…." and "my teacher that…." seemed to be our only dinner conversation. Even on the weekends she'd play teacher, complete with her pointer and blackboard. And if you happened to be one of her friends, good luck trying to play teacher. This was the role Elena was born to play. Poor Gracie, she did nothing other than raise her hand for the last four years.

When Elena came here and was subjected to a seemingly endless barrage of tests and drugs, you can easily understand her depression. Everyone was treating the body and no one was treating the mind. No creativity, no learning, no advancement. While her body recovered, her mind was at a point of atrophy. They offered psychological sessions, movie nights and even gifts, but none had any effect. So when we discovered the educational center at the hospital, we quickly knew the answer.

I've figured out that kids just aren't that complex. We think they need understanding and comforting when all they really need is a challenge and a bit of truth. A month ago, Elena craved both. She knew she had something very bad, why else would she get all this attention? So after two months of hiding our meetings behind locked doctors' doors, she made us discuss it in front of her. And in a way, it forced us to reconcile with the positives as well as the negatives of the disease. As for a challenge, she only had to be provided with the opportunity to learn and she was determined to take it from there. School was that answer.

Today her attitude is better than it has ever been before. She's not only happy with herself, but probably more confident now than she was back at home. And while she still hangs on to my legs at every doctor visit, she never forgets when it is time for school. It is the first question she asks when I get the schedule for the next day and I'm amazed at her grasp of time when she reminds me about her "school appointment" within minutes of its start. Then, without asking, she's off to the elevator and on her way to class. With her rolling backpack, she pushes past nurses and patients, leaving me follow. God help me if I get distracted – I know she'll never wait.

School is a purpose and a routine. It is what she loves about her life and what she needs right now to be a child again. It's not just about education anymore.

Day 51 – January 18

At the house you start as unknowns, only to become family. With its common kitchens, family rooms and support programs, you soon share experiences, memories and concerns with the other 50 families. When Elena and I first arrived, we were strangers, having moved to the house one week prior to the rest of the families at the hospital. While we were settling in, most of the other families were moving out. But then our generation started to arrive and one-by-one we began to understand their plights as well.

Five weeks later, everything changes. With most families nearing their six-week radiation protocol terminations, preparations have begun for the journey home. The first of these families goes home tomorrow. We go next Thursday. Another six families have started packing and preparing for school. But as we near the completion of radiation, our outlooks and regiments make us feel very far apart.

It seems that in our group there are two types of families. First there are those facing months, if not years of additional chemotherapy and surgeries. These families have two weeks to one month off to go home, but then they will return for another dose of severe chemotherapy and weeks in the hospital. And while they have the most difficult path ahead, their prognoses are relatively positive. Then there are those that are here for radiation only or combined radiation and chemotherapy treatments. They're going home for good, with the exception of an occasional check-up visit once a month. In some of these cases, the prognosis is still almost 85% survival. I envy both. We too will go home after our six weeks and return for only monthly check-ups. And while I certainly love being able to take my daughter back home, I'd spend weeks, months and even years if it meant that the survival prognosis would be better than 10%. In a way, we are our own class.

Happiness has now replaced despair. The same parents who haunted the halls at 2 a.m. every night, unable to find the sleep that they so desperately needed, now compete to see who will go back home first. Dinner is filled with conversations of school, basketball, work and travel. Gone are the endless Internet cancer searches, the bottomless cups of coffee and the pajama bottoms. Still, I don't feel any different. Today is just today and tomorrow is too far away. Hope is the eternal promise.

Day 52 – January 19

Therapy of the mind is just as important as therapy of the body. Today we concentrated on the mind and the hospital is no place to start. So after radiation therapy, we set off for another road trip – this time to the largest indoor complex we could find: The Opryland Hotel. You see, I had my fill of the museums, the malls and the hallways, and to tell you the truth, I could use a bit of therapy of the mind as well. If you couldn't tell from the journal, my thoughts haven't exactly been optimistic lately.

Obviously the Opryland Hotel isn't a young child's palace. You won't find amusement rides, cartoon characters or water slides, but it was perfect for Elena. She has never been much of a kid to begin with. If given the choice between a roller coaster and a library, she'd choose the latter. For her (and us), Opryland was heaven. From the moment she entered the room she ran to the balcony, opened the doors and declared, "Dad, come look at the jungle!" Then she had to call Grandma, Mom and Allyson just to tell them about her view. And she didn't stop with that – she also proceeded to tell all who would listen that this was "the fanciest place she'd ever been to."

For the next two hours, all we did was sit on the balcony, drink our exotic waters from the bathroom faucet and offer toasts to the view (thank you to my family for the "toasting" gene). Then after finding out that Mom took a wrong turn in Louisville and would not arrive for another two hours, we decided to take a quick tour for as long as Elena would last. An hour and a half later and after nearly six miles, I cried uncle. It turns out she has had much more practice in her therapy sessions than I had back and forth from the room to the kitchen. The walk ended with a race down the "jungle trails" of the hotel where Elena left me in the dust. And for the first time, she actually ran and felt confident enough to not just walk fast. Balance was always our last hurdle and it looks like we're starting to clear it. Another reason to celebrate.

It turns out that upon learning out about Elena, the crew of the Opryland Hotel decided to share in our celebration and join in too. Suffice to say, she was a princess and we were in awe. What a way to end a day and what a way to celebrate Elena's return to childhood. Cheers!

Day 53 – January 20

The princesses once again received the royal treatment at the Opryland Hotel. It seems the housekeeping staff has adopted Elena, bringing her gifts, breakfast in bed and now custom fit Opryland robes. This was great, especially considering that both Elena and Gracie no longer fit in their pajamas. There's nothing like having breakfast on the porch with their bellies hanging out and their pants up around their knees. The robes at least made us look like we belonged here. And they had pajamas. In a hurry to get on the road, Brooke forgot hers and spent the night in jeans and a t-shirt. Thankfully, they gave her a robe as well.

For a day we forgot about her condition and tried to be a family. It didn't work of course. Gracie wanted attention, Elena fought with Gracie, and Brooke and I forgot what it was like to have another parent around. Brooke says we need to relearn how to be a family. I know she's right. For the past two months, we've been in different cities, each with a child that we can't discipline or another one we won't. The result was a lunch where we spent chasing Gracie and Elena, all while struggling to have a conversation. I know that this will change when we get back together next weekend, but I also know that we desperately need some independent family time with just the four of us to get back to living. I fear that otherwise our lives will become even more chaotic with the passing visits of family and friends. And while the support is welcome, we also need to find our own way. Even though we've spent three days together, Brooke and I have not been able to speak to each other uninterrupted for more than five minutes. It will be nice to see her again next weekend if the situation allows.

Day 54 – January 21

Yesterday when we went to the mall, we went into an outdoor adventure store. We saw kayaks, bikes, snow skis and roller blades. Normally this would have been a store to dream, however, under the current circumstances, I did more soul searching than dreaming. It took walking through that store, hand-in-hand with Elena, for me to realize how much we never did. Elena and I talked about kayaking. Brooke and I have always wanted to kayak with the girls and dreamed of buying two-person kayaks and taking the girls with us on tours of waterways and lakes. Now I realize that summer may never come soon enough. We looked at the bikes and I remembered our bikes gathering dust in the basement along with the trailer we bought last year for the girls. I think we got one weekend out of the bikes before getting wrapped up in "more important" things. I looked at the snow skis and realized that Elena had never been snow skiing, let alone even experienced snow deeper than six inches. I realize that this time is lost. All the things I planned to do with her are now fading and I may never have that second chance.

Just like every other first-born, she'd never have the courage to try it alone. As a father, I'd have to push her, drag her and teach her to love every new thing. And then, after crying and cringing, she'd finally discover that she liked it all along. That was how it was with water skiing for both of us. Now Elena loves it, although is understandably fearful considering her lack of balance and therapy issues.

Will we have the opportunity to do these things? I hope so, but I will never know. And there, in the store, as I turn to Elena and explain to her about snow skiing, she tells me, "Maybe next year, Dad – when I get older." That would be wonderful.

Day 55 – January 22

Odds are fine as long as you're on the winning side. But if you're one of the unlucky ones, they're irrelevant. Facing cancer, I think every parent looks to the odds as a way of determining their actions. After all, odds are everything in buying stock, sports and business. Recently, however, I've come to the conclusion that our odds are immaterial.

Let's say she beats the cancer – why? Was it due to the odds? Or was it from our fantastic strategy, her outlook or a miracle? Say she doesn't. Was it because of our horrible strategy, our outlook or Murphy's Law? Maybe it was just a bad diagnosis. Either way, the odds were irrelevant in the final conclusion. And if she's one of the 9 in 10 who don't beat it, will it even matter in the end? In our mind, that's 100% after the fact. Besides that, what do odds mean after you've already lost the odds game and developed cancer in the first place? The way I figure it, we've already been a one-in-million shot. But who isn't?

Anyone with cancer makes decisions based more upon their personal attitudes and values than the odds anyway. In Elena's case, we also made decisions based on the moment and on her current condition. Religion also played a dominant role as well, although under the current circumstances, we have a hard time turning to religion.

In our short time here, we've met many families: the ones who are newly diagnosed, the ones who have relapsed, but mostly the ones who lost the odds. Every day you're surrounded by the chance to be discouraged and disheartened, but somehow you aren't. And while some may say that the communal lifestyle offers safety in numbers, I know differently. It is facing the impossible that hardens even the weakest soul. We will beat this cancer, we will see Elena graduate, we will beat those odds. I'll take that bet.

Day 56 – January 23

Today was Elena's last radiation treatment. She didn't want to go. But after telling her that she could go home in two days, she changed her mind. Unknown to me, this also triggered a long forgotten memory of a pledge that her mother made to her in Cincinnati, two months ago! If she would finish her treatments, Mom would buy her pink cowboy boots. At the time, I'm sure it was a good idea for Mom, but for me now, this would begin a journey of many miles. I'll spare you the details, but the results are a new pair of pink cowboy boots to match her pink cowboy hat. Suffice it to say, it took 5 stores to find size ten pink boots. Hey, what else did I have planned for the afternoon? Thanks, Mom. Two can play this game. I told Elena that if she comes back and completes her MRI with Mom in two weeks (they'll be here for just two days and without a car), that Mom will take her out that day and buy her a stuffed purple unicorn with wings. Good luck with that one. It's about as difficult as pink boots.

Day 57 – January 24

There's a tradition at the house. At the conclusion of their stay, every resident gets to leave their handprint on the walls of the kitchen. For the past eight weeks we've cooked under these colorful tributes, wondering when it would be Elena's turn. That time was today. So with paint in hand, Elena and I made her stamp on the kitchen. Of course, you can guess what color she chose – pink and sparkles. And in true Elena fashion, she had to do one better with a photo of her as well. Ultimately, I ended up doing most of the artwork as the staff decided that her space would be on a post eleven feet off of the ground overlooking our kitchen. With Elena's newly found fear of heights, this meant a quick lift in the air to stamp her left hand and then directions from the ground up to Dad on the ladder.

And just like all of the other kids before us, her name, diagnosis and date, and the date of release were imprinted on the walls. Unfortunately, many of the other kids had abbreviated "date of diagnosis" as "D.O.D." and knowing how I interpreted that for the first week before I figured it out, I was not about to use the same abbreviation. I'm not quite sure how we felt about cooking in a kitchen filled with memories. Some days the handprints were uplifting. And although we could only find three other diffuse brainstem gliomas in the kitchen, these showed us that we were not alone. Families wrestling with the same fears and hopes had also cooked in this kitchen and even burned most of their food as I had. Then again, it always ended with the thought of how many were left. About that point, you gave up cooking and went to the table without the last course. The green beans just weren't that important. As a result, I always had a 10-minute rule. If I couldn't prepare it in less than 10 minutes, I wouldn't do it. 10 minutes was all I cared to reflect on. Of course, I don't know if I even spent 10 minutes in my own kitchen at home.

By the time the imprint was finished, it matched Elena perfectly. Pink, sparkly, beaming and simple. Goodbye kitchen – hello home.

Day 58 – January 25

Today we left the house, hopefully for good. Not that it was a bad place (ask me again when I'm cleaning everyone else's dishes for the millionth time in the communal kitchen), but we didn't like what it represented. I gave Elena the option of staying another day and leaving early Friday morning, but she felt as I did, and we ran to the car immediately after her radiation appointment and started directly home.

Sure this won't be the last time we'll visit the hospital. There will be monthly visits for prescriptions, check-ups, and MRIs from now until she beats this disease, but each of these trips will be confined to a day and a plane flight back and forth. But hopefully, we will never stay more than three days ever again.

Fifty-eight days down and it seems like a lifetime. I wish it felt even longer. And through that time you never forget. I always thought it was just a line when people told me that they never stopped thinking about life changing events such as this. Now I know better. You think about it getting dressed, brushing your teeth, reading a book, working and especially when you tuck her in at night. Every minute is not an exaggeration. They also say this was the easy part – that radiation is the simplest part of the process. That part is now over and I wonder what is next. From here, you wait and see.

We've given her a lifetime limit of radiation and now it is up to the miracle. Radiation has given us time to understand, respond and react to the disease, that is all. Now we find out if our reaction is the correct one. In the best of scenarios, radiation has cut the tumor in half or even completely removed it. But every doctor tells us that even if it is gone, it will come back with time. That's where the experimental chemotherapy comes in. Hopefully, this is the magic bullet and we never utter the word "relapse." With relapse comes desperation and even more uncertainty for radiation cannot help then. My new favorite reading is "Clinical Oncology," a 1400-page manual on cancer. Knowledge is our crutch.

Today the clock starts and we look to remission as the goal. Now we are on our home turf.

Elena with her first IV to show her classmates

Elena being a child
at the hospital

Always a princess

Elena the night after we found out

Elena and Gracie
playing again for
the first time

Elena on plane with her dust mask

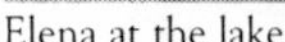

Elena at the lake

Kisses
for mom

"Queen of the Grass"
takes the wheel

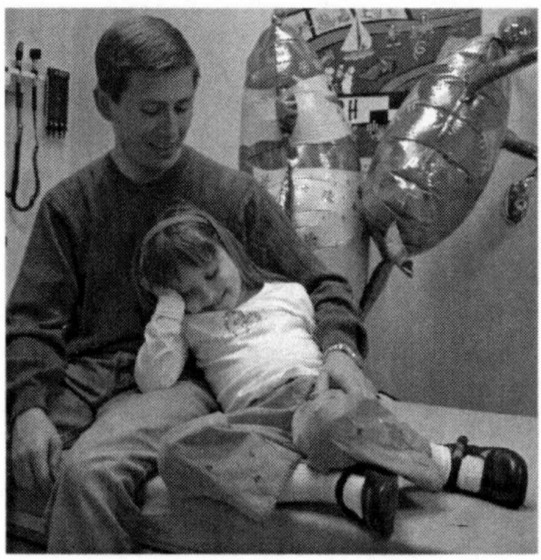

Elena before heading home for Christmas

All dressed up to see
"The Nutcracker"

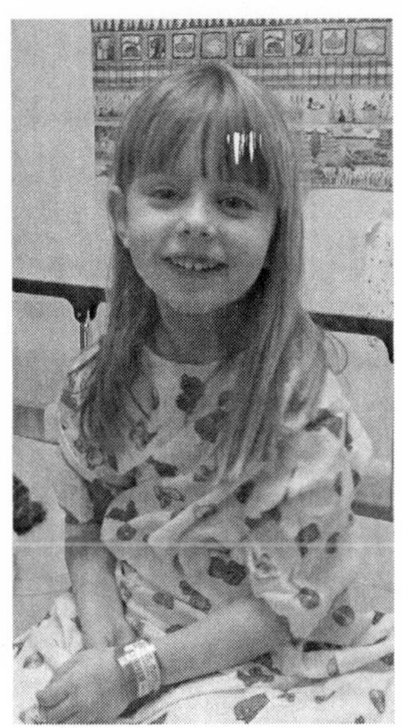
Elena on the first
day of radiation

Celebrating Christmas early
before leaving for Memphis

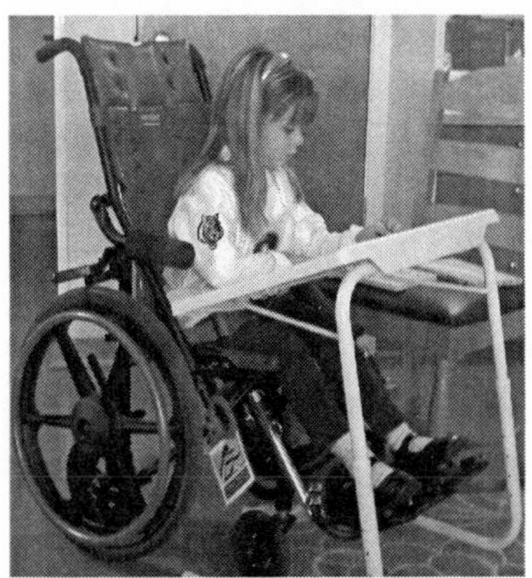
Elena remembers her cards

First day of school

Chapter 2 – The "Honeymoon"

Day 59 – January 26

Last night everyone slept well. When we awoke, it was normal. I went to work, Elena and Gracie went to school, and Brooke went for show-and-tell. Hey, someone had to help haul the 79 photos, radiation mask, and sticker chart.

After dropping Gracie off at preschool, they headed to kindergarten for the big presentation. There they were greeted by a 4x8 foot welcome sign and about 300 elementary students and teachers. It was everything that Elena needed, but never expected. We thought Mom would be the one who cried, but we were wrong. It was Elena. Thankfully kindergarten was calling.

By 2:30 p.m., it was time to pick her up. Well, maybe not quite, but I was tired of working. I quickly resumed my role as an over-protective Dad and roamed the halls outside her room. Finally, after one hour of waiting, it was time to take her home. I think I beat the rest of the students out the door as I tucked her under my arm and ran for the car.

This evening, we went looking for stars at the local observatory. There she saw the moon, stars and probably would have even seen Saturn if we had been able to stay up past 9 p.m. That's all right. My star is home tonight asleep in her own bed. Mom and I will sleep well tonight.

Day 60 – January 27

How do you go about living your life knowing what you know? More and more I wonder if modern medicine is a godsend or more of a curse. While we appreciate the advances and cures it delivers, at what point do you fear the anxiety it creates? I know this anxiety first hand, the uncertainty and fear. So what is a normal life? On any other Saturday we would have started it with a lazy wakeup at 7 a.m., breakfast with the girls and then proceeded into a litany of errands, house cleaning and home repairs. Sunday was reserved for family. Time was plentiful before – or at least so we thought – and our priorities were different. Cleaning, errands and repairs were more important than time with our children. These were our guilty pleasures and now there is no time left to waste.

Today we caved and bought two fish and an aquarium for the girls. After denying the girls pets and even claiming allergies for six years, Dad broke down and made the safe choice. Now it is our only choice considering Elena's medical restrictions, although I would certainly buy her any pet she desires if possible. By noon, the aquarium was assembled and the fish were at ease, while I fought off the urge to nap, check my phone, or work on the house. This was their time and I could wait – they had waited for me for six years. You see, every action, every decision is now weighed by severe consequences. Need to take a shower? Make it quick – you can save five minutes there. Need a haircut? You can go for another month – wait until she's asleep. Need to clean the house? That's what the night is for. Life is about them and nothing else matters.

When will it end? Will it ever end? Who knows, but I hope I have to keep making these decisions for the rest of my life. That's the curse of medicine. You can diagnose the disease, but God keeps the timeframe secret. I guess it's best this way to keep living and to see importance in every action. I see it now, but only hope that the lesson will soon be over and she will be cured. Until then, every weekend, afternoon and morning will be different.

Day 62 – January 29

Cereal kiss! That's what I get every morning before I leave for work. It's Elena and Gracie's way of sending me off and I can still feel the Lucky Charms residue on my cheek. First I get a normal kiss and a hug as they lull me into a false sense of security. Then, just as I'm about to leave, they run from the table and ask for one more kiss and hug. That's when I get the milk laden kiss as they run back to the table chanting, "Cereal Kiss! Cereal Kiss!" before I can catch them. They think I'm fooled, but the truth is I can't wait. Okay, maybe the first couple of times they tricked me, but it didn't take long to catch on.

It's these moments that a parent enjoys most about having kids – not even the trips to Disney World (although this is also fun), the first day of school or even birth is quite as exciting as the little daily moments. From age 4 – 8 is the sweet spot. This is the time that I feel is the most rewarding as a parent when you watch their creativity and personalities grow. Of course, I also thought 2 – 3 and 0 – 2 were the sweet spots. Maybe it just keeps getting better.

I keep reminding myself of this as I savor every day with a new perspective. Reminders such as "wash your hands – use soap" and "wash your hands – use water" no longer frustrate me quite as much. A little, but not as much as before. Who thinks that as a parent they have to tell their children to "stop pinching the banana," "don't lick the butter," and "don't brush your sister's butt with the toothbrush?" As if using a hairbrush would be any better. And to think I used all of these phrases today alone. I guess that's what being a Dad is all about.

Being a Dad is about more than the good and the bad, it's also about taking the time to treasure what you have and finding the humor in everyday life. Without it, you'll never make memories. It's true, I don't think I'll soon forget the image of Gracie licking the butter out of the jar.

Day 63 – January 30

Today we tried to go organic. With a gift card in hand, we headed off to the local organic grocery store. Little did we know that it was more than shopping, it was an adventure.

Keith nearly choked with the asparagus at $7 a pound, and it took all his might to bow to a pleading Elena for a bundle of the greens. Secretly I am sure Keith was trying to figure a way to slip a few stalks out of the bundle to save a buck. And after making a few cracks about how sandals and body jewelry were the uniforms of choice, Keith finally let us proceed. Then we desperately went through a day in the life of Elena figuring what exactly she ate and how to make her diet organic.

We weren't unhealthy eaters before; on the contrary, fruits and vegetables were staples in our menu, but there, in the aisle, I had a sinking feeling as I imagined all of the junk that we'd put in our bodies. Yet, we had an even bigger sinking feeling when we realized our grocery bill would double. For the past two years, we had followed a strict budget in our lives so that we could afford to live in the good school district and remodel our house. Every purchase was documented on the fridge door and if we went over budget one month, we bought less the next. We had decided that sacrifices needed to be made and priorities set. In November, those priorities changed and so tonight, we realized our new sacrifice.

Shell shocked, we approached the front to the checkout; I patted Keith on the arm and released him from the obligation of checking out. I don't know if that was for his benefit or hers, knowing that if he saw the total, he would have told the cashier that "surely they include the organic cow at that price" or given the cashier lint and told her it was his organic money. When I came to the car, Keith didn't ask the price and I didn't offer. We both realize that if it gives us an extra month, I will cook that $7 asparagus with $6 butter and not complain one bit (though don't expect the organic jokes to stop).

Day 64 – January 31

How do you measure time? When Elena asks how long she'll have to go to the doctors or have her blood taken, I reply "a while." Is "a while" a couple of months or will it be for the rest of her life? And what if a couple of months are the rest of her life? "A while" doesn't mean the same thing it did yesterday and I hope that one day "a while" will mean a lifetime.

As I walk through a day, I hear comments such as, "I wish my children were older," "I wish it was summer," or "I wish this day would end." These off-hand comments are how we relate to each other and how we grapple with time. But to me, I want it to just be today. As a matter of fact, I'd like it to be yesterday. Time has a way of sneaking up on you even when you don't want it to. I only wish it would also slow down.

A trip to the grocery store isn't the same. I not only shop for price (or organically grown), but I've also started to shop based on expiration dates. These dates have new meaning when you think that the food you're buying may last longer than your daughter. There's another reason to like organic foods; no preservatives, so they expire in a week.

I think that like all parents faced with this disease, you start to look for ways to impact the clock, even if it results in only one more minute. We're no different. I guess you can call this stage four of the journey. First comes denial, then comes anger, next comes depression and stage four is action. Today I finally received a delivery containing the 3200-page volume on clinical oncology that I've been anxiously awaiting. While at the hospital, I made it through the first 500 pages and now I can't wait to read the rest. Nothing like a personal experience to advance the learning curve.

At the same time, Brooke and I are contemplating the philanthropic side of this disease like so many parents before us. But rather than create a memorial we don't want or throwing money at the problem, we feel that awareness of the disease and creative thinking are the keys. I know that with Elena's interests and the fantastic support we've received, this will be possible. We just don't know where to start. I guess this is the honest answer of someone who never desired to be in this role. Either way, I know that this is about more than just Elena.

For now, the clock keeps going as we struggle to respond. I know the answers will come soon, but for now, we wait and fight the urge to react. This is Elena's time. Her days comprise school, tickle-time and lots of bedtime reading. (Tonight, the bedtime reading lasted an hour. It's certainly helping her reading skills. Brooke and I can no longer mouth out the letters to "needle," "blood," or "hospital" without her knowing. I guess fear helps the learning curve too.)

How long until the cure? I don't know, but I hope it's less than "a while."

Day 65 – February 1

Tomorrow is Groundhog Day. Trust me, I know. Apparently so does everyone else in Elena's kindergarten class. There Groundhog Day is a BIG deal. There were Groundhog Day puppets, Groundhog Day songs, Groundhog Day mazes, and plenty more. It was a regular Groundhog Day-palooza. And Elena loved it. For an hour after we picked her up, all we heard about was the shadow and the burrow and how funny it was that a groundhog was named Phil. And so the puppet went with us for the ride to the hospital as we sang the Groundhog Day carols. (I'll give you a hint; think "You Ain't Nothing but a Hound Dog" and insert the word "groundhog.")

Groundhog puppets are great at diverting attention in a hospital waiting room as well. Today Elena met the new hospital staff that will be helping us through the next phase. At first both Brooke and I were hesitant about returning home to the hospital that was the site of Elena's original diagnosis. After all, it was where we found out that a migraine was more than just a migraine and that a beautiful sunny day could be so miserable. Hopefully, now it can also be a place of hope as well. After meeting her doctors and the support staff, I have no doubt that she will be in good hands. And with them being ranked as one of the best in the nation for oncology, we find ourselves in the enviable position of having the best in both cities. At least this is of some comfort when dealing with a little known cancer diagnosis.

Day 66 – February 2

Well Keith and I have decided that Elena's teacher needs to expand her lessons on Groundhog Day to explain to the children that a groundhog will not see a shadow until the sun actually rises. No sun—no chance of a shadow. Well maybe we could have just instructed Elena to call her teacher at 4:26 this morning to ask if SHE had seen the groundhog yet. I know we certainly didn't see our shadow as we wiped the sleep from our eyes to see Elena waiting anxiously for this glorious event.

Today was the day of bridal dress shopping and Elena's aunt was more than willing to oblige. It's actually her wedding, but considering the circumstance, it was all Elena's day. For six years we drove past the local wedding dress store on the way to daycare and every time Elena would proudly announce which one she would wear when she got married. So it was only fitting that when Keith asked her what she always wanted to do after being released from the hospital, she responded with, "I want to buy a wedding dress." From the beginning we knew that this was going to be a tough day for Keith and me, but it was what Elena wanted. Luckily, with her aunt's wedding, we also had the occasion.

Thankfully we found a wonderful wedding dress shop that was nice and quiet - the perfect place for two kids strung out on sugar. We started off by having the girls choose the dresses they wanted to try on. And the only ones left were either too large or lime green. After finding the best of the best, we knew it was impossible to have the flower girls wear the same dress. These girls are so very different and not one dress fits all the personalities. Elena chose this pink, sparkly, ostentatious number that said, "I have arrived!" Gracie, for her part, chose a white number with pink flowers and tulle draped all around that says, "I am demure and dainty and belong on top of a wedding cake."

They twirled and pranced around, helping their aunt try on her own dress. Gracie helped by entertaining the boys in between the dresses. Bounding in and out of the curtain, she would announce the color and type of each dress, promptly falling back to the floor as her feet got caught in the lace and satin. We couldn't stop laughing at this little girl in a beautiful fancy dress falling all over herself every time saying, "I'm OK!" Elena was in charge of announcing the entrance of her aunt and giving us an update of the time remaining until the next dress appearance. She was our coordinator. Grandpa, on the other hand, was in charge of Keith. Luckily, he was there to teach Keith how to behave while a woman tries on clothes. Saying, "that dress looks like a pinwheel," "you could wear that to a disco party" and "that's my third favorite dress," are not the ways to a woman's heart – especially one who is about to be married in the dress of her dreams.

While Keith was unable to muster enough tact or patience for wedding dress shopping, every dress his girls tried on was "perfect," "beautiful" or "that is the princess dress." And when it was all over, I noticed that price was no object where his girls were concerned.

Day 68 – February 4

What do you do between the big moments in life? Is life made up of television shows, small talk and business? Or is it instead made up of charity, accomplishment and leadership in service? Do we ask our children, "what do you want to be when you grow up" or should we ask them, "what do you want to accomplish when you grow up?" And what is the total value of all the time we spend on diversions and distractions rather than the true purpose of living? Can one person change the world? Can one person cure cancer?

Too often the answer was no, but with Elena I've come to see the world differently. When this began, we were nothing but spectators, content to watch the world affect us. Cancer wasn't new to our family – quite the opposite, but you never understood it, let alone participate in the cure. Instead, you prayed for miracles and waited. And while prayer has its place, too often we ignored the reality that miracles also occur in people as well. After all, cancer was the doctor's job and we were just a family of cleaners. What did we know about cures, foundations and tumors? We were accidental victims and life now affects us in ways we could never imagine. After having spent the past 68 days in bewilderment, we start to see our responsibility in the destruction of this deadly disease. And just like Elena isn't, we too are not powerless, insignificant or immune to this challenge.

Last night I spent the evening paging through clinical trials and working through another 200 or so pages of my clinical oncology manual. Some things I understand, others I do not. Some parts seem logical, but others seem flawed. I am an uneducated mind in a sea of unknowns. I do not profess to understand or even be able to help remedy what so many, much higher educated people continue to puzzle over. In a way, I guess awareness is part of the solution. The more we are aware of characteristics of this disease, the more we will begin to understand our roles. I trust that time will be on our side.

Today we went to church. There, Mom and Gracie proceeded to church while Elena and I stayed behind to attend Sunday school. Church has never been my strong suit – I'd much rather find meaning in daily events than in sermons; and I could use a bit of Sunday school as well. First came the kindergarten "joys and concerns" where we learned that six of the ten children were experiencing loose teeth – not sure whether this was a joy or a concern. Then they prayed and sang. Next was a game to keep the interests of 10 six-year-old boys and girls. Then, before we knew it, school was over as we returned to the community hall.

There the chorus was rehearsing "Seasons of Love" from "Rent." Elena listened while I squirmed. Those of you that have seen "Rent" know why. Even after sleeping through half of the Broadway show two years ago on a date to impress Brooke, I caught enough to know the true meaning of the song (it helped that they repeated the song about 50 times in the show). Elena had no such context. To her, it was a pretty song that she continued to hum throughout the rest of the day. "Five hundred, twenty five thousand, six hundred minutes – how do you measure, measure a year?" There's meaning to everything now. Ignore the distractions.

Day 71 – February 7

It was time to go back to Memphis for a checkup. This is the next stage of the disease. Every MRI from here on out brings the hope of remission. Today was not one of those days. Not to say it was negative, but it wasn't positive either. It was what was "expected." The tumor was reduced about fifty percent by the combination of radiation and chemotherapy. And while this is a positive direction, it is tempered by the reality that radiation is over and chemotherapy is our only option to keep the tumor at bay.Now it is a battle to keep the tumor static and avoid a relapse. This is the new standard. It is also important to note they didn't see any presence of the tumor anywhere else in the brain.

In analyzing the tumor, the doctor also notes the presence of "specs of blood." And while this, by itself does not mean much, it does direct our relapse protocol options. With a potential of bleeding, our recommended protocol list is reduced from sixteen to two. Our knowledge of these protocols is limited, but we feel confident in the medical expertise behind these recommendations. I guess more research is in order. I know what Keith and I will be doing for the next week.

Elena and I decided to do our own preliminary research tonight as we loaded the MRI into my computer so we could view the "head disk," as Elena called it. This was an unexpected release as we ended up lying on the bed in fits of laughter. Elena was laughing because she could see her entire eyeball in the scans. I was laughing because it was ridiculous that I even began to think I could find the "bump" in those scans, though Elena kept prodding me to show her the bump.

After playing doctor, Elena decided that since we were ordering in pizza for the night, she was going to serve me. She laid out hand towels for the placemats, pulled up the chairs, and gave me a menu. She served me the pizza and asked me to wipe my mouth because " this is a polite restaurant." Apparently, she isn't a busboy though, because I ended up with dish duty. Thank goodness it was all paper and plastic.

On the holistic diet side, Keith and Gracie are graciously doing their part at home. With Elena in Memphis, it's time to rid the pantry of the junk food. From what I hear, it has been dinners of chips, pizza and fruit loops. Sounds like Keith has been doing a bit of gourmet cooking. It doesn't look like the holistic vitamins are working well either. Just as Elena is subjected to a holistic diet, so too will be the rest of the family. As part of that, we now take a host of vitamins. Apparently, the fish oil pills that we now take don't work as well as the other vitamins. After taking fish oil pills yesterday morning, I received a call from Keith asking if I smelled like rotten fish. Although I didn't, I guess Keith did smell like mackerel and Gracie didn't hold back in mentioning it to everyone. By the end of the night, after multiple showers and changing of clothes had no effect, he has resolved to "sleeping with the fish." Holistic in, fish pills out. I hope it gets better by the time we return home tomorrow. Otherwise, he'll be sleeping on the couch.

Day 74 – February 10

Today was our pre-Disney day and the girls couldn't be more excited. Brooke and I, on the other hand, were preoccupied with the task of cleaning the house and packing for every weather event and every emergency that could arrive. After six bags, we finally gave up and figured we'd buy the rest if we still needed it. Elena and Gracie, for their part, were anxiously awaiting the opportunity to play Disney tour guide to their "newbie" cousins. After all, they had experience and knew all the right rides. They even went so far as to set a division of labor where Elena would take the "babies" (her younger two cousins) and Gracie would take the oldest. Elena claimed that since she was a babysitter and planned on being a teacher, she was the right one for the task. Gracie was more than willing to oblige, and never really wanted to deal with younger children in the first place.

Elena has always had a passion for babies. Dinners at the hospital always went smoother when Elena could watch a baby at another table while we ate. Even when she could barely swallow and couldn't feed herself, I would take great pains to position her chair so she could be in view of a nearby baby. Then I'd watch her strain to make funny faces in an attempt to connect. Gracie, on the other hand, wants nothing to do with any child younger than she is at the old adult age of four and professes that when she grows up she wants "police kids, not babies." (You see, she wants to be a police girl when she grows up and I guess if you are going to have children, they must be "police kids.") Furthermore, she wants kids so that she doesn't have to watch them and feed them. Somehow, she believes that you can have kids born at the age of five and they will feed, dress and entertain themselves from day one. Gracie is our no-hassle girl, while Elena is our nurturer. Teacher versus police girl – I guess their dream jobs tell all. Maybe I can convince one of them to go into oncology over the next fifteen years.

At day's end, we decided to cap off our household activities with a bit of bowling with Elena and Gracie's neighbor friends. So, after being informed that the bowling alley was empty around 6:15 p.m. that night, we promptly showed up at 6:00 p.m. I guess their version of empty and mine were slightly different as we fought the onslaught of about 300 tournament bowlers and put our name on a waiting list for a bumper lane. Thirty minutes later and with a pink and orange ball in hand, the fun had finally begun. Little did I know how much Brooke and I would also need the bumper lane. Let's just say we're not taking up this sport any time soon. All that mattered, though, was that Elena and Gracie enjoyed it and we got to think about something other than cancer for an hour or two. And after being soundly beat by Brooke two games in a row, I decided that we were playing just for fun. She did not agree. Oh well. But the loudest cheers came for Elena, Gracie and their friend who celebrated 1 pin being knocked down with the same enthusiasm as they would a strike. And while it took 10 minutes for the ball to make its way down the lane, we knew that this was the reason we played. It was a good day. It's nice to be home – time to leave again.

Day 76 – February 12

This journal has become therapy for us. It never started that way. Seventy-three days ago, they told us that we had three months and six weeks from diagnosis. 135 days to be exact. And that was the original title. It was never meant for publication, discussion or anyone but Gracie. This was to be her journal. A way of recording the life with Elena that she might never remember. It was my gift to her. It was 135 days with her sister. Since then, it has become so much more.

For the first two weeks, no one knew about the journal. I would often write it in the early dawn when everyone else was asleep. Sleep was a convenience that I haven't had since Thanksgiving and I still don't miss it. After all, what good is sleep when all you need is more time? And so the journal continued. A collection of thoughts, dreams, experiences and wishes. I felt that it should contain our struggles, Elena's unique personality, and even some of the humorous aspects of life. It was my gift to Gracie and Elena's gift to us.

By week three, the depression kicked in as we ran through the barrage of tests and Elena started down the road of paralysis. Every day brought endless conversations with family and friends. How was she doing? What are they testing for? What does this disease do? And while the concern was comforting, every call brought another chance to relive our worst nightmare over again, further removing any chance at optimism. By publishing the journal, we could now inform and maintain some optimism as we marveled at Elena's courage. We could see the strength in her determination and the coldness of reality; all in front of our eyes. And by doing so, maybe, just maybe see an ounce of humanity in the struggle of our daughter.

Next week, Brooke wants me to stop – avoid the thoughts; avoid the constant preoccupation and anxiety. Still, it won't matter. This is a gift to Gracie first and foremost. Secondly, I still can't sleep.

So the journal will move on – truthfully and daily composing our thoughts as we live them. I welcome the day that I can label it "29,200 Days."

To Gracie: Your sister is a wonderful, intelligent, caring sister. She cares about you more than you can imagine and I know this by the constant stream of giggles that erupt from your joined bedrooms when you are supposed to be sleeping. She is and will always be your best friend and sometimes even an accomplice to your plans. And while you will always be different with your spontaneity and infectious squinting grin and Elena with her insurmountable will and application of detail, you will never find a better compliment than each other. You both represent everything that we love in our marriage, in life and in each other. You are our family and our reasons for everything we do in life. This is a journal about life and about you. Treasure the memories and embrace the future.

Every day is a gift.

Day 77 – February 13

The grandmas were playing for keeps today. That's the problem with combined family get togethers. That's why I never wanted them, despite the constant Thanksgiving and Christmas three party rituals. Inevitably, the result is a "Fight to the Finish Grandmother Contest" where the gifts fly as hard as punches. From the left comes gummy candy, from the right come books. Soon, the competition turns ugly with stuffed animals, firework inspired desserts and jewelry. And before we know it, the girls are spoiled beyond our best corrective efforts and there's no way to fit it all in a suitcase. Today was no different. Luckily, Brooke and I brought a fourth suitcase with this in mind. Hopefully, it won't get any worse. Though I know it will with Valentine's Day around the corner. Already I can see the love message hearts and the dolls arriving on the doorstep. And just when we're trying so hard to go organic and get antioxidants in her.

Beyond that, today was a soaker. At first we started the day with a twenty percent chance of rain. By 10 a.m. it had become a forty percent chance of rain. After the first downpour, the weatherman increased the chances to sixty percent. After the third thunderstorm rolled in and our ponchos became a permanent part of our attire, the weatherman went to eighty percent. I think he could have at least brought it to one-hundred percent by then. Either way, we spent the day in "It's a Small World," (I know you're singing the song now – good luck getting it out of your mind) and the "Haunted Mansion." "Thunder Mountain" would have to wait for another day when it was dry. By 4:00 p.m., the crew was ready for drier conditions as we headed to the luau at the Polynesian Resort. There we were greeted by leis and much needed alcohol and food – in that order. And for the first time, we sat together as a group of 15 and talked, laughed and ate. It was a lovely ending to the day and a wonderful way for Elena to enjoy her loving family. Then as the sun dropped and the temperature cooled, Elena asked to sit on my lap to watch the fire dancer show. Of course I could not resist as I watched her eyes twinkle in the light of the show. To be honest, I have no idea what happened during the luau; I spent the next hour admiring and holding her. It was the longest she had sat with me since she was just months old without squirming or running to Mom and I was not about to give her up. When it ended and it was time to go, I picked her up, laid her head upon my shoulder and continued to the ferry that would take us home – never mind that my arms had fallen asleep thirty minutes ago. And when we returned, my arms ached, but so did my heart. For despair forces you to live in the present while your mind races to the future. Regardless, tonight I was the luckiest father around.

Day 78 – February 14

Elena's never been what you would call "outgoing." She's never volunteered for anything, let alone a challenge. She won't sing aloud in the car or the bathroom, she won't talk to strangers, and she won't try new food. For her entire six years, her comfort margin has been restricted to what she knows and what we force her to do. Then, and only then, will she admit that it was good idea in the first place.

After the experiences over the past four months, we never expected anything different from her. She'd still resist and we'd continue to prod. And we were right. What we didn't expect, however, was how extreme it would become. Since her diagnosis, everything has become a challenge as she fights to remain in her comfort zone. And unlike before, this is now accompanied with tears, screams and a fear that we have never seen before. Today we discovered how deep this fear runs as we challenged her to a waterslide and to riding the Thunder Mountain ride – two things that she desperately loved the last time we came to Disney a year ago. And since that time, she has planned endlessly for her next opportunity at riding. But now, with her renewed fear, this is nearly impossible. For nearly an hour, Brooke and I attempted to convince, bribe and cajole Elena into going down the waterslide with her cousins. Surely, after both of them mastered the waterslide, Elena would make her way up the steps. After all, Gracie was always our ace-in-the-hole. As soon as Gracie did it, Elena would do it. No such luck. And after another thirty minutes of pressure, I pulled her close and began the climb. After ten steps, she pleaded for me to stop; ten more steps and she cried that she had to go to the bathroom; ten more steps and she complained that her right foot hurt; after the final ten steps, she told me that she was afraid of heights. I was not going to get the Father of the Year award this year this way. Finally, I did what any caring father would have done in her position – I pushed her down the slide and watched her turn the first corner screaming. Then I jumped in behind her and followed. I think they call that "forced fun." And although I knew that she did not want to go, I knew that she needed to try. After four months of needles, surgeries and paralysis, her confidence was tattered and the only way to fix it was with therapy or by force. I chose the easy route and it worked. No sooner had she reached the pool than she was on her way to the top again, telling everyone she met along the way how brave she was to try the waterslide. No confidence problem this time – she beat me to the top and even the fear of heights seemed to be cured. Forced fun parenthood is severely under appreciated. Tomorrow we will work on the other rides. Enough for today.

Day 81 – February 18

Today we board a plane for home. Bound for the land of the frozen tundra with eight inches on the ground and a covering of ice. What joy this brings to our hearts. But besides the weather, home brings no comfort. This entire vacation has been a struggle against time. Every ride brings a hope that it will never end. Every parade brings the chance that the floats will continue to appear. Every fireworks display comes with the wish that the lights will continue to float against the dark sky. But just as the rides, the parades and the fireworks come to an end, so must this vacation. But for us, these endings are more than the return to life – they are also one more step in a direction that we do not wish to travel. And as the days click by, our lives become more complicated and our hugs for Elena become more uncertain. I don't want this vacation to end because of the weather or the experiences, but because I don't want to lose this "honeymoon" as the doctors refer to it. This is the time when she can be a six-year-old again without the hassles of blood tests, MRIs and complex discussions with doctors where we avoid the "unmentionable words" in her presence. In truth, I don't think we could have done any more over these past seven days and I doubt my knees and back could handle much more walking, but my mind could have traveled much further had time allowed. But this is the reality of time; it never waits and it never repeats.

Today Elena looked at me and asked if she could get married one day in Disney World. This caused me to stop, look up and wonder to myself. My response was, "of course." I hope this is not a lie and the best answer I could ever give. Let time be on our side for a change and let me pay for that wedding. You are all invited.

Day 82 – February 19

Sunflowers are Elena's new passion. Van Gogh's "Sunflowers" to be exact. "Dogs Playing Pool" apparently just didn't have the same appeal as Van Gogh. And when we traveled to France this past Saturday (OK, France, Epcot), Elena immediately knew what she liked. There she saw Van Gogh in all of his glory – on postcards, on shoulder bags, on cutting boards, on switch plates and on prints. She especially loved the "Starry Night" switch plate, but she decided to settle on the "Sunflowers" print – especially when I wouldn't shell out the $18 for the switch plate. Of course, to tell you the truth, I wasn't willing to spend the $15 on the 8x11 print either. So she asked again and I said no. She asked again and I still said no. But when she asked a third time and gave me a hug, I relented and said yes. I guess the third time is the trick and she knows it. So she tucked it under her arm and made her way to the cashier before I could change my mind; never mind that she needed MY money. There we met with a French cashier who responded with "Bon jour, merci beaucoup." Apparently this means, "I can't believe you're about to buy this garbage." And yes, if you are wondering, Brooke helped me spell "beaucoup"; far beyond my abilities. Elena then took the opportunity to share with the cashier that her "Grandpa-Grandpa had the real picture at his house" and that this was just a copy. I think we got the cashier's attention at that point, regardless of the language gap. Never mind that the picture that hangs on my Grandfather's wall is also a painted copy of the real thing painted by my great aunt; to Elena, this was the original.

Tomorrow the print goes to school for Show and Tell, and from what I hear she needs not just one item but two things to share, for this is the responsibility of a "Star-of-the-Week." Brooke and I don't know if this is exactly true, but to be honest, I don't think either of us mind and neither will her kindergarten class. She can share the joy and beauty of Van Gogh with the class as she tells them how her Grandpa-Grandpa owns the real thing. Yes, there really is a $32 million dollar painting located in Cincinnati. We, on the other hand, will be plenty satisfied with the $32 million dollar smile it brings to Elena's face. Thank you Van Gogh.

Day 83 – February 20

A year ago I had never heard of the Caldecott Medal. Today, I at least know that it is an award for literature. Beyond that I still don't know what it signifies. But to Elena, any book that has won the Caldecott Medal must be special. These are the books we read first before bed. These books even have their own special bookshelf, just so they don't mingle with the "common" books.

Elena loves her books and it shows. In her room you will find three shelves of books and another two shelves in Gracie's room where wall space is more plentiful. Gracie, on the other hand, loves stuffed animals. She stores these lovingly all over the floor. Elena would never dream of doing this with her books. Each book is placed on the shelf, binding out, letters facing the same way with a filing system that rivals anything Dewey ever imagined.

To read a book with Elena is a methodical journey. First, you must do away with the book jacket if it has one. After all, in order to experience the majesty that is bedtime reading you must not only view the pages, but feel the cover as well. But be careful to place the jacket back on the shelf – you will need to recover it as soon as you finish the book. Next, always remember to mention the author's name, present the cover to the audience and then prompt them to tell you what they think the book is about. Never mind that the audience may only be Mom, Gracie and me. Third, open the book to the first page and review the copyright and the illustrator if different than the author. Now, we must pause at the copyright and discuss Elena's age at the point of original publication. Finally, you are now ready to read, but make sure to discuss the quality of the illustrations and how the author conveys movement with the pictures. Far away pictures that become close-ups indicate that the subject is traveling. Tonight we learned that a very talented illustrator named Donald Cruise does an excellent job drawing pictures to convey movement about transportation. (I guess she learned this at school.) It is also important to understand the illustrator's use of color. Bright colors convey happy feelings, while dark colors convey sadness. Once you have made your way through the book, close the book, set it on your lap and ask the audience to "discuss the book" with you. Then and only then have you truly enjoyed your bedtime reading. Now you know why it also takes us an hour or more to read three children's books every night.

When it comes to Elena's choice in books, there are those that have earned medals and those that are non-fiction. And she prefers non-fiction over fiction any day. I guess she figures that if she's going to spend the time, she might as well learn something important. Why learn about fairies when you can learn how to predict the weather?

Every day we learn from Elena. To tell you the truth, I've never looked at a copyright before or examined the colors of illustrations. While I am the parent, she is still the teacher. So when 7:00 p.m. comes around, it is time for us to sit in a circle Indian-style and listen. This we do well. When you ask her what she wants to be when she grows up, she tells you she wants to be a mom and then a teacher. And with her prodding, even Gracie now wants to be a teacher instead of a "police girl." As a mom and a teacher, I know that Elena will be excellent at both. Until then, I'm ready to be her student for an hour or two every night. Whether I know it or not, I learn something each and every day.

Day 85 – February 22

It seems that lately all of our serious conversations occur in the car. Yesterday was no different. At 2:00 p.m., I picked her up from school for a weekly check-up appointment at the hospital. Immediately, she knew what this meant; a blood test and she did not like it one bit. This time distractions fell short; she knew my game and wasn't about to be fooled. I talked about her day; she talked about needles. I talked about having popcorn after dinner and a movie; she talked about blue gloves. I talked about kittens; she pleaded to go home instead. And although I'd love to take her home, I knew that without blood test results we'd never be able to stay at home. Finally, I gave in and tried to reason with her. I explained that blood tests allowed her to go to school, come home to Cincinnati and be with her friends. I explained that by doing the tests we would know if the tumor was getting better. Besides that, she didn't want to go back to the way she was, would she? Now she can walk, talk and eat just like normal and these blood tests were part of the reason that she was getting better.

"But I am better, Dad," she responded. Yes, she was better, but just as it took a long time for the tumor to grow, it would also take a long time for it to shrink. This she did not understand. After all, she could walk, talk and eat, so why did she have to keep going to the doctor and taking the medicine? "Am I ever going to get better?" she asked. "Will the bump grow back and make me use the wheel chair again? I'm eating good food and taking the medicine, so it goes away." I paused. She waited. She asked again. "No, every day it will get better, but it will take a lot of time and a lot of trips to the doctor." I promised myself I was telling the truth. These trips, these tests, the medicine and her patience would ultimately win out over this disease. The rest of the trip was silent. No distractions could change her mind this time.

Today our topic was slightly more lighthearted. Today was President's Day. And as she entered the car, she proudly informed me it was George Washington's birthday. I pointed out it was also Grandpa's birthday as well, and offered my phone for her to call him. Was Grandpa as old as George Washington, she asked. No, not quite. After all, George Washington wasn't alive. With this, we made the call. But instead of wishing Grandpa a happy birthday, she instead told him he was "really old and thank you for being alive." Not quite the birthday greeting I imagined, but who was I to judge? I guess this is where it's the thought that counts.

Tomorrow I hope our conversation is more about kittens than our uncertain future. Regardless, it's during these times with Elena that I learn the most. She is both smart and painfully aware of her circumstances. I often wonder if she's on the other side avoiding the discussion as much as I am. Maybe she thinks I just haven't figured it out yet. She's much smarter than we can ever know.

Day 86 – February 23

Every step and every word with Elena now takes on new meaning. On Monday it was a slurred word. Tuesday brought a complaint from her about not being able to hear. On Wednesday, Brooke and I decided it was worth a visit to Children's Hospital to see if it was anything serious or if we were just overreacting. We were overreacting. But with her symptoms being as subtle as they were in the beginning and quickly progressing to a full blown paralysis in a number of days, we felt it best to discuss it with a doctor. I love being wrong. Hopefully we can overreact for the next 80 years.

With tonight came another attempt to overreact as we walked around the mall with Mom. Elena was complaining of being tired and the first thing we noticed was her right foot starting to turn to the outside. Then she caught her foot on the escalator and fell to her knees. For Gracie this would have been normal. For Elena, this was another reason for concern. I carried her the rest of the way. By the time we reached home, the foot had returned to normal and she climbed the steps to get ready for bed. Could I be wrong again?

The doctor says that glioma symptoms frequently reappear in the reverse order of how they returned after radiation. That would mean that the first to go would be the gag reflex, then the right leg and right hand, then the ability to speak and eat. Tonight she sits on the couch with a bag of popcorn – gag reflex fully intact.

Somehow I don't think this will ever change. She will continue to surprise us and we will continue to analyze her every move. I love being wrong, especially now. 79 ½ years to go…

Day 88 – February 25

For once Elena wasn't afraid - at least when it came to the water slides. Her fear of heights was another thing, and considering that all the water slides involved at least one set of staircases, this was enough ground to cover for one evening.

Today we went to the local water park as a gift from a friend of ours. Elena had always wanted to ride a water slide and she couldn't have asked for a better place to give it a try. With over 14 water slides, four pools and plenty of soaking guns, buckets and waterfalls, it was a kid's paradise. From the moment we entered the 120,000 square feet of chlorine heaven, Elena had her eyes on the three-story tube slide – a blistering 2-man ride down a yellow tube that took you through hidden curves until you landed in a white water rapid pool to soak any part of your body that you somehow kept dry all the way down. The only problem was that it required a trip up three flights of stairs to the top. Her solution: let Dad carry her as well as the double tube. No problem – I needed the exercise after a month of eating hospital food.

Thirty minutes later, after dragging myself up the last remaining flight of steps, careful to stay exactly in the middle of the steps to avoid any unnecessary glances over the edge, we boarded a tube for our 30-second journey to the bottom. She laughed. She giggled. She screamed. Then at the end, Dad labored up the steps again. And that was pretty much how it went for the next four hours. Elena had fun; Dad got exercise. What a small price I paid for a smile.

Finally after receiving the universal signal from my back muscles that we were having WAY too much fun, we made our way to the kiddie water slides. There Brooke and I soaked at the bottom of the slide while Elena and Gracie got an opportunity to climb five steps to get to the top of a 10-second ride. Somehow I felt cheated considering the three flights that we needed for a 30-second ride. Either way, we spent the remainder of the day watching them race each other to the top and then to the bottom.

For her part, Gracie quickly realized her potential as the family clown as she took a freestyle approach to the water slide.

Backwards, upside-down, head first, upside down head first, sideways and even twirling, Gracie came down the water slide laughing. Sometimes she'd come down with style, but more often than not, she came down in pure Gracie fashion with a mouthful of water and an, "I'm all right," yell. And while her technique frequently attracted the scorn of nearby lifeguards, she was looking for someone else's attention instead – Elena's. This she got and more as Elena would not only giggle at her antics, but often challenge her to do it again. Had we stayed for another hour, I'm sure we would have seen Gracie try a handstand on the slide; although I doubt she would have been successful. After all, the only part of Gracie that's graceful is her name.

At the end of the night, my family got what they came for. A mouth full of chlorine, a sore back, green hair and a couple of smiles to go with it. We'll all sleep well tonight.

Day 89 – February 26

We've never been "pet people." Correction, I've never been a "pet person." My hunch is that Gracie isn't either. Brooke and Elena, on the other hand, have a soft spot for cuddly kittens, playful puppies and just about anything else with fur. Recently, with Elena this love has reached new heights as she started decorating her room with just about anything pet related. There are magazine cutouts of kittens on the walls, puppy pictures in her scrapbooks and every imaginable stuffed animal littering her bed. I think we'll need to get a king size bed just for her and her nightly stuffed animal slumber party.

The reality is that I'm not really as anti-pet as I am a realist. After all, why get a dog or a cat when we spend the majority of our time at work or school? And with the multitude of trips that have become the new norm, the timing just hasn't gotten any better.

So for now, Elena must be content with her monthly visits from her aunt's Chihuahua, Sally, and the magazine cutouts that litter her room. Today, another picture made it to the wall of fame. It was a picture of two kittens inside of the mailbox. And while my mind immediately questioned the relevance of two kittens in a mailbox; her heart went to mush as she clutched the picture with an "Ahhhhhhh... look at this. They are soooo cute!"

In truth, I'm not really allergic to kittens, puppies or any other animal. The girls just think I am. You see, every five years when I'm out of town, Brooke tries to convince me that having a puppy is a good idea. And knowing that my answer would be an immediate "no," she does what every other spouse on a mission does – she does it anyway and doesn't tell me when I leave for a business trip. Only upon my return do I discover her secret, there in the family room making messes on the carpet. Welcome home. And however expensive these endearing experiences are, they are often quickly over as Brooke remembers the responsibility end of the cuteness and the puppy goes back to the breeding farm. There the puppy undoubtedly finds another family and so does our money, which goes along for the ride. And my allergies continue for another five years.

For now, pictures will have to do. With our house under construction and Elena in the midst of her disease, fish are as about extravagant as we'll get for a while. And while there isn't any fish on her bedroom wall and they aren't quite as soft and cuddly, they are certainly better for the allergies. The "oohhhs and ahhhhs" will have to wait a bit longer.

Day 90 – February 27

Next time the swim instructor will know better. And maybe, just maybe when she tells Gracie to jump out into the pool into her arms, she'll take a step back first. Second thought – maybe she'll take three steps back.

Today our pursuit of physical therapy brought us back to the local pool. We enrolled Gracie and Elena in swim classes. And while we'll never be able to go every week with Elena's continuing treatment schedule, we were anxious to inspire Elena in the midst of the wintertime monotony. Gracie was just an added benefit – call it "competitive drive" for Elena. And there, on the edge of the pool, their lesson began. Looking to assess their abilities, the first lesson was jumping in the pool. In response, Elena eased her way to the edge, ever so careful to avoid slipping, tripping or actually getting wet in the process. First came the toe, then the leg in pure hokey-pokey style. The teacher moved forward. "Jump into my hands," she said. Elena sat with her legs dangling and stretched out her arms. And in what seemed like an hour, she finally leaned forward and ever so gracefully drifted into the pool.

Gracie was up next. For this, the teacher figured that if the older one took this long, then surely the younger one would need more prodding. She took a step closer. Gracie waited with her back against the wall, fooling the teacher with her patented bashful look. For anyone who doesn't know better, this comes across as shy and timid. To everyone else, this is the look of scheming and mischievous intentions. She did not know Gracie. "Come on, jump into my hands," the teacher implored. Gracie didn't need prompting and she sure wasn't going to ease into the pool. After all, in Gracie's world (we call it Graceland), this was permission. And with that, she bent forward in a sprinter's pose, pushed off the wall and took off for the pool; too late for the teacher. She tried to step back, but Gracie was already in mid-air. And when she landed, Gracie not only made it to her hands, but also to her chest, her head and the hair the teacher had tried so hard to keep dry. Oh and the form! Legs and arms up – belly down.

It was the perfect belly flop; so perfect you would have expected her to continue skipping across the water until she reached the other side. She didn't of course, as the teacher was blocking her way. Instead, they both went under with Gracie on top. Suffice it to say, I think she passed this portion of the lesson, no matter that she still can't swim.

You don't realize how much Elena has lost until you see her swimming. Before her diagnosis, she'd swim across the pool unaided. Now she can barely manage 20 feet with a kick board. Funny how one month of paralysis can do so much damage. But I guess that's why we are here. The more she practices, the more she builds muscle to help her through the rest of this battle.

Day 91 – February 28

A dad's job is to protect. This is what I would tell Elena, from her first trip down the playground slide to her first MRI. It was my motto, and if you ask Elena what a dad's job was, she can tell you without hesitating. No matter what happened, Dad would be here to save and protect you. And I believed it. I believed that my hands were quicker than lightning and my skin tougher than armor when it came to protecting my daughters. No matter what the threat, I told them that their Dad would be there to keep them safe. Little did I know what lay ahead.

And somehow through the beginnings of this disease, I thought that by possessing the powers that come with fatherhood, I would somehow be able to protect her once again. I would be able to cure cancer, or find the miracle doctor who had the solution, but just didn't know how to tell the rest of the world. That power today is now quickly fading as I come to grasp with our declining options.

Today we learned that her chemotherapy protocols may not be as positive as we might have hoped. We're not totally sure, but with a trip to Memphis in the cards for next week, this will be our single biggest issue. The implications of such a result are discouraging to say the least. The drug that we have pinned all of our hopes on may have zero to little impact on the growth of the tumor in combination with radiation; this is according to another patient on the same trial who met with their doctor last week. Simply put, we might have wasted the best opportunity to beat this tumor. Now all we can do is pray for chemotherapy, but with her radiation lifetime maximum dosage already exhausted, this is a long shot at best.

And so today a new fight begins. A fight that we must understand and prepare for, and ultimately win. And while the time and direction that we must travel will ultimately be decided by the disease alone, as a father I take little reassurance in knowing that we are doing all we can do. Elena's time for miracles is upon us as the medical community is losing options daily. But just as a dad's job is to protect, it is also to never give up. I plan on keeping the promise I made over six years ago when I held her for the first time. A dad's job is to protect.

Day 92 – March 1

Gracie and Elena are more than just sisters, they're also best friends. With only 22 months between them, they share more than clothes, toys and hobbies; they also share their lives. This was the way Brooke and I intended it from the beginning. Having both come from families where we were three or more years apart from our siblings, we felt that our children would benefit from being two years apart or less. Little did we know how right we were.

At 22 months, Elena had no idea how much her life was about to be impacted, but she did know she was now a big sister. Proudly wearing her "I'm a New Big Sister" pin at the hospital, she took to her duty as bottle feeder as she gave up her room and her toys for the new addition to the family. And although they would play with each other and spend hours on rug patrol in the family room, we soon realized how much they would come to love each other the day we heard Gracie laugh for the first time. Around six months after her birth, we found Gracie giggling in her swing while Elena danced and made funny faces in front of her. It's never been the same since. Now Gracie returns the favor daily with her staged antics and infectious smile.

Even today, Gracie is the comedian while Elena is the comforting mom. Just this morning while Gracie was upstairs in the midst of a temper tantrum over her clothing selection and Brooke and I had all but given up, Elena quietly climbed the stairs to calm her sister. Five minutes later, she came downstairs holding Gracie's hand remarking to both of us how wonderful Gracie looked this morning, while Gracie wiped away tears. Not only had she managed to calm Gracie, but she also dressed her in the exact clothes that we had failed to get her to wear 20 minutes earlier.

Friends don't have to be the same in order to get along. Sometimes it is the differences that make a friendship work. In Gracie and Elena's, case it is also what makes them perfect for each other.

Day 93 – March 2

We call them "rusty eyes." It's the moment in the morning that you wish you had gone to bed earlier the previous night. For most people this lasts until the first cup of coffee or after the morning shower. For Brooke and me, it lasts all day and into the next. And it's more than just a lack of sleep; it's a weariness and exhaustion that have become our lives. After the diagnosis we couldn't sleep. Night after night we'd try, but from 12 – 4 a.m., we'd look up at the ceiling wondering how to wake up from the nightmare. Now it's different. Now we can sleep, but don't want to. This is the new norm. Whenever we aren't working, eating or spending time with the girls, we're reading e-mails from other parents, researching the Internet for protocols or reading our stack of oncology materials. And by the time 11:00 p.m. comes around, we've only gotten started. So we continue in our desperate search for options. The doctors tell us to enjoy the honeymoon. Other parents of previous DIPG children tell us to prepare. We want both. There's always the looming question of "why her." That's where faith comes in. But instead of questioning through faith, we choose to have faith that the solution will present itself and so sleeping is not an option. The "rusty eyes" continue; night and day. This is our God.

Day 94 – March 3

Sometimes things just happen. Without reason – without consequence. Sometimes everyday doesn't have a moral and isn't neat and tidy. Yesterday was one of those days. It started with our family on opposite ends of the country. Gracie was still sick at home after recovering from a cold. I was making my way home from California from a business meeting. Mom was home with the girls, struggling to balance business and family. Elena was at school suddenly feeling tired and overcome with headaches. Everything else could wait for now.

By noon, Brooke had received a call from kindergarten that Elena was tired and missed Dad. But upon picking her up from school, she also discovered that Elena was suffering from severe headaches. And after three hours of trying to force liquids, treating with Tylenol and allowing her to sleep, the headaches only got worse. It was then that she decided to make her way to the emergency room.

One hour later, Elena's condition worsened. Her right leg started to drag again, her voice became garbled and her right hand was less than perfect when put to the test. It was not good news. And by the time I arrived, three hours late thanks to airport delays, an MRI was already in the plans. The good news was that she went through the MRI on her own; no sedation, no problems. The bad news was that the tumor had grown in the last month. We are now in what they call a "recurrence" – the end of the honeymoon.

To understand what this means, you need to understand what we expected. From the beginning, we were told to expect anywhere from three to seven months from the end of radiation. In time, this was upgraded from seven to fourteen months from diagnosis, as we met with more specialized doctors. Even at the worst, we expected the tumor to possibly come back in late April. At that point, we would have enough time to evaluate alternatives, assess results and spend time with our daughter; if you can somehow believe that three months from radiation is enough time. And if it grew, somehow, it would be small growth. We received nothing of this sort. One month from the conclusion of radiation was not nearly enough. Worse yet, the tumor didn't seem to be growing by small amounts or even affected by the chemotherapy. Nothing can convey our feelings and I won't even try.

Where do we go from here? The most promising protocols need weeks to formulate and I doubt we have even two weeks to work with. The fact is we didn't work fast enough. Our options are limited and our understanding of this disease is minimal. We may have just missed our best chance to beat this cancer.

There is so much more work to do, both for us and for Elena. We need more time. The chance for miracles is today and the cure starts now. Tomorrow may be too late. I love you Elena.

Day 95 – March 4

After a careful review of the MRI, discussion and much deliberation, we finally had a verdict: we just don't know.

Welcome to the "grey area." The experts cannot tell whether the growth in the area is swelling from radiation (you can have effects of radiation for up to six months after treatment has ended) or progression. Our team determined the increase was small enough to call it stable. Elena also woke up with a fever and a headache on Monday, so perhaps all the symptoms were caused by getting sick, rather than a symptom of the swelling. We'd love to believe that that was all. Next month we have a follow-up MRI, so we will be watching that very carefully. We also got a go-ahead on our nutritional plan for Elena. As long as it is natural, we can give it to Elena.

At the hospital we decided to eat lunch before heading back home. While eating, I think Elena discovered the diagnosis for her headache. "Mom, I had three weeks without a headache and one week with a headache." Brilliant! I have an email out to our doctor to find out if I need to enroll her in medical school. For three weeks, she was taking her chemotherapy meds. This week she had an "off week" where she didn't take meds. Perhaps these are the withdrawal symptoms! Every day Elena amazes me with her intelligence and ability to simplify the most complicated situations. And while she's still working on her M.D., she practices doing the nurses' job every chance she gets.

Today, while receiving her monthly port flush through an IV tube, she calmly informed the nurse that she had missed a bubble in the syringe and she should elevate it and squirt a little bit of liquid out the top to clear it. The nurse looked at me, looked at Elena and then looked at the syringe. Elena was right and there was no doubting it. As if to assist further, Elena gestured at the syringe the nurse was holding just in case she did not clearly understand her. "Wow, she certainly is perceptive isn't she," the nurse commented as she cleared the syringe and continued. I asked her if she wants to be a doctor or nurse when she grows up. I don't think I have seen her shake her head "no" faster. Maybe we can still convince her to cure cancer before moving on to becoming a soccer player.

Day 96 – March 5

I remember now why we hated steroids. Aside from the bloating, insatiable appetite and the propensity to aid tumor growth, there is no better way to turn a sweet girl into a monster than with a 2mg tablet of dexamethasone. Overnight, she started growling, hitting and fighting with her sister all over again. Immediately we lost our daughter and invited moodiness back into our home. Frustration is accompanied by anger, which is followed by mood swings, and immediately, she becomes a teenager. Don't get me wrong, I still love her, but there's just something about the sight of your daughter sitting in the backseat of the car on the trip from Memphis hitting herself in the forehead with a plastic calculator. Why – I have no idea. Something about not being able to push the right buttons.

Today 'Roid Rage' took on a new form as it combined with a fever and sickness. At 100.1 degrees, Elena wanted nothing other than her bed and to be left alone. Who were we to argue? Just as soon as she finished her green tea and fruit smoothie, we would give her the next dose of steroids and tuck her in for the evening. Good luck. The fruit smoothie went down – no problem. But it was that green tea that got in the way. First came, "I don't like it." Next came, "I can't drink it all." Then came, "I'll have some later." Finally came, "You drink half." I did (she's right, it's horrible – but I smiled the entire time. I don't think she believed me). Little did I know that the "you first" routine would mean that I would be the only one drinking it tonight. I guess she figured that if I liked it that much I wouldn't mind another taste. I gave up. She went to bed.

Better luck next time. She's right – she needs the sleep. With all she's been through in the past four days, I can't blame her.

Day 97 – March 6

Abnormal. That's what they call Elena's tumor. Normally the thought of having an abnormal tumor would strike fear in the hearts of parents. After all, "abnormal" conjures up images of instability, deviant growth, and untreatable conditions. And while some of these may even be correct, for us, "abnormal" also means hope. You see, "normal" brain stem gliomas have a poor survival rate - no treatment protocol and plenty of despair. So being "abnormal" must certainly be the opposite of despair – right?

From the beginning, they've referred to her tumor as abnormal. Abnormal in how it takes on contrast (in MRI-speak, contrast is what they use to identify necrotic (dead) tissue and blood vessels) in the center. Abnormal in how fast it grows and in how they are unable to identify the most recent source of growth. And while abnormal also breeds uncertainty and fear, it also gives us hope that somehow this is a tumor that no one has ever seen before. Yes, we are actually hoping that this is a tumor that no one has ever seen before. Imagine that.

Maybe, just maybe, abnormal will also mean that it is curable. Surely, the 10 percent of children who survive this disease must have also had abnormal tumors. One can only hope.

Day 100 – March 9

For the last couple of days, Elena has been talking to truckers. The voices haven't been clear, but occasionally we make out a song or an inquiry about traffic coming from her Hello Kitty walkie-talkie. Now a CB radio isn't the best toy for a 6-year-old, but up until now, we always figured that she was picking up signals from a kid down the street. That was until she took the walkie-talkie with her on our trip to the Home and Garden Show. A mile down the interstate we finally connected the dots when the signal became clearer and her questions of who is this were met with names like "Tina Ray," "Big Mac" and "Diesel Duo." Little did they know that the person on the other end was using a $25 Hello Kitty radio and couldn't care less about the southbound accident at the bridge. Never the less, Elena kept on talking, asking questions and relaying traffic information as we passed the truckers heading northbound. Like a rancher herding cattle, she directed them to the right and then the left lanes, no matter that she had no clue as to which lane was closed up ahead. Traffic probably took an extra hour that night, thanks to our little girl. And by the time they discovered it, I planned on being out of range. Who knew that a Hello Kitty walkie-talkie could connect you to the world of trucking?

Day 101 – March 10

I'll never look at a hot dog the same way again. After a solid week of reading my 150-page packet about all of the foods and supplements that help brain tumor patients, I look at hot dogs and feel an overwhelming urge to gag. It is appalling to read all the things that we eat which may contribute to cancer like lunchmeat, veggies and sugar supplements. OK, almost everyone has heard the warnings on the news each night about this food and that one. Yet only after you are fighting for your child's life with only a pot and a spatula as weapons, do you start to really fear the contents of everything you put in your mouth. Eating is no longer for the taste, it is for the nutrients. Today we went out to dinner and I just couldn't stand eating the food because all I could do was picture in my mind all of the nasty preservatives and hormone infested meat. It reminded me of when I was at the height of my dieting and I could give you the calories of every food item I would put in my mouth. Each day I calculated out my meals with meticulous detail. Now, the only difference is that instead of calories it is nutrients.

Every night I spend at least an hour or two reading about nutritional strategies for Elena. Anything natural is fair game and the list of beneficial foods is endless.

It has now become a fine art of trying to stuff as much "goodies" into a meal as I can.Rice and veggies are cooked in green tea to sneak a bit more into her diet. I have become skilled in cutting shitake mushrooms into millimeter slices to hide them into her dinner. The whole mushroom hiding thing is especially hard because Gracie is horribly allergic to mushrooms. I wind up cooking two separate dishes so Gracie doesn't break out into hives. Elena caught on one day when I lunged to snatch a plate from Gracie when she sat at Elena's chair at dinner. I even make the girls leave the kitchen when I make the morning smoothie. I don't think they would even consider drinking it if they knew what I snuck into that puppy! Actually the girls love these smoothies. I guess it is a little like sausage; you don't want to know what goes into it as long as it tastes good.

Some nights I long for my convenience food, my Rice-a-Roni, my chicken nuggets, my 15-minute meals, my school lunches, my dinners out without scrutinizing the menu and my sleep! I hate having to ask the grandparents to take back their candy they brought for the girls or ask my brother not to order the hamburger for his daughter because Elena would want one. But then I realize that if this is the only battle I am fighting right now, I will take it. Next week is rosemary tofu with leeks sautéed in garlic and lemon zest-yumo!

Day 102 – March 11

Today was the beginning of Elena's wish trip. She was offered the world – swim with whales, go to the real Eiffel Tower, anything. But after two weeks of discussion, all she could settle on was to swim with dolphins – and that was with Gracie's input. I guess it just goes to show you the simplicity of Elena's wishes. And although I realize the value of this simplicity at a time in her life when control is critical, I can't help but wonder if her concept of vacation will ever expand beyond Florida. With the Grand Canyon to the west, whales to the east and plenty of ground to cover, would she appreciate these more if we took her elsewhere? After all, she has been to both Disney and SeaWorld before. Still, this is her trip and for now it is an easy trip given the circumstances. She has never been swimming with dolphins before so at least this will be a new experience. Tomorrow will be the best day ever for sure.

For Brooke and me, the vacation takes on a different meaning. This trip brings on feelings of hesitation and melancholy which are accompanied by pure and total exhaustion. I realize this now as I am too tired to sleep and too hungry to eat. But instead of craving cookies and my pillow, I yearn for the moment when she's in total remission and I can rest. The moment I can stop experiencing every second of life and live it instead. Our trip to Orlando is particularly significant as this is our last planned vacation in our foreseeable future. Pre-cancer this was not anything special; we never took enough vacations and never planned for them more than three months in advance. But now, with the possibility of this being Elena's last vacation, I'm so apprehensive that I don't want it to begin. After all, if it doesn't begin, it can never end - right? Two weeks ago, Brooke and I came to this realization as we stood on the deck of the train station at Disneyworld for the last time before leaving the park for home. There we realized that it's impossible to stop time regardless of how much you love your children. You take pictures, dry the tears, relive the moments and hope that you never forget. But at the end of the day, you look forward, stop thinking and keep moving for it is the only way to survive. This is ultimately what it's about when you deal with a terminal illness; you deal in the present and you never stop for fear that you will never get back up. And then tomorrow, you begin all over again. It's a type of exhaustion that you can't rest from and a feeling you will never forget.

This time I want the vacation to be perfect. So far, it is. Not one frown, not one tear, not one missed moment. This is the impossible mission, but the mission never the less. Life is about living and I know this. Living is about both the good and the bad. Living is about the present. We will live when we are at home and we will live when we are in Orlando. It isn't so much where you live, but how you live. For us, it is every minute until we ultimately fall asleep at the computer or at the foot of her bed. We can do both in Orlando just as well as here. Bring on the dolphins!

Day 103 – March 12

Dolphins feel like giant rubber bands. At least that's what Elena says after swimming with them. Although she insisted that yesterday was the best day of her life as we sat waiting for Daddy and Gracie, she let me know that today was the best day of her life and that *this* is what she had been dreaming of. I have to admit, this was in my top five days as well. There is nothing like holding my daughter as she experienced one of the most amazing adventures of both of our lives.

The day started by standing in line to get our passes and Elena endlessly asking, "Can we go yet?" I think that voice was stronger today. Then when waiting for the photographer to take our picture, "Can we go yet?" Then they took us on a tour of the park, "Can we go yet?" We got fitted for wet suits and masks, "Can we go yet?" When we finally reached the edge of the coral reef, with snorkel gear in hand, and took the first step in the water, Elena screamed, "I don't want to go!" You see, the water was a frigid 72 degrees

– even for pasty white Ohioans on spring break. So after about five minutes of Elena wailing that she was going to freeze to death, she got used to the cold and found a new topic to whine about—"I don't want the fish to touch me." I figured now wasn't the time to remind her that she was three hours away from having to touch a 400 pound fish. After ten minutes of convincing, we snorkeled in the depths of the two-foot sandy area to see two-inch guppies. Fifteen minutes later, we were floating and skinning our knees on the "sea floor" as we made our way out to the deep end. I am sure we were a sight with two little girls flailing, screaming and riding on the backs of Keith and I as we desperately tried to swim in 15-foot depths with no life jackets. But then, something magical happened, as Elena suddenly became a snorkel queen. Even when she saw the stingrays, I could hear muffled screams through the snorkel, but she kept her head down and headed in the opposite direction. On the other hand, when I saw the stingray, I ripped my mask off and wildly swam to the shallow end. Elena was back in her element. In Tennessee, Elena would swim for hours without tiring and today, she was as good as new.

After a bit of lunch and Gracie grooving to the sounds of the lunch buffet reggae band, we were off to the dolphins. Unfortunately, Gracie wasn't old enough to swim so this one was for Elena and Mom. As we inched into the water (because it was still a balmy 72 degrees – again, not as warm as you think!), the dolphins starting swimming and splashing around. Elena then said, "Look how excited they are, they must know I like dolphins so they must be excited to see me!" The trainers told us tidbits of information on dolphins, while Elena ignored them and squealed in delight as she got to pet the dolphins, Coral and Roxy. Next, we got to do our dolphin ride and this was one activity in which Elena had no fear. Coral decided to take Elena on the long trip and instead of going straight to the trainer, she zig-zagged through the water to make the trip last longer and Elena LOVED it! Only after we were done did I realize Keith and Gracie had disappeared. Apparently, Gracie had to go to the bathroom right before the dolphin ride started. Obviously Dad was a tad disappointed. Luckily they had a professional videographer who captured the moment for only $50 plus tax.

That night over a dinner of ice cream, we recounted the experience of a lifetime and then returned to the hotel to enjoy our $50 video of the swim. Then I tucked Elena in and she whispered to me, "This is everything I wished for." Enough for me.

Making one
of her wishes
come true

Elena swims with
the manta rays

Elena reading no
matter where she was

Flowers for mom

Elena and Gracie at Disney World

Elena after walking the Opryland Hotel

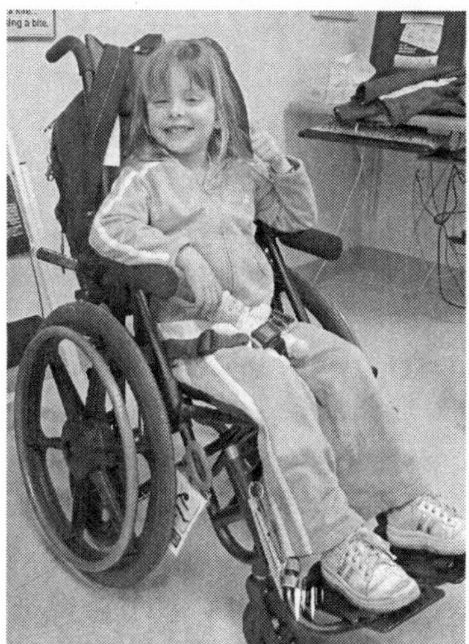

Elena at check-up with her "wheels"

Elena and Gracie in the playhouse they helped paint

Chapter 3 – Life After Progression

Day 106 – March 15

They say that Elena's symptoms will not vary. The doctors say that when she experiences a muted voice and difficulty walking it will be constant and unwavering. Today I had to wonder. After a spectacular day yesterday touring Disney, Elena awoke this morning with a whisper and trouble with her feet. At first we thought she was looking for attention so we ignored her hand signals for more juice and forced her to talk. She tried, but we could tell she was having problems. Coincidentally, today is the third day after her last dose of steroids.

Brooke says I'm wrong to expect that Elena will fully recover. That a muted voice and a slight limp should be the least of our worries in the face of this type of cancer. The worst part is that I know she is right. Still, there's nothing harder than seeing your child be the victim of something you and she cannot control. As a father, nothing short of perfect health is acceptable in your child. After all, isn't that the gift of childhood perfect health and a lifetime of opportunity? And now Elena is being robbed of both.

Still we stay positive and focus on the present. But Elena knows better. Every morning she rises with a smile only to succumb to depression when she climbs out of bed and remembers that her foot doesn't work the same as before. This is more evident than ever before as we share a room with her on vacation and see her respond to these difficulties. And when she turns to us to say good morning, her smile quickly turns to sadness when she has to instead pantomime her morning greeting when we can't understand her words. From there the day brings her depression and frustration as she tries to eat breakfast, tries to tell us what she wants to wear and what she wants to do. And by lunch, she's tired, aggravated and angry. By dinner, she can barely eat and only wants to go to bed. Not because she can't eat but because she just doesn't want to fight it anymore. Tonight was one of those nights as we struggled to keep her up past 7:00 p.m. and keep her stomach full. She ate one egg and a half a sausage today. Every other attempt was met with tears.

This is certainly not our most difficult battle and both Brooke and I know that we are only at the beginning. But how do you tell a 6-year-old to keep going when all she wants to do is stop? We let her make daily choices such as her clothing, her activities and her food in an attempt to give her back some control, but even this is met with tears. Tonight we could care less about organic food and just wanted her to gain back some control by eating anything. Fast food would have been enough. She refused and instead chose breakfast at Denny's. But even there, we had to force her to eat more than three bites of her egg.

Today was not a good day, hopefully tomorrow is better. And with the rain coming into town, it looks as though our trip to kayak with the manatees may be cancelled.Today the beach was good, but with high winds and 70-degree temperatures, we barely spent 30 minutes on the beach in the sand before retreating for the warmth of the hotel room. Not what we had planned, and considering her frustration, it is not what she needs right now. Comfort, relaxation and control are the keys to regaining her esteem.

Day 107 – March 16

Elena has always been the nurturer and Gracie has always been the entertainer. When it came to babies, puppies and kitties, Elena's brow would scrunch up in awe. As for Gracie, she never took notice; she was never interested in anyone younger than she was, or anything of the furry persuasion. After the diagnosis, Keith and I had serious concerns about how Gracie would take the inevitable increase in attention towards Elena. Gracie has always craved the spotlight and Elena was happy sitting on her own doing her drawings or reading her books. But fate had forced both of them into a realm they were not accustomed to and did not enjoy.

After three months of the new environment, Elena has learned that she simply has to smile, hide behind Mom or Dad, and eventually the attention will shift elsewhere. With Gracie, she was still struggling with the new norm.

As Elena's weakness began to grow in her right side today, Gracie has become the best of both personalities. After a full day of Elena being pushed around in the wheel chair, being given the front seat on the roller coaster and being given a taste of cotton candy (even though Gracie's 20 previous requests to taste cotton candy were met with a strong, "Not on your life!"), Gracie walked through the entire park, asked Elena if she liked riding in the front and even thanked Elena for sharing the cotton candy.

When we returned to the room and Keith and I began to pack while the girls got ready for dinner, we overheard a very eye-opening conversation between the "ladies." Elena was fretting about getting her hair combed and going to dinner. Gracie very calmly spoke to Elena in the quiet controlled voice of a skilled negotiator. "Don't worry Lena. Mom can put your hair in the ponytail so it doesn't tangle. Do you want that?" and she continued, "Do you want to pick the restaurant tonight, Lena? I will let you pick out the restaurant so that you can eat what you want. Will that make you happy, Lena?" She even offered to hold Elena's new coveted Shamu lunch pail while Elena struggled to get into the van for dinner.

Gone is the bickering; okay, the constant bickering and now we have two very grownup little ladies. We always looked at Gracie and pondered whether she would ever grow up with her silly antics and infectious laughter, but she has done it much faster than we could have imagined. She had taken over the role as big sister in light of Elena's condition. I am in awe of the selflessness she has displayed on this trip. She knew this trip was for Elena and not once did she complain that we weren't doing what she wanted. Only tonight did Gracie nicely ask if we could do pirate putt-putt at home, when our planned trip to the enticing miniature golf in downtown Orlando was called off by Elena's exhaustion.

In some ways, I am grateful for the new enlightenment and the hope that Gracie will be able to handle the increased focus on Elena. In other ways, I fear how this new and grownup Gracie may handle whatever is to come. In some ways it was easier to have the girls bickering than to have them so dependent on each other. In a new world where our girls are forced to grow up beyond their ages, I'm proud to have them as my own.

Day 109 – March 18

Four months ago, "tickle time" was our only nighttime ritual. This was the time at the end of the day when I connected with the girls and chased them up the stairs to bed to tickle and tuck them in. Gracie would always play the victim, acting like she tripped on the stairs just so that she would be caught first and get the most tickles. Elena, never shying from competition, would race to be first in bed and then heckle Gracie over her victory. Then at the end of the night after closing the doors and turning off the light, she'd call out for me and calmly inform me that Gracie had gotten more tickles than she did and she was due since she was the first one in bed. Of course, I always obliged.

Tonight our nighttime ritual involves much more than just a simple tickle and a kiss. First we must read. Junie B. books are still the favorite, as long as Mom is doing the reading. She always has that certain knack for the Junie B. accent that the girls equate with the character, while Dad tends to use far too much baritone in his narrative. My responsibility instead is to now offer foot massages.

I guess I don't need an accent for this duty. Of course, we can't forget Gracie, so I get to do two more feet. I'm waiting for the day that Brooke asks for hers as well.

Then there's the holy water. For the first month it came by the gallon. And while I never professed to be the most religious person around, I can't help but believe that this also has an effect. And with four types of holy water from places I didn't even know existed prior to this entire religious experience, we have quite a selection to choose from. So we move from bottle to bottle and sometimes use all four types, depending on her mood during the day and our emotional state. How to apply it I have no idea, but I figure it's best to get it close to the tumor so on the back of her neck it goes. Tonight, for the first time, Gracie noticed and now she also gets a dose of holy water on the back of the neck. I wonder how long it will take before she wants Elena's chemotherapy treatments as well.

Last but not least, there's tickle time. And as always, Elena is the first in bed. And Gracie still falls on the floor just so that she gets caught first. I often wonder if this is the most effective treatment of all. I know that it is the one I will never forget. You see a successful treatment should be about more than just treating the tumor; it should also be about treating the patient. And nothing brings a bigger smile to Elena than a dose of tickle time. Of course, it also brings a smile to me as we connect once more. Sorry Gracie, Elena was first.

Day 110 – March 19

The sign language has returned. With Elena's voice becoming increasingly congested and her vocal ability decreasing, she is back to resorting to hand signals and spelling. And while she has been able to hide her right leg weakness pretty well, it's her speaking and gag reflex that we're worried about now. Meals are no longer simple since portions must be cut into small bits and she has started to avoid hard foods for fear of choking. And while we're not quite at ice cream and applesauce, it is discouraging to say the least. Both Brooke and I pray this is still swelling and not progression. With the MRI scheduled for the first week of April, we will soon know.

Unfortunately, this was also Elena's first day back at school after the Make-A-Wish trip. And after the introductory tears, she finally went into her classroom to start all over again. Mentally, she's no different. Physically, she's a bit of a novelty in kindergarten. I quickly learned this upon picking her up from school and noticing that she stopped speaking altogether. Apparently, she'd overheard some of her friends talking about her voice and so rather than to confront the issue; she decided it was better to stop talking completely. Obviously, I don't ever want to lose her sweet voice again so I spent the car ride home convincing her to use her "alligator mouth" and practice her words. The "alligator mouth" is a method of talking that her therapist told her to use to overemphasize words by moving her lips and jaw completely. The idea is that by moving all of her mouth muscles she is able to compensate for the loss of the vocal cord function that she is experiencing. Hopefully she never stops and this is enough.

Day 112 – March 21

Our life has become a web of contradictions. A paradox of what is and what we know to be. It was a beautiful day. Sunny, warm and just the hint of spring stirring from the bulbs unearthed by our home's remodeling project. Any other day it would have been perfect. Brooke and I took advantage of the opportunity and left work early to pick up the girls. From there, we went home to enjoy the waning afternoon hours pushing the girls on the backyard swing and playing "Old McDonald's" fast food drive through in the windows of their playhouse. This marked the first time we ventured into our backyard since late October, when our lives were much simpler. And right now we needed a taste of that. Elena and Gracie climbed, swung and practiced penny-drops, while Brooke and I longed for ignorance, bliss and idealism. They, along with their friend, ate graham crackers and released their pet butterflies into the air, while I watched every step that Elena took with concern and fear. Hopefully the limp would just go away and we'd be left worrying about mosquito bites again. No such luck.

Today Elena's mood improved, but her condition deteriorated. The limp and loss of voice worsened and it was now joined by a slight headache, drooling, trouble swallowing and double vision; all symptoms we've seen before. And while we're still working under the assumption that this is the result of swelling, we increasingly have to come to grips with the reality that it may be progression and our time frame may no longer be a matter of months, but weeks.

People ask us how we're doing. We tell them, "Fine," but today that will no longer suffice. They ask again and we know then that they want the real answer. Then we shake our hands, shrug and utter "you know." Still the truth is that they probably don't know and we don't want to be reminded. So we go on with our days and find solace in routines. It's the simple things that keep us going. Folding wash, emptying the dishwasher, holding meetings, calling customers; these are distractions we can hardly concentrate on, but distractions which allow us to function. And for a minute or even an hour your mind stops focusing on the future while your heart never stops reminding you of Elena. How are we doing? Fine, as long as we keep going. Fine as long as Elena keeps going.

Tomorrow, "fine" will not do. Elena is scheduled for another MRI. This one was not planned. With her recent symptoms, our hunch is that the tumor is growing. Where do we go from here? If it is a progression, do we stick with the chemotherapy? And if we don't, what options do we have? Other protocols may not be available for another month, so do we go a holistic route? Starting today, no options are favored because no one knows. Doctors, social workers and family tell us that we have to be confident in the decisions we make, which is another way for saying that no one can make these decisions for us because they just don't know. This is the part of medicine that they don't study for, the part where medicine stops being about science and starts to verge on faith. Still, what is faith? Is it faith that we will make the right decision or faith that it is in God's hands? And while we can't just walk away from the decision, we are increasingly realizing how little impact we have on Elena's situation and how much we just can't solve. I'm not satisfied with this, but it just doesn't matter. Once again, we have little control and this is what I must accept. Yet, in some way I know that Elena could accomplish so much more if given the opportunity, and I pray for this chance.

Ultimately, we will make this decision and it will probably come tomorrow. Beyond that, God will show us the way. Hopefully He will also give both Elena and our family the opportunity to do more for this type of cancer in a way that cures it for all children. All we ask for is time and guidance. Sunny days don't come often enough.

Day 114 – March 23

So this is how it feels. I got a taste of it when they first broke the news to us of Elena's tumor about three months ago. Of course we didn't believe a word of it; after all, you always wake up from nightmares. But the nightmare did not end and we're starting to come to grips with the impact of this disease. When they told us last night that the tumor had nearly doubled in size, we went through denial, anxiety and anger all over again. Only this time it was real. This time, I looked around the room, but couldn't see; I heard what they were saying but never understood; and my writing was blurred as my hand shook with fear. And during the entire consultation, all I could do was tell myself to look serious, concentrate and breathe. Somehow I would begin to understand. Somehow it would all make sense. Yes, the tumor area had enlarged, but what it meant I had no idea. Sadly, even today, after spending the entire evening last night reading everything I could get my hands on, I still feel no more confident in our decisions. Do we bail on chemotherapy? Should we try another protocol? Are any really available to us? Should we stop treatment all together? Yet, all I can do is focus on the facts. Each of these offers more treatment options than cures. And in the slight chance that they work, they will only give us extra weeks to us, not years.

Now we need to also examine Elena's quality of life. Do we risk it all and go for yet another cure, regardless of her condition? Do we go the safe route and try the drug that gets another week, but we know will not work? Or do we give up on medicine, provide comfort and try the natural route? Sadly, we never predicted that we would need to make this decision now. Not with our daughter and not before the start of the window they gave us when she was originally diagnosed. But this is an abnormal tumor and this has meant a perfect storm of cancer. The worst tumor, the least understood, growing in the worst place at the fastest speed, exceeding all expectations. I'll take normal any day right now.

Where do we go from here? On Monday, Brooke and I will be faced with a decision that we can't fathom and are not prepared to make. The experts tell us that they just don't know, while everyone else tells us to follow our hearts. I've been listening, but my heart isn't talking. All it does is ache. I had always thought a heartache was an expression. Now I feel it every day. It is an emptiness in your chest that your try to fill with work, shallow humor and sometimes food, but the reality is that you'll just learn to ignore it over time. Right now, I keep trying to fill it with hope, but every time I do, doctors who tell us that they too cannot find survivors immediately dash our hope. Whatever happened to the 2% survival rate? Was that merely a psychological lie designed to allow us to sleep for the past three months? If so, why not make it 98% instead? So now we make a decision based on no numbers and no information. If we believe it is swelling, then we should stick with the chemotherapy. If we're right, she'll have a few more months of survival. If we're wrong, she'll be lucky to last two weeks. If we believe it is progression, then we switch to a new drug regiment. If we are right, then she may last another month. If we are wrong and it was truly swelling, we'll lose the few months we would have gotten if we stayed with the previous chemotherapy and get a couple of weeks instead. And while each option is a matter of weeks, they are precious weeks. New treatments and possible cures come out every day and it is only a matter of time until the cure is tried on a patient like Elena. So in the long run, even one week can mean a lifetime.

The decision is ours alone, but for now we take advantage of every moment.

Day 116 – March 25

It is all about the quiet moments now. With Elena's voice still quite weak, whenever we are around a large group of people or around strangers, Elena withdraws into her shell. She will nod her head and that is about it. She knows she can't speak above all of the voices and that strangers can't figure out what she is saying, so she says nothing at all. In one of those quiet moments she asked me why I don't let her paint the walls. I am not sure where it came from, but I could certainly change that. So with four pure white walls in our playhouse crying out for decoration, we searched for old clothes. You never realize what a girlie girl you have until Elena stood crying in her bedroom because she didn't want to wear old clothes. She wanted to look pretty. After convincing her that it was only temporary, we set out through the puddles of mud in our backyard and made it to the playhouse Dad made back in the days when we had free time. We opened cans of bright colors and the girls set to work. It only took about ten minutes before the girls tired of painting, so Mom hurriedly painted flowers and birds and clouds to finish the empty sections.

The girls put their handprints all over the walls and then we ran back inside to clean Elena's hands from the pink paint that was giving her fits. And to think we would have given her every wall to paint if she only had the time.

Day 117 – March 26

The emotional roller coaster continues. And while Elena's condition is improving every day (thanks to a healthy daily dose of steroids that would make even a baseball player blush), we are continually reminded of the uncertain future ahead. Starting tomorrow, we expect the paralysis to return and the voice to weaken as we start to reduce the dosage to a manageable level. Once achieved, we fully expect that this dosage will continue for days, weeks and hopefully months and years to come. Moodiness, bloating and sleepless nights will worsen as the effects of steroids take hold.

With the MRI indicating tumor swelling or growth, we received a call from her doctor with his impression of the film. This much anticipated call was not only a source of worry for Brooke and me over the decision ahead, but also every grandparent and relative who called us hourly for a status report. And somehow we figured that this call from Elena's doctor would put our minds at ease.

If he told us it was progression, Brooke and I were prepared to react with a switch in chemotherapy treatments immediately (of course this decision is always easier when you have almost no options to turn towards). And while feelings of depression would reign, somehow we would scrape together the courage to prepare Elena for the battle ahead. If he told us that it could be either progression or swelling and no one could offer us a clear determination, Brooke and I were planning to also make a move to higher ground with a change in chemotherapy treatments. Either way, we figured that a change was necessary in light of the minimal results. What we didn't anticipate was a call telling us that they felt that the interior of the tumor *may*be growing, but that it may also be dying. Essentially, the dead portion of the cell mass expanding could influence the growth that we may be seeing. Don't ask me how this is possible, that's what we still have yet to decide, but needless to say, it significantly changed the equation. So now we have an opinion that it might be progression and another opinion that it may be radiation causing dead cell growth or necrosis. Now we're squarely in the middle. A tough decision just got tougher. Tonight will be a long night.

Day 118 – March 27

How much does one smile cost? Exactly $229 + tax. And you pick one up from the toy store in the bike isle. But make sure to bring a big truck to haul it in because you'll need to fold down all the seats to fit this smile in the back of the car. Then prepare for "some assembly required." Smiles take lots of bolts, nuts and miscellaneous pieces to put together. Of course you'll have the customary extra screw and bolt, but don't worry, you'll find out where they go soon enough when you take the smile out for a test drive. Three hours later, there it will be. And for the rest of the day you'll bask in its glow.

I caved. It's purple and pink, has four wheels and a battery to help it move. It's a Barbie Jeep and it's exactly what Elena always wanted. Even with the steroids, I managed to induce a smile or two. Too bad I lost the camera after recording them. Hopefully I'll find it tomorrow, otherwise, that smile will get more expensive.

Too many times this journal has been used to record the "last" things, instead of the "first" times. I guess when you go through a struggle like we do, as parents, you start to think in this way. You start telling yourself that "This is the last time she'll visit her Grandparent's house," or "This is the last time she'll go to Disney World," or "This is the last time she'll go to the Nutcracker." In a way, this is how you prepare yourself for the worst. Then, if the worst happens you won't get hurt. If it doesn't, you'll be surprised. Either way, the pain won't kill you. Still, it's this daily mindset that ruins hope and lives. Instead of talking about "lasts," we have to start talking about "firsts." After all, the first three years of her life was all about "firsts": her first step, her first bike ride, her first words. Why can't this time also be about "firsts": her first dolphin swim, her first fancy dress, her first waterslide? It's a much better way to think about life, if you can do it. It only requires hope.

Tonight that hope was challenged by reality. It's day three since the news and Brooke and I still haven't made a decision on our course of action for Elena's therapy. Not because we can't or because we don't have all the information. Actually we have more than enough information and plenty of expertise coming from all sides. Our difficulty stems from conflicting information that still suggests either radiation swelling or progression. We find ourselves in the unenviable position of deciding Elena's fate. Worse yet, not one opinion has an edge on the other one. One doctor suggests that the tumor might be growing. If this is the case, a change in chemotherapy might be in order. Another doctor suggests that the tumor is "stable" and any variations are the result of radiation. If this is the case, it makes sense to stay with the existing protocol and allow it to work. What makes this even more difficult is the reality that the alternatives are unproven, limited and have some nasty side effects. So where do we go from here? No change might be the best course of action.

In light of Elena's recent recovery resulting from her steroid regiment (she now walks, talks and swallows much better), we might decide to take a "wait-and-see" attitude and reevaluate next week. That's when we'll make our monthly trip to Memphis and have the benefit of a fifth MRI. Perhaps then, the decision will be clear and another week of steroid dosage reduction will give us hope of swelling. There's that hope thing again...

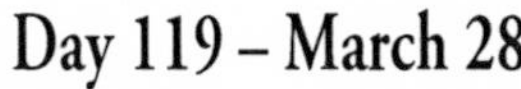

Day 119 – March 28

Dad's a fool. Smiles are free. While he needs a Barbie Jeep, I get them for free all day, especially today. You see, reading this journal you'd think Elena and Gracie are Daddy's girls; not so. In this household it's still very much three versus one. Daddy still gets the punches and I get the kisses. Take today for example: Gracie cuddled and scratched my back, while Elena practiced her therapy with right-handed punches to Dad's stomach. One day he'll learn that kisses work much better than tickling. Until then, Elena gets her daily therapy session. I can see this coming in handy with her eventual boxing career.

Today Elena was genuinely happy. And except for when Dad had to drop her off at school, everything else went well. Lately, Elena has developed a strong attachment to both Keith and me in the mornings. The result is an emotional goodbye at the schoolhouse door. It's not that she doesn't want to go to school; she loves school and can't quit talking about it when we pick her up. It's that she doesn't want to let us go. Tonight as I prepared her for bed, she told me that she didn't feel that we spend enough time together as a family. I agreed. But I also know that Elena loves her friends and her teacher too. Trust me, dropping her off is one of the toughest parts of the day for me as well (although I think I handle it much better than her father, "Mr. Mush"), but I know that this is just what Elena needs to come out of her shell. In a way, it has become more than just an education but also a bit of emotional therapy. For us, it is a chance to return back to life as well, as we pretend that all is normal and just like it was four months ago.

Day 121 – March 30

We call her "Steroid Sally." She's up and down all night, perpetually shy, incurably hungry, and irritable. And she's not our Elena. That's why we call her "Steroid Sally." Last night Steroid Sally started out the day early. More specifically at 12:10 a.m. It was my turn to sleep in Elena's room.

I went to bed at 11:45 p.m. She was up at 12:10 a.m. Chapstick was the emergency of the moment. Suddenly she remembered that she had left her Chapstick in her pants from the previous day and she needed to get it out now! For my part, I had just reached the deep sleep stage. My logic was fuzzy, my memory was worthless. And before I truly awoke, I had already walked halfway down the hallway in search of her jeans from last night. Ten minutes later, I found them and returned to her room to find her sound asleep in bed. So much for this being an emergency.

At 1:30 a.m., she was back up again. This time she sat up calling my name from across the room. "Dad, Dad, DAD, DAD, DAAD, DADDDDDDD!" I was awake. She said, "I need my plain skirt." I heard, "I feed my trained bird." Obviously this wasn't why she woke up again. And she doesn't even have a trained bird. She said it again, getting increasingly frustrated with her limited voice and my poor attempts at reading lips in the dark. After the fifth or sixth time, I finally got it. Still, a plain skirt didn't seem like enough of a reason to awake in the middle of the night. I reassured her that we would pick a plain skirt in the morning. Two minutes later she was back asleep. I was awake for the next hour.

At 4:18 a.m., she was up again. This time she sat up, called my name and said, "I have to tell you something." I sat and listened. She said nothing. I walked across the room, wondering if this time it was about a plain shirt or a penny in her coat pocket. She said nothing and instead turned to rest back down on her pillow. The next sound I heard was her snoring. Great, now she was not only waking me up, but also having a dream about waking me up. Just like her mother. Who knew it could be genetic? I gave up and switched off the alarm. Someday I'll actually use it.

Mom's up tomorrow night. But by then, the steroid dose will hopefully be reduced and she'll again start to sleep through the night. Either way, we'll take it. Goodbye Steroid Sally.

Day 123 – April 1

The steroids are wearing off. After dropping another milligram of steroids from her daily dosage, we are starting to see some increasing symptoms of the tumor. Her right hand has weakened slightly, her voice has gotten worse, but fortunately this is about all. Now we find ourselves at the point of wondering if further actions to limit her steroid dosages will bring it all back. Any further decrease in steroids will no doubt improve her disposition, but it may also result in difficulty walking, swallowing and even loss of sight. It is a balancing act that we cannot avoid.

Later that afternoon, we visited Grandpa-Grandpa. In his company, it doesn't matter that Elena can't talk clearly, he doesn't understand anyone else either. But somehow it never matters. His sociable and enthusiastic appreciation of your company is the only thing you notice, except for the jokes. But be prepared to hear them over and over again. Just pretend you don't know the punch line. ("Did you hear the one about the potato that told the news? He was a common-tater.")

It was there that Elena got her first taste of Easter: organic style. And let me tell you, when you take the candy out of Easter, you're not left with much more in the basket except that annoying plastic grass that clings to your rugs and shoes. Still, my family was not to be outdone and considering that this was the last time they would see each other before Easter, Elena's great aunt and uncle went to great pains to make it special. And special it was. Some eggs had coins. Some eggs had dollar bills. Some eggs had rubber balls. Some eggs had rocks. And some eggs had firecracker smoke bombs. Yes, smoke bombs. Try telling the girls why the Easter bunny decided that smoke bombs were appropriate seasonal gifts. Not to mention the fact that they're also age and gender appropriate to two little girls under 7 years old. As a matter of fact, not just a few eggs had smoke bombs – 23 of them to be specific. Orange, green, purple and yellow smoke bombs.

As we made our way home later that night, it was the smoke bombs that they remembered most. Call it a new tradition, or even call it the crazy idea of a pyrotechnic uncle, but either way it worked. Who needs a chocolate bunny when you can have fire, smoke and even a little boom? I just feel sorry for the grandparents next weekend now that expectations have been set. Fireworks for Easter. Candy eggs for Independence Day? Only with my family.

Day 124 – April 2

Hope comes in many forms. Today it came in the form of a limousine. This time it was a white one. And to think we were expecting a school bus. At school on Friday, Elena's teacher asked if we were ready for Monday. Little did I know that her teachers had plans for Elena's first day of spring break. When the limo arrived at 10 a.m., we didn't know what to expect. And after a six-point turnaround in our 30 foot wide street with a 40-foot limo, we were on our way.

Along the way, we not only discovered clues to our afternoon, but I also discovered my family. We found Elena's hidden laugh, Mom's tears and Gracie's love for gizmos in a limo. If there was a button to push, she pushed it. If there was a drink to drink, she drank it. And every seat not occupied called her name, at least for ten seconds. Thank goodness Mom found the seat belts.

Soon we had arrived at our first destination: the art museum. Immediately, Elena recognized it as she turned and told me that she had been there three times before. This was the fourth and since the museum is normally closed on Mondays, this time she would be the only guest allowed. Knowing that Elena would be at the hospital for the remainder of the week, her teachers pulled some strings to get the museum to allow a solitary visit on Monday. And so dodging the army of custodians, floor refinishing crews and curators, Elena received a personalized tour of some of the museum's most prized possessions. There she saw American art, contemporary art, sculptures, impressionist art and even multimedia art installations. She also spent a little quality time with her friends, Vincent and Pablo, as she now calls them

Back in the limo, we learned that a picnic at the park overlooking the river was up next. But not any picnic meal would do, in our case the teaching staff had prepared an organic lunch for Elena in a traditional picnic basket, no less. Apparently, they had studied Elena's packed lunch selections over the past month and meticulously purchased all of her favorites for this special picnic. Eager to accept and still on steroids, Elena gladly sampled every plate while enjoying the beautiful weather. Then it was finally time to return home as we boarded the limo one more time.

Our memory of the day was beautiful weather, fine art, a perfect picnic and time with our family. And as we prepare for our trip to the hospital tomorrow in anticipation of news that Brooke and I do not want to hear, we find ourselves bolstered by the support of Elena's teachers and classmates. You see, what we also found in the limousine was a handcrafted quilt made by Elena's teachers and classmates. A quilt of love and support designed by a community that we are proud to call our own and emblazoned with the handprints of every student from her school. In a way, this was the true art of the day and enough by itself. It was hope, a hope we desperately need and a hope that we must continue throughout Elena's life every day until she is 100 years old. Regardless of our setbacks and regression, we realize that today we had more than a family of four in that limousine, for covering that quilt was a community of hundreds.

Day 127 – April 5

I've never had a hero before now. Sure, I've had role models and even mentors, but I can't say that I've ever really had a hero. In my mind, a hero was always someone who epitomized strength, courage, integrity and an ability to do the impossible. And now as a father, I have a hero in my own daughter. Her strength and courage throughout her treatments have been nothing short of amazing. Throughout the past four months, she's seen her speech, walking and feeding abilities disappear, only to have them return and now disappear again. Still, her resolve has never faltered and her courage to continue smiling seems endless. Her integrity is without question, Elena has never been able to lie, and her concern for others in the face of her struggle is miraculous. All I can hope now is that she will do the impossible. She will overcome yet another hopeless regression and she will triumph over the disease that has taken so many others. Then she can help others to triumph in this struggle with the impossible.

That's the dream and what my hero is capable of achieving. And with Easter around the corner, I can see no better opportunity for her to start her recovery. Today, this is all Brooke and I can hope for. Her condition is no better than yesterday and we fear that it has worsened. Still, neither of us wants to admit what we see, for fear that it will become a reality. Tomorrow we will be forced to confront this and question our actions. Religion plays a very important part of our lives, not just as occasional prayers, but also to continue a hope that we have trouble seeing on a daily basis. So in the meantime, we prop each other up and move forward, hoping that tomorrow will be better. On this Easter weekend, hope will be our only prayer for our little hero.

Day 128 – April 6

It took all day, but I finally got a spark. Right now Elena can't roll her tongue, talk clearly, walk without assistance, or move her right hand, but the smile is still there if you try hard enough. And boy, did we ever try.

At breakfast this morning, Brooke and I recognized Elena's "million mile stare." Sitting at the table in our newly remodeled efficiency (we lost our kitchen today to the remodeling efforts and now have a temporary sink and oven in the dining room), Elena stared off into space while tediously attempting to eat her oatmeal. But without the use of her tongue, she's no longer able to manipulate her food in her mouth and resorts to poking her cheeks with her fingers to push the food between her teeth. She understands what's happening even more than we do, and also understands that there's nothing that either she or we can do to prevent it. Still she continues to eat and reaches for a napkin to dry her shirt of the drool.

It isn't a pleasant sight, especially when it's your child, but the good part is that Elena is smart enough to know what she can and can't eat and does so without an argument. She knows that when we ask her to eat this type of food or take her medicine, it is her best interest, so she does it without our asking.We are grateful to have such a courageous and intelligent. We only wish we could do more.

Today it was different. At the breakfast table, I commented that she was looking better than yesterday. It was a lie, but one that I hoped would boost her confidence. She didn't even look my way, she knew better. I asked what she wanted to do today. She continued to push her oatmeal around and stare into the distance. I asked her if she wanted anything else to eat. She ignored me. Looking across the table, I saw the look of defeat; the stare that says she is going through the motions. The look that says she's accepted her condition and there's nothing she can do about it.

Gone was the spark, the casual gaze across the table to see what everyone else was eating or the look of interest as we asked a question. She knew she had to eat, but she was only going through the motions.

I remember this look. And although her circumstance may be bleak, I knew that we must change her outlook if we were to have a chance.

Tonight we would go see the "Lion King" Broadway show; this would be the answer. Brooke bought these tickets months ago, even before the diagnosis. And even though it started an hour after her bedtime, we knew that this would give us the spark and the smile. We were right. For three hours, she sat on my lap and watched the show so she could see over the people in front of us. The lady next to us told Elena that she had the best seat in the theater. She was wrong; I had the best seat in the theater.

Elena laughed, smiled and even stayed awake until the end at 11 p.m. This in and of itself is quite an achievement for a girl that never stays awake past 7:30 p.m. And for one night, we broke the rules, we stayed up late and I even treated her to a blue slushie. Pure sugar, but I think attitude will fight more tumors than sugar will promote. Now my pants have blue stains on the legs, but I wear them as a badge of honor. What was most important was the blue smile I saw in the mirror as we drove home from the theater. That was worth it all.

Tomorrow we will continue the "million mile stare" fight. I think chocolate chip pancake smiley faces will do the trick. If not, maybe a little blue food coloring in her milk might help too. So if you see me walking around with blue stains on my leg or see Elena with blue lips, you'll know what it's about. It's about courage, it's about smiling, and it's about not surrendering.

Day 134 – April 12

Every morning it's something different. First it was her voice. Next it was her balance. Then it was her foot. Brainstem glioma robs Elena of something every day. Some days it's something critical: her voice, her sight or her ability to swallow. Other days we're lucky and it's something minor: her ability to roll her tongue or a ticklish spot.

Three days ago as Brooke and I sat down at the breakfast table with Elena, we noticed her right index finger curled under. Her hand had been weak since we returned from the hospital, but this was new and it was scary at the same time. Never before had she lost total control of something; weakness was as far as she's experienced so far. This was the true reason behind our therapy regiment and our religious determination to push Elena to exhaustion. Somehow we thought we could fight progression and ignore the onslaught.

Today our efforts were rewarded. As I picked her up from school and reached out to hug her in the hallway, she reached back with open hands and an open finger. And although her hand is still weak, she can now move the very finger that had curled with lint for the past three days. Little victory, but one we will cherish and will push us to continue the fight. So far it has been two days and no changes. Two and counting...

Today Brooke accompanied Elena with the intention of seeing how she would adapt. We expected to leave an hour later, fleeing for the comfort of home. Elena stayed. Then we figured she'd make it to lunch. Still she stayed, and before we knew it, Elena had stayed for the whole day. Of course by 3 p.m., her eyelids were half shut, her leg had strayed far to the right, and she begged to be carried to the car, but I knew we had made progress. Chalk one up to her will and determination.

Today we learned a lot about Elena's resolve instead of learning more about the symptoms of brainstem glioma. I'll take that lesson every day. She'll just take the lessons at kindergarten instead.

Day 135 – April 13

135 days ago, our lives changed forever. 135 days ago, we asked Elena what she always wanted to do. 135 days ago, I sat in the dark holding her hand in the ICU ward. 135 days ago, they told us

that she had three months and six weeks to live. 135 days. That was when we started a journal for Gracie that would tell the story of her sister. It was titled "135 Days with Elena." Today is that day.

135 days tells the story of a girl and her family: a family involved in a struggle that we fear, but one we hope never ends. Tomorrow we will start a new journey and most certainly a new phase. On November 28th we began stage 1: distress. This was when we first learned of the cancer and discovered medicine's inability to cure her. Stage 2 brought anger: anger over why it was our daughter and how this was allowed to happen. Stage 3 was when we learned to fight. And with countless books on oncology and early morning Internet searches, we truly began to understand this disease. Stage 4 brought desperation, fueled by the information we had collected. It's something to feel overwhelmed by the complexity of the disease, but it is another thing to feel powerless in the realization that we know almost nothing about how it grows or how to cure it. You can have all the best experts, the best hospitals and even unlimited resources and still be lost without a cure. There is no way to learn, travel or buy your way out of a terminal disease. Determination, faith and a little bit of chance are your best hope. Stage 5 saw us attempting to preserve Elena's life. We bought concrete handprint pavers, had her paint walls and kept every last scrap of paper that she scribbled on. But now, at day 135, we realize that these stages were both premature and irrelevant. Elena is still fighting every day and will continue to do so. She now does so exceeding expectations, just as we had hoped she would. Stages end here and living begins.

The journal was started late one night and continues today late into the night. Interestingly, Elena started a diary of her own today from a journal she received in her Easter basket. I guess she figured that if I could write, she could draw. Her experiences with Carson Palmer formed her first entry. Not to be left out, Gracie started her own diary too. But instead of calling it her diary, she calls it her "diarrhea."

Tonight at dinner, she proudly announced that after she finished her green beans, she would need to "start her diarrhea." So much for the sanctity of the situation. Once again, Gracie teaches us to live in humor and with a smile. And that's just what we plan to do. Every day starting now is a gift. The cure starts now.

Day 137 – April 15

A good day is relative,and while they certainly don't measure up to the good days of last year, our perspective and appreciation have changed. Today was a good day. We had nothing planned and we wanted it that way. For the first time since Elena's diagnosis, we sat around the breakfast table and actually asked what the girls wanted to do instead of telling them what we had planned. And after a plateful of pancakes and a bowl of oatmeal (in Elena's case, bowls of oatmeal. She claims everything that Gracie doesn't eat), we decided to go to the museum for a relaxing afternoon of play. There, Gracie played in the tree house and Elena shopped from the selection of plastic fruits and vegetables in the play grocery store of the Children's Museum. Two hours and a belly full of ice cream later, we arrived home with two very sleepy girls. Gracie retreated to her bedroom for a little three hour nap, while Elena decided to relax with her books on the bay window seat.

I agreed with Gracie and decided that I would take a little nap on the couch. Thirty minutes later, Elena succumbed to her exhaustion and made her way to the couch to join me. This was the best part of my day. For the first two years of her life, napping with Dad was a Sunday tradition. During the fall and winter, we'd turn on the football game and lay on the sectional with her in my arm.

Now four years later, napping with Dad is still a Sunday tradition. And when Mom came home from errands two hours later, she found us lying on the couch, her head resting on my shoulder, both of us wide awake but very comfortable. Who can sleep when you're afraid of missing a moment of this quality time? Either way, with Gracie awake and Mom pushing us to leave for the next errand, Elena and I pledged to continue our Sunday tradition next week too.

Day 138 – April 16

Tonight we moved the girls to Elena's room to sleep. With the removal of joists below Gracie's floor during the reconstruction, we thought it best to move them for the night. But instead of Elena sleeping in her bed with Gracie tucked in on the floor mattress, Elena asked to instead sleep on the floor closer to the ground for fear she would fall out. Any other time, Gracie would have leapt at the opportunity to sleep in the "big kid" bed. But this time, the girl who anxiously awaits any chance of bunking her beds and getting the top bunk looked to her sister for guidance. After all, this was Elena's room and Elena's bed, why would she want her to sleep there? So while Elena quickly succumbed to exhaustion, Gracie tiptoed downstairs to consult Mom and Dad. After all, why did she have to sleep in the "big kid" bed? "When was Elena going to get better?" Some questions were impossible to answer; others didn't make sense. "Will the house be finished when Elena gets better? I want presents just like Elena." Either way, we realized that Gracie had noticed.

Today it was her turn to be the big sister. Proudly, Brooke and I have seen Gracie not only express love for her sister, but grow far beyond her years. In pictures, Gracie now wraps her arms around her sister and pulls her close, just as Elena had done for the past four years. When we get in the car, Gracie now leans over to buckle Elena's seatbelt and make sure she is comfortable before we leave the driveway. When they brush their teeth, Gracie now helps Elena open the toothpaste and apply it to her toothbrush. Tonight she tucked Elena in bed and gave her a kiss on the cheek. In all ways, she has not only assumed Elena's role as the big sister, but has been there to help her "bestest friend in the whole world."

Somehow I know this is not the last time we will need to console Gracie, nor will it be the last time she will fail to understand the changes in her sister. What I do know is that Gracie will never disappoint us or her "Lena."

Day 143 – April 21

Before cancer (otherwise known as B.C.), we had three square meals a day: breakfast, lunch and dinner. After diagnosis (otherwise known as A.D.), we have a fourth meal: medicine. And with eight pills and six formulated liquids twice daily, this has become Elena's largest meal of the day. Sometimes she even gets full from the medicines alone and never makes it to breakfast, at least that was the case before steroids. What once took us twenty minutes to prepare breakfast has now become an hour as Brooke rushes down to prepare the drug cocktails, while I get the girls dressed in the morning. And if Brooke forgets to include the occasional pill or antibiotics, Elena is the first to notice and remind us with a handwritten note indicating the type and color of the drug we forgot. Still, even with a 5 a.m. wake-up, we still find ourselves rushing out the door 30 minutes late and with the last pill in hand.

The one consolation is that Elena has always been an "eat-your-vegetables-first" kind of girl. With a motto of "why put off till tomorrow what you can do today" she's the one child who actually chooses to take the worst tasting medicine first. If she could, she'd even take all of her weekly medicines in one sitting, just so that she could be free of it for the rest of the week. And considering how some of the medicines taste, this is no small accomplishment. Brooke and I try to make it sound appealing by comparing it to the taste of root beer or to bubble gum, but the truth is that we can't even stand the smell of it as we pour it from the bottle. The worst smells come from the medicines that the pharmacist tries to flavor to make more palatable. And while their attempt is noble, the result is often a hideous combination of cherry flavoring and antibiotics that separates in the cup and smells like a dead skunk. Still, Elena takes it without complaint, even offering up the occasional "cheers" as our glasses thud against her multitude of plastic medicine tumblers. Then it's bottoms up, six times over and the quick shiver as she pushes it down her throat over the objection of her taste buds.

Returning from a day at the hospital yesterday, she not only walked away another two drugs heavier, but she also showed signs of extreme exhaustion from the infection. So while Gracie and her cousins broke in the new concrete driveway (band-aids were in short supply at the household), Elena looked on from the shade of the framed garage. Today she preferred the company of adults and resisted any activity that might require energy. Partly out of embarrassment for her handicaps, and partly because of exhaustion, she sat on the sideline until Brooke or I pushed her to get involved. But even then it was met with frustration and cries to return back to her seat.

Today, however, we relented and allowed her to relax in hopes of a quick recovery from the infection that still has us watching her temperature diligently. Luckily, Sally was able to visit with Elena for the day. So from morning until evening, Sally slept in Elena's arms and Elena scratched Sally's belly, ears, and back until the fur ran the other way. For now, we'll have to just borrow Sally.

Day 144 – April 22

I miss those warm sleepless nights. Not that we don't have our share of sleepless nights now, but then it was different. We'd go to bed around 9:30 p.m. and listen to sounds of the neighborhood children laughing and playing tag in the backyards of local homes. Of course at the time we'd curse the screaming and kick-the-can calls, wondering what kind of parents would let their children play outside after dark on a school night. After all, some of us have to be up at

4:30 a.m. But soon I would realize that my girls would also grow up and torment our neighbors with games of tag and screaming long after nightfall, just not on school nights. So I'd flip over, cover my ears and promptly go to sleep.

Tonight I hear the familiar screams and games being played outside our open windows. Although somehow, this time it is different. At a time when I should be hearing my girls playing outside, I only hear their friends. With Elena sick, there will be no late nights, no games of tag and no screams. And without Elena, Gracie stays indoors by her side. At a time when I should be relaxing bedtime rules (all the while making the girls think they are getting away with it), I'm enforcing a 7:30 p.m. bedtime so that Elena has the proper amount of sleep to aid her recovery. And Gracie, never one to pass up a good nap, obliges and accompanies Elena to bed.

By 8 p.m., our house is silent. The girls quickly succumb to exhaustion and Brooke and I sit on opposite ends of the living room; she with her diet planning and I with my journal. Four hours later, we say our first words of the night to each other and head off to sleep. Four hours later, we're up again starting the process anew. It's a strict schedule, but one that squeezes every last minute from the day. Elena is our purpose and everything we do must move towards that mission.

Tonight after putting the girls to bed, Brooke and I sat on the top step of the stairway and listened. Listened to the silence and listened to the breeze blowing through our windows. It was in that breeze that we heard the first whisper from Gracie to Elena. She had a plan: Elena will press the doorbell hanging from her headboard and make up something ridiculous. Never mind that we installed the doorbell for emergencies and bathroom runs; the girls use it as their personal call button.

Elena pressed the button and I entered the room, pretending to be worried only to find that Elena wished to have toast in the morning. I feigned frustration and left the room. The doorbell rang again. This time she wanted to make sure I put all the money back in her bank that we had used for physical therapy that morning. I told her that I had, and I asked her to only use the doorbell for emergencies. She and Gracie giggled. And by the time I closed the door, I heard the doorbell once more. I waited. It rang again. I waited. It rang again. As I opened this time, they both burst into laughter; Dad was wrapped around their fingers and they knew it. Elena had no reason for ringing it this time, she just wanted to see my face as I raced in and started to tickle them.

Twenty minutes later, we were still playing the doorbell game, only this time they would ring the doorbell and then hide under the sheets. Too bad I still knew where they were. And tonight, if only for a half an hour, it was our house making all the noise in the neighborhood. There were screams, giggles and even an occasional doorbell. Bedtime may be a little late tonight.

Day 145 – April 23

The leap from age six to thirteen occurs much sooner than you think. While her body and mind are still in kindergarten, her attitude today was pure teenager. She ignored adults, cut in front of her classmates in line, and even engaged in a bit of backtalk. Ignoring adults I expected. When her music teacher came in to visit at recess, I justified the behavior by explaining that she was embarrassed about her voice. And while this has been true in the past, after hearing her talking to her classmates at snack time, I knew she was getting used to the sound of her voice. Suffice it to say, after her teacher left, we spent the remainder of the recess discussing how being sick does not excuse rudeness. Even at this, she did not make eye contact. At least she heard it.

It seems that Elena has also increased her knowledge of sign language at the same time. In the absence of a strong voice, she has discovered unique ways of talking back with her hands. Her favorite is the gesture where she circles her ears and calls us crazy. I received this several times today, usually when she thought I had turned my back. Then there is the wave of the hand as if she's brushing us off. This usually comes when I correct her or ask her to try harder. I guess I can't really be too mad; after all, she certainly is increasing her vocabulary. Still, I know we have some work to do. Without a positive attitude, recovery will be much harder.

It's when I see this determination and stubbornness that I begin to become hopeful that she will make it through this as the one-in-a-million child; the one who beat the impossible cancer. After all, if she can outlast me, why not a little disease? And while I know this is a distorted view, it's this strength that buoys our spirits. But then, optimism can be dangerous. As a parent, somewhere deep within, you prepare yourself for the worst. You protect yourself; you protect your heart. You look at her rebelling and find your mind wandering towards the future: her wedding, her children, your grandkids. Then you awake and realize it's still today and you're no further than you were two minutes ago. The fight is for today and it is one step at a time. Hope is what fuels you, but hope is also what discourages you. So you continue the day looking for hope, but careful to not take it too far and fall into despair.

Elena is strong; stronger than I will ever be. If there is to be hope, it will be with her. In the meantime, it is our responsibility to support her, love her, and teach her. Tomorrow we'll start with manners first.

Day 146 – April 24

How do you sum up such a complex, thoughtful little girl into a page of instructions? If any child is worth an instruction manual (in multiple languages), Elena is that child.

Today I had to shrink it down to a small list of instructions. This was an exceptional feat even more so now than before. Our new aide at school started today by shadowing me to learn what exactly I did in kindergarten to help Elena. With most kids, you can simply give a daily schedule of activities and you are done. With Gracie, I simply give her a full bottle of juice and a kiss and she goes with the flow from there. Elena's list of instructions are packed with ways to keep her involved, techniques to keep her talking and methods to force her to move her right side. I am a caregiver, a therapist and a psychiatrist. How do you teach that, how do you write it in a list, how to you pass that torch?

It has taken me six years to figure out how Elena ticks and how to help her excel and be happy, and then I spent the last four months relearning everything all over. In the end, I realized the best way to teach someone about Elena is to let Elena teach them. Over time, this will not only allow her teachers to understand her better, but may also help Elena come out of her shell and rediscover herself. There comes a time in a parent's life when you learn you must let go: first at daycare, then it on the first day of kindergarten. I am pretty sure tomorrow will be even harder than the first day of school. Most likely she will go to school and she will cry, and I will cry. And as I walk back to the car, I will realize that that time with her friends may be her best chance at recuperation.

Day 148 – April 26

I've heard them all. "God has a plan, though we may not understand it." "God works miracles." "God only burdens those he knows can handle it." From friends and family, they come without offense and are meant to comfort. I know this, but somewhere deep down I can't help but question.

Right or wrong, I've always found religion and God in my family. For me, I've never looked to the church, statues or the Bible for guidance. Instead, it was in the faces of my family that I've always found comfort and solace. These were the true gifts in life and somehow I always envisioned that I could seek virtue through my actions and commitment to my family. When Elena and Gracie were born, I knew that this was my mission. This was God's plan and I didn't need a sermon to tell me so.

Today I find myself not only questioning my faith, but also God's plan. I look at Elena and I have a hard time believing that this is part of a "plan." Since our visit to the hospital a month ago, Brooke and I have seen her decline daily to the point where she can no longer walk on her own. Now in recent days, we have begun to see her improve slightly with therapy and schooling, but far less dramatic than the decline she has experienced over the past month. And so instead of writing about her condition, I now find myself writing about general commentaries and entertaining stories in order to avoid re-living what I already know might happen.

Tonight as the storms passed overhead and I kissed the girls for the final time before bed, I stood on the front porch searching for meaning. I looked to the east, to the south, to the north and finally to the west. I looked across the horizon and to the impending storm front approaching. Still, I could not find what I was looking for. To me, God is still in the faces of my children as I think He will always be. No sky, church or priest can tell me otherwise.

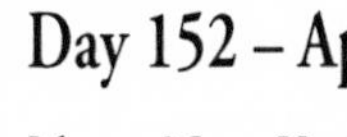

Day 152 – April 30

I hate New York. I hate Cleveland even more. Nothing against the cities, personally I've never spent enough time in either to develop an opinion, but for today they symbolize something. You see, Elena listens to every conversation we have now a days. When we say MRI, her ears perk. When we say bleeding, she turns to look. When we say progression, she stops. Today we said "progression" quite a bit. All the doctors agree, the tumor has grown and she is officially in progression.

With an overall growth of over half a centimeter, the chemotherapy is no longer an option. In her case, it will provide no more hope and we must move quickly. But with pinhead bleeding, an established protocol is off the table. What options we had a month ago when her MRI showed no signs of bleeding are now nonexistent. Instead, thanks to the help of the hospital, we will pursue a new chemotherapy outside of trial and at our own risk, or rather Elena's. Unfortunately, this may also mean without the help of health insurance.

No one truly knows how this new treatment works or if it will work on diffuse gliomas, but when you have no other alternatives, nothing else matters. Together the hope is that it will provide the success that we once thought the previous chemotherapy would bring three months ago. However, with this treatment, bleeding is a serious concern. It doesn't help that brainstem gliomas have a history of abnormal bleeding on their own. When combined, the bleeding risk is severe and life threatening. And with Elena listening in, we've started to refer to this bleeding risk as "going to New York." So when we say that she could have a very good chance of "going to New York," we must accept the risk before proceeding. Unfortunately, a "trip to New York" will most certainly result in a "trip to Cleveland," which means that she may not make it.

There, I've said it. And while I cringe at the callousness of these metaphors, with her in the same room as we continued conversations with her oncologist, I can't dare let her know the seriousness of the situation. As far as she is concerned, we will improve each and every day, despite the fact that for the last week, I've been struggling to find any improvement. Sadly, she may already know. Whereas before she would question every discussion we had with her doctors, she now sits in the corner motionless with her eyes locked on the floor. I know she is listening and I fear she even understands what we say when we talk about "going to Cleveland." She is smarter than I could ever know.

Today we realized that decisions come much easier when there are no alternatives. The former is not an option. And with Elena now wheel chair bound, unable to talk and for the first time experiencing left side weakness, we know that we have only weeks to go without trying something else. So tonight we will stay in Memphis and return every two weeks for an IV treatment of the new chemotherapy. But this time the treatments will be more difficult and with more side effects. She will experience vomiting, a chance of bleeding and possibly hair loss; this is conventional chemotherapy and all of its problems. Hopefully, it will also include some of its successes.

In one way, Brooke and I thank God that tonight we had at least one more alternative and not a dead-end. Still, we are painfully aware that this is our last option and our only hope. We are not prepared to give up yet and neither is Elena. Improvement each and every day. I hope we never see New York or Cleveland.

Day 155 – May 3

She's hardly the artsy type. She loves numbers and details, doesn't wear eclectic glasses and has both ears, but somehow she's made it into the art museum right next to the likes of Picasso, Renoir, and Van Gogh. Okay, so I do know how she made it into the art museum, but to her, it is the ultimate wish. And although you may not notice her smile through the fog of a tripled steroid dose and the extreme exhaustion that accompanies a first dose of chemotherapy, trust me, this means the world to a 6-year-old girl.

Today we took her painting to the museum to have it "installed." While we simply hung it on the wall of our living room, at the museum it would need to be "installed." It was then that I wished we had spent a little more than $30 on the framing at the local hobby store. Somehow the "50% off frame sale" frame didn't seem worthy of an "installation." Who knew that this little painting would mean so much more?

There at the museum, Elena also had her first look at the gallery where her painting was to be displayed. Somehow, in the back of my mind, I envisioned her painting occupying a corner near the bathroom where "Dogs Playing Pool" had been the previous masterpiece. But as we approached the gallery, we soon discovered that Elena's painting would take center stage in a room of giants. Picasso took the skinny wall by the door, while Elena's "I Love You" would reign supreme on the main wall flanked by masterpieces that otherwise could have had a gallery to themselves. And as if this was not enough, as we arrived, curators were desperately preparing the wall for Elena's picture with a fresh coat of paint and plaster. At home during our renovations, we'd be lucky if it even hung straight. I guess that's the difference between an installation and a plain old nail.

Since Elena's diagnosis, her artwork has taken on new meaning. Pictures that we'd otherwise toss were priceless. Even scraps of paper that filled her school bag became testaments to her love. Now everything must be saved: every picture, every note and every card. Sometimes this is too much. In our desperation to save every memory, her room has become more of a shrine than a bedroom, forcing her to sleep in her sister's room for fear of the avalanche of stuffed animals, artwork and Bengals memorabilia. But how do you clean a room when you don't want to give up anything? You can't, so we spend our time rearranging, all the while convincing ourselves that it looks cleaner than when we started. One day I fear we'll need to add another wing to her room. But then, I guess that is a good thing as it will mean that she'll still be with us.

For now, we'll continue to archive her pictures and she'll continue to paint. Without a voice and even a right hand, this is how Elena communicates with us and how she shows us her love. I guess that's why the title "I Love You" is so appropriate. Simple, plain and exactly Elena.

Day 156 – May 4

So many people spend their whole lives focusing on issues that don't really matter. I only wish we still made the same mistake. Today I am so grateful to God for something very simple, a thank you. Today was the long awaited kindergarten field trip to the zoo. At the beginning of the week, I fretted over mentioning this event to Elena for fear that we would not return to Cincinnati in time to attend. This morning, we were dressed in record time and she even ate all her breakfast pretty quickly (less than an hour). We packed our bags and started out the door until Elena stopped me, and feverously made a sign I had never seen before. She desperately tried to say the words, but after four hours of sleep last night, my brain could not wrap itself around what she was trying to say to me. Finally she pointed to paper and she wrote out, "I wut to sho mi snak." To clarify to those parents not skilled in kindergarten phonetic spelling, she was not asking for a Chinese snack, she wanted to take her new stuffed snake to show her friends.

While we were at the hospital, and as soon as we left the recovery room, Elena reminded us of our tradition of visiting the gift shop (or as Elena spells it "gft sp") as a reward for a day at the hospital. This time Elena chose a bendable snake. I have no idea why, but that little girl dressed in a pretty pink dress beamed her way through the hospital with a brown snake twisted around her wheel chair armrest. We kept her smiling by bending the snake in funny positions throughout the day, including around her ankle and then pointing it directly at her within inches of her face. With nine heaping milligrams of steroids raging in her veins, things like this typically result in an angry spat, but for some reason, this time she simply smiled and left it be.

Today she insisted on taking it to school. I think she was hoping that the kids would focus on the snake rather than the wheel chair the snake was coiled around. While it worked, I think it also helped that the kids were so preoccupied with the field trip. Her new wheels were low on their radar. Her mood was so improved that she even volunteered to say the Pledge of Allegiance over the intercom this morning. Elena didn't open her mouth the entire time, but she was smiling ear to ear as her three friends made up for her silence.

The rest of the day was a blur. We followed her classmates through the bears and monkeys. Elena requested that we visit the reptile house and she smiled at the irony as she showed her snake the other snakes. How I wish she could talk and tell me what hilarious joke was surely going through her head. We stuck with a small group of four girls from her class. As usual, they held doors and walked holding onto her armrests. Children are amazingly accepting, and her classmates have been able to make Elena feel more normal than we ever will be able to. After lunch we treated her friends to a carrousel ride and after a quick picture, we left a little early. As I drove home from the zoo, Elena was attempting to talk to me. Usually I can figure out what she says to me if I hear her and watch her lips. (Let's just say that this is a tenuous feat while driving a car.) So at a stop light, I pulled down the rear view mirror and asked her what she was saying. She looked at me in the mirror, smiled and signed "thank you." My heart melted. Through all the nasty moodiness that the steroids cause, she was genuinely happy and I was so grateful I could find a way to bring that to her.

Day 157 – May 5

Elena's self confidence is waning. Every morning she brushes her teeth with her eyes fixed on the floor. She buries her face in the corner of her wheel chair when we attempt to take her picture. She cries when we cut her hair. It's her cheeks and she's become increasingly self-conscious about the swelling that ensues with every steroid dose. At 4 mg per day, the swelling was manageable. And while Elena never loved the way she looked, we could draw her out of her shell enough to get a forced smile. But now, with double the dosage, the swelling has doubled as well, and Elena can't stand the way she looks. Mirrors and cameras are her enemies.

Today at the art museum it was no different. And although Elena has always been the classic introvert, she never had difficulty with a crowd. But with steroids in tow, it was a totally different experience. She shunned family, friends and strangers alike as she recoiled into her shell. And in the same room that just two days before she had giggled with excitement in, she now cried. Not because she did not want to be there, but because she did not like the way she looked. Only knock-knock jokes from Grandpa-Grandpa and a promise to visit her precious Sally dog were enough to calm her anxiety if only for a minute. Finally, we gave up and left the museum early.

As a parent, what is most frustrating is seeing her concentrate on her cheeks when she has made so many wonderful advances in the last day. Today she walked her first ten steps in over a week, she ate her food by herself and she began to gain control of her left hand once again. Yet, all she sees are her cheeks. Sadly, it is this one-track-mind that allowed her to paint this picture and it is this compulsion that leads her to fear the attention it creates.

For Brooke and me, Elena's painting represents more than just a heart. It represents her ability to illuminate a disease that destroys so many young lives. It represents the vibrant colors and emotions that define our daughter. It represents her view of the world at this young age. Tears or not, we know that she appreciates the support and the one chance for her to see her painting at the art museum next to "her Pablo." This she admitted as we boarded the elevator back to our car.

In the end, the painting was beautiful. Not because it was the best in the class, for I doubt it was. And not even because it hung in an art museum. It was beautiful because it symbolizes everything we love about our daughter: the power to illuminate and the willingness to share, all while smaller and more reserved than the paintings around it. I love you Elena.

Day 158 – May 6

I'm known as Elena's Dad. Nothing else matters after today and I'm okay with that. After having her artwork displayed at the art museum and her story carried on the front page of the newspaper, Elena has become a bit of a hero in her own right. Hopefully the most that I can ever aspire to be known as Elena and Gracie's Dad.

Elena's recovery continued today in a manner all her own. The leg is still weak and the right hand still hangs lifeless by her side, but her appetite has returned and her voice is improving. Not that she's giving up sign language anytime soon. She's still busy teaching us two to three new signs a day. Where she learns it from we have no idea, but a quick check of the Internet confirms our suspicions: she's a sign language savant. This is her new voice and sometimes I wonder if she'll ever give it up.

As I kiss her goodnight, I try to remember the sound of her voice. These are the moments that a camera doesn't capture. There's the smile, the face and the memories, but the voice is forgotten. Funny how you can forget something so important so quickly. For six years it was the sound of her voice that welcomed me home from work, the sound of her voice that begged to go higher on the backyard swing, and the voice that wished me goodnight. Now it is the sound I can't remember.

But tonight as I see Elena taking her first steps and eating her first real food in over two weeks, I yearn for the chance to hear her voice once again. The progression chemotherapy seems to be working, although this can only be confirmed by an MRI 20 days away. And although her chances are still remote for a full recovery, we will take each day one-at-a-time and hope for it to be slightly better than the rest. Then, maybe one day I'll get both of my wishes: to hear her voice and always be known as Elena's Dad. This time I won't forget.

Day 159 – May 7

Elena's chances are called "grim." Her prognosis is "dismal." And although certainly harsh, these words serve as daily reminders of the battle she faces. It is in confronting these overwhelming odds that we find solace now in Elena's improvement. This is not a battle of terminology so much as it is a battle with the horrific disease we know as diffuse intrinsic pontine glioma (DIPG). To the rest of the world, it is simply known as brainstem glioma cancer.

DIPG is a disease that strikes at the heart of childhood and it is a disease in desperate need of a cure. And in my mind, I can see no better place to start the cure for cancer. Lung cancer has a survival rate of 80% if caught in the early stages to less than 5% if caught in stage 5. Breast cancer has typically an 80% survival rate. Leukemia has a 48% survival rate. At the same time, less than 10% of DIPG children will live longer than 18 months from diagnosis. Meanwhile, "survival" statistics aren't even quoted for DIPG, since virtually all children will never make it to the five-year milestone that is generally understood to be remission.

Often we consider the race for a cure a matter of numbers. After all, what better way to attack a problem than to focus on the cancers that afflict the most number of people? And while this may seem like a good idea, the problem is that often cancers that afflict the most people (generally lung cancers) also have an 80% to 5% survival rate.And while most people with lung cancer may choose to pursue aggressive treatment options, it is those with slightly better survival statistics who may consider "quality of life" options as well. After all, if the prognosis for survival is 80%, does it make sense to pursue a treatment protocol that has risky side effects such as a stroke or coma? Maybe not.

Now consider the impact of age. Overall, children may respond more positively to aggressive drug therapies than adults. And while they may not be subjected to the same dosage amounts based upon their weight, the fact that children are growing and their cells are continuing to develop often helps to overcome most drug side effect issues. They might even be able to pioneer drugs that might have failed with most adults. So are children the best place to invest our resources and efforts in the pursuit of the cure?

Surely no one advocates making children our testing ground for new cancer cures, but DIPG represents an opportunity to pursue cancer in ways that we might not with other forms of the disease. With a "dismal" prognosis and virtually no recognized survival, it would seem that this is the place to establish a cure. After all, what parent would not want every chance at seeing their child beat cancer and actually survive where others have not? And while "quality of life" options would still have to be at the heart of every parent's decision, I think you will find that the scarcity of survivors would resonate in all actions regarding protocols. When discussing the cure, the word "dismal" should represent "opportunity," although in my mind and most other DIPG parents' minds, it will still underscore the horrific nature of this disease.

In the end, numbers don't matter. Overall annual diagnosis numbers help us to prioritize, but they do not help us to cure. The cure will start with the form of cancer that has the most to gain, for it already has lost the most. Five months ago, cancer was an invisible enemy and DIPG was an obscure illness. Today I see it as the key to a cancer cure and the key to winning back my daughter.

In the end, I sadly realize that it may be too late for my Elena, but my viewpoint remains unchanged. DIPG is where we will find lasting cures and where we will advance medicine. I am not a doctor, but somehow I do not think that this point is lost on anyone. DIPG is a window of opportunity that we cannot afford to ignore. The cure must start now.

Day 160 – May 8

Every night when I clean out Elena's school folder, I pull no less than two notes from Elena saying, "I love you Mom Dad Grace." I find the phrase on the back of her worksheets and on meticulously cut hearts. Just recently with her increased reliance on Mom and Dad to do the simplest of tasks, she has become ever more thankful for our help. Each time she makes the sign for potty and I approach to lift her, she smiles sheepishly. When she requests a toy or her fifth course of her meal, she signs "I love you." When I carry her to the car for school, I get endless kisses as a thank you.

Elena has always been an independent girl, and now she is painfully aware of her inability to control anything in her life right now. Yet, despite being miserable in knowing that she needs assistance to simply play with a toy, she is always quick to show us her appreciation. Just today Elena was sitting behind Keith as he talked to me about her upcoming medical appointment. Elena secretly signed "I love you" with a broad smile on her face and I returned the smile just as brightly. Keith looked at Elena and back at me, questioning what we were smiling about. Elena simply smiled back at him and rolled her eyes towards the ceiling, happy to find a way to tease Daddy.

Each day that shows a little bit of progress, a few extra steps, spontaneously using the right hand, or even using her tongue to lick off the corners of her mouth is a major development to us. We are overjoyed that she continues to improve as we back off the steroid doses little by little. Despite the grueling days of therapy and simple daily tasks, Elena remains a caring and loving little girl. I count down the days to when we will be off the steroids, her voice will be back, and we have far more opportunities to verbalize our feelings. Until then, I will take the notes and tuck them in my briefcase for a quick dose of happiness when she is at school, and savor every kiss and smile.

Day 162 – May 10

Elena is an author. And at two books a day, I think she'll soon eclipse most authors. Still, Elena's kindergarten teacher thinks that Elena should write less non-fiction and more fiction and instructional books. Apparently kindergarteners now need a writing portfolio. A lot has changed since my kindergarten when I scribbled a crayon line on a piece of construction paper and went back to eating paste. Of course, I guess all that paste may also be why I never wrote prose. Still, I wonder if a journalistic expose will be next.

Either way, Elena was determined to cure this problem and she started this morning at breakfast. The title: "How to be a Kindergartener." It was for her sister. You see, Brooke and I recently discovered that Gracie is fifteen days shy of the kindergarten cut-off for next year. And while we've always prided ourselves on not being overly aggressive parents, pushing advancement for the sake of advancement, we've decided that Gracie is ready. I think Elena agrees.

So somewhere in the midst of our discussions, Elena figured out that Gracie would be attending kindergarten and she decided that this should become the subject of her instructional manual. Then, armed with this new textbook, she decided she would coach Gracie on the finer points of kindergarten etiquette. So starting on the first page with a heart, she decided to show her the ropes. First, she determined that Gracie would need to learn to sit on the rug. This was where every good kindergartener must begin the day, sitting cross-legged and quiet as they would begin to share. As if to help illustrate her point, she continued with a detailed drawing of the carpet squares, complete with marking to signify Gracie's place at the front of the room (do you think Elena knows something about Gracie's personality that we don't?).

On page two, Elena figured that Gracie would need a floor plan to better understand the elementary school campus. There are three areas at school: the top, the blacktop and the lower playground. This was where recess was held and she went to great effort to not only list the areas, but to also draw a diagram to help her understand how they relate to each other.

Page three was blank. I guess we must have skipped a page. Maybe she just left it with the understanding that she would add to it later.

Page four was dedicated to the complex kindergarten schedule. You see, not only do you have to worry about sitting on the rug, but you also have to balance art, PE, "muizc" (music for all you non-spellers), and "libre" (that's Spanish for "library").

Page five contained only the simplest of instructions: "be qiit in the cafuteryu" or "be quiet in the cafeteria." I think all teachers would be proud of this lesson, although I expect they'd want quiet in more places than just the cafeteria.

Page six was the most important page. Even with her limited voice, this was a subject worthy of elaboration. Ten minutes later, she was still instructing Gracie. This one was about Razzle Dazzle, the all important honorary status bestowed on only one special child per day. The responsibilities are endless, the privileges are coveted and the daily tributes are legendary. He or she is the line leader, the password chooser and the weather forecaster. Best of all, it comes around only once every 21 days (there are 21 children in her kindergarten class). Elena's lesson to Gracie was simple: you get to be Razzle Dazzle. Who knows, you might even get a song named after you...

"Her name is Elena,
She's like the sun,
Her Razzle Dazzle has just begun.
Razzle, dazzle, sparkle and shine,
Razzle Dazzle, sparkle and shine."

And trust me, after the first time your child becomes Razzle Dazzle you know the song. Elena sang it all the way home.

Page seven was simple. No words, just a picture of Gracie and all the friends she will make at school.

Page eight was blank. I guess she left more space to add to later.

Page nine was about calendars. Every good Razzle Dazzle girl needs to know how to read a calendar for news and weather time. Elena would later educate Gracie on the finer points of calendar function as she referred to her highly detailed diagram that continued on page ten.

Page eleven was all about attitude: "Smil Gracie." Apparently Mom and Dad's endless prompting for Elena to smile regardless of her steroid dosages had finally taken hold.

Page twelve was about centers. This was always Elena's favorite; after all, this was when she got to write the non-fiction books that she loved. Now it was her turn to pass it on to Gracie. Writing, reading, word study, puzzles and math; the choices were endless.

Page thirteen was her tribute to her sister: "have a grat tim at knidrgrdni."

Page fourteen continued with a mission to "do gret weth ur tchr." Just like Elena, I have no doubt that Gracie will be the teacher's pet.

Pages fifteen and sixteen were all about the benefits of kindergarten. First she noted that in kindergarten you have poetry books. Then she noted the role of special activities like special guests and programs.

Page seventeen and eighteen summarized Elena's experience in kindergarten with "we have los uv fun" and "knidrdnd is los uv fun." And by the time she finished reading, Gracie was already packing her school bag. For Elena, kindergarten is fun and she couldn't imagine anywhere else she'd rather be. To her it represents new experiences, new friends, and a routine that she so desperately needs right now. She always wants to be a teacher and now she gets to be a mentor. Good thing Gracie is a fast learner.

Day 164 – May 12

For Mother's Day, the girls gave Brooke tomatoes. Well, not exactly tomatoes, but tomato plants. And they didn't exactly give it to her, I bought an upside down planter on the Internet and my Mother planted the plants for me. Oh, and I didn't really think of it myself; Brooke sent me an e-mail last week asking for me to buy an upside down planter for tomatoes for her on Mother's Day. The e-mail even told me how much to spend and how early to purchase it to ensure timely delivery. Then when I forgot, (which I did) she sent me a reminder e-mail (I blamed it on the girls, after all, this is their Mother and they should have ordered it over the Internet, right?)

So there we were, parading around the yard in our muddy gym shoes, with muddy socks, wiping our muddy brows and doing our best to find some plantable clay. Real quality time. It occurs to me that I have never really grasped the meaning of the Mother's Day holiday. After all, for Mother's Day, Brooke asked for tomatoes, and she hates tomatoes. So why would she want tomatoes? Simple, it was for the girls. You see, my Mother has a tomato plant at her house and the girls love picking the ripe tomatoes directly off of the vine and popping them in their mouths. Sometimes they'd actually sit on the porch waiting for the tomatoes to turn red just so that they could eat them. Now of course that never happened, so occasionally they'd pop a green one. This was more often with Gracie; she never had patience. Elena, on the other hand, would wait patiently until it was just perfect but with Gracie around, her tomato selection would be limited.

On a day when we honor our mothers by rewarding them with any whim they can imagine, Brooke can only think of her girls first. No pedicure, no facial; for Brooke it is enough to simply ask for a planter for the one food that she hates the most. This was when I realized how lucky we are. Not only does Brooke think of her daughters first, but she also knows that her husband barely gets anything right, so she even sends him reminders. How lucky we all are. No card, no breakfast in bed, just tomatoes.

Finally it occurs to me why she does what she does: for the smiles. Skip the card and the pedicure, a smile is so much better, even when it comes with tomato seeds in it. The tomato planter is a way to delight the girls and in turn generate smiles. Maybe she isn't so selfless after all. No, she probably is. The smiles are all hers.

Day 165 – May 13

They say that the world always looks better through rose-colored glasses. Now I know what they mean. On the way home from the amusement park tonight, Elena donned her rose-colored sunglasses and moaned with excitement. And after about ten minutes of gesturing, we finally figured out that with her glasses she was able to see without double vision again. One of the symptoms of DIPG is double vision as a result of not being able to fully move your left eye. When it first occurred in early March, Elena would have double vision when she lay on her back or when she would look to her right. Slowly, her left eye became increasingly paralyzed until about a month ago, when the double vision became a permanent symptom. But now, with the aid of her rose-colored sunglasses, apparently all was cured. So during the drive home, she called out signs, cars and colors as if she was seeing them for the first time. But as we continued down the road, she eventually became silent, removed her sunglasses and tossed them to the floor. Quick as it had left, the double vision was back. The euphoria was over. Rose-colored glasses seldom offer lasting solutions.

Today was the day for the "Eiffel Tower." And if you've been following Elena's wish list, you know that this was the wish — well, other than the chili parlor. 165 days ago, after receiving the news that Elena might only live for 135 days, she and I stayed up all night at the hospital and talked about what she wanted to do when we left. Little did she know what this list was about or that I would be committed to making it all come true. On that list was wish number two: a visit to the Eiffel Tower. But not the Eiffel Tower in Paris; instead, the Eiffel Tower at the local amusement park just north of our house. Having driven by it on the way to her Grandmother's house for more than six years, she always wondered what it would be like to look out from the top. So today, with clear skies and a perfect 72 degrees, we finally went to the park to climb the tower. Of course, it didn't hurt that the park staff had heard of Elena's wish and donated tickets for the cause.

About an hour into our visit and after overcoming Gracie's overwhelming desire to ride some rides, we finally boarded the elevator to the top and perched her wheel chair next to the glass wall as we ascended the 354 foot tower. But with her newfound fear of heights that we acquired somewhere during the disease, she was decidedly less than excited and wanted to be at least five feet from any overlook. That limited her appreciation to mostly east, west, north and south horizons, but the effect was the same. For Brooke and me, the occasion symbolized a triumph over the 135 day timeframe. To Elena, she just kept looking for her kindergarten teacher's house (apparently at school, her teacher had told her that she could see her house and dogs from the tower). We never found the house with the two dogs in the backyard, but we did at least get a picture to remember. Soon it was time to board the elevator again, this time with our backs to the glass wall of the elevator and continue our visit to the park.

From there we went from ride to ride with Gracie taking the lead. Fast, slow, inverted or the sickening Scrambler, no ride was too wild for Gracie. Elena, looking for less excitement and more rest, preferred to watch. With Brooke and me taking turns volunteering each other for the worst rides in the park (I suggested that Gracie take Mom on the log flume and Mom suggested that Gracie take me on the stomach turning Scrambler), we made our way through the park. The winner would get to stay with Elena and seek the comfort and shade of a nearby tree.

While she had made tremendous progress in the last two to three days, today I noticed a decline. The finger no longer moved as it had previously, the right foot dragged once again, her speech was slurred and her breathing was labored. In my head I told myself that it was allergies, lack of sleep or even the sun. Never wanting to admit that it might be something else, I looked for excuses and even tried to ignore the signs. Somehow I think I wasn't alone, for as I returned from a ride with Gracie, Brooke was also staring at her limp leg and asking her to pace her breathing. With so many positives in the past week, neither of us wanted to see her this way. And while we may be over anxious, tomorrow will tell the true story. Either it was sleep and sun, or it was the tumor. Alone, none of her symptoms mandate further action, but collectively they cause us concern as we prepare for bed tonight. And still, as if in denial, Brooke and I have not discussed the symptoms that I'm sure we both have noticed. Today was a good day and I don't think either of us wanted to lose that feeling.

In three days, Elena once again will go for her chemotherapy treatments and I pray that they will bring the same promise they did two weeks ago when we saw her improve for the first time in a month.

Until then, we will watch her walk, talk and eat with the anticipation that only a parent can know. Tonight, rose-colored glasses are more than just a way to see without double vision. For Brooke and me, they are a way to make it through one more day.

Day 166 – May 14

A wise lady, who also has a child with DIPG, once told me, "Never look at a day and think it is a bad day, because this may be better than tomorrow, so just thank God that you have the day at all." I can't tell you how many times this has gotten me through a day. We have always joked that our girls could never jointly have a good day. If Gracie acted up, Elena would be an angel, and vice versa. Today, Gracie was perfect, even dressing herself, putting on her own seatbelt and letting me drop her off at preschool after only 10 minutes of goodbyes. Elena, on the other hand, was having a hard time, especially as I noticed her breathing had become very shallow during breakfast. On the way from dropping off Gracie and heading to Elena's school, she burst out into a big long paragraph with great excitement. I can never decipher what she is saying without looking at her lips, so I asked her to hold that thought until I got to the school and felt quite excited that she was attempting to talk so much. I got her settled in the classroom and her face immediately went deadpan. No smiles, no expressions, no more talking. I asked her what she needed to tell me and she put her hand up in the stop position and shook her head "no." Enough said, or not said. I asked her aide to take it a bit easy on her today, and I guess that is all Elena needed to hear to shut down for the day. I picked her up at lunch to find out she did the minimal amount of participation for that morning. Two days and counting until the next treatment, I can't wait.

Day 167 – May 15

Every day we believe that we are doing our best. That our efforts are stretched to their limits and that we can do no more.

The goals and struggles we endure today are the most we will ever carry. That someday it will get easier, but it never does. What we believe today to be impossible will be inconsequential tomorrow. And so it continues.

It is called a survivor mentality. And for those who accept this responsibility, life is both a burden and a pleasure at all times, and at the same time, particularly with our experience with Elena. I have come to understand what being a survivor means. It is a title bestowed on those who see a glimmer of light in a hall of darkness. It is a person who has no doubts, no fear and only confidence, that at times seem irrational. It is a person who believes that he or she alone can find the solution and that at the right moment, it will become evident. It is a confidence that exudes optimism hand-in-hand with faith.

I often wonder if we have what it takes to be survivors. Could we stand alone on a deserted island secure in the fact that we would find our way home? Or would we be relegated to scanning the horizon for a hope of being rescued? And would we then feel the constraints of pressures for which we had no solutions? No food, no shelter, and isolation. Would this be too much? Would we think it could get no worse, only to discover that it did?

Being a survivor must be more than just an ability to find solutions, it must also be an ability to cope. Suddenly I understand what it means and I wonder if we are up for the challenge. I have no doubt that Elena is. At a time when she is at her worst and seemingly unable to accept any other burden, she still takes the time to be a sister to Gracie. And through it all, she helps her prepare for kindergarten, get ready for bed and even brush her teeth. For her, being a survivor is also about being human.

Some days, as I look across the table at her laboring to breathe or struggling to drink from a straw, I wonder how much more I can take.

Would it be better to just have calm, regardless of the outcome? Or is life about more than being comfortable? Somehow I know the answer, although I ask it daily.

Life is about the struggle, the passion and the love that we share for our children. Still, I'm struck by the fact that somehow I think I'm the one struggling when it truly has nothing to do with me. This is Elena's fight and I am merely a spectator placed here to support and love. She is the true fighter and the true survivor. Ultimately Brooke, Gracie and I are left to embrace Elena and make her stronger daily. We do not have cancer, we do not experience paralysis and we do not have to face this terminal battle. Elena does, alone. And when she succeeds, our family will be one. If she fails, we will be lost and left to cope, as survivors. Life is about the battle and belongs to survivors.

Day 169 – May 17

They say to not expect too much out of the first days after chemo. She may have diarrhea, she probably will have nausea, and she will be exhausted. If Elena can give attitude to her parents, she can definitely be defiant to those doctors, and she certainly was. I let Elena sleep in this morning. For me, that only lasted until 7:30 a.m. when I needed to see her face. Now there is no thought that escapes my mind as I open that door. Today I crept into her room and found her staring at the ceiling, and I held my breath. But instead of heavy breathing or groaning about her right side not working, she simply turned her head to me with a huge smile. My heart soared; it didn't just make me feel good, it made me float on air. I haven't been greeted with a smile in such a long time. It didn't stop there and she smiled through getting dressed and through breakfast.

I asked her if she felt up to going to school. She nodded yes and said, "No PE." Apparently, her gym teacher had her doing bench presses with a one-pound bar and doing arm stretches trying to help her with her physical therapy during her last class. I asked her, "Don't you like your teacher?" "No," she said very clearly. I told her he must be doing right. I reminded her that she didn't like her physical therapist at first either, but that was because she was working her hard to get results. By the end of our stay in Memphis, the therapist was our best friend. So I relented, not willing to push the envelope, no PE this time. But I told her next time he would have the barbells and mats waiting. She agreed and smiled.

We got to school just in time for PE. It appears that her teacher had been asking if she was coming in today because he had new tricks up his sleeve. We rolled into the gym and he begrudgingly agreed to let us sit and watch the ultra amusing game of "Scoop It Up." The rest of the day I didn't transfer her from the wheel chair too many times; I figured a good attitude was better than walking today. We lasted about two hours, until the only thing left was recess, writing and lunch. Upon hearing this, Elena quickly wrote her book in about two minutes, and said "Home." Instead of going home, we surprised Dad for a lunch date, flashing Dad smiles the entire time and then off we went for our nap.

Day 172 – May 20

Exhaustion has set in. I've experienced physical fatigue many times before. I've been simply tired; lacking my normal sleep. But exhaustion is a completely different matter. I awake every morning too tired to sleep, realizing that I haven't had a dream in months. I get dressed only to realize halfway through the process that I've put on two different shoes and I'm not quite fully awake. I drive across town but can't remember what route I took. I sit down to eat and can't bring myself to eat even though I'm hungry. Or worse, I eat just to eat regardless of the fact that I'm already full. I've resolved myself to writing lists throughout the day in order to keep track of my schedule, only to later lose the list. I find myself struggling to remember names of people that I've known for years. And in my mind there is only one thought, every hour of the day: Elena.

I'm sure Brooke feels the same way. Often we joke about it. Today we counted out balloons for the art show, only to realize that by the time we finished counting, we had already forgotten the total number. And so it goes with no end in sight. It is an exhaustion that we cannot avoid for it is a result of our circumstance, not how many hours we sleep, although I'm sure this does not help it any.

I often wonder if Elena experiences this as well. Fatigue is certain; we see the effects of chemotherapy on her face and in the number of naps she takes every day. Exhaustion is another thing. Today I think we saw it for the first time. We did our best to counteract it with aggressive physical therapy and an optimistic outlook, but the lines on her face tell a different story. After all, lines don't belong on a 6-year-old's face. I could tell in the way she dragged her foot more while walking today despite being able to flex it during therapy more than ever before. I could tell in her hand as she let it slump over the armrest of her wheel chair no more than an hour after using it to hold down the corner of the prints she signed in preparation for the art show. And despite our best intentions, I watched as she gave up and went to sleep on the couch. She never truly naps during the day.

We ask her what she is thinking, believing somehow that by knowing her thoughts we will be able to give her peace. It's a dangerous risk, and if she asks the one question we hope she won't, we'll have to lie. So we hold our breath and ask. Today she told us that she loved watching everyone buy her painting and that it made her happy to see it at the art show. Thankfully today the answer was a good thing. Still, her exhaustion as well as ours is taking its toll. Sadly, there is no way out and no end, or at least not one we want.

Day 173 – May 21

We needed today. After spending yesterday watching Elena struggle to breathe and cry with every movement, Brooke and I were ready for the worst. We contemplated increasing her steroid dosage, forcing her to stay home from school and even thought about calling for the hospice consultation that we had been putting off for the last month. But Elena had other plans for today. And not only did she improve from her previous depths, but she finally made progress in freeing herself from the wheel chair.

Today we started small. Five years ago, she learned to walk by first learning to crawl, so we thought this was the best way to start. The wheel chair became a method of transportation and nothing else. If she wanted to sit at the table, she had to walk to the chair and sit down. If she wanted to draw and make a craft, she would do so on the floor. And when her pen was out of reach, she would have to crawl to get it. But when you've been in a wheel chair for the past month and a half, even the simplest activities become a challenge. A five-foot crawl to get a bead took 10 minutes and involved falling to her belly more times than you can imagine. Still, by the end of the day, she realized that slow and steady movements were better than larger ones and when you stop crying you really can concentrate better.

In a way, Elena's easy to work with. You can explain how bending a knee is better than swinging a hip when she walks and she'll stop and listen. And when I told her to concentrate on keeping her hands under her chin when she crawls, she did it. Five years ago, she figured it out on her own. This time she needed coaching even if I didn't quite know how to explain when you bend one knee and not the other while walking. Try it and see. We know how to walk, but try to describe each and every motion. Then you'll know what it is like to be Elena. What came naturally once must now be learned again.

But what had changed most of all was her attitude. Today she awoke with a smile and ready for a challenge, even if her body wasn't quite willing. She talked, she stopped gasping for breath and put all of her efforts into getting better, and this is what made her better. When she was first diagnosed, we were told that DIPG is a progressive disease. That what you lose will stay lost unless you're going through radiation. But the DIPG that we know is nothing like that. Instead, it is a roller coaster with bends and turns that we never expect and can't prepare for. So too are our emotions, which follow the track wherever it might lead. Get ready for the next turn.

On a side note, the next time you see Elena, ask her about Earl the Squirrel. It seems that at breakfast Elena made a bet with Mom that even the squirrel sitting outside on the retaining wall wouldn't eat her medicine. Mom held the moral high ground and put $5 on it. Tonight the medicine still sits on the wall and the squirrel is nowhere in sight. Tomorrow, either Elena will be $5 richer or you'll soon see a squirrel roaming our street with a bad attitude. Looks like Mom is going to lose again.

Day 175 – May 23

One peanut butter and jelly sandwich, a cookie and chocolate milk. Sometimes a strawberry on those days when the steroid hunger would set in. Elena loves the picnics in the backyard. The breeze is cool, the grass is warm and the respite from the living room couch is always appreciated. This is the beginning of Wednesdays with Dad.

Sometimes we hear the hawk from above as she builds a nest in the oak tree overhead. Other times we can barely hear each other over the pounding of hammers and the scream of circular saws as the carpenters build the untimely addition on the back of the house. At one point, it seemed like a good idea but now after her diagnosis, it is nothing more than a distraction that we don't need. Still we move on, only this time reworking the plans to accommodate for a first floor bedroom and a handicap accessible bathroom just for Elena.

I ask her over lunch what color she wants to paint her new bedroom. She just shrugs. Maybe pink, I suggest. She looks away. We sit in silence. Somehow I think she knows more than I want her to. The house will be finished in October but her disease tells us to expect no longer than July. It is June. Somehow I doubt she will ever be able to decorate her new room.

We try to talk about something else, but small talk is all about the future. Questions like where she wants to go on vacation, are you looking forward to school, and what do you want for your birthday all seem frivolous. I think even she knows that she'll never make it that far. So we sit in silence.

It was the same way with Christmas. Every present was a chore. Each gift was another thing that she didn't want. Couldn't everyone see that the only thing on her list was to get better? It was the one gift we couldn't give her and the only one she desired. What's the use of a new doll when the paralysis prevents you from hugging it?

We give these children gifts and vacations when we can't give them hope and a cure. And they know the difference. I believe that Elena does. I can see it now in her smile and in the pictures she draws. The themes are of love, but also finality. "I love you Mom, Dad and Grace," she writes, as if she'll never see us again.

After the picnic, we lie on our backs and look at the clouds, her head on my arm. We exchange no words, just a passing glance and silence. I love you too, Elena.

Day 177 – May 25

How does cancer affect a child? How does it affect my child – aside from the clinical effects? Over the past two weeks, I've started to notice changes in Elena that I fear will never heal. Where there was once a child, there is now an adult. Where there was once innocence, there is now cynicism. Where there was once a smile, there is now scorn. The moments are fleeting but becoming more and more dominant over a 6-year-old's carefree manner. Now I wonder if we will ever be able to bring back the child in her.

To question her future attitude is to assume a cure. That is the good thing. And maybe the loss of a childhood will be the only thing we have to fear if the cancer goes away. That, by itself, is a leap of faith. But as she starts to recover again for the third time, we are back at the top of the hill with a view of the horizon and suddenly we start to question future prospects. At the bottom, you can only see the ground. So tonight as I washed her hair and put her to bed, I find myself searching for the girl I once knew. But in her eyes, all I see is emptiness and suspicion. After being poked and prodded, cut and bled, stretched and poisoned, she no longer can feign innocence. She is more of an adult than I will ever be.

Cancer or any terminal illness makes martyrs out of heroes and hollows souls out of survivors. Bringing it back will be impossible. No candy or flowers will allow her to forget this struggle, it is part of her life and part of her future forever. Still, it is the best that I can hope for, for survival is the only objective.

As a parent, you also begin to wonder how far to push. If this is not the cure, do we go beyond experimental and verge on improbable? And at what point should we give up? Can survival be worse than death? Right now, survival is our goal, and I will never be able to answer that question until it occurs. I pray to never see that day.

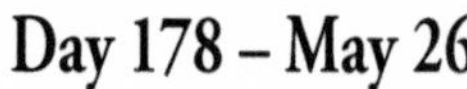

Day 178 – May 26

Every summer for the last few years, we have gone to Tennessee several times during the summer to met Keith's family for weekends at the lake. I still remember when Elena went to her Kindergarten orientation. She was so proud to tell her new teacher how she had water skied that summer at her Grandma's house. The girls have always cherished summers with the family, especially their two cousins. Elena has always gravitated towards her youngest cousin as Elena was pretty sure that she needed guidance through life. With everything going on, we have been hesitant with taking trips, but with a long weekend and Elena feeling pretty good, we took the risk for a weekend of fun. Elena and Gracie were more than ready as we had not been there in about eight months.

Before traveling, we had to get tests done to make sure everything was ready for chemo on Tuesday. After three hours at the hospital and the all clear, we got on the road. Gracie let me know she loves sleeping on these trips because when she opens her eyes, suddenly she is in Tennessee. I won't tell Gracie that I do the same thing and suddenly Keith is left all alone for the entire drive. I love my husband! We were just glad that we were able to go to Tennessee without the threat of having to go to a hospital when we arrived.

I think Grandma and Grandpa have been planning this weekend for the last two weeks complete with a refrigerator of organic foods to feed an army, if the army were concerned about hormones and antibiotics in their food. Grandma had crafts scheduled for several times a day; just call her Grandma Cruise Director. Grandpa custom outfitted the dock for Elena's needs with water misters and fans to stay cool and a giant canopy to keep her out of the sun. But what took the cake was waiting outside on the deck after breakfast. In a valiant attempt to make the weekend perfect for the girls, Grandma's efforts didn't stop there. You might want to sit down for this: she actually sewed tomatoes onto her tomato plants because her plants had not produced any tomatoes yet. The girls loved the gesture and Gracie was excited to find the "real tomatoes" that were still green and not ready to be eaten. Never mind that the "vines" were actually made of thread.

Later that day, Gracie was the first to the dock after lunch. With water skis on, she was ready to go. Elena would have been content under the canopy, but we weren't, and made her get into a floating chair. The kids jumped and played just like every other summer weekend in the past. Elena's most daring feat today was when I slipped her off the floating chair to swim in the water with me. She was okay with it. I think after a full day of insisting on not swimming, she wouldn't actually let herself enjoy it. I certainly enjoyed the few minutes of hugging as we walked through the water. Elena, as always, enjoyed watching the crazy antics of her cousins.

Tonight we put the girls to bed and finally were able to have the New Year's Dinner we never got to have this year. There we talked of Gracie skiing and remembered that we were pretty confident that this year Elena would be off of training skis and learning to ski. Today, I was more proud that she was strong enough to be able to stand for the first time this week without pain.

Day 180 – May 28

In my family, you know you've made it when you get posted on the back of the bathroom door. The television stations pick up anything, the newspaper may fill space, Nobel prizes are commonplace and even the Pope can recklessly choose a saint, but being featured on the back of my Grandfather's bathroom door is a legendary honor. Why the bathroom door? Why not the kitchen bulletin board or the living room shelf? Who knows, but the back of the bathroom door has always been a place to feature the "movers and shakers" of the family. There you'll find a newspaper picture of my Aunt and Uncle as they participated in a breast cancer cure walk, an article on a relative who earned a "Teacher of the Year" award, and a newspaper picture of my sister combing the tail of a horse before a show. These are the heroes of my family and these are the ones who will be honored for all of eternity on the back of the bathroom door. As a child, I could only wish to be that lucky.

Tonight, I have been informed by my Grandfather (or "Grandpa-Grandpa" as Elena knows him), that Elena has taken her rightful position as a bathroom door honoree. Now we know that she has truly touched lives. Effective last week, her newspaper article and "I Love You" masterpiece will grace all who seek respite with the gods of indoor plumbing. Forever to enhance the color scheme and decorating of a bathroom ripped from the '70s, Elena's brilliance of colors and shades of blue and pink will forever call out to visitors of my Grandfather's bathroom to seek the betterment of themselves. And now, her impact will increase ten-fold, mostly just because of the size of my family.

Kidding aside, the bathroom door represents something. It represents an achievement and the selfless impression that she continues to leave on my family. And while it may not measure up to a debut at the art museum among the likes of Van Gogh and Picasso, a front page story in the newspaper, or even being the featured artist at the local art show, it is the one recognition that means the most because it is from her family.

On June 1st Elena will be honored by the city with a proclamation declaring it "Elena Desserich Day" for her impact on the city and its residents. Never before did I figure my daughter would have this much impact or be appreciated by so many. And in the beginning, I didn't even know what a "proclamation" was. But after reading the text that the City Manager sent to me late last week, I now understand its significance. Even without the proclamation, we knew that we were the parents of two very special girls. This Friday, when it is presented, I have no doubt that Elena will be impressed and honored. And if we're lucky, she might even smile through the steroids as she is given a copy of the proclamation complete with a large blue ribbon. Eventually they tell me that it might hang with a copy of her picture at the local recreational center lobby for all to see and appreciate. To Brooke and me, this is more than we could ever hope for. Elena, on the other hand, would be perfectly happy if it were to only hang on the back of the bathroom door.

Day 181 – May 29

Is it too early to be optimistic? With the prior failure of the last experimental chemotherapy drug and Elena's recent progression, we are hesitant to declare a success when the reality is that we've seen no changes. But isn't "no change" a positive in the face of a tumor that can grow overnight by a centimeter or more and paralyze her entire body? Better yet, at a time when we're supposed to be preparing for hospice, we are instead preparing for Elena's next day at school. And just this past weekend we were confident enough in her improvement to reduce her daily steroid dosage by a third. Clearly this is a positive sign, but the journey is far from over.

This morning, Elena woke up in a good mood. Without this, no recovery is possible. She knew what she was capable of and put her mind to the task. Her back pain is nearly gone, her right hand can now assist the left, and she tries to walk short distances with the help of either Brooke or myself. Two weeks ago, she wasn't capable of either and even eating was a struggle. Now it is a distant memory.

As I look back at the over the past several months, I'm struck by how miraculous her recovery was during the first three weeks of her radiation. I remember what it was like to feel desperation, but see the first signs of her recovery. And somehow I wonder if this will happen again. Back then she was unable to speak, walk and eat, just as she was unable to do a week ago. Back then she started with small steps, small bites and small words. Today she does all of this. And later she'll free herself from her wheel chair and return to her idealist 6-year-old exuberance. Hopefully next week she will begin this next step.

Day 183 – May 31

I have recently found it impossible to look at pictures. As the end of the school year approaches, we start to get sentimental. I wish I was like every other parent, busily thinking ahead to summer camps and play dates, but instead of looking forward, I find myself looking back. I walked into Elena's classroom today and looked at the bulletin board full of pictures of the kids on their first day. Each kid looked pretty much the same as today, minus a few teeth or some hair. I just stared at Elena's picture and thought how beautiful and young she looked. I never knew a disease could age a girl five years in five short months. I am not even referring to her newly bulging cheeks. I look into her eyes and my heart sinks as I see how tired they look, how "experienced" they appear. Gone is the innocent sparkle that you see in all the kindergartners. She knows more about this world than any of those children will for years to come, the good and the bad.

We picked up Elena's yearbook today. Prominently on several pages, Elena's bright smile and those big beautiful eyes that we knew would melt every boy's heart, made her picture stand out. I couldn't control my emotions as I flipped the page and saw Elena decked out in her Indian headdress from their Thanksgiving lunch. That was the last day of innocence. The last carefree day. The last day of school before we whisked her away to endure endless days of doctors and treatments. Through her already strained voice that day, she told me of the food they ate and things they did. She excitedly told me about why she chose to be an Indian rather than a Pilgrim. I miss how she got so excited about learning. I am sure she still gets excited about school, but she just doesn't show it much anymore.

Throughout the day, we struggled with Elena not being able to open her mouth too wide and her left hand weak from either the tumor or exhaustion. As I get ready to run to the store for "easy to eat" food, I wonder what I did with my time before all this. The doctors are pondering whether this decline is due to the steroid reduction or progression, but luckily there are no signs it is bleeding externally. We watch and wait to see if the treatment will kick in before we have to increase the steroids again. I really wanted to continue lowering steroids to a manageable dose. Just today, her cheeks deflated significantly which eased the pressure on her nose so she could breathe better. We even stood for a good amount of time with no pain. If we bump up the steroids, all of that will be gone. I want so much to see progress...

Tonight I have been given the task to find a picture of Elena from around the beginning of the school year. I looked at the picture and the ridiculous notion crossed my mind that all I wanted to do was crawl into that picture and stay there forever with her as she was. No limitations, no worries - just happiness. God, I wish it were that easy. God, I wish for so much but I think my shooting star is on vacation.

Day 184 – June 1

Holy cow she has a sign! Gracie was as surprised as I was as we drove home from work this afternoon. There, prominently displayed on the community recreational center billboard for all to see was the message "Today is Elena Desserich Day." They were serious about this proclamation thing.

The day began with an early wake-up call from Gracie at 4 a.m. It seems that "Lena Day," as she calls it, deserved as much anticipation as Christmas. Perhaps she might have been disappointed by the lack of presents or tree, but Gracie was content to jump out of bed and snuggle up to her sister and wish her happy Elena Day. Elena barely budged. Still, Gracie patted her cheek with her hand, kissed her and offered Elena her coveted "low" (her satin pillowcase that she sleeps with every night) as comfort. And after seeing the affection she presented her sister with, I didn't quite mind the early awakening.

By the time Gracie and I were off to school and work, Elena would finally awake with a smile on her face and a hunger in her belly. It seems that her dinner of one lonely meatball was not enough to fuel a growing little girl. Thankfully this morning, she was able to pry her mouth open far enough to fit in a couple spoonfuls of banana and a quarter of a pancake before getting frustrated with her inability to chew and giving up. Hopefully this will give us yet another day of nutrition to fend off the steroid and feeding tube options. But regardless of her hunger and chemotherapy fatigue, she insisted on going back to school to see her friends and teacher. Only later did we discover that she needed two naps to make it through the day. Perhaps next week we might explore some home schooling, but with it being the last week, I doubt Elena will want to miss one moment.

At school's end, she returned home to help Grandma with her afternoon nap (it seems Grandma also was a bit weary and needed Elena's comfort for a mid-afternoon siesta). But with Gracie's return two hours later, it was time for swimming. After all, the new swimming pool hadn't escaped Gracie's eye and she was ready to go. The sign declaring it "Elena Desserich Day" was just icing on the cake. So without delay, we packed up the girls and headed for a couple of hours of swimming before attending Elena's formal declaration of her ceremonial day.

There at the pool, Gracie practiced flips and turns off of the diving board, taking notes from the pubescent boys trying to outdo each other. So Gracie, all 40" of her, stood holding her place in line among a crowd of five foot, lanky, awkward teenagers all vying for attention, not that Gracie didn't want attention too. And of course Gracie got it; first with a belly flop and then with a series of cavorted twists and flailing arm movements which were anything but graceful. Still, the splash was the same and the cheers from the crowd gave her unnecessary encouragement. So up she went again, this time to do it higher and bigger.

Elena, watching from across the pool in the comfort of Mom's arms, stared in amazement, wondering when Dad planned to stop her sister before she hurt herself, all the time never knowing Mom's secret plan to weave a bit of therapy with a bit of fun pool-time. And before she knew it, she was on her feet walking the bottom of the pool balancing with the help of nearby hands. But just like anything else, the ruse was soon up and smiles turned to pouts as she understood this to be therapy and not fun.

By 6 p.m., it was time to dry off and head to the official proclamation ceremony in which her painting would be officially mounted in the recreational center lobby alongside a notice declaring June 1 as Elena Desserich Day, as long as you live in the city. And there in our bathing suits, sunglasses and cover-ups, Elena was honored for her courage, bravery and inspiration. And after a few "whereas," "therefores" and "hearkens" thrown in, it was made a legal and official proclamation for years to come.

Tonight, as Elena Desserich Day reaches twilight, her proclamation hangs on the wall of the recreational center as well as her bedroom for all to see. Still, in our hearts, tomorrow will always be more special than today, regardless of our newly certified holiday. Tomorrow brings promise, today brings hope. In the meantime, happy Elena day! Holy cow she has a sign!

Day 185 – June 2

Lately we've resorted to distraction to relieve stress. Instead of concentrating on her frustration with eating, we read the headlines in the local newspaper. When she can't even sit without falling over, we pick paint colors for the new addition. When her left hand fails, we try cleaning the house. Still it never works. Headlines don't matter, colors are irrelevant and the house will never be clean again. Our thoughts are with Elena and the future no matter how hard we try to protect our sanity and ourselves.

It is a feeling of being out of control that hurts the most. After all, from the very beginning of life you are taught that if you do good, good will come to you. When you bring in the trash, you get an allowance. Good grades bring the promise of ice cream. But all along, control is the one thing that eludes you. Now we truly understand how little control we exert on our lives. As we look at Elena, we wonder to ourselves what we did wrong and how we can make it right. I'd like to believe that we've lived lives devoid of sin and to the benefit of others, but still I wonder if we could have done more.

It's a ridiculous notion, it doesn't happen for any reason at all to any particular person, but in the back of your mind you just can't shake it. You never will, regardless of how many times people tell you otherwise. Still, you want it to be true. Not because you want to find fault with yourself, guilt has nothing to do with it, no matter how many people make this assumption. Instead, you want it be true because it will give your life meaning and grant you the faith that you crave.

After all, if life is about consequences and charity, you are back in control. You can excuse away tragedy on the basis of sin and perfect yourself in the pursuit of fortune. No longer will you fear life and question tomorrow because life can be what you want it to be. And in doing so, time is endless and without true value. Good deeds mean more time.

In reality, it is better without control. For without control, time is the ultimate reconcilable factor. Good deeds are done not because of a promised fortune, but because they are the right things to do. And today is the only thing to be lived for. This is the lesson of Elena and the tragedy of a terminal illness. Sadly it is a lesson I wish we never would have to learn.

Even our journal is a distraction. On tough days, we turn to self-reflection and on good days, we talk about how we spent our hours as a family. Today was not a good day. She couldn't stand, could hardly eat and couldn't even sit without falling over. And while they tell us that we need five days from treatment before making any conclusions, Brooke and I wonder how much longer we can wait. Tomorrow is the fifth day and we have not made any tangible improvement from the depths of Wednesday. So we watch television, write a journal and look at paint swatches, all while thinking the one thought we still can't talk about.

Day 186 – June 3

The people at the gas station thought I was crazy. No, not just because I pulled up in a truck when gas was at the highest price all year; that was about the only sane part of the fill-up. No, the looks came when I circled the car making faces and banging on the windows. Of course, what they couldn't see through the tinted windows were Gracie and Elena in the backseat smiling in delight at Dad's antics. You see, I'm not really crazy (at least not yet), so much as I'm looking for smiles. And in this game, it's all about the element of surprise and cheap visual gags. So I run from side to side, popping up in a different window each time with a different funny face. Then it's down again as I hunch over and run to the next window, careful to avoid tripping over the gas hose. This time I pop up over the hood and they see me through the front windshield. Next I bang on the rear, creating a shriek of surprise and laughter that only I can hear from outside the car. But after three trips, my back and legs scream out for relief, while inside the girls scream out for more. Too bad for me that I didn't buy the economy car – at least then the fill-up would be over. Instead, I'm only $40 into the visit and with a truck this is only half way. Now I'm left with the old tricks. I start with the stairway trick and then the elevator. Brooke rolls her eyes, but the girls want more. "Over here Dad," yells Gracie as she points to her window. Apparently, the experience has special meaning if it is in her window. I oblige and move to the other side. Nearing the end, I finally hear the click of the gas pump and realize it's time to leave.

Once again, I'm an adult with composure and maturity as I make my way to the pump to retrieve the receipt and return the nozzle to its holder. But while I was busy entertaining the girls, the rest of the gas station customers had also taken notice of my antics. To them, I had lost it. I looked around only to see them quickly look away and back at the ground. "Don't look at the crazy man – he might hurt me," they fear. I want to tell them about my girls in the backseat, but somehow I still don't think they'll understand. After all, Brooke doesn't even get it. "Stop that before someone we know sees us," she says. "You'll make a fool of yourself." Isn't that the point?

In the end, it's a smile and a laugh that I'm after. So next time you see me running around my car with arms flailing and banging on the windows, you'll know the girls are inside and I'm working for smiles. Stare all you want – then try it with your kids. Together we'll be the crazies at the pump.

Day 188 – June 5

She always listened to Mom more than she listened to me. I guess it's Mom's soothing nature, or maybe it's because Elena and I are one in the same. Her hair, her nose, her personality and her compulsions all come from me. Gracie, on the other hand, is just like Mom. Brooke and I always said we don't mix well. Either way, after her conversation with Mom yesterday about taking control of her life, Elena listened. Back again were the orders for breakfast, her clothing selections, who she wanted to pick her up from school, where she wanted to sit, and what she wanted to do. Oh, and yes, that included not taking a bath. Thank goodness we chose to not listen to that one. Still, for the first time in over a month, she was in charge of her life and it not only changed her attitude, but her willingness to fight.

This was the Elena that we know and the Elena that we will need to beat the cancer. And while her physical condition didn't change much (she still can't walk and move her right side), we know that in time this too, will change. Our biggest concern is keeping her involved and focused on her recovery. I guess it is like riding a bike. You can peddle fast, you can even have perfect balance, but if you don't look ahead you'll never go far. Attitude will be her balance, stubbornness will be her legs, but our next battle will be to keep her eyes on the future. And even for us, this will be difficult. After all, having been told for the past seven months that she will not outlive the goldfish, it is hard to think about tomorrow. But this is exactly what we must do if we are to convince her to fight. Tonight we started for the first time.

In the stands of the local tennis court with Gracie playing nearby on the playground, we started the conversation. When she started walking again, would she like to take tennis lessons? "No," she replied. Did she want to take swimming lessons instead? A bigger no. How about soccer lessons? Gymnastics? "No" to both. Ballet? Finally, a yes. Now we had a start. And did she want to take it this summer? She looked at us like we were crazy. After all, did we really think she'd be walking that soon? We pressed the issue. All we got was an "I don't know" shrug. In truth, neither did we. Still, it didn't matter; at least now she knew that there was a chance. And knowing that she might take ballet lessons in the summer, she finally agreed to therapy. She would try to walk again, not just today. We'll take it.

Tonight as we prepared the girls for bed, we took a moment to look at pictures from the past six months. We saw pictures from the day after diagnosis when we thought that she was at her worst. We saw pictures from the hospital when she couldn't eat. There too we thought she was at her worst. We saw pictures from the last day of her wish trip. There, we knew that it was as bad as it could be. That was also the day we figured that the progression started. But the one thing that each of the pictures had in common was that at the time, she wasn't the worst that she could be. And that goes for today as well. Someday we'll look at today's pictures and remark on how lively and happy she was as we sat at the tennis courts in the sun. Or, for the first time, we might actually be right and this will have been Elena at her worst. We just don't know. But as long as we plan for the best, we can't go wrong. Just like before, we will never be able to predict what is the "worst." Register for the ballet classes – here we come.

Day 189 – June 6

You can feel the excitement in the air. It is the day before the last day of school. I am actually sad I wasn't able to make it to the last "real" day of school today. Elena's aide wrote of all the fun things they did in class and it must have been pretty riveting stuff since this was the first day in a week that she didn't fall asleep during school. I have such mixed emotions about tomorrow. I wonder if she'll make it through the full day of field dayfestivities; I am sure I will break down a few times before we pack up her things. I am certain it will take several hours to say our goodbyes, and I am scared that she won't be able to come back in August. I hate tomorrow because I don't want school to end, and the progress to end, and the learning to end, and the purpose to end. Three months is an eternity anymore and I so desperately want to be standing there with her next year waiting for the school bell. I must have stared at the flyer to order school supplies for next year's class for about 20 minutes. I haven't wanted to fill out a form as badly as that one. Then I put down the form and got on the

Internet in a desperate attempt to find just one survivor of DIPG. If only I could have hope.

Day 190 – June 7

What a wonderful day. Elena was a little quiet when I dropped her off at school, but I think the excitement from her classmates was infectious. Elena completed her desk work independently and participated in all of the activities. Elena's sense of humor shines through some days and today she faked being asleep to get out of gym class. Only after her teacher promised no calisthenics on her last day, did she peak out and smile sheepishly. I arrived in time for the picnic lunch and Elena ate exceptionally slowly, again I believe trying to find a way out of the field day festivities.

After the kids were gone to start the games, we retreated into the air-conditioned office to finish the meal. We chatted with the teachers and Elena was content not to join in the activities during the hottest day of the summer. Finally her teacher coaxed us out to participate in the parachute game where Elena was given the coveted center spot under the parachute. We paused on the way back in to watch the custodian literally hose down the students. They loved it. We rejoined the teachers in the office and I convinced Elena to sit on my lap and close her eyes for a nap to make it through the rest of the day. Let's just say she didn't protest.

After popsicles and cleanup, we listened to one last story and then we had our goodbyes. All the teachers visited for their hugs and Elena's soon to be first grade teacher came to tell her she could come in next year to pick out her desk before any of the other kids. We assured him that we would be walking into that classroom in the fall. The teachers were so insistent that there would be a next year for Elena; our goodbyes weren't nearly as hard as I thought they would be. We made plans to see some of them when we got back from Tennessee, and we were on our way. By the time I got home, I had a renewed desire to get her moving again and optimism crept back into my thoughts.

When she asked for help feeding herself at dinner, I told her that either she could straighten out both hands while I do it or feed herself. Miraculously, that hand quickly grabbed the fork from me. Keith and I stood her up to change her clothes and then made her walk to the bathroom. She complained and whined as we forced her to tell us why she didn't want to walk. Did it hurt? No. Was she afraid of falling? No. Are you afraid you can't do it? Yes. I reminded her that five months ago at the hospital we had to do the exact same thing. It is hard enough to rehabilitate a six-year-old once, but to have to do it twice is heartbreaking. The therapists at the hospital were amazed with Elena's fast progress in December; I hoped reminding her of that would motivate her even more. So with words of encouragement, she made her first ten steps in the last three weeks, took a bath without crying, and showed Dad how she could turn herself in bed. Today we finished our first year of school and started our first summer of therapy. Watch out first grade, here we come.

Day 191 – June 8

It's been this way for over six months now. Every night, whether we felt like it or not, we've ended the day reflecting on Elena's experiences and chronicling every action. Some days are better than others. Often you can tell by the first line of the journal. Good days come with a diary (or "diarrhea" as Gracie calls it) of the day and Elena's experiences. Bad days are followed with generalizations and commentaries about anything that offers the possibility of distraction. Maybe you can tell from the first paragraph what today was like...

Some people tell us that we should make a book out of the journal. They say that the journal helps them prioritize their own lives. And while flattering, this journal was started for Gracie in order to know her sister better. But with time, as we see Elena progress from a victim to a survivor, we begin to see the journal in a new light. Maybe now it will be a book for Elena as well as Gracie. I guess that is the best way to see it.

Or perhaps the journal has even more of a purpose. This was the lesser known effect. It is in times like this that even Brooke and I need a release and no drug or psychologist consultation can do better. The journal has a way of crystallizing our thoughts and forcing us to reflect on the positives in a field of negatives. And even tonight as I strain against the pressure to fall asleep at the keyboard, I know that this is more important than an extra hour in bed. It is through this that I truly learn to relax and prepare for tomorrow. Maybe then I'll be able to write about her experiences rather than generalizations.

Day 194 – June 11

Last week we found the underwater camera we had taken on the wish trip, and I got the pictures developed today. I am shocked I didn't get hit by a car on the way to my van. I was excitedly opening the package as though it was Christmas as I weaved through cars in the parking lot. I didn't even mind the sweltering heat of the car, or sweat dripping from my forehead as I flipped through the pictures. That day was her last day of having all her abilities. I remember how she was so strong and happy just swimming around in the water and playing with her sister. I still look back on that day and feel such a sense of calm. At the end of the day, we sat listening to the birds and watching the dolphins. We had nowhere to go and nothing to worry about. Even though that was three months ago, it seems like an eternity. The day after those pictures were taken, she slowly started her decline. It almost seemed like a fairy tale that her last day free of symptoms was such a magical day for all of us.

Today Elena and Keith are on their way back from Memphis with some renewed hope. Keith spent the majority of his short time in Memphis working with the therapist to find new ways to get Elena moving. More than anything, we made sure she heard the therapist, whom she respects very much, tell her it was necessary to do these activities to get walking again. I think in the back of her mind, Elena was pretty sure therapy was our punishment to her. Now she knows what she needs to do. The therapist stressed the perfect activities for her would be water exercises. No matter how many times we told her, Elena never believed us when we suggested this. Now that an expert suggests it, she is willing to give it a try. One day my children will listen to all of my expert advice, right?

Day 195 – June 12

Through her life, Elena has constantly been complimented on her stunning eyes and beautiful hair. To emphasize her long locks, she had the world's most eclectic variety of ponytail holders, clips and of course, the headbands. Headbands of every color and most of them sparkled with rhinestones or sequins. Elena never wore gaudy clothing, but she always knew the "bling" belonged in her hair. Just this year, she asked to start the honor of brushing her hair before school and she meticulously made sure it was smooth and shiny before placing the chosen ornament of the day.

When we met with the doctors in the beginning, they warned of the possibility of having thinning where the radiation beam would enter and exit her head. Even though we had slight thinning, she had such thick long hair she could easily hide it.

Elena's first chemo was a low dose oral variety that did not cause hair loss. It was actually a bit weird to walk around the hospital with hair. Most days there were boxes of brightly colored knit caps at the front counter where the kids could choose their daily accessory piece or do-rags made of fun material patterned with their favorite character. I still remember the time Elena, after noticing she was in the minority with hair, asked if she was going to lose her hair. After reassuring her she would not, she actually asked to pick one handmade hat that caught her eye.

Unfortunately this new chemo is much harsher and it is likely that she too, will join the majority of her friends at the hospital wearing fun head coverings. Tonight, for the first time, I noticed a lot more hair in the brush. We asked her if she wanted to try a new hairstyle and she emphatically shook her head, "no." We suggested she just look at different styles to see if there was something she would like better and she just shrugged. I can't imagine how she would take losing her beautiful long hair after she had such a tough time with the swelling in her face. Perhaps her thick hair will be forgiving and she will just have thinning. Either way, we will still have the most beautiful girl with big bright eyes and the most lovable face. We will just have to expand our repertoire from hair ornaments to the fanciest head coverings anyone has ever seen.

Day 196 – June 13

It's a rollercoaster: chemotherapy – decline – recovery. And the cycle begins again. Today was day two of the decline. This will last about another two days in which our biggest concern will be dehydration and nutrition as we fight to feed Elena without choking her. Today she had two strawberries, a couple spoonfuls of baby food and half a glass of milk – and we considered this a success. At this same point after chemotherapy last time, we were contemplating a feeding tube. Now we're just contemplating IV hydration. Success is measured in baby steps. Two steps forward; one step back.

Overall, Brooke and I judge Elena's progress by what we don't see. We don't see the tumor progressing, we don't see her struggling to breath and we don't see the depression. Most of all, we don't see her worsening. This alone is a major accomplishment considering that the past three months have been filled with all of the above and in the end, the tumor was almost double the size of what it was originally. In this way, her new protocol has given us time and we now find ourselves two weeks away from the impossible. At first they told us to expect three months. Then they told us that we might get 7 months. On June 28th, it will be 7 months. We plan on celebrating this as we would a birthday, for on that date, she exceeds the average. Bring on the balloons and candles.

In the meantime, blowing out the candles may be our greatest accomplishment over the coming week. And as the roller coaster proceeds, by next week she will once again be strong and ready for therapy. First we'll work on rolling over in bed. Second, we'll work on eating and talking. Then we'll walk in the water and practice balance. And somewhere along the way we'll get to blowing out candles. By then, the recovery will be in full swing – for one week only. Next on to chemotherapy, and it starts all over again. No matter how many times it takes, or how many rides on the roller coaster, one thing is clear: it is better than the alternative.

Day 197 – June 14

You desperately want to forget. These are not the memories that you want to keep when you remember your daughter. Instead, you want to remember her laughing as she chases her sister across the backyard or cradling a baby ever so gently in her arms. But today was not for memories. Today was about surviving. Still the hours and moments are priceless and you hold them near.

Recovering from chemotherapy, Elena was unable to both eat and drink today without extreme difficulty. Every effort to bring a cup to her lips was met with gurgling and coughing, signaling us to stop for fear of causing pneumonia. The lips and teeth were equally resistant, clenched tightly together preventing the passage of both spoon and straw. So for now, we concentrated on nutritional drinks delivered via dropper, one drop at a time. And when we weren't forcing food, she spent the balance of the day sleeping in her bed staring at the ceiling. I don't think she really slept, but to her it was an excuse to do nothing and she liked it. Thank goodness Grandma and Grandpa visited to take her out for a bit of swimming therapy or she would have spent the better part of the day getting to know her new favorite color – ceiling white. From what I hear, she kicked and floated the hour away. I wonder if they too, have ceiling white at the pool.

Somehow I never imagined that I'd feed my daughter with a dropper or that I would also succumb to the melancholy of her situation and allow her to stare off into the distance. It is not the memory I wish to remember and I never plan on repeating it. This was a day devoid of moral lesson and message. And for the first time I wondered what were to happen if it were to end. Would it be fast or slow? How would we react? Was it our fault? And in that instant, I also wondered if I could protect myself from her loss. Could I teach myself to ignore my feelings and fool myself into believing that it really didn't matter? But it was in asking that question that I found my answer. The very act of posing this question proved that it did matter and I couldn't stop caring or remembering. Still, today was not a day for memories or to be remembered. This thought process had to end. It did. Tomorrow we will make memories.

Day 198 – June 15

Comfort Care, Star Shine, Palliative Aid. Apparently there are endless names for the most dreaded step for cancer families. We started hospice today with great trepidation. Our doctor had hinted around about hospice for the last few weeks and urged us to meet with them, if simply just to talk. We fought it and insisted that we had it under control. After three days of dropper feedings, we started to wonder if she was getting all her medicine down, and if four millimeters of liquid was enough for a day. So we decided to be preventative and ask for some IV hydration and medicine as we waited for the rollercoaster of chemo to start uphill so she could regain control of her mouth. Rather than having us stuck in the hospital, our doctor suggested we have hospice come hook her up at home so she could get fluids while she slept.

So grudgingly, we relented and signed up for hospice, if simply to prevent putting Elena through a night in the hospital. As soon as we made this decision, Elena instantly started drinking more and ate two bowls of ice cream and two pretzels. Miraculously, the mouth that couldn't find a way to open for Dad's mashed bananas was wide open to accept the frosted donut holes Grandma brought for breakfast. Also, on a positive note, her hand and foot were looser than they have been in weeks. Nevertheless, we went ahead with our plan to get her recovering faster.

This afternoon we met with the hospice team and our doctor. Now we have a special relationship with Elena's doctor. He is very talented, which is essential, but almost as significant is that he has built a very strong relationship with our family. Over the past four months, he has gotten to know our personalities. We have a special way of handling stress and problems, we try to remain positive and we always laugh. Elena's doctor thoroughly appreciates this need. I can't say it will be the same way with the hospice team. We talked about what we could do to make her comfortable and were amazed at what hospice actually offers. Only now do we realize why our doctor was so intent on us meeting with the team. I only wish I didn't fall into the trap of thinking hospice was giving up. I was excited to find out they even have a massage therapist for Elena. Somehow I know this will be her favorite.

They also spent the hour trying to teach two overly tired parents to remember the 100-step process to get an IV bag connected. Then we spent the next hour giving them the 100-step process to deal with Elena. We assured them they had the harder task at hand. They welcomed the opportunity to help Elena get back to her bull-headed and independent self. I suggested that if the nurse wanted to make friends quickly tomorrow morning that perhaps she needed to come with frosted donut holes. What started out as a dreaded conversation surprisingly gave me hope. This wasn't the beginning of the end; it was us accepting we may need some help from time to time.

Day 199 – June 16

So much for being a police girl or teacher. Gracie informed us tonight that she's officially changed her career choice and this time it is final. Instead of "shooting bad guys" and teaching, she's made up her mind to be a doctor. But not just any doctor – she wants to be Elena's doctor. She wants to be a pediatric oncologist. After all, they get to wear blue gloves, use loud beeping machines and help kids. What could be better? And as she dangled her feet off the hospital bed, she whispered to Mom that the best part about being a doctor would be that she "could wear a big white coat." Time to start saving for college – and the coat.

Little does Gracie know how much she'll have to learn. Elementary, middle, high, college, graduate school and residency – it's a lifetime of learning. Good thing she'll be off to an early start. Effective today, Gracie will now join the ranks of kindergarteners this upcoming fall. And while her academics have never been questioned, our reasons for enrolling her stem from Elena's situation. Considering Elena's prognosis, Brooke and I felt it best to make the change now while there is still a possibility of some home stability. And while Brooke and I certainly feel the strain of uncertainty, Gracie has little to no idea of what lay ahead. And for her, this is a blessing as she attempts to hold on to the remaining threads of innocence. But as time progresses, we fear that this will soon change and so we felt it best to quickly acquaint her with new surroundings sooner rather than later. That way the school would be "her" school rather than "Elena's school" and she could form friendships and a nucleus that could help her make it through tough times ahead. Thankfully, she also has the academics to support this decision or we would have never had this option.

This is the daily challenge: to care for Elena while supporting the innocence of Gracie. Elena knows too much and Gracie knows too little. So while we attempt to distract Elena from her condition, we must also take care to preserve Gracie's childhood. It's the constant battle between soothing and tickling that requires dual personalities on behalf of Brooke and me. Some days this is easier than others. But today, as we fought to improve Elena's condition with a combination of physical therapy and distraction, the last thing we wanted to do was run and play doctor with Gracie. So we tell ourselves that there will be time for that tomorrow and Gracie will have her day, all the while knowing that these were the same phrases we uttered a mere eight months ago with Elena. No, there will be tickling for today as well. Gracie is our balance and our relief. Innocence is a good thing as well.

So donning her blue latex gloves that she deftly stole from the hospital and hid in her jean shorts pockets, she made up her mind. She was to be a pediatric oncologist and she had to "hurry up and grow up." After all, Elena needed her help and Gracie was determined to be her new doctor. "Doctor Gracie," she now refers to herself. But in the car, Elena only shot her a stare of disdain. After all, wasn't this the girl that told us last week that she didn't want to feed the fish and we could flush them? OK, so she'll have to learn some bedside manner along the way. In the meantime, she does have some nice blue gloves...

Little does Gracie know how much we wish that were true: that either Gracie could grow up quickly and be our miracle working doctor or that Elena would survive long enough for her to finish college. It makes me wish sometimes that I had stayed in college and chosen oncology over carpet cleaning. I can get a nasty stain out of your rug, but don't ask me to save a life. Hopefully Gracie will make better choices. From what it sounds like, she already has. Bring on kindergarten. We've got a lot of ground to cover in a very short time.

Day 200 – June 17

Lately, we've lived in fleeting moments. As the days grow, Elena's condition seems to be a contrast of alternatives. She has not recovered the way we hoped from the last chemotherapy treatment and now we consider what we had hoped to avoid. I know now what those before us have been through. Still, there are those signs that give us hope: the unintended smile before she coughs, the arm curled around my neck as I take her down the stairs, and the yawn. They say that her yawns are reflexive, but Brooke and I live for them. Whereas she can only open her mouth a quarter inch normally, with each yawn it opens completely. But what is most heartening is her voice, which reappears with every yawn to its fullest power and melody. Why, we have no idea, but with every yawn we hope that Elena's abilities will return and this will all be a distant memory. It isn't. Still, her yawns are moments to celebrate as we turn to remember the sound of her voice and the sweet song of innocence. We try to force a yawn, mimicking our own and feigning an exhaustion which we already have, but it is without result. So we are left to wait for the next occasion.

Try as we might, we are unable to remember Elena or her voice the way it was. So late at night we watch our 30-second video clips from the hospital recorded on our digital camera. And while it still isn't her real voice, it's close enough for us to reminisce. Some days I wonder if we will forget the beauty of her face in this same way, or if we will we just remember how it ended. I've been there before, as has virtually every other person that reads this – I just fear the thought.

I've also found that I've started to live between blinks. What is too painful to watch causes me to close my eyes, only to quickly open them for fear of missing a moment. I guess this is natural, but lately, as she falls to the floor, chokes on noodles or cries from exhaustion, I have spent more of the day with my eyes closed. Maybe once when I open them, she will suddenly be better. But this is only a dream. Somehow I do not think it will get better tomorrow.

Tonight it finally rained, if only for a little while. I've forgotten what rain feels like.

Day 202 – June 19

I feel like I've run a marathon. For the past few days I have felt things I never wanted to feel, cried myself into a constant headache, and probably tied my stomach into a knot a boy scout would be proud of. Keith and I have stayed up late each night trying to figure out how to make Elena eat so that she doesn't have to use a feeding tube. Tonight I started the two-hour process of trying to feed her for dinner. We tried to broaden our horizons and branch out from our constant yogurt consumption and try chicken and stars soup. After ten bites of this, she didn't want any more. I asked her if she wanted plain old milk, not the vitamin packed milk we've been trying to force her to drink. She picked up the medicine cup and practically chugged it. She still coughed afterwards, but it didn't stop Keith and me from standing dumbfounded.

Keith opened the cupboard to put away some food and Elena lifted a shaky finger. After playing twenty questions, we found out that she wanted goldfish. She carefully chewed three goldfish. We then opened the refrigerator and cupboard for her to choose what she wanted. Her dinner was three goldfish, half a slice of cheese, a scoop of ice cream, and as a reward of a mouthful of whipped cream. So much for healthy – at least it isn't a feeding tube. Each "course" was carefully chewed and she coughed often, but it went down.

After Dad took Gracie up for bed, I asked Elena if she wanted more to eat. She shook her head no and pointed to her cheeks. I finally figured it out, she was afraid if she ate too much her cheeks would grow bigger. I told her she was beautiful and she shook her head no and pointed to her cheeks. We tried to explain that it was the steroids that caused the cheeks to swell and not the food, but she refused to believe us. If she only knew.

Day 203 – June 20

This isn't science. It's not really medicine either. It's more trial and error, but it's how cures are made. For other families faced with cancer, when your doctor says, "I don't know," it's just not enough. And before long, you're looking for that second opinion. But when you face a disease like DIPG where the prognosis for survival isn't even known, you start to feel different about medical science. You become accustomed to the "I don't knows" and take pride in the abnormal. And this is how a cure is found; not just for diffuse intrinsic brainstem glioma cancer, but possibly for all cancers across the spectrum. It's found by those willing to risk it all for the alternatives, which are far short of dismal.

So far everything they've told us was wrong. They said she'd live three months beyond radiation or 135 days. We're on day 203. They told us that she'd make it maybe seven months. Next week she'll surpass that marker. They told us that after progression, we might have three weeks left. She's already made it nine weeks beyond that point. And now when we are told to prepare for the end after her recent bout with respiratory problems and contemplation of a feeding tube, we now find ourselves again taunting the inevitable. This morning she awoke, drank two glasses of milk and ate a full breakfast. By lunch she had crackers and cheese and was asking to go to the mall. Tonight the doctors tell us that they just don't know, and that's exactly what we want to hear.

The abnormal is our best hope. Normal is terminal, so abnormal must be life. Regardless of how it happens or the extent to which we can explain it, abnormal might also deliver a cure. This is how medical science is written – in small steps, abnormalities, and trial and error. It's not that our doctors are inexperienced. On the contrary, I believe that they are the best in the nation across all cancer specialties. Elena's doctors in Memphis had the courage to fight the impossible and give hope to the needy. Her doctors in Cincinnati took that fight one step further, offering to help us when nothing else was left. And even if Elena didn't quite fit a research protocol, they still bent the rules and offered it anyway. It may be this very treatment that revolutionizes the medical community. I truly believe that if we find a cure for DIPG, we will find a cure for ALL cancers. The solution lies in the most dismal cases and in the endearing spirit of our children.

In the end, pioneering medical science isn't so much about education or research – it's about courage and finding the ability to say, "I don't know." So tonight when her doctors took the time to come to our house during their free time, we found faith in their sincerity. And when they called Elena's condition "abnormal," both Brooke and I found comfort. And when they said, "I don't know," we cheered. Neither do we. Let's find out together. We're in very good hands.

Day 206 – June 23

Today we needed an excuse to pamper Elena. With the loss of the hair and the swelling in her cheeks, she needed all the indulgence we could offer. Gracie, ever the adventurous one, went first. Pink and red nails and Shirley Temple curls – what a sight! And knowing Gracie, nothing like you'd expect. No more tomboy – at least until the curls fall out. Elena, ever the timid soul, was fascinated with the stylist's wife's red highlights and finally decided to get some of her own. After three trips to the hairstylist for curls, braids and beehives, she needed something different – something that screamed rebel. Besides that, she just liked the color red. And I mean red! Permanent coloring red! So be it. Mom and I were not about to say no to a girl who just spent the last seven months getting poked and prodded going in and out of hospitals from state to state. We'll hold the line at tattoos and piercings – at least for now. Somehow I think if she returns to the salon, a request for piercings and tattoos will soon follow.

Two hours later, Elena had her new style and cut, as well as a four-foot stuffed dog and a berry smoothie, all courtesy of the salon who went out of their way to make Elena comfortable despite her ever raging back pain. Maybe tattoos aren't all that bad – as long as they're not on my daughters. Either way, the trip was most certainly worth it and Elena loved showing off her new flair. Maybe this will take her mind off of her cheeks, if only for a little while.

Day 209 – June 26

We call them wildcards. And they usually happen at 2 a.m. She wakes up, pokes Mom and moans something unintelligible. We ask her if she wants to lie on her side. She shakes her head. We ask her if she wants to lie on her back. She shakes her head. We ask her if she wants the covers pulled over her arm. She moans again – this time we know she is saying no. We ask her if she wants another stuffed animal. She shakes her head. We ask her if her leg is hurting. She moans no. Now she's getting frustrated. We turn on the light, searching for any clue she might hold in her face as to what she wants. We ask her to say it again. This time we think she's telling us to "leave grandma's coat off." We know this isn't it, but we don't dare repeat it for fear that she'll get angry and then the huffing and puffing will start. Time to wake up the house.

Before long, all the lights are on and it's an early morning game of charades. She tries to spell, but with her paralysis, all we can make out are E's and L's. Somehow this won't help. "Get the pad of paper!" Two minutes later, with paper in hand she draws a small "U" with a line over it. "Is this a picture or a vowel?" She just shakes her head. We ask if it is in her room. She shakes her head. We ask if it has something to do with her body. She moans no. That's when we ask the most important question of the night: "Does it have to do with tonight?" She shakes her head no.

This is why it is a wildcard. Most of the time she asks for something simple like a drink or to go to the bathroom. Other times we get lucky and get it on the first or second try. But it's the wildcards that are the most difficult. This is when she wants to tell us something that has nothing to do with what she is doing at that time. Frequently it's just an observation and she doesn't want anything at all. She just wants to let us know about something she saw earlier that day. Other times, she wants to tell us about something she wants to do tomorrow or the next day. She'll tell us that she wants pink socks tomorrow or that she counted five flags on the way home from the hospital. Either way, it's nearly impossible to guess. Still, when she first lost her voice, we promised that as long as she never gave up, neither would we. Our reward: the largest and most precious smile you will ever see as she realizes that she can still communicate with us even through it all.

The speech therapist visited Elena today to help us improve our communication. Realizing that sign language will no longer work, we are turning to a picture book of symbols and words to help. So today we took pictures of nearly everything in the house that she could possibly ever want. We took pictures of her animals, her chair, her pillow and even her ice cream. Then we took pictures of her in bed – lying on her side, on her back and with the blanket over her body. The last group of pictures will go in a separate section of the book marked "Nighttime." Maybe now we can get a little more sleep. Last night alone, she woke up eight times. Seven of those times she wanted to be repositioned. One time was a wildcard. That one wildcard took longer to figure out than all of the seven combined.

If you're wondering, the wildcard took us about thirty minutes to figure out. It turns out that earlier in the day while Gracie was feeding the fish, she forgot to put the cap on the fish food. Don't ask how we finally figured that one out. So after a half an hour of guessing, we went downstairs, put the cap on the fish food and brought it upstairs as proof. She smiled and promptly went back to sleep. It took us another hour to do the same.

The speech therapist didn't understand why I asked her to take a picture of the fish food jar with the cap off, but Elena did. We put that in the "Nighttime" section. Somehow I think we might soon have a "Wildcard" section as well.

Day 211 – June 28

Seven months is too short. Still, we never thought she'd make it. After being told she had 135 days to live and then later being told to expect seven months, we now have reason to celebrate. Nevertheless, seven months is too short.

I guess Elena now crosses over into undiscovered territory. I don't think anyone actually keeps statistics on pediatric high-grade diffuse intrinsic pontine glioma, but informally we've been told that a seven month survival is the average. But just like anything else in this field of pediatric cancer research, I don't think anyone really knows. And if they did, they're most likely handicapping the number so that as a parent you feel grateful when your child exceeds the "average." That's okay, we'll take the handicap and celebrate.

Elena's anniversary comes at a time when there is little to celebrate in the field of pediatric DIPG. As I write this, I hear of yet another child who has lost his life to this horrible disease. The cancer strikes again. And while I am happy for Elena, I am painfully aware that if she beats the average, there is another child falling victim to it. Such is the law of averages. So tonight as I hug Elena a little longer with a hint of joy in my heart, I know that the battle still awaits us ahead, looming with uncertainty and holding no mercy.

Earlier today as Elena received her chemotherapy and I held court with the imminently qualified and compassionate team of doctors, I asked the questions I never wanted to hear myself ask. If she were to die, how would it be? Would it be peaceful? Or would it be the way I fear; the way that your mind paints a picture of when you read other parents' accounts of their child's last moments? Of course, they never say how, but as a parent facing the same challenge, you can read between the lines. When they say, "it was a long night," you know it was more than just sleeplessness. When they say that their child had headaches, you know that it means so much more. It is a code that you never wanted to learn.

Sadly, their response was not unexpected. They said to expect breathing problems. They said it may also be nutritional or lack of fluids. They said that it may be internal bleeding. They said it may be a seizure. I didn't want the answers, but I knew I had to know. My worst fears would be much worse than reality.

Through it all, I listened while they spoke in measured sentences, slow and deliberate. I concentrated on the matter at hand while each doctor's reaction indicated that they expected more. Maybe a tear, maybe a touch. I had neither. And while Brooke and I say we ran out of tissues six months and thirty days ago, and we started the fight at that very instant, I know that this is not the truth. In my heart, somehow today was different. She was upon her seven-month survival anniversary and hope had returned for once.

In the roller coaster of her chemotherapy and the roller coaster of our emotions, tomorrow I am sure it will change. Still for today, we relish in the joy that she is with us and that we can beat the odds. I only wish I could pass this on to other DIPG parents.

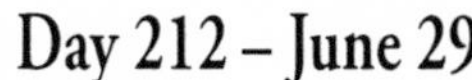

Day 212 – June 29

What do you do when you have no alternatives? After despair came education. From education came options. On one coast, we had surgery. On the other coast, we had chemotherapy. In the middle, we had protocols. All we had to decide was which one was best. And we did – twice. But now the alternatives have vanished. It's not that we're looking to switch; we still don't know what her current treatment is capable of. But we want to be prepared and have something lined up just in case the tumor starts to grow again. However, this time, no matter how hard or where we search, we come up empty. No protocols, no chemo and no surgery.

Our problem this time is that we know too much. We know that other protocols are not right for Elena's tumor and we know that some of the other treatments have already failed. For the first time, we are well informed. For the first time, we are on the front lines. Where we once watched other children enroll in other treatment programs and could predict our results from what they did, we are now the ones that must set the course. She is a survivor, but this is a very intimidating position to be in. Now I know how the other parents felt.

I am also frustrated with the lack of research and protocols available to DIPG children. When we first started, we had at least five experimental protocols to choose from. Now we have two for a progression. At a time when a parent would try anything, there is nothing to try. Have we lost an opportunity to advance the search for a cure in the name of research publicity? True, children with progression are less likely to survive, but are researchers so busy trying to hit a home run and focus on newly diagnosed children just so their studies aren't doomed? Since when is the research more important than the child?

The cure will start when we put children first.

Day 214 – July 1

Two hours of sleep is just not enough. It wasn't enough for me when I was at the hospital with Elena, although then I was running on adrenaline with a mind racing through scenarios. Two hours isn't enough now when Elena sleeps with Brooke. But this time the adrenaline is nowhere to be found.

With chemo still pulsing through her veins, Elena is a nocturnal animal. When the doorbell goes off and she pokes you in the back, you pretty much know it is one of the following:

1. She wants to sleep on her side
2. She wants to sleep on her back
3. She wants to sleep on her other side
4. She wants her hand brace
5. She doesn't want her hand brace
6. Her right leg has locked straight and needs a pillow
7. She wants to put in her breakfast order
8. She wants to tell you that she wants to sleep with Mom tomorrow night (never Dad)
9. She wants to tell you that she wants Mom to stay home with her tomorrow morning (never Dad again)
10. She doesn't want therapy
11. She's reminding you that the fish food cap is off
12. She wants her blanket adjusted
13. She's just testing your reaction speed to the bell (she loves this one)
14. She's still asleep and laying on the bell
15. She has to go to the bathroom
16. Or a wildcard…

Either way, you are always assured that she never wants Dad and that it's certainly worth a call in the middle of the night. At least the first five times you hear it. And that is only before 10 p.m.

Last night we knew it was going to be a long night when the doorbell rang three times within the first five minutes. Apparently, she had a lot to tell us and she waited all day to do so. And since she slept the entire day, the only reasonable time to tell us was during the night. Thankfully, she wanted Mom more than Dad. At least I had an opportunity to pretend to be asleep in the other bed, while Mom played charades every five minutes. It's tough not being the favorite parent. So during every other wake-up and poke to Mom, I'd pretend to wake from a deep slumber and moan something unintelligible just so that Brooke felt that I was helping, even if I did get my share of sleep. Never mind that a moan wasn't what she needed as she strained to read hand signals by the light of the 40-watt closet bulb. Eventually she figured out all of the requests – even the one requesting eggs for breakfast and the one telling Mom that she wanted to watch a video on the way home. Impressive indeed.

By 3 a.m., I had lost count at ten rings. Somehow I knew that Brooke hadn't. I had to be sympathetic or risk Brooke's wrath the following morning, so knowing the list well, I picked out one that Elena had not mentioned and tossed it in for consideration from across the room. Surprisingly, I even got three right. Elena's nothing if not predictable. Maybe Brooke would be so thankful for my help that tomorrow she'll tell me to sleep in while she wakes up with the girls. Not a chance.

Such is the life of the second-best parent. And as long as Elena requests Mom and she obliges, I will sleep a bit longer. Still, that's not what I want. I will happily assume the long nights and the bags under my eyes for the chance at getting another couple of hours with my smiling little girl. Two hours of sleep is plenty when you consider the reward. I know Mom thinks the same way and wears the bags under her eyelids with pride every day; at least for another couple of nights. Elena has already put in her requests.

Day 215 – July 2

Somehow I guess I never figured she would improve. After hearing from all the doctors and reading countless web sites, I never once considered that she might make it. And while I occasionally posted messages of hope and positive thinking, I never really believed it would happen to us. Maybe because I was never given hope from the beginning or maybe because I was trying to protect myself from disappointment. Either way, the thought of a cure never really crossed my mind – until tonight.

I had resolved myself to soaking in the final moments. After the new chemotherapy treatment and the consequential arrival of the oxygen tanks and IV poles in the home, we figured that this was to be Elena's last treatment. We figured that either we would have to discontinue all future treatments out of concern for her health or that she just wouldn't make it another two weeks. But just like everything else about this disease, it looks like we're wrong. The day started out normal, at least as normal as life gets in our home. We awoke Elena by 7 a.m. and worked together to dress her and comb her hair, this time stopping four times to clean the brush of dead hair before proceeding. Then we went downstairs and attempted to feed her. But since she is only able to open her mouth less than half an inch, she is again relegated to a meal of yogurt and milk. What was most surprising, however, is what occurred after we left for work. That's when Kelli and Grandma took over and Elena began a recovery.

The plan was to take a trip to the community all-access tree house. A tree house for children of all ages and all disabilities, we felt that this was not only an excuse to get out of the house, but an opportunity for Elena to look at something other than the ceiling as she ate her lunch. So, packing a lunch basket, Gracie, Elena, Grandma and Kelli left for the day. There I'm told that Elena ate far more than her recent staples of yogurt and milk. She ate a peanut butter cookie, some chips, a couple of blueberries and some ham and cheese. And while three months ago this would have been normal, today it was a crowning achievement. Small steps, but definitely in the right direction.

By the time I returned home from work, Elena was not only ready for dinner, but for the first time in over a month, she started to communicate through words instead of sign language. Best of all, the decision was all hers. And while the only things she said were, "I want Mom to help me tomorrow morning," "I'm trying to lift my head," and "I don't want a bath," both Brooke and I knew we had made progress. She was reaching out, taking control and finally able to craft words with her previously paralyzed vocal cords. Best of all, they were sentences – not just words.

I saw Elena improve and it wasn't just because of radiation. It was because of her will and hopefully because of her treatment. And tonight for the first time ever, I'm wondering what a cure will look like. Will she gain something every day instead of losing something? Will she get it all back or just some? How long will a recovery take? Either way, it's nice to go to bed for just one night and pray for positives rather than curse at circumstances. And while I don't want to go too far, I'll take just this moment to wonder what it can be like to have her back just like she once was.

Day 218 – July 5

I've always felt like the kid. At least around Elena. True, I'm a lot older than she is, but for the past six years, she has been the adult, with a wisdom that transcends generations and a unique balance of emotions and common sense. Even when she was a baby, I had the sense that I was being judged by her and coached to be a better father. And let me tell you, she is an excellent coach.

From the very beginning, she taught me to say I'm sorry (Mostly to Mom. Sometimes I wonder if Mom had a hand in this) and to spend a little extra time with the family. Work and the chores can wait until tomorrow – family comes first. And even today when she struggles to eat and can't imagine her first steps taken for the third time in her life, she stills takes a moment to improve Dad. This time she focused on a bad habit – cracking my knuckles. And whether she did it because she was trying to help me or because she grew tired of hearing the endless snaps as I nervously paced the hospital room floor on chemo days, she was determined to break me of this habit.

This morning as I lay on the couch with her cradled in my arms after breakfast in the fleeting minutes before Kelli's arrival, I cracked my knuckles and she moaned, looked up and placed her right hand on my finger. Shaking her head and gesturing to her own fingers, I knew what she meant. I would try, I told her. It's a nervous habit, but I will try. And I did, at least for another five minutes, as she fell asleep and I unintentionally cracked my toes within my shoes. Little did I know that I was being tested as she opened her eyes and motioned this time to my shoes. "No," she moaned, and held up her hand to signify stop. "I understand," I told her.

Even today as Elena struggles to eat and talk, she takes the time to improve others. Ever the teacher, mom and angel, Elena is more worried about my fingers than she is about her own condition. She may be only six, but what she lacks in years she makes up for in compassion.

Day 220 – July 7

Despite endless talks about what she wants to do, she simply shrugs her shoulders. In spite of my assurances that I could overcome all of her physical limitations so that she may do anything, she simply looks away. We provide endless lists of suggestions and she only wants the mall or a movie. Not even drawing seems to interest her. When you push her she cries, but still can't or won't tell you something she wants to do. Suddenly there's a wall between us. On one side it blocks me from understanding what she wants to do, and on the other side it stops her from understanding that I can to anything to make her desires a reality.

Today I worked with Elena to stand for some therapy. She responded with huffs and puffs and pouting. When I asked her if she was in pain, she said no. I asked if she was scared she would fall and she said no. I asked her why she was making such a fuss and again she shrugged. She could stand for five minutes with my help, but she just didn't want to try. For the first time, I can't connect with my daughter. I can't decipher her moods and feelings. I feel so helpless that at a time when I want to do anything and everything to make her happy, and I can't find a way to do it.

Tonight Gracie found the chocolate bars my mother left behind for making s'mores. After dinner we gave the girls a half of a bar. It was like gold to Elena. I haven't seen her smile that big for a long time. With each bite, she simply grinned from ear to ear. By the end of the day, we determined that we would provide chocolate therapy three times a day and research a chocolate protocol at the world famous Hershey's Hospital. Do you think they provide it in IV formula? Actually that may take all of the joy out of it. Maybe each day I will make a trip to the store to buy bars in bulk and in her chocolate stupor, she will start drawing again. Perhaps we can finger paint with melted chocolate.

Day 221 – July 8

We are constantly asked how Elena is doing. Fortunately our roller coaster has recently become a kiddie ride and the dips and valleys haven't been quite as severe. Now I am going to go knock on wood while rubbing a rabbit's foot and tossing salt over both shoulders. She has her good moments and can stand with our help. She is eating, as long as it slips past the half an inch opening between her teeth. She drinks like a champ...out of a medicine cup using her own hand. We are back to taking pills, as long as I sandwich them between two little slices of American cheese. She can now sit up in only a few special chairs as she watches television with an eye patch over her right eye.

We have spent the days recognizing her deficits and figuring out how to get around them. Some days I feel like an inventor and can fashion a wheel chair from a few rolls of duct tape, toothpaste, and a paperclip. I have tapped into a part of my brain I have never used before. I've always been a lateral thinker. But every day I have to start over from the beginning as we figure out how to overcome new obstacles. Gracie and I tried to figure out how to help Elena find things to play with, so she and I climbed the stairs to the playroom in the attic and took pictures of all of the toys. Tomorrow we will print out pictures of all her toys and pick a toy out of a hat to play with for the day. She needs the challenge and desperately needs to be a child once again.

We tell Elena that if she doesn't give up on us we won't give up on her. There is nothing she can't do; we just have to modify it to make it work. Still by the end of the day, I sit exhausted from trying to decipher her needs, from figuring out how to make those needs a reality, and from finding new ways to keep her happy. Most of all, I can't imagine if I am this exhausted, how completely spent Elena must feel. But this race is about her and for now it is all I can do to just keep running.

Day 222 – July 9

I now know why Elena doesn't talk much. It has nothing to do with the tumor, depression or even a lack of something to say. It's because she can't get a word in edgewise. Of course, neither can we.

Lately, Gracie has developed a vocabulary and she never resists the opportunity to use it. With sprinklings of words like "of course" and "most certainly" she tells us of her day with Grandma and all of the reasons why she'll be good in kindergarten. (In case you're wondering, Grandma helped her paint a whale, which was really an eye and a smile on a blank piece of paper. Don't you know, a whale is too big to draw on one sheet of paper? And she'll be good at kindergarten because she already knows how to sing.) And when she's not talking, she's singing. But not just any song, typically a song with a familiar melody but with completely different lyrics. "Little Johnny Brown" is still her favorite.

Sure, there are breaks to breathe and even breaks to sleep, but other than that it's pretty much constant talking. Tonight Brooke tried to time Gracie's pauses and the highest we were able to count to was five. And if you don't answer her immediately, don't worry. Every one of her questions is meant to be entirely rhetorical and she usually fills in the answer before you can anyway. As a matter of fact, while I'm writing this, Gracie has come down for the second time tonight to tell me that she's worried about the silence and doesn't want me to feel lonely. She says that Elena has fallen asleep and there's no one to talk to, so she decided to come downstairs for one more kiss and hug. But as she pulls up a chair at the dining room table, I know that my silence is to be shattered once more. This time she tells me about a walk that Mom promised her and how she wants to walk to school and walk to God (this is her way for referring to the church down the street). She says that we should wait for a cooler day and then go because Mom says that it won't be so hot. I listen, smile and offer up a kiss and a hug. "Now it's time to sleep," I remind her and I've now told her twice to go back to bed. "No Dad," she replies, "you've only told me two times – not twice." Okay, I know when I'm beat.

In truth, she was right. I was lonely and I really didn't need the silence. As for the "twice" thing, I think I was right on that. And even if she does come down a third time, I don't think I'll mind. Somehow Gracie always knows when she's needed and it's when we're without her that we miss her the most. (Okay, so how do you miss someone when they're right by your side? There's a Gracieism.) And tonight as I sat down to write the journal, the only things that came to mind were Elena's worsening inability to eat and my continuing struggle with religion in the face of her unfair battle. Either one would have been the wrong choice. Gracie knew this and it's why she couldn't sleep as Dad sat downstairs in silence. I'll take the constant talking and singing. So will Elena. Silence is our worst enemy. The kisses and hugs were good too.

Day 225 – July 12

Therapy is a negotiation. Of course with Elena, nearly everything is. Her determination and perseverance can also translate into stubbornness when she wants to. I guess if I went through what she has, I would be the same way. I think part of her difficulty is in having to start all over again. This is her third attempt at recovery and just as soon as she gets some of her functions back, she immediately loses them and more. She initially lost her voice and right hand. With therapy she improved, only to lose her voice, her right hand and her ability to walk. She then fought back, gaining back part of her voice and her right hand. Within months, she was able to use a walker to help her navigate the hallways of school. But now, she has lost her voice, right arm, right leg, her left eyesight and her ability to swallow and open her mouth. This time I think she's just tired of fighting.

Still, we press on and she fights us, either with a blank stare, falling to the floor, or complaining of a headache. Granted, she's not really falling and she's not really in pain, but she knows that it might just get her out of therapy. It worked once with Mom and Dad, so why not everyone else?

Insert Kelli, a studying occupational therapist and my cousin. Knowing of Elena's struggle, she bravely volunteered to help throughout the summer, giving Brooke and I a break and offering a chance to try some proven occupational techniques rather than our futile attempts at sewing cards and play-doh. But while she knows infinitely more about occupational therapy and therapist-patient interactions, she knows little about Elena. They definitely do not cover this in class. So begins the battle of the century: Kelli with training and creativity against Elena with pure brute force and a determination to do nothing.

Today, for the first time, Kelli expressed frustration with Elena's disregard for her efforts. She'd spent nights and weekends preparing creative activities and crafts only to have Elena see through to their therapy component and refuse to participate. In a way, it is like a chess game, only Elena has you figured out before you move the first pawn.

This is the way she's always been. On trips home from school, even at four years old, she'd ask if I had any money. I would reply, "a little" and ask why. She'd ignore the question and comment on how hot it was today. "Can you wind down the window, Dad," she'd ask, "I'm a bit hot." I'd roll down the window, immediately knowing that she had ulterior motives. Soon it would come, but only as we neared home and the local ice cream stand. "Dad, we need to stop and get some ice cream to cool us down." There it was. Unlike any other child who would simply ask for ice cream, Elena built her case from the time she buckled her seatbelt and made sure to eliminate any excuses I might have. Did Dad have enough money? Would Dad agree it was hot? Wouldn't ice cream be the perfect solution? How could I say no? I had been played.

So you can understand Kelli's difficulty with Elena's therapy. With Elena, it is all about planning and setting the ground rules. And just as Elena used them with me, I now use questions to get her to agree to therapy. Does she want to work with play-doh or does she want to walk up the stairs? Obviously she'll take the play-doh. Does she want to spend three hours of therapy with Dad or one hour with Kelli? Once again, the choice is clear. No wonder she hates Dad. I'm just like her. Then I offer rewards. When she completes her therapy, we'll go to Skyline for some chili. But even there she knows Dad will work in additional therapy. She'll have to feed herself and talk through the entire meal. Still, she knows at least she'll get her chili.

Watching me work with Elena this afternoon, I think Kelli had her doubts. Negotiating is not part of her therapy classes. I forced the issue, Elena protested with moans and screams, but in the end she did more than even Elena thought she could do: she picked up two pens and rubbed her motionless hands together. Small steps, but part of a larger path to improvement. In the end, Kelli will be better and smarter than I have been and will achieve more over the coming weeks than I have over the past months. She will harness her creativity and realize that it's okay once in a while to force Elena to do more. Alternatives, rewards and creativity. All the marks of improvement. Maybe one of the rewards can be ice cream.

Day 228 – July 15

I've become a Daddy Handkerchief. And I don't mind. I have eight shirts in my drawer: five black collar ones, one blue, and two T-shirts. All of them have snot on the right shoulder. You see, now that Elena can no longer walk, we need to carry her to the kitchen table, to the bathroom and to bed. And with Brooke's bad knee, I'm the designated carrier. So picking her up from bed, I cradle her head over my right shoulder and start down the stairs. But before I can make it down the steps, Elena is blowing her nose on my shirt. What started out as cough weeks ago has now become Elena's little joke.

Next time you see me, take a look at my right shoulder. If you're like everyone else I meet during the day, you'll comment about the white stuff on my shoulder and ask if it is paint. No. Is it drywall? No. And before you ask, all of my shirts look this way. Not only does Elena use me as a handkerchief, but now she uses my shirts as a napkin too. Today my right collar has strawberry yogurt on it. No matter how many times I wash my shirt, it will always have a pink stain on the collar. I know, I've tried and will again tonight.

In a way it's my badge; my medal of daddy service. It's also Elena's little joke. Today alone, on the way to the kitchen table, she spit out her yogurt and blew her nose twice. As I sat her down in her chair, her smile gave away her secret. This was no accident and she loved it. This was her way of getting back at Dad for all the therapy and teasing. Filling her cheeks with milk, yogurt and applesauce, she asked to use the bathroom and grinned. I knew that this was part of her plan. Looking at my shirt tonight, I was right. So the next time you see me, please excuse the shoulder. It's permanent and I can't buy enough shirts to stop it. It's Elena's little joke.

My little joke was the tire swing. After two weeks of appeals by Gracie for a tire swing, today we chased down a used tire and climbed twenty feet into the air to tie it to the 60-year-old oak tree in the backyard. Then it was time to test it with Gracie clutching the rope. Perfect. Next was Elena. And although she would never admit it, I think she actually enjoyed it. We'll see if she wants to go tomorrow. That's Daddy's revenge.

Day 229 – July 16

Tonight my wife said the words that I didn't want to hear: "We have to at least try and make her happy while she's here." Sure the past weeks have not been Elena's best. Her condition has taken a turn for the worst as the tumor has put its full bear on the nerves that control her head and face. In a seemingly ironic manner, the hands that were once curled and lifeless have now regained partial function and for the first time, she possesses enough knee strength to stand with assistance while we dress her. But it is her head that we are most concerned about. Speech – even moaning – is impossible. Feeding and swallowing are tedious at best, as we struggle to nourish her with droppers and whatever amount of yogurt we can squeeze between her teeth on the tips of our fingers. The lips and tongue are motionless, left to only obstruct every chance we have at feeding her. Her eyes, which at one time served to communicate simple yes's and no's, can no longer move side to side and are fixed straight ahead, giving her permanent double vision. Worst of all, just yesterday, she lost her ability to support her own head and is now at the mercy of her unstable shoulders. Clearly this is not where we thought we'd be.

Still, it is better than yesterday. She ate a half a jar of yogurt yesterday and today she ate a full one. And whether it's because she improved or we simply became more skilled at feeding her, it is not enough to continue to fight this tumor. Yet tonight as we put her to bed, she was well enough to sign one identifiable sign as we kissed her goodnight. Raising both hands to her face and then pulling down she told us, "sad." She was sad that she was sick. And from lips that wouldn't move for dinner an hour earlier, she now frowned.

No amount of comfort can soothe Elena's sadness. No trip to Disneyworld or elevator ride to the top of the "Eiffel Tower" can make her happy again. She knows what we know. Still, we will try to distract her with a trip to the bookstore tomorrow and an ice cream. The day after that we'll try a trip to the mall or a trip to the zoo. And for the next week, we will find any excuse to get her out and away from the cancer. Will it work? We don't know, but it is the only thing that we can do.

Still, Brooke's concern about Elena's happiness was normal. Her admission that Elena will not survive was not. For months, we've fought to keep hope part of our everyday lives. And although we both privately questioned her chances, we never dared discuss it between ourselves. But now, with reality casting a harsh light on our hope, it is nearly impossible to ignore. She's right. And although I still plan on fighting and never once giving in, we now need to consider Elena's comfort as well as her treatment. Today we can pursue both of these goals. Someday, maybe tomorrow, we will have to choose. Sadly enough, some day may come very soon.

Day 230 – July 17

Tonight I redeemed myself in Elena's eyes. I went from Daddy hatred to Daddy apathy, and that was nothing short of miraculous. All it took was a frozen pizza, a six-pack of Mountain Dew, some breakfast sausage, a package of strawberries, a box of cheese crackers, and a lunch packet. She can be bribed.

It was Elena and Dad's big secret. With Brooke and I alternating days at home due to her increasing need for constant care, today was Daddy day. And I wasn't about to let her spend the day on the couch. So pulling her from a breakfast of frozen yogurt pellets (we freeze slices of yogurt small enough to fit between the gaps of her molars and then push them one by one into her mouth to eat. Mealtimes are counted in hours, not minutes), I packed her into the truck for a trip to the grocery store. I was determined to rid her diet of yogurt and find something she really craved.

While pushing the wheel chair with my right hand and towing a cart with my left, we took our caravan into the isles of the grocery store on a food scavenger hunt. She'd moan and tilt her head to the right or left to direct me, but without being able to control her head, she'd start falling to the side and towards the floor. By the second time, I quickly learned to hold her head with my left hand, push the wheel chair with my right and drag the shopping cart with my left foot. Looking back, I now understand why we were greeted throughout the store with offers to help. It's not too often you see a girl in a wheel chair being pushed by a hopping man with his foot caught on a cart. Nope, thank you for the help – we were just fine.

In the end, her choices weren't nutritious or practical, but that didn't matter. I was looking to spur her appetite and change the scenery. $61.29 later (she wouldn't accept the generic brands I suggested), we had both. Now our pantry (or the shelf in the dining room/kitchen/ medical supply room that masquerades as one) looks more like a dorm room closet than a budding family of four's food supply. Mountain Dew, frozen pizza and cheese crackers, all the main food groups and nothing like the organic diet that we've insisted on over the past seven months. Hey, nothing else matters when she can't eat.

In the end, the food sits unopened in the pantry. We tried the pizza and she couldn't swallow it. We tried the Mountain Dew and it dribbled down her chin. We didn't even attempt the Goldfish for fear of choking. So much for good intentions. Tonight it was back to frozen yogurt pellets and little cups of milk. Three-hour meals indeed.

It was after lunch that we finally connected. It turns out that cuddling is much more important than food. And for two hours, we sat on the couch with her sleeping in my arms, a permanent smile painted on her face. Meanwhile, my mobile phone rang abandoned on the dining room table and the e-mail piled up. Still, nothing else mattered. This was all I wanted for the past seven months. There will be time for Mountain Dew and pizza later.

Day 231 – July 18

I feel like I lived a week in only 24 hours. The day started with my 3:50 a.m. wakeup call as our IV fluids ran out. I wish they would give us just 100 mg more in the IV bag so I could wake at a decent hour. Unfortunately, by the time you get the first meds going and you slide back into sleep, 25 minutes later the alarm goes off to switch meds. An hour later, it is time to start the day. This morning was Mom's turn to stay home and the calls and visits didn't end.

That's when the phone call came in that brightened our day. We had submitted an application for a companion dog for Elena to aid her inside the house. The dog can help to alert us if Elena needs anything, as her voice has gotten too weak for us to hear if we leave the room. We didn't have much hope we would be chosen, as thousands of people need these highly trained dogs, so we figured our chances were nil. But the wonderful people recognized our urgent need and by chance, just the right kind of dog became available as they received our application. We got the call from the organization that they could match us up and we'd be training by August 1st. When I told Elena the news, I saw the first twinkle in her eyes that I had seen in a while. We made plans to shop for a toy for the dog and I explained the purpose of the dog was to help her. Elena smiled. I told her she was responsible for caring for the dog, brushing and keeping him happy. She complained by lifting her hand, but when I assured her I would help her do this, she twinkled again.

Day 236 – July 23

This morning, the girls and I went to my parents' house in Columbus for the day. Gracie packed her bags as though it was a one-week stay, not an eight-hour visit. She didn't care as long as she could spend the whole eight hours swimming in their pool. We actually got through breakfast in record speed and soon knocked off 180 calories of our daily requirement. Funny how I struggle to minimize the calories and with Elena we try to find any way to maximize the quantity and quality of calories. So with full bellies, we loaded everything into the truck.

We got to my parent's house and Gracie instantly found Grandma's world famous fruit rollups. I watched Elena's eyes follow Gracie as she walked around the room peeling the pressed fruit off the cellophane. Finally, Elena signaled that she also wanted some. So we tried and it went down. Well, that opened the floodgates of indulging in all of Grandma's delicacies complete with deviled eggs, Swedish fish, turkey, and peanut butter cups. With each bite of food, she drank an ounce of milk or soda. Grandma kept offering up suggestions and Elena took her up on each and every one. I literally fed her from the time I got there until I begged for a break about an hour-and-a-half later. Then lunch crept up on us and she tested everything on the table. Her mouth dutifully opened and she was swallowing without a problem. I asked her if she wanted the frozen yogurt I had prepped when we arrived, and she gave me the "you have got to be off your rocker" look. Eventually, I had to pry her from the table to take a walk, while Gracie rode her bike. Afterwards I excused myself to start packing up the car, and when I returned I found Elena again at the table eating chocolate.

I think we hit our 500 calorie goal for the next week! Elena is too smart not to take advantage of her abilities when she has them, because she doesn't know when they'll disappear again. We got home and Elena didn't want to lie down, she wanted to be seated at the table, surely ready for the next meal. She successfully blew Daddy away with her newly recovered ability to eat. I have a feeling that for the next few days, our kitchen is going to resemble a 24-hour buffet in Vegas. But if it helps our lab counts so she can keep doing this chemo that is giving us such hope, I will break out the warming plates and get some more comfortable dining chairs. Even though I spent my entire day with a fork in my hand, it was such a welcome change to the past week's trials of sliding slivers of yogurt into a small space between her teeth. We are not quite sure what may be fueling the changes we saw today, but we celebrated nevertheless.

Day 239 – July 26

These past nine months have been a giant waiting game. We started in November when we were impatiently waiting for the bulldozers to arrive. In December, we nervously waited to see results of the radiation. In January, we eagerly awaited to go back to school. In February, we were endlessly waiting to go to Disney. In March, we were excitedly waiting to swim with dolphins. In May, we happily waited to see Elena's beautiful painting in the art museum. In June, we constantly waited to visit the lake in Tennessee. In July, we seem to be waiting for everything and nothing at the same time.

The girls have been waiting for their favorite friends and family to come and visit. Mom and Dad have been waiting for some peace and quiet. Elena and Gracie have been waiting for their new dog, a hope for Elena to have some control in her spinning world. Mom and Dad wait to see the smiles this new member of our family will provide. Gracie has been waiting for any free moment to go swimming. Elena has been waiting for any free moment to snuggle with Mom or Dad. We wait to see if treatments have an effect. We don't have great events or wish granting to wait for anymore. We wait for the little things now: the smiles that a good day brings, the crazy things Gracie does to make us laugh, the small steps we take in completing our home, and the small improvements we see in Elena or the absence of decline in her condition (during progression, no decline is considered an improvement).

Life doesn't seem to just happen anymore. We don't have control of our lives, instead they are dictated by what the tumor decides to give or take away each day. I feel like I watch life coming in slow motion, while I sit and wait for it to reach me. All of a sudden I am acutely aware of every aspect of life that affects my day. It is almost like being in a hypersensitive state at all times. People talk about being pumped with adrenaline during a moment of crisis. So what happens when you are in a constant state of crisis?

Tonight, Elena called me to her bedside to tell me her left arm hurt. Most parents would give medicine and send her to bed. But I can't focus my thoughts on just that arm. I think of the blood transfusions and the pages of precautions they gave us, I think of the brace and what that could do and I worry about what this problem could indicate. I finally called Keith inside, panicked by what was going on. In the end, a "medicinal" cold washcloth on the arm seemed to soothe her woes.

I wait for a time in my life when a hurt arm is just a boo-boo. When I can wake in the morning and not have to think out the entire day of medicine and feedings. Today we reversed our normal post-chemo trend of decline. Elena ate like she did the day before treatment and was awake the better part of the day begging for her cuddles. This was the day we had been waiting for. Maybe it's the waiting for the little things that keeps this uncontrollable situation slightly manageable.

Day 240 – July 27

They were all wrong. Mom thought Elena wanted to sleep with her, not Dad. Grandma thought Elena was upset that I made her eat breakfast and lunch. Grandpa guessed that she wanted to watch television. It was obvious that Elena was irritated and growing more frustrated by the second. Within minutes, she went from apathy to tears and it all started when I came home from work. And knowing my reputation with Elena, everyone immediately guessed that somehow Elena did not like me. As I said, they were all wrong.

From therapy drill sergeant to mealtime dictator, Elena has never hid her hatred for me. And ever since our final days at the hospital in early January, it was Mom who received all the love. I was good at the feedings and okay at foot massages, but Mom was the cuddler and sleeping buddy.And so relegated to the couch, floor, or Gracie's second bed, I spent the last six months waiting in the wings while Mom took center stage. Not that I minded, in my mind, anger was a form of therapy just the same. After all, if she punched me (which

I encouraged her to do), she built up right arm strength. If she was angry, at least she was active and involved. But somewhere deep inside, I missed Elena. She was always Daddy's girl for the past six years and now I had lost that as well.

When she cried this afternoon, I figured once again I was the reason. I even guessed that she wanted me to leave. But this time it was different. I asked if she wanted me to leave. Her eyes said no. I asked if she wanted me to stay. She said yes. I asked again, certain that she did not understand. And again, she said yes. I asked if she wanted me to hold her. She said yes. I asked if she was hurt and needed help. Yes again. Now we were getting somewhere. And with another five questions we had the answer. Elena wanted therapy. Elena wanted Dad. Thinking that she was mistaken, Mom asked again. Still yes. Daddy's girl was back, at least for tonight.

In the end, her back hurt and she turned to Daddy for help. And before long with a couple of stretches, the back was feeling better and the tears had dried. I was a hero, if only for a moment. Tomorrow I think we will try a new therapy, cuddling with Dad.

Day 244 – July 31

I've always feared that Elena would become a face of cancer, that her disease would be her identity and perhaps her legacy. Events, tributes and memorials would soon become memories. But the longer we struggle with cancer and the more people we meet, we quickly realize that we are not alone. A disease is not an identity, but an obstacle. At the same time as we're fighting our own battle, we meet people who reach out to us with their battles. They have children with cerebral palsy, children who died in accidents, or even their own children with cancer. And despite their pain and their struggles, they still find the time to reach out to us. This is perhaps the most telling example of all. And in a way, it is this attitude that is the true identity of the disease, the way in which you gain comfort by comforting others.

This weekend as I took Elena to the pool, I saw this first hand. I saw her friends circle around her in her wheel chair and talk to her like a friend, not like a patient. And while they asked about her new chair, her hair and why she couldn't talk, they spoke to Elena, not me. The very children who we coach on dealing with handicaps and instruct not to stare end up teaching us about caring. For to look away is to also ignore and disregard. They did neither, they asked and they cared. And Elena responded. They saw her as a friend and not as a disease.

Tonight as I looked to the couch, I fear that Elena's identity is disappearing. Her left hand and foot have joined the right with partial paralysis and she now drools from the right side of her mouth. Feeding and drinking are increasingly difficult and with every passing hour, we begin to fear that these symptoms are less the result of drug side effects and more the symptoms of another progression. And so in response, we dig in with web research on our next course of action and take little comfort in the fact that there is nothing left to try. I beg for tomorrow when she'll become her old self and I curse myself for over-reacting once again. I love those days. What do I learn from the children? Love Elena for who she is. Let the lessons and legacy come tomorrow.

Day 246 – August 2

For the past nine months, she's been a pincushion. Prodded, poked and stuck. First for tests, then for treatments and now to understand her condition. And each time, she has shed a few less tears and fought back a little less. Tonight, as we relented and they inserted a feeding tube, she welcomed the change. No tears, no fight.

What started out as a quarter-inch opening between her teeth yesterday became much worse this morning when she woke up with her jaws locked closed. And whether it was from exhaustion, blood counts or tumor related, we knew that this would be an uphill battle. Last time we went through this, mealtimes lasted four hours and we still couldn't get more than about 200 calories in the day. But with her condition continuing to deteriorate and her left side now weak, we knew this was a battle we could not win. Two weeks ago, Mom was ready for the feeding tube, I was the hold out. I thought that the moment she had one, she'd stop fighting and give up. But tonight I realized that the battle was impossible to win and to fight it would sacrifice the very time we treasure so dearly. Still, what was most interesting was Elena's reaction. Instead of resisting, she saw the installation of a feeding tube for what it was: a way to make her life easier. Without hesitation or anticipation, she waved "yes" with her eyes and lifted her head up for the installation. And then without a tear or a flinch, she watched as they inserted the fourteen-inch tube through her nose and into her stomach.

Tonight I realize that the feeding tube will improve our days. Where we spent eight hours a day forcing food, we can now spend six hours cuddling. Still, I cannot ignore the hint of defeat in our actions and I doubt that this will improve her willingness to fight. In the end, I again find myself at the whim of consequences I cannot control, but must have faith that they guide us in the right direction. For a man who believes in the power of individuals, this is not an easy realization to make. Somehow, some way, I still hope and feel that Elena will be more powerful than the cancer and smarter than the circumstances. If so, then today will be nothing more than a stop on the way to a longer and easier life.

Day 247 – August 3

As I look through pictures of Elena, I'm reminded of how every trip to Grandma's involved a haircut. Sadly not one of Grandma's haircuts ever looked good. Crooked bangs, uneven sides;

sometimes I wondered what my mother was thinking. Each trip her hair would get shorter and shorter until her bangs would disappear leaving only a few crooked hairs remaining.

It never really mattered to Elena. For her it was just another opportunity to spend time with Grandma. Brooke and I tried to hide the scissors. My Mom just bought another pair. We tried to scold her. My Mother just feigned ignorance. We even instructed Elena to run when Grandma came near her with scissors. But Elena never ran and never said no to Grandma. As the oldest, she never ignored the attention. Sometimes Grandma would promise to only "even it up a little" or "thin it out" and at first we believed her. But after seeing the results, we knew that "evening it out" was nothing less than two inches shorter.

Only with our trip to Memphis did we ever see Elena's bangs grow out and her hair even out. At least in Memphis she was able to get a real haircut, eight hours removed from Grandma's scissors. And now, looking back, it is easy to separate those pictures after diagnosis from those before. Just look at the bangs.

Seven months later she now begins her decline and has lost even the pink highlights as a result of the chemotherapy. And for a girl who loved her hair, this was never easy. Her hair makes her feel pretty and healthy. Even after Grandma's haircuts, it would grow back again ready for the next day they would spend together. Brooke and I would cringe – Grandma and Elena would laugh. A day at the salon – Grandma's way.

Day 248 – August 4

Walk slowly. Throw petals. Don't step on your dress. Don't move and be quiet. All the essentials of flower girl etiquette and Gracie knew it well. "I know, I know. Walk slow. Throw petals. Don't step on my dress. Don't move and be quiet," she'd say on the way to the wedding, on the walk to the church and while she stood in line ready to enter the sanctuary. Who told her these things we have no idea, but apparently our advice wasn't necessary; someone had gotten to her before we did.

Today was Kelli and John's wedding (Okay, it's always the bride's wedding. The groom is just along for the ride.) As Elena's caregiver for this summer, Kelli's wedding was something she looked forward to for the past three months. Personally I think Elena was a shoe-in for the flower girl position all along. Gracie, thankfully, was also included to make our lives easier. But that didn't keep Gracie from stealing the show.

This was Elena and Gracie's first opportunity at flower girl status. And somewhere in the spectrum of little girl honors, this falls no more than two steps below princess. Needless to say, the dress was picked out early, even before Kelli's announcement, in preparation for yet another wedding (her aunt's wedding in less than a month). And in the mass hysteria of wedding-palooza that will rock our family this year, it was decided that the girls will wear the dresses of their choice, as long as they were white. That way, they could go with any color in the wedding party. So in accordance with bridal protocol, Gracie picked out a white dress with pink flowers and Elena chose a completely pink dress with ruffles. So much for wedding protocol. But who was going to tell Elena no? What Elena wants, Elena gets. Kelli chose green for her bridesmaid's gowns. Her flowers were red and white. Even the men wore green cummerbunds. Still, Elena wore pink.

In the days before the wedding, the air was thick with anticipation. Plans were made and rehearsed. Dresses were inspected daily. Every little detail was obsessed over. The night before, however, was sleepless. At least it was for Elena. Somehow, I think Kelli slept better that night before. For a girl who had once stacked her books according to size and color on her bookshelf, we once again saw the obsessive habits rise to the surface. I never thought I would be as pleased as I was to see them once again. Finally she cared about something other than sleeping with Mom that night.

From Grandma to Aunt Jenny and Aunt Jackie, everyone seemed eager for Elena's big premier. And while we worried that Kelli's wedding would soon become Elena's flower girl presentation instead, it was Kelli who also went out of her way to include and encourage Elena's participation. I don't know if this was intended as a distraction for Elena or just an excuse for ceremony, but for this we are eternally grateful. It's not too often that you get to see your daughters walking down the aisle. Even once is enough for any father.

By evening's end, the wedding went off without a hitch. Elena was attentive and excited. Even with her paralysis, we could tell through her eyes with every "yes" and "no" nod. For her part, Gracie walked slowly, stayed off her dress, and threw petals. So many, as a matter of fact, that by the time she reached the seventh pew, she had dispensed the majority of petals and the rear of the sanctuary resembled a rose slaughter. This did not prevent her from throwing imaginary petals in their place. As I said before, she stole the show once again.

Today was a welcome relief from the events of the past week. At every step, we've tried to encourage Elena and coax even a hint of her personality from her lips or eyes. But with paralysis now affecting everything other than her eyes, we have received no such sign. And so begin the inevitable thoughts as you see her close herself off from the rest of the world as she no longer reacts to even the most loving touch or your goodnight kiss. It's then as a father that you begin to wonder if she's really there. Does she know what you whisper in her ear, does she know that you're holding her hand? Or are you inserting this feeding tube and continuing these IVs for your benefit and not hers? And what about quality of life? Or is that just a fancy way of giving up the fight while rationalizing your true intentions away? And if you do give up, will you say one day it was for the best, while wondering secretly what would have happened if you were stronger and kept up the fight? I do not profess to know these answers, nor do I think I want to hear them from someone else. Still, after a week of seeing no response, I wonder if this is what makes it easier to stop the fight. Had I already lost my Elena when she stopped responding a week ago? And while I know that thinking, feeling girl still resides under that lifeless face, what is life without communication? Oh, how I needed a sign from her tonight.

Tonight I would learn how little I knew. Through the wedding, she finally responded with excitement and passion. In her eyes, Brooke and I saw her watch, wonder and dream of a wedding of her own. Complete with flower girls and her own white flowing dress (or possibly pink). Still, it was at the reception that we finally communicated, this time as a daughter to her Dad.

As we sat watching the girls twirl with abandonment on the empty dance floor, twirling themselves endlessly and then falling to the floor, Elena motioned to me with her eyes. Did she need to use the bathroom? No. Did she want a pretzel? No. Was she uncomfortable? No. Was she cold? No. I was out of questions. So we sat, quietly watching Gracie twirl and fall once more, this time laughing all the way down. Did she want to dance, I asked. "Yes," she nodded. Did she want to twirl? No. Did she want to dance with Mom? No. I paused. She never before wanted to cuddle with Dad. She never wanted Dad's comfort at the doctor's office. She never even wanted Dad to tickle her before bed. Still, I asked, "Do you want to dance with Dad?" "Yes," she nodded, enthusiastically. I asked again. Obviously she must have misunderstood, but the answer was still the same.

One song. Two songs. A third song and finally a fourth. Through it all, she kept nodding yes and asking for more. This was Dad's dance and no one was about to take it away from me. It was the dance I had always wanted, just not at the wedding I expected. So there on an empty dance floor to Lionel Ritchie songs that I was sure must have been free at some garage sale to the DJ, we danced with Gracie, Allyson and Michelle, twirling until dizzy. My dancing was shoddy, the atmosphere was less than perfect, but it was a night I will never forget. And by the third song, I slowly felt her hand open from its paralytic clenched fist and move to pat my neck. Communication. Not by words and not by eyes, but by love. One day I pray to get that dance again, this time at her very own wedding.

Day 249 – August 5

Wake up early. Eat two bowls of breakfast. Play fetch with the dog. Go for a walk with the family. Visit more family. Read five books. Go to bed. For any normal child, this would be a full day. For Elena, it was nothing short of miraculous.

After spending the past three weeks unable to open her mouth even enough to sip milk, Elena began the day without restrictions. Hinting that she was hungry the moment she woke up, we jumped at the opportunity to try and feed her without the help of the feeding tube still hanging from her nostril. Never mind that she had already eaten the equivalent of a day's worth of calories through the tube since the moment she went to sleep last night, she was still hungry. And when we found out that her teeth had finally relinquished their vice like grip, we knew we were in for a day of surprises. Quickly, we pushed everything we could find in the freezer into her awaiting mouth before it could close and disappear forever. Thankfully her mouth cooperated as she not only inhaled a cup of yogurt, but also a few pretzels, some strawberries, some cereal and two glasses of milk over the course of the day.

From there, it was nothing but pure excitement as we watched our daughter blossom once again, complete with her obsessive intentions and her drive to be normal. Her paralysis started to fade with an occasional lift of her head and a motion with her left hand. Surely even she could be satisfied with her progress over one day. So when we found her crying at the dinner table at her Grandpa-Grandpa's house, we were puzzled. It turned out that to her, part of being normal was also to play in the backyard with Gracie and the other kids. And so, lifting the wheel chair in our arms, we carried her on her throne down the deck stairs to the waiting game in the yard below. And although no one kept score, we all knew who had won that day.

Tonight as we put the girls to bed, we recapped today's successes while reading our favorite collection of knock-knock joke books. The punch lines weren't new and the jokes were clean, but to Elena and Gracie, it was a wonderful way to end the day. Gracie would begin with the knock-knock, to which Elena would respond with eye blinks to spell out each syllable of "who's there" and "Archie who?" Even Pueblo, our new resident canine sibling, joined in with the occasional bark to prod Elena along when she fell off to sleep. And by the time Gracie delivered the punch line, funny or not, we all laughed, including Elena.

"Knock-knock."
"Who's there?"
"Sue."
"Sue who?"
"SURPRISE!!!"

Yes, definitely a surprise and a very special one. Let's do it again tomorrow.

Day 250 – August 6

My mother was in town to help us out today; realizing I could not juggle Elena, Gracie and a new dog. I sat down with Elena for breakfast and I was overjoyed to find the mouth open even wider than yesterday. We had Cocoa Pebbles, eggs, smoothies, and milk. Then to add to my shock, she started signing a letter, "d." Donut? I guessed right immediately and nearly fell off my chair because first of all, she was using her hand to sign and second, she was asking for things again. So Grandma was sent on a mission for chocolate donuts. This, "Name That Food," extended to lunch when she asked for a Happy Meal. All day long she signed and made requests. And although she only had two small chunks of a nugget and a fourth of a fry, she was content to be able to get them in her mouth. Yet, I was ecstatic to waste five dollars for the constant "yes" being conveyed in her eyes as she held the food in her mouth. You could almost imagine her internal sigh of pleasure. The best part was when she yawned several times and the mouth opened all the way as her voice squeaked out a sound. You would think we had won the lottery the way we were hooting and hollering.

Day 251 – August 7

Mom is the alpha male of the family. The kids know it and now so does the dog. I don't think I ever stood a chance. When Brooke barks a command to Pueblo (Elena's new companion dog), he immediately perks up and obeys. Sit, down, bed, shake, get, give, let's go, stay, visit, jump, car, lap and hurry - it doesn't matter. When Brooke says it, the dog knows she means business. I guess two days at obedience school teaches you that; speak with authority and you'll never have to repeat yourself.

I'm more of the poop-picker-upper. I guess this is the opposite of the alpha male. When I speak, the dog is trained to ignore. Brooke says that Pueblo's trainers told her that this might happen. "Have him feed the dog and the dog will start to see him as its master," they said. So I feed him twice a day. Still, it doesn't matter. Now I'm not only a poop-picker-upper, but also a doggie-chef. At least he responds to "Pueblo, food."

It's not that I really mind; I've never been a dog person in the first place. And what makes Elena happy is what makes me happy, so we now have a dog. It turns out what makes Elena happy also makes Gracie and Brooke happy too. Three for the price of one. So the dog stays. Still, something tells me that the dog knows I'm not a dog person and so he has decided to not be a Daddy-dog.

Staying home to take care of Elena today, I quickly realized how little influence I have over this dog. I tell it to sit and it stands. I tell it to lie down and it follows me. I tell it to go and it sits. I tell it to visit (this is to let others pet it without licking) and the dog licks. I might as well let the dog choose its own commands, he already does. What makes matters worse is that Pueblo is a designated companion dog because he was unable to be a service dog. Apparently, he was easily distracted in public. So on day two, after seeing Brooke demonstrate Pueblo's wonderful abilities, I took it upon myself to show my parents his abilities. "Watch this," I'd say, "he can pick up this toy and bring it right to your hand." But of course, it was me telling Pueblo the command and him being distracted by the audience. "Look," I'd say, "he'll let you pet him without licking." Almost immediately, he'd jump up and lick them in the face. After a while I began to feel like I might as well have a talking dog. (Of course, he never talks when anyone is around.) I give up.

Today, as Elena and I were cuddling on the couch, trying to coax her to sleep after spending yet another sleepless night changing out IVs and chasing bathroom runs, I threw some more commands at Pueblo. "Down," I said, "go to bed." I pointed at the rug in the corner covered by doggie bones, a squeaky toy and a blanket. Pueblo, knowing my status, looked at the bed, then at me, and bounded onto the couch and into my remaining lap. "Pueblo, NO!" I shouted. Pueblo didn't move. "NO!" Pueblo licked my hand. But then, before I could react, out of the corner of my eye, I glanced at Elena. Where once was a static frown now resembled a grin. She was laughing at me.

Apparently, Pueblo was right all along. Maybe this is his true purpose. Maybe down, sit, stay, jump and shake are secondary to a smile in the code of a companion dog. And maybe this little act of rebellion is nothing more than an act after all. Then again, maybe I'm giving him too much credit. He is, after all, just a dog.

So if you want to see Pueblo at his best, ask Brooke. If you want to see him make a fool of his master, watch me. And if you want to see Elena smile, watch her while she watches me try to control him. After all, I'm not the alpha male.

Day 253 – August 9

I fear that Elena knows more than we do. Over the past three days, she has asked to dance with Dad, play in the backyard, eat a happy meal and chocolate ice cream, go swimming, take a bath and play a card game. But what's more interesting than her sudden burst of energy has been the fact that for the past several months, she's shunned each and every one of these activities. She chose Dad, over Grandma and Mom as her dance partner; the same man she spurned when it came time to cuddle, eat or sleep. She wanted to play a game she never played before, a game in which her paralyzed arms would prove useless. She wanted a Happy Meal, despite knowing that she could never even eat the smallest fry. For her, just the sight of it was enough. She asked for chocolate ice cream, which for a pure vanilla girl was nothing short of astonishing. She actually asked to go swimming, an activity that she came to fear as she began to lose the use of her arms in early January. She wanted to take a bath, despite her recent fear of any activity that might result in the loss of more hair. And finally, yesterday, she wanted to play a card game. Out of necessity and because it was the only thing we could usually fit in the little remaining space in our backpack, this game was the game of choice at the hospitals during chemotherapy treatments. She never really enjoyed the game. To tell you the truth, neither did I, but it was something to distract us as we passed the day from waiting room to waiting room. To both of us, it came to represent everything we hated about hospital life.

Together these activities symbolize everything that Elena either feared or never did. And for three days, she was well enough to experience it all. She could finally open her mouth, move her left hand and communicate with us through blinks of her eyes. But this morning, all of that stopped. The hand is again motionless, the mouth is limp and her left eye is completely blind and paralyzed. She feeds from her feeding tube and drinks from her IV. And now our vital link of communication with our daughter has been severed. What was once three days of celebration now has the potential to be our best and final memories.

Today we made another trip to the emergency room. Brooke and I hold Elena's hands as we watch her chest rise and fall with every breath. We've been here before and pray for the opportunity to do it over again. But as I hear her breathe from across the room with a whine and hesitation, I realize that somehow, this time, it is different. My little girl who has surprised so many and stolen life from this tumor four times before at the last moment, no longer has protocols, treatments or antibiotics to help her. It is up to her and we can only stand by and watch. Tonight will be a long night. I now know that she knows more than we do, I just pray that she also has the courage and will to match.

Day 254 – August 10

There's something about the inevitable. You anticipate the end but it never comes soon enough. Tonight the inevitable is all we have. No longer do we have the medicines, the chemotherapy or control over own lives – we are powerless. Powerless as we grapple with Elena's sickness. Powerless as we sit by her side holding her hand. Powerless as we watch her struggle to breathe.

Tonight Elena began the inevitable. After an hour of opening her eyes this morning, she slowly succumbed and fell into a coma. And for what seemed like a lifetime, we watched each individual breath as she hesitated and coughed. And for the first time, both Brooke and I realize the struggle has been lost. I guess that happens during a coma. When the last thread of communication is lost and the distance begins. The distance between Gracie and Elena. The distance between Elena and us. The distance between her and a cure. The memories start to fade as our hopes turn towards a painless end for our brave little girl.

For the past seven months we've watched and waited for our turn. Watching as child after child became a statistic. Knowing the end and how it would come. Now we wonder if [*called to Elena's side by Brooke*]

Day 255 – August 11

Today we know what it's like. The empty feeling; the one that cannot be pacified and aches to be filled. Last night as Elena fell into a coma and her breathing became short, we decided to finally tell Gracie about what lay ahead. So there, in the backyard on the steps of Elena's playhouse that I built for the girls, we told Gracie that her sister was going to die. We explained that Elena was going to be an angel in heaven. And tonight she would have to say goodbye. Gracie, in her own fashion, asked if Elena would get wings and then suggested that we bring Elena out so she could show her her rock collection.

The rest of the evening was spent by the playhouse with Elena struggling to breathe and our entire family around to comfort her. And with Brooke to her right and me to her left, we held her hands under the tree she help us plant when we first moved to our new house. It was her tree, her choice: a brilliant scarlet maple.

Throughout the night she was at peace. At times, she strained to breathe under the pressure of the tumor, but through it all she continued to sleep. Brooke and I lay by her side in bed until early this morning when she finally relented and left us.

Today Gracie has remaining questions and so do we. I'm sure all will be answered in time, but not by any person and not today. All that remains is our love for our daughters and our desire to remember her free of cancer. The house is now quiet and so are our hearts.

This morning I carried Elena to the waiting ambulance in my arms. She is still my daughter and I know she would appreciate being carried in my arms rather than being placed on a stretcher. She will also be our daughter and a part of our family forever. And although all traces of medical supplies and equipment were set outside our door within hours, her pictures will always grace our walls as a reminder of the inspiration she was to all of us.

In the end, we decided on an autopsy to garner any information about this tumor in the hopes of helping other children inflicted with this hopeless disease. We pray and will work to continue Elena's fight in pursuit of a cure and make sure that her life continues to inspire long beyond today. The service and tributes will come later.

For today, the memories and tears continue. We now sit at a table for three and sit in the backseat of a car as a family. The bed isn't as small as it once was and our house is too large. And in our hearts we continue to be reminded by notes hidden throughout the house over the past nine months by Elena: "I love you Mom, Dad and Grace." We love you too, Elena. More than you can possibly imagine.

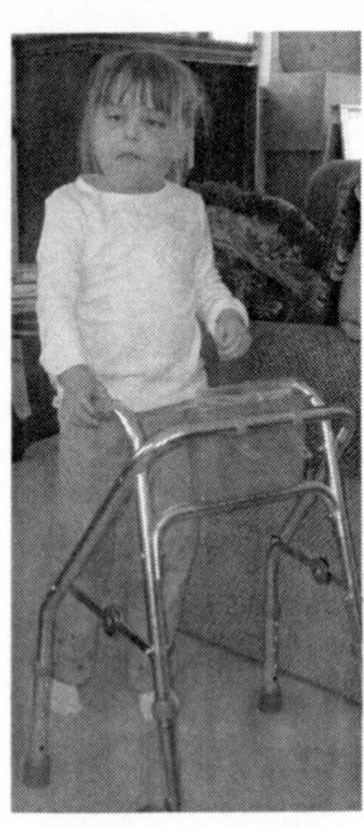

Elena taking her first steps with the walker

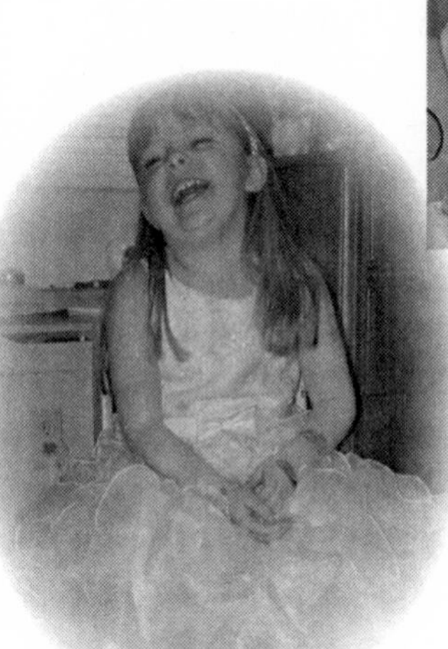

Elena and Gracie sharing jokes before bed

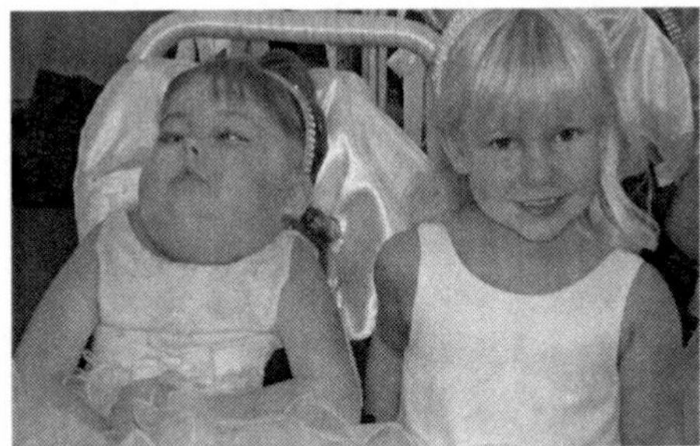

Elena and Gracie ready to throw petals at the wedding

Mom and Elena at the Cincinnati Art Museum the first day of the exhibit

Elena and Dad on July 4th watching the parade

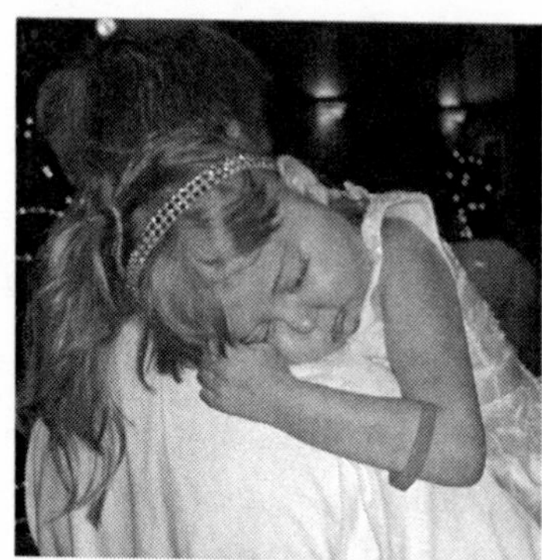

Dad and Elena's dance

Elena and Gracie
showing off their wheels

Elena and Sally take a ride

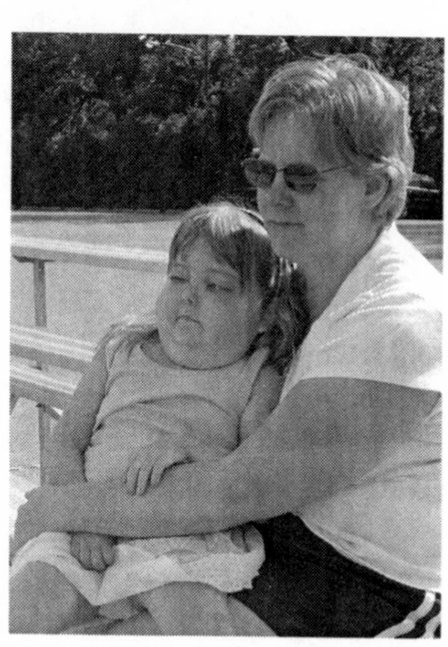

Elena and Mom talking about what
she wanted to do during the summer

Chapter 4 – Fearless

After Elena Day 1 – August 12

Today we ache. Elena's favorite animals, her dresses and her sparkly shoes remain in her closet untouched. We can't make it through even a sentence without pausing to reflect. Where we once said "come-on girls" we now have to stop and say "Gracie." It's amazing how even the smallest pronouns make you stop and wonder what could have been.

I've also discovered that while still a family, we've all mourned at different times. Grace did her mourning in March when Elena first stopped playing with her. That was when the paralysis started and Elena's fear took over. Gone were the swim lessons, the races down the slide, and the ride in the Barbie jeep. Brooke did her mourning in May after Elena's first progression. At that very moment, a lifetime was reduced to three weeks as we were told that she might not make it to June. To see Brooke at that time was to see the essence of a mother's love. From that moment on, every day was a gift.

I mourn now. I guess I was so busy putting on a strong image to Elena that I never bothered to consider death as a reality. Sure I questioned why and wondered the extent of her will to fight, but deep down I ignored every urge to confront it. Now I can barely make it through an hour without holding a picture tight or making a trip to her room to remember. I guess I just don't want to forget. The sight of her beautiful eyes, long eyelashes, the sound of her sweet voice and the smell of her hair (thanks to the dyed red locks from her friends at the salon).

Brooke keeps asking if I'm all right. I don't answer. She knows because she's going through it too. We go through our day wondering what to do with our new found time after being a caregiver 24-hours a day. Busy is better and helps to keep us from thinking. I apologize to all of my family who come to comfort us. For Desserichs, mourning means work.

So while they expect to sit inside and recount her life, I prefer to clean out the garage. Whatever I can do to keep me from breaking down is best. So if you come to our house, make sure you wear work clothes.

Today Brooke convinced me to put away the broom and shovel and go back to the amusement park. There, we could not only give Gracie a chance to run with her cousins, but also take the time to climb to the top of the "Eiffel Tower" to pay tribute to Elena. But somehow, the tribute was not what I expected. Without Elena, nothing is. I guess somehow we want to be whole once again. We know that this will take time, but after the past nine months time has a new importance. We want to be healed now and we want to be happy once again.

Last night as the sun faded from view and the last visitor left our driveway, we sat as a family of three on the front step and looked to the horizon. In the parting moments of the sunset, pink clouds covered the sky. Gracie was the first to make the connection. "Look Mom, Elena's clouds," she said. She was right. And so for the final minutes of daylight, we were a family of four once again. Pink was always her favorite color. Thanks for the show Elena.

After Elena Day 2 – August 13

Tonight as I put Gracie to bed, she gave me the first hint that she truly knows about Elena's death. Standing in the doorway to Elena's room as I brushed her hair, she motioned to Elena's bookshelf and told me that a musical wind-up princess doll on the top reminded her of Elena. Sadly, I had never before noticed this princess doll, but I picked it up and all became clear. With a lift of my hand, the final notes of a long last melody were released. I knew the tune all too well. Gracie asked me if I knew the words. I did. Did she know the words, I asked. "No," she said. So sitting down on the floor of her room I wound the pin and released it with a sigh all too familiar in the past three days, the sigh that says I don't want to cry anymore. I began.

My voice wasn't perfect and my singing cracked somewhere between baritone and bass with frequent jumps in between, but before I could make it through the first line, Gracie joined in. It turned out that she knew the words after all.

"You Are My Sunshine
My only sunshine.
You make me happy
When skies are grey.
You'll never know, dear,
How much I love you.
Please don't take my sunshine away."

And then, without even asking, Gracie told me that the song reminded her of Elena because Elena was the sunshine. "That's why she could make the skies turn pink yesterday," she said. Little did she know how right she was. "Yes," I replied, "Elena was my sunshine as well." Gracie then asked if one day she too could be my sunshine. Oh, if she only knew how much she was at that very instant. "You already are," I replied. In truth, Gracie has always been the sunshine of our family. Elena was our compass. Elena gave us a path and Gracie showed us the light. Tonight it was she who illuminated our memories.

After Elena Day 3 – August 14

I've been told that the best therapy for losing a loved one is to see the impact they've had on the community. They're right. Tonight, if only for a few hours, Brooke, Gracie and I didn't feel so alone. The church was filled and so were our hearts. We spent the evening hugging family, friends, co-workers and even people I've never met before. And in a brief second, they shared with me how they connected with Elena and came to see their own lives in different ways. Some parents hugged their children longer, some shared experiences with their own losses, and others explained how they came to value the simplest moments in their lives. I was touched by their stories and comforted by their sympathies. Still, I am the lucky one to meet these loving strangers and be a father to the best girls in the world.

I am constantly amazed at how a 6-year-old girl with no voice, partial paralysis and an imposing sense of humility could do so much in such a short time. She wasn't famous, she wasn't powerful and she wasn't outgoing. Still, with humility and on a personal level, she changed so much, including myself. I became a better dad under her direction and with her love. And all we ever wanted to do was to tell the story to Gracie. A story of love. A story of life. A story of Elena.

Tonight at the memorial service, Gracie turned to me and told me that she wished she could "start the days all over." That she loved Elena and wanted to go back to before she was sick. In truth, I don't know. I want to say that it was all worth the pain, but it's just too close right now to agree. Maybe tomorrow my answer will be different as the pain lessens. Still, tonight I'm in awe of the lives she touched in such a short time. I am also forced to reconcile with the reality that had she never developed cancer, most likely she would remain unknown except to our family. And in this way, her inspiration outweighs the pain that I feel.

In the end, tonight was a step towards healing and the very people who help us are the same people who were helped by Elena. In time, the pain will fade as we learn through her inspiration and let her go. Tonight was step one. Tomorrow will be step two. Gracie knows best.

After Elena Day 4 – August 15

Yesterday morning I received a call from the chaplain of the hospital. Elena's remains had been cremated and she wanted to personally deliver them. It's funny. Throughout the entire process, I always thought this would be the moment I would dread the most. I had envisioned that when I held her ashes, I would come to the realization that she was really gone - forever. Instead, I was relieved to have her home once again. It's not that her body holds any true significance, her soul is always with us. Still, her body was a tangible symbol of what was left of my daughter and I wanted to have her back home. Carrying her to the ambulance after her death was the hardest. For the first time in her short life, she was in someone else's hands. Minute after minute, I'd wonder where she was. It permeated my thoughts and invaded my nights as I worried about her body, all the while wishing that somehow she would come home soon. Finally, she did.

Then I was left with a pewter canister containing her ashes. Small, cold and simple. Nothing like my daughter, but I still couldn't make myself let go. I sat on the couch and held it in my arms for what seemed like hours. Somehow you never think this will happen to your daughter. I envisioned holding her in the palm of my hands as an infant, cradling her as a toddler, consoling her as a child, hugging her as a teenager, and walking her down the aisle as a young woman. But never did I think I would hold her in this manner.

Brooke and I decided long ago to spread Elena's ashes; no urn and no burial. In our minds, this was the only way to continue. Simple ceremony; Mom, Dad and Gracie. Elena, in all of her humility, would have preferred her ashes to be placed close to home. So looking to the backyard, we found our answer.

Three years ago, Elena was barely three years old. Gracie was still on Mom's hip. We had just moved into the house and knew that a remodeling project was imminent. But with no money, all we could do was plan for trees. Besides that, if we planted trees now, by the time we were ready to remodel they would be mature and help shade the yard. We picked an ash, a willow, an oak, a sugar maple and a magnolia. Partly a product of budget and partly because we figured that with more diversity, we were guaranteed that something would grow, thus we planted trees that didn't necessarily match. When Elena suggested that we also buy a pink dogwood, we figured that we'd better stop while we were ahead. "No," we told her. It would never survive the deer that raid our backyard every night. Still, Elena pressed. "How about a red one?" she asked. Okay, she wanted a tree, so be it. So slogging back through the mud at the nursery we picked a scarlet maple. At least two of the trees would match and this way it would at least be green most of the year. The tree was scrawny, but it was also cheap. So we bought it, never expecting it to survive or flourish. Three years later, it's the strongest tree in the yard and also the prettiest. Still, fall after fall, it never turns red. Instead, it turns burnt orange two days before dropping its leaves.

Tomorrow, Elena's tree will also become her final resting place. In preparation, we built a stone fence around the bed and planted pink mums in her honor. I only pray that I am strong enough to let her go when we release her ashes there tomorrow. And maybe this fall, the tree will finally turn scarlet red, but knowing Elena, I wouldn't be surprised if it is pink.

After Elena Day 5 – August 16

We spent the last months using this journal to document what happened in our lives with Elena. We shared with countless people the ups and downs of helping her courageously live her life to the fullest. I go through my days anymore thinking about what Elena is doing. Whether on this earth or not, I love to envision what I think she is busy doing in heaven. Promptly at 6 a.m. Elena jumps out of bed with a smile. I hear the drawers open and shut countless times as she finds just the right outfit for the day. She grabs one of her purses and fills it with the smaller toys she wants to keep near to her for the day to show anyone she meets. In the bathroom she brushes endlessly, loving the feeling of clean teeth. Carefully she combs her hair until it is perfectly straight. She smiles, very proud of herself as she picks out a pink headband to perfectly match the pink streak she got in her hair the minute she walked into Heaven. She slips on her pink fancy shoes and off she goes to find her Great-Grandma to have breakfast. Even though they have told her in Heaven you can eat anything you want, she opts for a full glass of milk, a bowl of fresh fruit and a chocolate chip pancake.

I can feel in my heart that she spends her days to the fullest in Heaven, just as she did here. She sits, cuddles and plays with her two baby cousins who left this world before they could open their eyes and see its beauty. She reads them stories and tells them all about their families they never got to meet. After making sure that her cousins are happy, she grabs her books and art set and sets out to find her new friends. Through the day she runs through the fields playing games. Her room is filled with books beautifully written by her own hand, each graced with a proper copyright and dedication to "Mom, Dad and Grace – mi Famle."

Every once in a while, she peaks in on us and giggles as she leaves us a sign that she is with us and thinking of us, whether it be the tinkle of a wind chime or a nicely timed breeze. Probably her most favorite part of her day is the honor she has to draw on the biggest canvas she has ever seen. She thoughtfully molds the clouds just so, making animals she hopes we recognize. Some nights, when she thinks we need some extra happiness, she opens up her paint set and paints the sky with her beautiful colors. The other kids tell her she should do it every day, but Elena reminds them you should save them for special occasions. She certainly doesn't want to run out of that prized paint set that God gave her when he welcomed her to Heaven.

At the end of the day, she climbs into bed and lies really still and quiet so she can listen to the stories that we read to Gracie. Then when we are done, she sends down the tightest of hugs. When she hugs Daddy, he pretends to fall over. When she hugs Mom, she doesn't stop kissing her. When she hugs Gracie, together, they simply laugh and giggle. I have no problem envisioning what Elena does every day in heaven. Each day she spent on earth before diagnosis, she never regretted a day. She never wished we had done something else. I know she isn't lonely and whenever she misses us, she comes to visit in her own little ways. I am certain she will be busy working magic in little ways for Gracie, Keith and me for the rest of our lives.

After Elena Day 7 – August 18

It has been a week. A week since our family became three. A week since the IVs, feeding tubes and oxygen tanks left the house. A week since we lost Elena. The pronouns and habits haven't changed: I still call up the stairs "c'mon girls, it's time to go" and I still find myself putting toothpaste on two pink toothbrushes in the morning instead of one. Sometimes I wonder if this will ever go away. But now, a week later, the feeling is different. I'm more reflective than emotional and more bored than relieved. On one hand, I'm glad to be free of the medical obligations. Free of the endless parade of pills, the constant opening and closing of the wheel chair and the two-hour meals. But then there are those things that won't go away. I still massage Gracie's feet in the evening and find myself practicing physical therapy on her ankle for no reason at all. I comb Gracie's hair after bath slowly and carefully; fearful that with every knot, I will pull loose a wad of hair. And just this past Thursday on a trip to pick up Elena's death certificate, I found myself instead pulling into the hospital parking garage, a mere mile from the county records office. And while these are just routines, they are also a sign of my thoughts. Her death still weighs heavily on my mind and comes back to bear every time I get up and walk down the hall past her bedroom door.

Still, I am a man torn between two very different feelings. With Elena's death came a desire to finally be happy. To laugh, play and indulge in trivial pursuits. Now, I could finally start working on the house again: finish the floors and paint the walls. We could get away for the weekend, swim at the lake, or just enjoy a dinner out. I could play tickle-time with Gracie on the floor, running circles around the couch until we both collapsed on the floor to rest again. I could take Brooke out on a date, get to know her again, and rediscover our love. But no matter how strong my desire to return to our pre-cancer lives, I also never want to forget. I want to remember the sound of Elena's voice when she read her first book, "The Piggy in the Puddle." I want to remember her face lying in our bed early on Saturday mornings as she watched cartoons. I want to feel the touch of her hand as we walked up the stairs to her school. Still, it's the pre-cancer memories that are the toughest to recall. So I walk around the house staring into family photos for a glimpse of her personality, hoping that if I look hard enough I'll hear her voice. I hug her stuffed animals close, smelling their fur just for the opportunity of reliving one last minute. I sit in the corner of the room and try to remember even the smallest detail of her life. But no matter how I try, nothing comes. Her voice is lost, the memories are hidden and her personality is buried deep within my mind.

Last night after everyone went to bed, I spent an hour trying to remember. In the dark, I sat staring at digital pictures flashing on a screen, wishing that I had taken more. I don't know what I was expecting, but I guess in some way I just wanted time to pay tribute and pray for my daughter. I wanted to know that without me, she was all right. I wanted to know that I would never forget and that her memories would be emblazoned into my heart forever. I wanted to know that it was OK to stop mourning and start living once again. But by the time the pictures had finished their loop, I felt no different – only tired.

I guess this never ends. Every laugh is accompanied by a wish that she was sitting beside me laughing along. Every falling star that I see will be accompanied by a wish that she could see a sky as beautiful as I saw. In the meantime, we continue day-to-day acting out routines rather than actually living.

After Elena Day 10 – August 21

Cancer affects us all. Lung cancer, breast cancer, colon cancer, brain cancer and cancers of the blood, some people experience one type, others, like us, have experienced several. But regardless of the type of cancer, the effect sends shockwaves through our families and our lives. And for those who ultimately lost a loved one, the effect was somehow permanent. Survivors talk about the fight and how they prevailed. The family of a victim talks about lessons learned. In my family we talk about both.

How cancer affects you ultimately doesn't matter, the impact is the same. Still, as we've fought alongside Elena over the past nine months, I've noticed the comparisons between cancers. "This one is the worst," they say. "This one has the most difficult treatment" or "this one is the most painful" or "this one affects the most people" are also used. But living with cancer, I've developed a new way of looking at this sinister disease. Instead of comparing its effects, I consider its impact in finding a cure. So instead of talking about the "worst," I talk about the willingness of the victim to advance new experimental treatments. After all, if the prognosis is poor or "dismal," drug side effects, even the worst ones, are better than the alternative. And so the search is advanced one more step in the direction of a cure.

To look at cancer in such a way is cruel. In a way, it is a "hit and miss" strategy that suggests that our family members are guinea pigs in the field of cancer research. But somehow I think those who have lost their lives to cancer would agree. And while I'm not suggesting painful or even useless procedures, I'm fully aware that this chapter of medicine remains unwritten and uncharted. Whether we like it or not, medicine is a science and science is about trial and experimentation. To ignore this most basic point is to never advance the science.

Ultimately what I see in DIPG is an ability to advance oncology because the prognosis is so "dismal." You do not have a 20% chance of survival. Even when they give you a 10% chance of survival, hardly anyone can give you one example of a childhood survivor. 10% is a number to give you hope. So when you have DIPG, you don't consider drug side effects and you don't consider future complications. And if you can buy time, you take it as it comes. Yes, this is harsh. It is also callous. But then again, she was my daughter. My beautiful, precious daughter. My children are my greatest love and my true devotion. Her life and her well-being superseded anything that I could want for myself. Still, knowing the previous impact of cancer, I knew that this was a fight and a fight that needed to be approached with every bit of power we could muster. You do not get a second chance.

Often when people asked me about my daughter's cancer, they would always ask another question as well. "Do you have any other children?" It was an innocent question, even an instinctual one. After all, anyone confronted with this news always feels the need to reassure and comfort. And somehow, if you have another child, the pain would be lessened. But the logic never works. When a loved one has cancer it doesn't matter if it is your father, mother, child or even yourself. The pain is always different and never comparable to what other people think you feel. Part of the time you feel anger and other times you strive for solace, but cancer transcends any normal pain. It is an emptiness that is indescribable. Until now, I never understood it. Now I do. And now I try to fill it with a passion, a passion to make Elena's life worthwhile and to prevent any other parent from having to answer the question we all come to hate. DIPG makes sense because you are able to risk it all, even if it means risking your child. It is as good a place to start on a cure as any other cancer. Fight the fight where the battle is already lost and you will find courage where you never thought possible.

After Elena Day 12 – August 23

Life doesn't stop. Gracie understands this better than anyone else. There was a time when we wondered how she would take the news of her sister's death. Would she remain oblivious, failing to understand the ramifications of the loss? Would she simply not remember and go through life thinking that she never had a sister for her first four years? Would she grieve, left as the only child in our empty family? Or would she grasp not quite enough, leaving the balance to be discovered over the coming years in frustration and through a never ending series of questions? But what we discovered we never expected. Gracie understands and knows more than we could ever imagine.

Since the beginning, Elena's disease has always been a factual matter to Gracie. She had a "bump in her head" and she was very sick – that was all. And when Elena died, she saw it in the same light. Elena went to Heaven and became an angel. She regarded the loss very matter-of-factly. God needed Elena and she would miss her very much. No tears, no probing questions, no wondering when Elena would come back. Death was permanent and easily understood. I wish for me it could be that easy.

Sometimes I think we spend so much time anticipating death that we fail to realize the simplicity in life. Maybe our kids have it right. There's life and then there's death, nothing more. Focus on the present and forget the rest. In times like this we wonder how to answer children's questions. We plan out therapy sessions, consumed by the possibility of questions we can't answer. But in the end, is it really us who desire the therapy? Maybe we look to the questions that they might pose as an opportunity to instead explain it to ourselves. Maybe simply by talking about it with children we find the answers we need to heal ourselves.

Today, for the first time, Gracie followed me as I entered Elena's room. I didn't really need anything, only a look around. It's amazing how many feelings are trapped behind her door. Sometimes I wish they would stay there, allowing me only a little time to myself between the distractions. But they leak out a few at a time, finding a way into my words, my thoughts and my actions.

With Gracie in the room, I didn't know what to expect. Was this when the questions would start? Would she wonder if Elena was coming back from Heaven in time for dinner or to read a book with us before bed? Instead, Gracie had other thoughts. "Elena had such a pretty room," she commented. I hung on the word "had." She understood. She walked to the mantel, then to the bed and finally to the dresser. She opened Elena's music box and turned the key. "Can I have this?" I resisted and closed the box. This was Elena's sanctuary. At her death it ceased to be a bedroom and became a memorial. On her mantel sat her collection of snow globes she made me buy on every business trip I made. On her headboard hung the medals from the past two years of the "Flying Pig Marathon" where she ran the last half-mile with me. (I think they thought she ran the whole thing with the way she collapsed at the finish line.) In her closet sits a pile of quilts, each made by a mother who read of Elena's story and made her something to keep her warm. We swore that in the winter she'd cover herself with a new one every night. In her drawers are her tights, tights with leopard prints, butterfly designs and stripes of every size and color. She loved her tights. And the shoes – oh, the shoes. Elena loved her room. Pink, pink and more pink. Princess pictures of every kind line the wall. "Can I have Elena's room? It reminds me of her. And I want to sleep in here."

I'm not ready.

I'm not sure I'm ready. It's too soon. Where would we put Elena's stuff? The excuses kept running through my mind. Still, deep in my heart, I know it is the best answer. I just don't think I'm ready. I know Elena would be. She would be the first one to give up her room for her sister, and somewhere in the clouds I think she's ready to do it now for Gracie. But I'm not in the clouds and I don't think I'm ready. I hugged Gracie and didn't answer.

Turning back to the bed, she pulled back the covers and cradled the urn containing Elena's remains. "What's this?" she asked. Yet another question I didn't want to answer. Still, I swore that I would never lie and never avoid Gracie's questions. After all, this is what they tell you is the best way to help your children through the grieving process, even if you need the therapy more than they do. "It's an urn and in it are the remains of your sister," I responded. It didn't make sense to her. I explained that in the urn was her body but her soul was in Heaven. "Oh, I see," she said, "I was wondering where you put her body when you carried her out to the ambulance. Are we going to bury her?" Simple questions, simple mourning. The burial was something else we weren't ready for. She hugged and kissed the urn.

In the end, grieving is about reconciling your feelings and finding a way to move on. And today, Gracie's therapy session with me took some steps that I wasn't prepared to take. So I ignored her questions, patted her on the head and we went to the pool. Still, I think she was right once again. Maybe the best way to help us and help Gracie is to have her move into Elena's room. If we don't, the room will always be a memorial to Elena. If we do, it will be a celebration of her life. Celebrations are always better. Elena would like that.

After Elena Day 16 – August 27

I can now see that Gracie's return to school will be littered with a minefield of questions. Questions that she cannot possibly answer and questions that she hasn't yet considered. They are questions about life and death and they are questions about Elena.

Today after dinner, Gracie decided that another trip to the pool was in order. She is keenly aware of the fading summer season and wants to savor as much chlorine time as possible. I guess her hair isn't quite green enough. So after finishing dinner we packed a quick bag and made our way to the pool. Everyone knows Gracie there. We tell her it is because she's such a great diver, she says it's because she had the "sick sister." She's right, but we don't let her know it. "Hi Gracie," the girls from the lap pool yell out. Gracie shyly waves back and runs off to play. But as Brooke and I drop the bag and walk to join her, we start to hear the questions. "So what did they do with her body," they ask. "Do you have cancer too?" Gracie stumbles. Maybe she doesn't know the answers either. Maybe she is just uncomfortable talking about it. Either way, these are not questions that any child should have to answer. Brooke jabs me and suggests that now may be a good time to chase after Gracie and play the tickle monster game. Thankfully, it is still easy to distract Gracie. As for the other girls, they are relentless. "What symptoms did Elena have? Do you have those symptoms?" This must be the daughter of a doctor. I don't ever think I've even heard the word "symptoms" from a seven-year-old before. Time for the tickle monster again.

In the end, I spent the evening chasing Gracie around the pool. No more questions tonight. Brooke suggests we have a talk with Gracie and prepare her for school. She's right. But how? To do so would open a floodgate of thoughts that we've all kept to ourselves. Still, I think Gracie will understand. Talking about it with her friends is another thing. Oh, how I miss the days when the most complicated conversation involved bullies, why you can't wear sandals when it is snowing or why Santa has a fake beard. Even the questions that will come during her teenage years seem minor in comparison to the ones we face today. No script or brochure tells us how to handle this, we know, we have them all.

Somehow I don't think the teachers will appreciate me chasing Gracie around school as the tickle monster. So tomorrow we will have the talk and raise all the questions. At the same time, we will also tell Gracie how to stop the questioning when she wants to. It's her decision and she's old enough to make it.

After Elena Day 20 – August 31

It seems real now. The picture of the smiling girl with the headband that graces our walls, the girl on the web page, the angel in the newspaper; she's the daughter I lost. Three weeks of shock, disbelief and the vision that I'd wake up and hug her again are over now. What lasted so long now leaves my mind like the dream it was. She's not coming out of school at the end of the day, she's not getting out of the caravan on the right side and she's not knocking on our door in the morning. We've cleaned out her closet, moved Gracie into her room and taken her lunchbox down from the top of our refrigerator.

When I'm not moving or preoccupied, it is the only thought that I have. I stand fearless with the knowledge that I've lost what I thought was most sacred. Failure and death threaten my actions no more. When you've been through the worst, everything else is a distraction. But what is most interesting is the significance that religion plays upon my life. Elena's illness drew me closer to religion. Her death pushed me away. Yet now, I feel that I must believe once again.

When she was first diagnosed, I sought the security of prayer. I believed that somehow I could pray enough, kneel low enough and make a difference. And at that point, you just can't help it. You're surrounded by people and symbols that give you comfort in the saving grace of God.

Eventually comes desperation and death. Anger was soon to follow. I cursed religion on the basis that no God of mine could take a life so precious. And then the same people who told me to take faith in God's healing power once before, now tell me that Elena was lost because it was beyond God's power. That sometimes it's just what happens. He needed another angel.

So what was I to believe? Was I to believe that my God chose inaction over compassion? Was I to believe that sometimes God's power is powerless? Instead, I chose disbelief. Then there was anger. Plenty of anger. It still lingers even today. I doubt it will ever disappear.

Now I find myself seeking refuge in religion once again. But this time, not because I need to, this time I want to. With Elena gone, I want to believe that she's somewhere better. I want to believe in her as an angel. I want to see her in my mind at peace. I want Heaven to exist just so I know that she continues to change lives each and every day. So I continue to pray, not for myself, but for her. Maybe she's on the other side doing the same thing.

Events like these have a way of forcing you to question faith. Death is a natural part of life, it's just never supposed to happen to those who never had the chance to live. At least that's my opinion. But reality has a way of ignoring what we think should happen. Good things don't happen because they should; they happen because they do.

For now I'm left wondering. She's gone and all I have is prayer. Somehow I don't think it will ever be enough.

After Elena Day 29 – September 9

Last night Elena's kindergarten aide told me that she doesn't want to empty her reading bag of Elena's books quite yet. I guess there's a certain amount of permanency in even this. These were the books she read to Elena in her final days. Books on children with disabilities, books with rhyming lyrics and even books with farting dogs. Each had its place, whether it was to make Elena feel normal, to help calm her after being accessed with an IV for the second time in a day, or to just make her laugh. She chose each book deliberately, knowing precisely which one to use at the right time. In a way, it was a teacher's toolbox, custom built for Elena. But now, after her death, it was a haunting reminder of the void that we all have. For us, it was the closet of tights, hats and hundreds of brilliantly shiny shoes. And although we were finally able to move Gracie into Elena's room, the closet contents remain untouched. We know we need to do it, but tomorrow always seems like a better day than today. But at this pace, tomorrow will never come. Somehow I guess we fool ourselves into believing that a full closet or a bag of random books is better than emptiness.

After Elena Day 31 – September 11

It is an anniversary I hate to celebrate. One month ago Elena passed. Thinking about that makes my heart break. I have spent the last month crying about losing my little girl. I have spent my days celebrating her life by sharing stories of Elena with as much pride as I had when she was alive. I have used those days to change the way I live so I don't waste a moment or take it for granted. Mostly, I have spent this month missing each and everything about Elena. I think in the last month I have composed in my mind the longest greeting card in my head.

Gone are the bad memories of the disease. All that is left are the beautiful happy memories of Elena. I don't miss all of the amazing things I did with Elena during the last few months. The time we spent completing her wish list isn't what makes my heart ache. It's the quiet moments and the little things. And so starts my Hallmark card.

I miss her smile.
I miss the feel of her hair.
I miss how girly she loved to be.
I miss the big bear hugs she would give me.
I miss the motherly way she would lead Gracie.
I miss listening to her sing the songs on the radio.
I miss her telling me something she learned that day.
I miss watching her pick out her clothes every morning.
I miss her telling me what she would do when she was a mommy.
I miss how grateful she was for every little thing that was given to her.
I miss how she made everyone feel important, no matter who they were.
I miss how she made me feel like the most wonderful, perfect mother in the world.
I miss how proud she was to be the first person to make Gracie laugh.
I miss every way she made Gracie laugh from then on.
I miss how she never quit, no matter what she faced.
I miss the "I Love You" notes she would write for us.
I miss how she would carry herself with such poise.
I miss how she always wanted to hold my hand.
I miss the whispers of secrets and new ideas.
I miss how she always wanted to cuddle.
I miss her face when she saw a baby.
I miss her reading books to me.
I miss her infectious laugh.
I miss those huge eyes.
I miss her.

I wonder if I will stop counting days, or noticing anniversaries. I am pretty sure I will never stop missing her.

After Elena Day 35 – September 15

This week I started working on the house for the first time in months. Up until now, home improvements were the domain of subcontractors and general contractors we hired to take my place as I stood by Elena's side. Where I was once passionate about remodeling, I now consider it little more than a chore. It is an opportunity for distraction – nothing more. But today as I finished installing shelving in the family room, I felt unfulfilled. You see, any other Saturday a year ago you would find Brooke in the kitchen cooking with Gracie by her side. And whether it was cookies, a new dinner concoction or just simply brownies, Gracie was there to lick the spoon, mix the batter or play with her own kitchen play set nearby. Elena would always be with me. Donning her tool belt she'd offer me tools, read me a book or compliment me on the beauty of my craftsmanship. Every screw, every nail and every coat of paint would be met with praise wonderment as Elena expressed her appreciation for everything I did. I relished her company and her admiration. No matter how bad it looked, no matter how badly I screwed up, Elena was always quick to tell me just how lovely she thought it looked. With her hands to her cheeks and in her most sincere voice, she'd tell me that she loved the change and thought I was the best. I think this, above all, I miss most about Elena.

After Elena Day 38 – September 18

It's five weeks later and feels different. I walk past her picture in the hallway and smile. I remember her laugh as she threw back her head, her crouch as I chased her around the house tickling her, the way she crossed her legs like a lady when she read me a book and her oh-so-soft cheeks as I brushed my fingers up against them as she slept. The tears don't come the same way they did and I can slowly feel myself settling in our new way of life. The wound is still fresh, but today I find solace in having spent six wonderful years with my little angel.

Midway through her disease and immediately prior to progression, I spoke with another father of a DIPG child who had passed away. I never truly understood what he said at the time. Today those words resonate through my body. It was on that phone call that I told him I couldn't imagine life without my daughter and that if she died, the memories and the sound of her name would be too much. "Don't fear the memories," he replied, "for the worst day of your life will be when people stop talking about Elena." Today I feel what he knew. Her picture no longer adorns the bulletin boards of the local supermarket, people no longer mistakenly ask, "how are the girls," and I'm no longer known as Elena's dad to her friends. Instead, people simply nod their heads and ask how we're doing, they talk about my "daughter" rather than about "Elena," and I'm known as Gracie's dad. In truth, there's still a part of me that wants to hear her name, be always known as "Elena and Gracie's Dad," and encounter that one remaining person who still doesn't know. I guess it's my way of preserving the idealism one more day.

I must never forget that Elena was about actions. For six months she spoke not a word and craved humility. Privately she loved seeing her painting hanging on the wall at the art museum and she regarded this as her highest honor, but publicly she shunned the reception and the compliments that people graced her with. She saw beauty in simplicity and kindness in everyone, from babies to dogs and to even her dad. She melted my heart like no other person ever has. Now I see she has had this effect on my family, my community and strangers we've never met. She embodied courage, true love and simplicity.

After Elena Day 53 – October 3

Brooke has her note. I have mine. They are tucked away in our briefcases; always with us, never out of reach. I found mine in the black backpack that we took to Elena's wish trip. On the cover of the envelope is a lopsided purple heart, just the way Elena drew them best. On the side she wrote DAD in clear pink letters before sealing the envelope and hiding it in the hidden pouch of the backpack. Brooke found her letter in the side pocket of her briefcase, where she had put it many months before. These are two of many letters that Elena hid for us in the last nine months of her life. They are constant reminders of her determination and her inspiration. She knew somehow that one day we would need them to continue.

I love the heart. I yearn for her handwritten "Dad" is written on everything from printer paper to scraps of paper around the house. Still, I can't get beyond the envelope. Her last letter told me she was sorry she was sick. I found this letter two weeks after her death in the drawer by my bedside. I cried for the week following, concealing my tears in the sounds of the shower or within the walls of the playhouse that I built for her at the rear of our yard. I can only imagine what this letter says.

In a way, the heart drawn on the front of the envelope says it all. She communicates with nothing more than a heart that tells us she loves us, even from beyond the boundaries of life. This is all I need to know. Tomorrow I will most likely find yet another note and it too will remain unopened, tucked away in the side pocket of my briefcase. One day I'll take the time to read them from the comfort of Elena's playhouse next to the tree under which we scattered her ashes. I'll cry and I'll wonder what she knew. But in the end, I'll discover that what she knew was us. They are her words, her pictures and her inspiration. One heart – one message.

After Elena Day 62 – October 12

Tonight Elena gave us hundreds of reminders of what we missed most when she died. As we searched for CDs for Gracie's new birthday gift of a boom box, we discovered hundreds of letters and notes scattered in between the dust-covered cases on our shelves. There were cutouts of hearts - pink, yellow, white, green, blue and purple paper; all with the words "I love you Mom Dad Grace Elena." And in her customary style, each word was spelled carefully except for the "Elena" that was purposefully spelled backwards. This was her signature and as she told me, she liked the way it looked. There were notebooks, eight of them. One was used for food orders, a necessity developed from her steroids in the last months of her life. Another was a listing of school news; an hour-by-hour account of what centers she participated in, what she drew in art and who was the "Razzle-Dazzle" helper of the day. A third notebook was a book of games Elena created for herself. On one page she created a maze and then drew her way to the finish. On another page was a crossword puzzle, complete with the words "Grace," "Dad," "Mom," "Dog" and "Love." Another notebook was her working notebook that she took to work with me every morning. In it she drew graphs, scribbled accounting numbers from her time with Mom, and stapled nearly every corner of every page. For two hours, Brooke and I read each page and remembered what we loved most about Elena. At times we laughed, but mostly we cried until we finally stopped for fear of never again finding another note from Elena. Somewhere deep in our hearts we long for more but realize that one day the notes and the letters will no longer hide in the corners of bookcases or in the pockets of briefcases and we will be left empty.

When hospice left us that fateful day, they gave us a box to hold the reminders of Elena. But on the first day, the box was already overflowing. Today, Gracie, Brooke and I all have a box to ourselves and we've filled another three boxes with just the letters and artwork that she hid from us over the past year. In a way, it was her way of touching our lives each and every day, slowly and purposefully with her own treasure hunt. Tonight we filled box four and we're on a quest to find a trunk big enough and worthy enough to hold all of Elena's letters and artwork.

After Elena Day 72 – October 22

I can't tell time. For ten years I wore digital wristwatches; the cheap kinds. Some had timers, some could tell me the time in England if I were to ever travel outside of Ohio and one had a calculator (that was the expensive one: at least $35). Telling time was easy: look down and read the display. They even had a backlight if I was ever in the dark. Then came the pager and suddenly the watch was redundant. And for the next five years my watch was on my belt. Then I got married. Brooke thought I should wear a watch once again, but this time I would get an elegant watch. No more black plastic, this one would be made of metallic silver and decorate my arm. She said that I needed to look sophisticated and the watch was the first step of many to come. So like a paper doll, I bought a new watch and wore it again for the first time in five years. This time it had hands and no numbers. I suggested a compromise. How about one with hands and a digital display? That's when I realized it wasn't my choice.

That was ten years ago. And for eight of those years I wore a watch I couldn't read. Sometimes I'd show up an hour late, other times an hour early, but never on time if I relied on my watch. Some people would ask the time and I'd look at my watch puzzled. "It's this time," I'd say, offering them a glance at the silver piece of jewelry hanging from my wrist. Sometimes I'd quickly look at my phone as they looked away to confirm. A watch without numbers was always pointless.

Then the watch battery would die. Still, I'd leave it on my arm for weeks, never noticing until Brooke asked me for the time. During time changes it would go a week or two before I'd finally change it; usually when Brooke would as for the time. Then came Elena. One of the last things that she learned in kindergarten was how to tell time. And while she too never comprehended the purpose of a watch without numbers, it never prevented her from trying. When we went to the Memphis, her teacher told her to practice telling time. Good thing, because when you're waiting for your "always late" radiation appointments it's about the only thing you do. So she and I would practice together, counting each arrow on the face. In time she mastered the hours and I filled in the minutes. She had found her skill and I helped her with mine. Cooperatively we knew the time. We were no longer an hour ahead or an hour behind.

Last week my watch battery died once more. This time I noticed immediately. I still can't tell the time and part of me never wants to. Still the watch hangs from my wrist and serves as a reminder of the way she touched my life. And whether I never change it from eastern daylight time to Eastern Standard Time, each second that clicks by signifies a part of me that never wants to forget. Together we could tell time, just as we could do so many other things as team. I will never buy another watch with numbers, just don't ask me what time it is.

After Elena Day 89 – November 8

I see life in a new way since Elena's passing. I see shadows in life where I previously only saw sunshine. It is the life of a parent who has lost a child. Still, somehow I feel that it is different with DIPG.

The loss of a child is always painful and the grief is always the same. A parent who loses a child to murder blames the offender. It is a senseless act without meaning and never understood. There is blame and raging anger that offer some path to recovery but never a chance to forget. Solace is discovered if only for fleeting moments in the prosecution or forgiveness of those involved. I never want the pain that these parents carry each and every day.

A child lost in an accident forces a parent to question why my child. It is a question of odds, chance and circumstance – nothing more. There are no offenders, no one to blame. Once again the grief strikes deep and never heals. Still there is some comfort in the reality that had the day been different, they might have been spared. Of course, it is the same reality that haunts these parents for the rest of their lives of what might have been.

A child lost to any other disease suffers the same question of chance. Doctors tell you that there is a 20%, 30%, or even a 90% chance of survival. Still, your child is not one of the lucky ones and you lose him or her to the very disease that you abhor. For these parents, it is a question of why my child, but a lingering understanding that your child fought the courageous battle. There is always comfort in knowing she had a chance and fought the good fight.

But DIPG is not just any disease. The view from the other side of the battle is decidedly less optimistic. Doctors admit that the 10% chance they once told you wasn't quite accurate and that even those who last 18 months or more might have been misdiagnosed. The same people who told you they knew of a survivor now tell you that there never was a chance. I guess I can't blame them, it's what we needed to hear when we went through the fight with Elena. Still, the view from here is much different.

I see the parents of children lost to DIPG now as they are. Thoughts of suicide, running away and breakdown flood their minds as the memories of their children pass behind their eyes. Powerless, they suffer in ways that others will never understand; even to parents who have lost their children in other ways. It is one thing to lose a child but quite another to know that you could do nothing had you been able to relive their life. You are powerless.

I write this not because I wish for some way to find concern or attention, but instead because it is a view that I hope no other parent will ever share. If anything, I admire Gracie and Brooke for their courage in our own battle and recognize that we have bonded together in order to survive. I am thankful for this strength and for Elena's example.

Tonight, hug your children. Read that long book. Hang their artwork all over your home. Ignore the thought of predestined lives and live in blissful ignorance. It's how you must live one day at a time. I too know the value of this and wish all the world to have it back with Elena peacefully asleep back in her bed.

After Elena Day 100 – November 19

It was a simple job. It defeated bullies, darkness and nightmares. A dad's job was to protect. For six years this is what I told Elena and Gracie as I tucked them in and turned off the light. One simple job...

With Elena's death I discovered that the job of a dad is never over. Cancer has scarred my family forever, for the third time. I should have seen it coming. I should have done more. I will never make that mistake again. Never again. Tonight I stand at the edge of Gracie's bed making that same promise.

Brainstem cancer made sure that Elena never had a chance. Now Gracie is left. History tells me that she has a 43% chance of getting cancer, just like so many women in my family have chanced before her. If she does, she has a 66% chance of getting brain cancer. And if she gets brain cancer, she has a 100% chance of dying from it. I will never make this mistake again. My job is to prevent the inevitable and my time is limited.

Awareness, research and funding are not part of a job. This isn't a hobby and it isn't a way to somehow justify Elena's death. It doesn't start at nine in the morning and it doesn't end at five in the afternoon. I don't go to bed thinking about something else and I don't wake up in a dream, not anymore. The search for a cure is a passion, the kind of passion that burns in your veins endlessly. I will never have enough time, enough money or enough determination to do what I know I must do. It encompasses two lifetimes for which I only have one remaining. Still, I never again want to powerless – just fearless.

Time slips through my fingers, one second at a time. I sit at stoplights and count the seconds, knowing how precious each one is in the search for a cure. Could I raise one more cent; maybe a dollar in the time it takes to drive home? I brush my teeth wondering if maybe I should instead be checking my e-mail for another grant, another donation or another idea. Work is something that occupies time and pays bills – nothing more. Food and sleep cease to be necessities and instead become distractions. I need neither to continue – the passion is my fuel. It is the pain that only a parent feels and only the determination of a father who has failed. I will not fail again.

The Cure Starts Now is a promise. A promise to Elena that I wasn't able to keep, but a promise that I will never again break. Gracie deserves this. So does every other child afflicted by brain cancer. For decades we moved without purpose and focus on minutia. Today we have a purpose. Change the world one child at a time. This is where it begins...

After Elena Day 103 – November 22

Last month we spent more than $48 on tissues. By my calculations, that's 3600 tissues – or 120 tissues per day. And considering Gracie is only good for about six a day, that leaves 114 between Brooke and me. That's about ten tissues per hour. Today Brooke easily fulfilled her quota. She just hides them well.

There are tissues in her sleeves, tissues under her pillow, tissues in the cup holder in her car, tissues in her pockets, tissues on her desk and even tissues in the empty cookie jar on the counter. Some she hides just in case, others ones are used but she's just tired of walking to the garbage can. Even in the time since I began this journal, she's used three more as she checks on other DIPG children around the nation with her computer.

The tears are quiet now. There's the occasional dab of the eyelid between phone calls at the office, the preventative dab as she greets people at the door and then the all-out soaker when she sits alone in the office at night. If it weren't for the tissues, you'd never know, but with the garbage cans overflowing it's hard to miss. Today was a bad tissue day, partially because she has a cold and partially because last year this was the last day we lived in ignorance. The day after Thanksgiving was when we learned the news about Elena for the first time. It was the day we first heard the words diffuse intrinsic brainstem glioma. It was also the first day that tissues became scarce in our household.

She doesn't want Gracie to know. Neither do I. So we paint a smile and turn away as she blissfully sings the months of the year to the Macarena dance theme song (apparently this is the new song for kindergarten). It's not that we're sad, well, not completely. Instead, it's that we remember. We remember yelling at her to sit up, quit faking her alto voice and to hurry up and get in the car. Then late into the night we remember putting her to bed as she complained of feeling dizzy and tingling in her arm. We were convinced it was a cold, nothing more. All she needed was sleep. Now we wish that's all it had been.

By now Brooke's on tissue number eight since I started the journal and they pile up next to her as she reports on yet another DIPG child experiencing progression. By the end of the night we'll be on to the next box as we recount our own experience with Elena through the eyes of another desperate set of DIPG parents.

In two hours, Thanksgiving will be over and our minds will immediately focus on the next anniversary date: one that will bring happier memories but undoubtedly more tears. Next month is Elena's birthday. Last year we celebrated her life with family and friends at the local chili parlor, just as she always wanted. This year we hope to do the same and honor our daughter over a "2-way" with cheese and spaghetti. On our refrigerator hangs the phone number for the hospice nurse who suggested that we release balloons in honor of our daughter. It was a good idea, but her funeral was too soon and the Walk-a-thon was at the airport where it was prohibited. Maybe after school, her birthday might be the perfect opportunity to send her a little birthday greeting to the heavens with some birthday balloons. We could use the help and the cheer. I'll pack a couple of packs of tissues along for the ride.

After Elena Day 106 – November 25

There are questions that I can't begin to answer. Tonight as we drove home from dinner with my family Gracie began to ask them all. And for the first time, she realized Elena was never going to come back.

It began with, "I really miss Elena," and then came the tears that she'd held back for months began to flow. "I want her to come back down – I really miss Elena," she cried. "Why did the doctors make her die?" I answered that they didn't. Elena died from a tumor in her brain. "But why didn't then they cut open her head and then tape it back up?" "Because it was in a place that they couldn't remove it," I replied. "Is she an angel," she asked. "Yes – she always was," we told her, "even when she was your sister." "But she didn't fly when she was my sister." Even we couldn't argue with the logic.

"If God knows how much I miss her, why doesn't He let her come back down," she asked through the tears. Even we wondered why. She asked again. "I guess He needs her help taking care of other children," we finally answered. It was a truth that we didn't even believe.

The hardest part of Elena's death came tonight. The pain that we feel ourselves is nothing compared to the pain we felt as we watched her sister cry in the backseat for what seemed like hours. There's nothing you can do. No answers suffice. All you can do is offer your hand, a tissue and your love. She too feels the pain that wounds us all yet brings us together as a family with our memories. For the past four months Gracie has brought us joy and love, now she also brings us memories that will never fade. Now we are powerless to help her.

In the end, it was Gracie's resilience and questions that made us smile as we tucked her warmly in her bed. "Why does God give us headaches? I have one right now and it's not nice," she said. Yet another question we couldn't answer. We too had headaches.
We love you Gracie. Dream about Elena.

After Elena Day 124 – December 13

She was a six-year-old girl. And if you want to know about Elena, here is all you need to know:

- If you asked her if she was asleep, she'd tell you yes.
- She'd always eat her vegetables first and save the candy for months later.
- You can never wear enough pink.
- Shoes are always better when they sparkle.
- She'd always write her name backwards – not because she didn't know how to write it, but because she "just liked the way it looked."
- Why sigh at Dad when you can roll your eyes?
- Always, always shy away from attention, except when you are about to have your picture taken.
- Why settle on one Halloween costume when you can switch it the day before, and then switch it to a third the day of?
- Always cross your legs when you sit.
- Red highlights in your hair are a great way to rebel against Dad.
- There is nothing better than art class, except, of course, a trip to the library.
- A belt is the perfect accessory.
- Fiction is better than non-fiction.
- Skip the pop, give her milk. And pour it in a wineglass and say "cheers."
- She loved "squibble-squabbles" (lace and ruffles).

- She was the perfect sous chef.
- Tights are best when in jungle patterns or polka dots.
- No pants, only dresses.
- She LOVED babies.
- When you played school, she was always the teacher.
- Avoid Dad during "forced fun." (water skiing, tubing, water slides)
- Mom was best for cuddling.
- She loved to sing, but couldn't hold a tune. And please don't ask her to dance.
- Sally (a grumpy old Chihuahua) was the best pet she never had.
- You can never have enough headbands.
- Write at least three love notes to your family a day and then hide them for finding later.
- All she ever desired in life was to be a mom.

She was simple, she was a sister, she was Elena. She is our inspiration.

After Elena Day 134 – December 23

We put on an act. Smiles cover up tears and both Brooke and I complain that our eyes are red because of the allergies. On Elena's birthday she went upstairs; I went outside. We took our turns, neither one talking with the other about what we knew we were both feeling. Meanwhile, Gracie sat on the couch cradling the picture of her and Elena taken two years ago in the hallway of our disassembled house.

Gracie told me that morning that she wanted to wish Elena happy birthday. Brooke and I decided that a balloon message would be the best way for her to help say goodbye. So after finishing work, I went to the local card store only to stare blankly at the wall of balloons. Somehow each seemed too cheery and trivial for the occasion. Most had happy birthday messages written over backgrounds of fireworks, party hats and even Disney princesses. These were balloons for happier times, nothing like the occasion we were celebrating."

How do you say goodbye with a balloon? How do you say, "We miss you and will never have another "moment" with foil and ribbon?

In the end, I knew that I'd spend my life waiting for the perfect balloon and finally chose two foil heart balloons and two pink latex balloons to mark the occasion. The clerk would never understand my deliberation and hesitation when she asked if I wanted to write my daughter's name on the balloon to surprise her with. I simply replied "Elena" and she set to work making out the stickers to personalize the balloon. I rationalized that maybe it would allow Elena to see the balloon and instantaneously know it was meant for her. Yet, I was fully aware that the stickers would ultimately do little more than litter a field somewhere as the balloon eventually made its way back to earth.

At home, Gracie was hard at work on her message. She had chosen an "I Love You" card proudly displaying Elena's artwork on the front panel. In it she wrote, "Happy Birthday Elena – we miss you" and signed her name. Then we folded up the message, placed it in an envelope bearing Elena's name and tied it to the balloons. It was a pretty message, but one that was symbolic and nothing more. It was a way to pacify our anxiety and serve as an outlet for Gracie's grief. Yet, the message would remain in our hearts no matter how many times we wrote it or how many balloons we released.

Outside it was a beautiful day. For the first time in a long time, coats were left in the closet as we walked to the yard hand-in-hand with Gracie and her balloons. Then, without a thought, we released the balloons into the sky to deliver Elena her birthday message. Drifting side to side the balloons fought the gusts as they moved westward. And no more than 50 feet from the ground, they collected in the waiting branches of the neighbor's 80-year-old oak tree.

Two days later, there they remain. The pink balloons deflated; the card blowing in the wind drenched by the nightly rains. Gracie asks when they will reach Elena while Brooke and I struggle to find meaning. But in the end, there is no meaning and no symbolism. To Gracie it is a daily reminder of the message that Elena never got. To Brooke and me, it is just another missed opportunity to heal. The balloons are now too high to reach and too tangled to ever fall down.

They say that latex balloons can decay in a matter of weeks. Ribbon can take up to a year. Foil balloons, on the other hand, can take upwards of twenty years to decay. I don't know if I can wait that long. As much as I wanted the balloons to rise to the heavens, I now equally want them to fall to the earth. The daily reminder as we cut the grass, rake the leaves or return home is one that we don't care to acknowledge. And for the past two days, Gracie never fails to notice. We tell her that in time, they will rise and get to Elena. I just wonder if she'll believe me twenty years from now.

After Elena Day 169 – January 28

255 days and all I can think about are the minutes. Minutes spent at work, minutes spent watching television, minutes spent in hospitals, minutes spent sleeping. God gave us 367,200 minutes after diagnosis and we wasted 146,880 of them. I look back on the pictures and it's all I can think of. If only I had one of those minutes back.

On day one, I promised we would make the most of her life. I would take her to the "little restaurant," take her wedding dress shopping and we'd go see the view from the top of the Eiffel tower. Living a life in 255 days. Days 2-5 we spent in hospitals. Days 5-14 was spent in fear as I fed her Jell-O and soup in a desperate attempt to keep her nourished and we contemplated our options. On day 15, we raced to radiation realizing that she would not make it through the next week. By day 18 she started her recovery. From there we started living once again.

In the beginning you want to know the chance for survival. In the end, you start to ask how long. I can't even begin to wonder the questions that Elena must have had. Either way, it's a race to maximize every minute to its fullest. You tell yourself you can skip sleep, ignore the wash and find a way to pay the bills without a job. The minutes are worth more than any of that. Six months after her death they're worth even more.

Ultimately, I will never have those minutes back. Instead they serve as a reminder of how I must live my life with my family now. Live your life as if you have 135 days and minutes to lose. Thank you, Elena.

After Elena Day 176 – February 4

No matter how old or how young, cancer touches everyone. Frequently it's deep within. Other times the wound is still fresh. It motivates, inspires and haunts, all at the same time. You can tell them apart by the understanding in their brow, the way they ask all the questions others avoid and how they respond with silence when you tell them about your loved one instead of with parables and metaphors. They know what it's like to lose a mother, a father, a sister, a brother, a spouse or a child. They know what it's like to fight cancer.

But it's what you do after cancer that's most important. We all make promises in life, but none more sincere than when we bargain with God in the face of death. Even tonight I sit on my porch in the darkness and cold, promising God I'll find the cure if He will only bring back Elena. The irony is that I'll never know if it is true until I find that cure, despite the voice in the back of my head explaining away the irrational part of the deal.

Almost 20 years ago, I was introduced to cancer for the first time. My grandmother was the first to fight what became a generational battle with cancer that would eventually infect nearly every woman in my family. At the time she was still young and had ten grandchildren of her own. Her battle was with brain cancer, at a time when the "dinosaur" drugs of the early chemotherapy age ruled. Hers too was a terminal prognosis, plagued with a loss of her abilities and memory. And in time, it took her life and the heart and soul of our family.

Then, as I do now, I questioned my priorities. If God would save her I would learn about cancer, become a doctor and change the world. But then again, I was too young. How could I ever hope to make a difference? Besides that, everyone had cancer and there were bound to be plenty of people smarter, more determined and better positioned. In time the promise faded as I thought I had seen cancer for the last time.

Less than ten years later it was my mother's turn. This time it was breast cancer. Suddenly the promises all came back. She sought treatment; I sought refuge in the library in the medical sciences/oncology section. And then, as before, I feigned understanding about the differing types of radiation and exactly what a biopsy hoped to discover. I swore this time it would be different. I'd change my studies and do what I promised before, this time with passion and with diligence.

Unlike my grandmother, she won the battle with cancer and seven years later she was in remission. I still read books on oncology, but over time they lost out to better books on business and leadership. Suddenly it didn't seem so important. She lived and I moved on. Once again the promise faded. Little did I know what lay ahead.

The promises mean nothing. In my heart I know that they are little more than a way for me to grapple with the lack of control that comes with every terminal illness. Still, they are promises to myself even if they are not promises to my God. Now it may be too late for me to change a major or refocus priorities. I cannot find the cure looking through a microscope or by identifying DNA strands. Instead, I must accomplish it with awareness and on the shoulders of people still more intelligent and better positioned than me. And this time it will not fade.

After Elena Day 193 – February 21

Prayers at the dinner table will always hold special meaning. In truth, we've never been diligent in our prayers. Scripted words of thanks and blessings never seemed heartfelt. Instead we left our prayers to our actions and the love we had for our children. So when we'd say the occasional "grace" around the holidays or on Sundays at Grandpa-Grandpa's house, the girls would never know how to act. Gracie always thought we were talking about her when we'd ask who wanted to say "grace," while Elena waited for her opportunity to fold her hands and be the leader. Soon the anticipation was too great. Elena had her turn.

The room was silent (or as quiet as it gets with 20 loud relatives) as Elena began. "I pledge allegiance, to the flag, of the United States of America...." No one said a word. Aunts flinched, Grandmas nodded while Brooke and I couldn't help but laugh. At the time, no one thought it was funny except us. It seems that with all of her practicing to say the pledge of allegiance at school in the morning, this was the only prayer that she knew. At least it contained "one nation under God."

I think about this now as we sit down at the dinner table at home. God is on our minds with the Lenten season in full swing. And while we still don't fold our hands in prayer as much as we should, the fish brings back memories of the seat left vacant by her death. Gracie and Mom always ate meat on Fridays, unfazed by my Catholic presence, while Elena happily joined me with a plate of fish and plenty of tartar sauce. She too hated fish, but would never leave me eating alone. That was my Elena.

After Elena Day 197 – February 25

There will always be one picture I hold close to my heart. It's a simple painting, but one that I'll never forget. It's about a girl named

"Rita" and it is titled "Rita the Boot Necked Girl." And the title tells it all. In the picture you will find a girl with a dress and a boot drawn where her neck should be. How she ever imagined such a picture I will never know, but it's classic Elena. Imagination with deadly accuracy. Creativity without limits. A boot drawn where a neck should be.

The name "Rita" comes from the school we passed every morning on the way to preschool. To Elena, St. Rita's School was more of a castle befitting a princess than a school for the deaf. Over four stories in height with towering steeples, it hardly looked like a school at all. As far as she was concerned, it was Rita's castle. Where the boot came from, we may never know.

When she drew the picture, Brooke and I stood with amazement. It was the first picture she had drawn that didn't look like a spider. Overnight her drawing advanced months. And from there it never stopped. There are pictures of Rita the Boot Necked Girl in the park, a picture of Rita the Boot Necked Girl at the lake and a picture of Rita the Boot Neck Girl on the see-saw. And in all renditions, the boot remained where her neck should be.

The boot wasn't a mistake; Elena would tell you so if you asked. It belonged there. Weeks passed and soon Rita disappeared from her drawings never to be seen again. Hearts took her place and pictures of Gracie and Mom became her new passion.

Rita the Boot Neck Girl was Elena's first artwork and I'll never understand the reasoning behind the boot in her neck. Now I wish I would have asked. Somehow I imagine that the explanation would have been more interesting than the picture.

This May, Elena's heart painting, "I Love You," will go back on display at the Cincinnati Art Museum. For four months, it will be part of an exhibition on the anniversary of its original presentation one year ago. Along with it will display the heart paintings from her kindergarten classmates created at the same time. I can think of no group more worthy of such an honor. Their courtesy and love for my daughter in her hardest of times were nothing short of wonderful. I can think of no better symbol than hearts to demonstrate the power of that one kindergarten class. Gracie, forever her best friend, will also have her picture displayed to represent our family and the influence that continues on today in her sister. They are and will always be the perfect pair.

When asked what she named her picture, Elena simply responded with "I Love You." It was simple, yet perfect. Just like "Rita the Boot Neck Girl." That was Elena: simple, honest, humble and gracious, with an imagination I'll forever love.

After Elena Day 206 – March 5

The chair swing on the back porch was always for Elena. I had always imagined the two of us swinging to the sounds of crickets as we waited for Gracie to return home from a night with friends. If she were anything like me, she'd rather stay home and read than spend an evening with friends. If Gracie was anything like her Mom (which we know to be true), she'd spend her time with friends and playing sports. We were the quiet ones; they were the sociable ones.

When we built the house I couldn't wait to build the porch. And even before the house was framed in, the porch swing was painted and hung. It was the only thing finished on the entire house. Then, on that third week of July, I carried Elena out to the porch and we sat on the swing. Nowhere else other than in her bay window seat was she quite as comfortable. It was one solemn hour as she rested her head in my arms, too weak to even sit.

Last night I sat on that swing for the first time in seven months. This time it was alone. And as I do each and every night, I wonder what it would be like to sit next to Elena. Now she'd be seven years old. She'd be starting math, frustrated with boys and looking forward to summer.

She'd be taller, her hair would be longer, but the jeweled shoes and pretty headbands would remain. And we'd use the porch swing each and every night.

It's the same way with her bed. And her bicycle. And her seat at the dinner table. In my mind, she's seven years old and smiling. My heart will never let my mind forget. Every time I smile, every time I laugh, my heart pulls me back and forces me to remember. The smile fades as my eyes turn towards her empty chair.

When she died, I wanted no memorial and no grave. Within weeks we cleared her room, hauled the medical equipment to the curb and put away her dresses. We feared that if we waited, we would never be able to heal and would lock ourselves away in a corner of our house. What we did was wrong. Her ashes were buried at the foot of the red tree she planted with me four years before. At the time, I wanted to remember her with pictures and with memories, not gravestones and a hearse. What I never expected was that the monuments would become her porch swing, her bed and the empty chair at dinner.

Now I find myself searching for a place to visit, something to touch as I clear the memories from my head. Something that says she'll never be forgotten. Something permanent and just for her that says love, humility and joy. Something that says Elena. But today I have no place to go, every chair in the house is a memory, every picture is a tribute and that maple in the backyard is a grave.

Where I once shunned tributes, my mind now creates monuments out of everything I see. It's a desperate search for memories in a battle for my heart to never let my mind forget.

After Elena Day 213 – March 12

"Survivor" is how I wanted to see Elena. Strong, bold and victorious. We view cancer survivors as more than just heroes or winners in the game of luck. Survivors get where they are through positive thinking, faith and determination. At least that's what we tell ourselves in our game of deception somehow imagining that we have much more control over our fates than we really do.

Once again, the anniversary of Elena's death weighs heavily on our minds. This time, however, it came eight hours later, postponed by the trivial distractions of the day. Only when attending a dinner to celebrate brain cancer achievements did the irony of the day present itself. I could see it in Brooke's eyes and in the blank stares that we traded hoping the other one had somehow forgotten and was in ignorant bliss.

There at the dinner we talked of advances, trials and of survivors. They asked who knew of a family member or friend affected by cancer. I raised my hand along with everyone in the room. They asked if we treated and cared for someone with cancer. Everyone raised his or her hands. They asked if our child was a survivor. Suddenly I didn't know how to respond – neither did most of the other parents.

It's the painful reminder of those who lose a loved one to cancer. The label "survivor" is emblazoned on your daughter from the moment of diagnosis. They talk of diagnosis, the struggle and the eventual remission. And as a dad you try to think of nothing else. But there are some parents who will be faced with another word: "Victim." This word comes with no pride, no comfort and empty promises. To be a victim is to be weak, unlucky and dead. It is not worthy of Elena's legacy.

And so our hands went halfway up, not knowing quite where Elena fit in. And the same justification that we used to award her the status of "survivor" we now find ourselves rationalizing away as luck. In truth, she is a victim, a victim of a merciless disease that knows no boundaries. But to me, she'll always be an inspiration, regardless of whether she was a survivor or a victim.

On this day, seven months from her death, we are the survivors of cancer and Elena is our inspiration. She always will be. Elements of fate will never take that away from any other children affected by DIPG. They are the ones who force us to advance the cause, raise awareness and fight for the cure. Without our children, this fight would be groundless and our efforts in vain. Survivors vs. victims: the labels are meaningless. They are all inspirations to you and me.

After Elena Day 227 – March 26

It all seems so surreal, until you walk by her picture. I guess this is where the shock sets in. Cancer research is no longer a hobby, it is now a passion. A passion that overrides every other priority beyond my family. For me it is a chance to be close to Elena once again. A chance to reflect on the values that she instilled in us all.

At the same time, you never want to forget. But I do. At least for a minute. And then I look at her picture resting on my desk, I glance at her heart hanging on the wall, or I see her notes littering my dresser. And then it all comes back – in pieces. I remember forcing frozen strawberry juice cubes between her teeth when she lost all ability to eat. I remember carrying her over my shoulder as she struggled to breathe. I remember the sound of the IV machine as the beeps pierced the night. I hated that damn IV machine.

Brooke wants to only remember the good days. I only remember the bad. But to me none are bad. And I don't know why. Brooke only displays the good pictures before diagnosis. In my mind I hold the exhausting days after radiation, the moments we struggled to get her to swallow her steroids, the nights I sat in the corner of the room and watched her sleep. Maybe it's because I want to always remember why every moment is important. Maybe it's because those were the days that we were alone together. Maybe it's because I know no different.

Either way it's these thoughts that permeate the shock. In my heart I hope it's a nightmare and tomorrow I will find her asleep in her bed. I know that these thoughts will never end. But when I remember the bad days, I know tomorrow her clothes will still be tucked away in the guest room closet and her stuffed animals hidden on the top shelf. And then I know that it was my daughter. The memories of bad days remind me that it was my family. And the shock wears off. It's the pinch of reality that brings me back.

After Elena Day 274 – May 12

Brooke cries and I don't know what to do. Normally when someone cries you pull them near, hold them tight and tell them everything will be all right. Only this time it won't. It won't be all right because she'll never come back home. And this is the first Mother's Day without Elena.

She misses Elena and I understand. But it's the memories that bring the tears. Over six Mother's Days have passed and neither of us remember one memory about celebrating it with Elena. And so now, instead of losing her on that fateful day in August, we now lose her one memory at a time. For three hours we sat and tried to remember, but instead all that we could recall was a photograph amid a box of tissues.

Two nights ago Brooke had a dream. This time she heard Elena's voice. How I wish that I too would have that dream. Instead I find myself forced to remember memories that are fading all too fast. The memory of her first steps, the memory of her first words, the memory of our first vacation; I can't remember one. All I have are the pictures to fill the spaces in my mind. But those are just snapshots. With them I can no longer hear her voice, feel her hand or touch her soft cheeks. If only the memories remained.

It's more than being just about Mother's Day. It's about losing my child piece by piece and preserving the memories that I still hold close by. So I practice remembering each and every day in the hopes that I'll never forget. I write a journal, trade stories with Brooke and keep moving on. Maybe one day they'll all come back.

After Elena Day 275 – May 13

We still find notes – hundreds of them. Often I wonder how much she knew. Now I know.

For years, we went through the annual spring season practice of cleaning out closets. Gracie's summer clothes from last year no longer fit and it was time to put away the sweaters. This will be the last time she'll fit into Elena's old clothes, that is, if Brooke and I can handle the memories that come with them. So we fill a bag with jeans, wool socks, boots and sweaters and exchange them with shorts, jackets and sandals.

For six years, we stored the bags in the rear corner of Gracie's closet. Baby clothes to six years old. The last time we switched clothes was last May. At the time, Elena's condition had worsened. Unable to fit into her new summer clothes because of the steroid swelling and loss of balance to the tumor, the switch occurred late in May as she moved to Gracie's room where we could more closely monitor her sleep. There, she would sleep until late July when the IV machine would force her into our room. Apparently she knew about the clothes as well because through each hole at the top of the bag she had stuffed little notes with "I lov you Mom, Dad and Grace." From the top to the bottom, all six bags had one note each; all with a love note and all with a small heart drawn at the bottom in the same fashion as her "I Love You" drawing that she drew just one month prior. Even the bag of clothes packed in May when she first started using her walker had a small note tucked into the top.

Since her death, we've found notes with hearts, notes to Mom, notes to Grandma and notes to Gracie. Our only question was when. Now we know. Even as her paralysis took her leg and spirit, Elena still found the time to write us notes of love and tuck them away where she knew they would be safe, deep in the corner of Gracie's closet. We love you too, Elena. Thank you for the notes.

Book Club Discussion Questions

1. What is the significance of the title?
2. How does the diagnosis of a life-threatening illness change an individual?
3. How does it change those around him or her?
4. What does it take (mentally and/or physically) to fight a disease like cancer?
5. How did Brooke and Keith deal with the stress this situation created?
6. What do you think is the hardest aspect of going through this experience?
7. What role does hope play for parents in this battle?
8. How do you think Elena views the world after her diagnosis?
9. How did the relationship between Gracie and Elena change?
10. Were you surprised by the change?
11. Why do you think children with serious illnesses grow up so quickly?
12. Should children be told everything about their condition?
13. How do you think Brooke and Keith handled the day-to-day issues of Elena's illness?
14. What does Elena's artwork represent to her and her family?
15. How do Brooke and Keith describe survival and the survivor mentality?
16. How do you think Elena knew she only had a little time left?
17. What kind of impact did Elena have on her community and those who followed her journey?
18. How do you think Gracie dealt with Elena's diagnosis and her death?
19. Are children more resilient and understanding than we give them credit for?
20. What legacy do you want to leave for your friends and family after you are gone?

To learn more about Elena, order extra copies of "Notes Left Behind," learn about *The Cure Starts Now or donate directly to the fight against cancer, visit www.thecurestartsnow.org.

A portion of the proceeds of this book will benefit The Cure Starts Now in our mission to fight childhood brain cancer as the final frontier in our battle against all forms of cancer, both adult and pediatric.

**The Cure Starts Now is a non-profit, 501(c)3 organization.*

Printed in the United States
R3585200002B/R35852PG208239BVX2B/106-1425/P 9 780981 726458